The Birth of Intersubjectivity

The Norton Series on Interpersonal Neurobiology
Allan N. Schore, PhD, Series Editor
Daniel J. Siegel, MD, Founding Editor

The field of mental health is in a tremendously exciting period of growth and conceptual reorganization. Independent findings from a variety of scientific endeavors are converging in an interdisciplinary view of the mind and mental well-being. An interpersonal neurobiology of human development enables us to understand that the structure and function of the mind and brain are shaped by experiences, especially those involving emotional relationships.

The Norton Series on Interpersonal Neurobiology provides cutting-edge, multidisciplinary views that further our understanding of the complex neurobiology of the human mind. By drawing on a wide range of traditionally independent fields of research—such as neurobiology, genetics, memory, attachment, complex systems, anthropology, and evolutionary psychology—these texts offer mental health professionals a review and synthesis of scientific findings often inaccessible to clinicians. The books advance our understanding of human experience by finding the unity of knowledge, or consilience, that emerges with the translation of findings from numerous domains of study into a common language and conceptual framework. The series integrates the best of modern science with the healing art of psychotherapy.

A NORTON PROFESSIONAL BOOK

THE BIRTH OF INTERSUBJECTIVITY

Psychodynamics, Neurobiology, and the Self

MASSIMO AMMANITI
VITTORIO GALLESE

Foreword by Allan N. Schore

W. W. Norton & Company
New York • London

The Introduction and chapters 2–8 of this book were authored by Massimo Ammaniti. Chapter 1 was authored by Vittorio Gallese.

For information about permission to reproduce selections from this book, write to Permissions, W. W. Norton & Company, Inc., 500 Fifth Avenue, New York, NY 10110

For information about special discounts for bulk purchases, please contact W. W. Norton Special Sales at specialsales@wwnorton.com or 800-233-4830

Manufacturing by Quad Graphics, Fairfield
Production manager: Leeann Graham

Library of Congress Cataloging-in-Publication Data

Ammaniti, Massimo, 1941–
    The birth of intersubjectivity : psychodynamics, neurobiology, and the self / Massimo Ammaniti, Vittorio Gallese ; foreword by Allan N. Schore. — First Edition.
        pages cm. — (The Norton series on interpersonal neurobiology) (A Norton professional book)
    Includes bibliographical references and index.
    ISBN 978-0-393-70763-2 (hardcover)
1. Developmental psychology.   2. Neurobiology.   3. Motherhood—Psychological aspects.   4. Parenting—Psychological aspects.   I. Gallese, Vittorio.   II. Title.
    BF713.A466   2013
    155.9'2—dc23
                2013013901

ISBN: 978-0-393-70763-2

W. W. Norton & Company, Inc., 500 Fifth Avenue, New York, N.Y. 10110
        www.wwnorton.com
W. W. Norton & Company Ltd., Castle House, 75/76 Wells Street, London W1T 3QT

1 2 3 4 5 6 7 8 9 0

To Dan Stern, who has illuminated our lives
with wit, vitality, and lightness.

Contents

Foreword

Allan N. Schore

In the last two decades, a substantial amount of scientific and clinical data has been amassed highlighting the centrality of early development for both optimal brain maturation and adaptive social emotional functioning over the lifespan. Only a short time ago there was some debate about the relevance of interdisciplinary developmental studies and particularly neuroscience for clinical models, but at present both researchers and clinicians, of every therapeutic persuasion, are incorporating updated psychoneurobiological attachment models into the treatment of the entire spectrum of mental health disorders. Indeed, the clinical professions continue to show an intense interest in the psychotherapeutic applications of these new discoveries of the relational origins of the conscious, and even more, the unconscious mind.

This extraordinary book provides a significant contribution to that effort. The authors, both international figures in neuroscience, present a fresh, neurobiologically and developmentally informed model of intersubjectivity. The volume is a collaboration between Massimo Ammaniti, a developmental psychoanalyst at the forefront of functional magnetic resonance attachment research, and Vittorio Gallese, perhaps the leading neurobiological researcher on mirror neurons and creator of an "embodied simulation theory" of intersubjectivity. Intersubjectivity is a relational phenomenon familiar not only to psychoanalysts, but also to a large number of clinicians, especially those with an affective, developmental perspective. This book offers an integrated model of "the birth of intersubjectivity," which Ammaniti and Gallese locate in the continuous and reciprocal interactions and exchanges typical of human beings from their first days of life. Although this theme runs throughout the book, each of the chapters stands on its own as a new and exciting contribution to the study of relationally driven neurobiological development—that is, interpersonal neurobiology. In an exceptional feature, the chapters on prenatal and perinatal neurobiological development can be used as resources in their own right.

The chapters that follow describe recent developmental research that needs to be incorporated into clinical models. These include creative discussions of essential events in the prenatal and perinatal critical periods, such as biological and subjective changes in the transition into motherhood, a new assessment procedure for pregnant women, "Interview of Maternal Representations during Pregnancy," an updated neurobiological conception of Winnicott's seminal "Primary Maternal Preoccupation," the overlooked yet expanding discipline of "maternal fetal attachment," new information on maternal and paternal co-parenting during prenatal and postnatal periods, and the psychological impact of echography on the pregnant couple.

Moving to the postnatal periods of development, the authors offer the reader ongoing research on the neurobiology of motherhood and the transformation of the female brain into the maternal brain, including an overview of the interpersonal neurobiology of maternal love; a model of reciprocal, regulated mother-infant interactions that describes the theoretical relationship of attachment to intersubjectivity; a description of Ammaniti's functional magnetic imaging (fMRI) research on dismissive women; and the characterization of the interpersonal neurobiological mechanisms that convey the impact of relational trauma on the maternal and fetal brains. This new information about the intergenerational transmission of stress or resilience during pregnancy as well as in postnatal periods is not only offered in a clear and comprehensible fashion, but also integrated into a coherent model of intersubjectivity, grounded in a contemporary psychodynamic perspective.

In every chapter, the authors present a well-articulated model of the ontogeny of intersubjectivity, grounded in recent advances in developmental neuroscience, modern attachment theory, and relational psychoanalysis. They offer evocative descriptions not only of the alterations in brain development in both mother and infant, but also of the concurrent, relationally induced changes in the subjectivities of both members of the dyad. Summarizing the critical role of reciprocal affective communications in postnatal critical periods (a developmental stage for what the authors term "the primary matrix" of primary and then secondary intersubjectivity), with which the reader may already be familiar, the authors go on to describe in great detail the prenatal and perinatal events that set the neurobiological groundwork for these postnatal advances.

Over the course of the book the authors supplement the large amount of current interdisciplinary research with extensive interviews. They note that "deep changes are characteristic during pregnancy, with emotional upheaval and rapid identity oscillations, but at the same time women experience a growing sense of internal coherence, satisfaction, and personal integration" (p. 62). That said, they point out that this deep experience is impacted by personality variations, akin to attachment classifications. In discussing various typologies of maternal representations, they offer interviews of expectant mothers with integrated, pre-occupied, conflicted, and restricted/disinvested representations. Readers will note the similarities of these narratives to case vignettes, an effective device for highlighting the expectant mother's changing subjective states.

As mentioned, this work deeply delves into another matter of intense interest to clinicians: mirror neurons. Gallese offers a convincing critique of cognitive neuroscience as reductionistic in its narrow association of intersubjectivity with full-blown linguistic competence, social metacognition, symbolic representations that follow formal syntactic rules, and theory of mind—mental states that map beliefs and desires. Along these same lines the authors refer to current developmental psychology's "staging of social cognitive development almost exclusively by relying on children's verbal reports and language-mediated performance" (p. 4), pointing out, in contrast, that "intersubjectivity is not exclusively confined to a declarative metarepresentational third-person perspective" (p. 9), and suggesting instead that intersubjectivity involves "the mapping of the other unto the self, reciprocated by the mapping of the self on the other" (p. 8). "The other," however, is not so much a metarepresentational third-person perspective as a "bodily self." This is consonant with the construct of interpersonal neurobiology, and indeed with the work of many other authors in the Norton Series on Interpersonal Neurobiology.

The authors then offer the reader a detailed neuroanatomical and neurophysiological description of the mirror mechanism whereby action observation activates the ventral premotor cortex and the posterior parietal cortex, proposing that the mirror mechanism may play a role in imitative behavior, even perhaps in unconscious mimicry of body postures, facial expressions, and behaviors of social partners. They speculate that the perception and production of emotion-related facial expressions "can be hypothesized to be similar to the mirror mechanism. . . . When observing someone else's facial expression, we do not understand its meaning only through explicit inference from analogy. The other's emotion is first and foremost constituted and directly understood by reusing part of the same neural circuits underpinning our first-person experience of the same emotion" (pp. 16–17). They thus present a model of intersubjectivity that stresses not symbolic representations but intercorporeality. This conception is consonant with my own work on right-brain-to-right-brain bodily based affective communications, which the authors cite throughout the book (Schore, 1994, 2003, 2012).

Applying "embodied simulation theory" and motor cognition to the early ontogeny of human intersubjectivity, the authors cite classic studies of the neonate's imitation of tongue protrusion, a transitory phenomenon. But is this dyadic communication? They clearly highlight the critical mechanism of reciprocal bodily based communications of state in citing Legerstee's (2009) description of early contexts of social interaction in which "infants communicate with eye contact, facial expression, vocalizations, and gestures while assimilating the rhythm of their interactions to that of caretakers" (p. 2) and Trevarthen's (1979) observations of protoconversation (again, note that both are consonant with a right-brain-to-right-brain interpersonal neurobiological model).

The authors are candid about certain essential, thus far unanswered questions about the mirror neuron system: "We do not yet know when and how the mirror mechanism appears. We do not know whether mirror neurons are innate and how they are shaped and modeled during development" (p. 21). Why is this question essential? Because Trevarthen's (1979) relational-affective contexts of proto-subjectivity and secondary intersubjectivity occur, respectively, early and late in the first year, which are critical periods of "the birth of intersubjectivity." In fact, Ammaniti and Gallese admit the existence of only "indirect evidence" for the origins of the mirror mechanism, and report just four studies of mirror neuron activity in the first 16 months of life—none of these in the first 6 months or within a relational attachment context. In other words, there is no existing evidence that the ventral premotor parietal system is active in the 3-month-old infant's brain, or in the mother's brain, as they are intersubjectively communicating with each other. Also, no studies have been done on the epigenetic modification of these neurons, nor on mirror neurons in mothers with psychiatric disorders.

Although there may be unresolved questions about the role of mirror systems in very early dyadic attachment and intersubjective processes, neuroscience now strongly confirms the existence and importance of mirror neurons, especially when the mirror system operates in association with the limbic system and particularly with the right insula, the anterior cingulate, and the amygdala. But controversy remains on the matter of empathy, an essential mechanism in both mother–infant and patient–therapist intersubjective interactions. Due to the commonality of the word "mirroring" in psychoanalytic self psychology and in neurobiology, some claim that the mirror neurons were equated with psychological mirroring, that is, empathy. In the conclusion of the mirror neuron chapter Ammaniti and Gallese specifically refer to the interface of neuroscience and psychoanalysis, and to the groundbreaking work of their late colleague, Mauro Manicia (2006), on implicit memory and the early unrepressed unconscious. But do cortical mirror neurons influence the therapist's ability to empathize with the patient's not only verbalized but also unverbalized subcortically generated unconscious self-states? Affective (more so than cognitive) empathy is essential to the therapeutic context, and affective empathy is mainly processed by the limbic-autonomic circuits of the right hemisphere (Schore, 2012; see also Gainotti, 2012).

As the reader will soon note, chapter 1, in which the authors present an extensive and comprehensive exposition of the mirror neuron mechanism, mentions the term "empathic" only once, and only in reference to another research area, spontaneous facial mimicry. Indeed Decety (2010) now concludes, "While the mirror neuron system provides a physiological mechanism for motor resonance and plays a role in mimicry, current neurophysiological and neurological evidence does not clearly support the idea that such a mechanism accounts for emotion understanding, empathy or sympathy" (p. 206). Accordingly, in an overview of fMRI studies of empathy, Fan, Duncan, de Greck, and Northoff (2011) state, "Our meta-analytic results did not show consistent activation of these mirror neuron system regions at a corrected level, suggesting that this system is not centrally involved in empathy per se" (p. 907).

These matters aside, as the authors assert, "the existence of the mirror mechanism is now also firmly established in the human brain" (p. 14). To my mind, there is no doubt that the discovery of mirror neurons is a central event in modern neuroscience. There is still much to be learned, but my own sense is that the mirror neuron system becomes truly contributive to adaptive function in not the first but the second year, when the cortical motor circuits significantly increase their complexity, allowing for the onset of human upright locomotion, a period when the left hemisphere that is dominant for voluntary behavior comes into a growth spurt. In other words, the mirror mechanism and motor cognition may be centrally involved in the toddler's and young child's imitation and observational learning of the maternal and paternal caregivers' left lateralized instrumental (as opposed to expressive) gestures (see Gallagher & Frith, 2004), and thereby in early experiences of exploration and skill learning, especially in a social context.

This exceptional book breaks new ground on the matter of intersubjectivity. The clinician with an appreciation for developmental knowledge will find a rich trove of up-to-date information with direct clinical applications. Intersubjectivity is here elevated to the level of attachment, a central theme of Daniel Stern's lifelong work. In his groundbreaking 2004 book *The Present Moment in Psychotherapy and Everyday Life* (published in the Norton IN series), he argued that intersubjectivity acts as "a basic motivational system." In an important expansion of that idea, Ammaniti and Gallese propose that the intersubjective motivational system "is like a constant barometer that gives us information about our self and others in different contexts. . . . Intersubjective processes are like a blueprint underneath every motivational system and, in the case of the attachment system, they are activated when attachment needs emerge" (p. 143).

This volume will be invaluable to clinicians specializing in attachment disorders and relational trauma, child psychotherapists, infant mental health workers, pediatricians, and psychoanalysts, as well as developmental researchers. Increasingly, both mental health clinicians and researchers in developmental neuroscience and developmental psychology are moving into the very earliest critical periods, including prenatal and perinatal stages. The concluding chapters of the book directly speak to the clinical applications of the authors' model for early assessments and interventions, including interventions with pregnant mothers. Citing numerous studies, they conclude that "the maturing fetus receives and registers information about the maternal environment through most of the biological systems that later will mediate adaption to endogenous and exogenous challenges" (p. 159). They cite research showing that fetal cortisol concentrations are directly related to maternal concentrations, with a maternal–fetal ratio of 12 to 1, and that 10% to 20% of maternal cortisol passes through the placenta. Thus clinicians must now understand that the intergenerational transmission of resilience of susceptibility to later psychopathology begins in utero, highlighting the importance of working with pregnant mothers and patients with histories of prenatal trauma. The critical matter of early assessment and intervention is a focus of my own recent work (Schore, 2012, in press).

The Birth of Intersubjectivity presents a fascinating, rich amalgam of new information for a deeper understanding of the early intersubjective origins of our own and our patients' internal worlds. These worlds guide our external relational, intimate social-emotional interactions with others, especially the essential adaptive processes that occur beneath conscious awareness.

References

Decety, J. (2010). To what extent is the experience of empathy mediated by shared neural circuits? *Emotion Review, 2,* 204–207.

Fan, Y., Duncan, N. W., de Greck, M., & Northoff, G. (2011). Is there a core neural network in empathy? An fMRI based quantitative meta-analysis. *Neuroscience and Biobehavioral Reviews, 35,* 903–911.

Gallagher, H. L., & Frith, C. D. (2004). Dissociable neural pathways for the perception and recognition of expressive and instrumental gestures. *Neuropsychologia, 42,* 1725–1736.

Gainotti, G. (2012). Unconscious processing of emotions and the right hemisphere. *Neuropsychologia, 50,* 205–218.

Legerstee, M. (2009). The role of the person and object in eliciting early imitation. *Journal of Experimental Child Psychology, 51,* 423–433.

Mancia, M. (2006). Implicit memory and unrepressed unconscious: Their role in the therapeutic process (how the neurosciences can contribute to psychoanalysis). *International Journal of Psychoanalysis, 87,* 83–103.

Schore, A. N. (1994). *Affect regulation and the origin of the self.* Mahwah, NJ: Erlbaum.

Schore, A. N. (2003). *Affect regulation and the repair of the self.* New York: Norton.

Schore, A. N. (2012). *The science of the art of psychotherapy.* New York: Norton.

Schore, A. N. (in press). Regulation theory: A contribution to formulating early infant assessment and intervention. A response to Voran's clinical case. *Journal of Infant, Child, and Adolescent Psychotherapy.*

Stern, D. N. (2004). *The present moment in psychotherapy and everyday life.* New York, NY: Norton.

Trevarthen, C. (1979). Communication and cooperation in early infancy: A description of primary intersubjectivity. In M. Bullowa (Ed.), *Before speech: The beginning of interpersonal communication* (pp. 321–347). Cambridge, UK: Cambridge University Press.

Introduction

This book deals with the theme of intersubjectivity, which describes the continuous and reciprocal interactions and exchanges typical of human beings from their first days of life, in a process in which "humans come to know each other's mind" (Bruner, 1996, p. 12). In the past decades, the interest in intersubjectivity has grown in many scientific fields—from relational psychoanalysis to infant research, from social cognition to neurobiology—each one using its own research methods and theoretical models but nonetheless leading to interesting convergences.

The enormous amount of research data and clinical observations in the field of intersubjectivity makes it difficult to establish a unified reference model. The interaction between different and complex systems may be described with Sameroff and Chandler's transactional model (1975), in which the environtype (the source of external experience) and the genotype (the source of individual biological organization) interact together to produce the phenotype (the developing infant), which in his or her own turn influences and modifies the environmental context and the genetic endowment. Recent advancements in molecular biology, genetics, and neurobiology have shown the importance of studying multiple interacting systems. The same approach has emerged in the areas of infant research and relational psychoanalysis, which emphasize the complex relational network of the individual self from the beginning of the life, built on social reciprocity and on the development of "we-ness" (Emde, 2009).

The progress of research in molecular genetics, endocrinology, and neurobiology will be integrated and confronted with psychological and psychopathological research. In a number of research domains, multidirectional and interactional models are nowadays substituting reductionistic and unilinear models and emphasizing gene–environment interactions and epigenome relation experiences.

The developmental perspective is particularly important when analyzing dynamic and continuous interchanges in which single subsystems cannot be separated from the whole.

In this ambit, the gap between brain circuits and behavior is too wide (Carandini, 2012). It would be useful to find an appropriate level of description: an intermediate level of neural functioning, which occurs in individual neurons or populations of neurons.

This book is coauthored by a developmental psychoanalyst and a neurobiologist. Working conjointly, we have tried to find the interactions and connections between our theoretical fields of reference and, although using different strategies and methods of study and research, we have highlighted the significant convergences that have emerged during recent years. It must be noted that the writing of this book inevitably reflects the theoretic approach and language of each author, which we have chosen to maintain to reflect the dialectics that characterize today's scientific debate.

As we discuss in chapter 1, the intermediate level between the mirror neurons mechanism and the empathic resonance typical of parents–infant interactions is characterized, at the functional level, by the embodied simulation: "a specific mechanism by means of which our brain/body system models its interactions with the world" (Gallese, 2006, p. 2).

Chapter 1 addresses the topic of intersubjectivity by relying on a multidisciplinary approach, integrating and critically discussing relevant contributions from cognitive neuroscience, developmental psychology, philosophy, and psychoanalysis.

The social nature of humans has been acknowledged since the time of Aristotle; however, a solipsistic account has dominated the scientific field for decades. But during the last century we discovered that several thinkers of different traditions of thought have emphasized the necessity to assume a second-person approach to explain intersubjectivity (e.g., Buber and Merleau-Ponty). In the notion of intersubjectivity, the interaction between the Self and the Other is crucial, as is the role of the body with its peri-personal space.

If confronting intersubjectivity with neuroscience, conclusions may be divergent when neuroscience adopts a classic cognitivism-inspired theoretical assumption based on localizations in the brain. However, if the neurobiological approach explores brain functioning during ecologically plausible interactive behaviors, the confrontation could be more reciprocally enriching. In this work, the importance and function of mirror neurons in the brain are presented, clarifying the mechanism of embodied simulation.

A new model of intersubjectivity emerges from the joint application of a developmental psychodynamic perspective and an embodied cognitive neuroscientific approach, which sheds new light on the birth of intersubjectivity, the main theme of the book.

In chapter 2 we discuss the evolutionary origins of maternal care that have stimulated, especially in mothers but also in fathers, the capacity to be sensitive and more attuned to their children.

In the past decades, the traditional family, as described by Freud, for example, has undergone great changes. Today there are a number of family pathways, often responding to different and overlapping needs, which do not find adequate answers within the traditional structure. Because of this, different and more fluid family solutions have emerged. Tradition has mixed with deep changes brought about by a number of movements that have appeared in the past decades, from feminism to gay and lesbian movements. Often the head of the household is a single mother or a single father (Tyano, Keren, Herrman, & Cox, 2010), as is confirmed by the fact that 40% of US children spend their nights in a home in which the father does not live.

Within this framework, the number of gay and lesbian families, in which both partners are of the same sex, has increased rapidly. Notwithstanding some prejudices that still exist, research has found no systematic differences between children reared by a mother and father and those raised by same-sex parents (Patterson, 1992); this is further confirmation of the importance of intersubjectivity and attachment between children and their caregivers.

This intersubjective matrix begins at pregnancy and runs through the infant's first year, as was also documented by Freud and Winnicott. During pregnancy, deep transformations occur in the maternal body with hormonal and neurobiological change on one hand, and the maternal psychic world and the identity on the other, with the activation of mental representations of self as a mother and of the baby. The transformations of maternal identity are illustrated and discussed through three interviews with mothers who show different and prototypical maternal representations and psychic constellations during their pregnancies.

In chapter 3 we start discussing the concept of maternal–fetal attachment by examining research contributions in this area and pointing out the strengths and limits of this conceptualization. During pregnancy, mothers develop a capacity for concern for the fetus and the pregnancy, described clinically by Winnicott. A further observation from Winnicott highlights a special state of mind during the last phase of pregnancy, the primary maternal preoccupation, which implies a heightened sensitivity toward the baby and the pregnancy. Recent research has confirmed these clinical observations by evidencing a modification of the brain in the last period of pregnancy. While primary maternal preoccupation is a physiological condition during motherhood, more severe preoccupations and fears can appear in this period, as we will show in excerpts of an interview with a pregnant mother which documents these psychological reactions during pregnancy.

In chapter 4 we widen the previous perspective of motherhood, stressing the role of fathers and of coparenting during pregnancy and the postnatal period. Coparenting dynamics are investigated, considering and confronting both the psychoanalytical and the system perspective. The study of the emerging triadic capacity during pregnancy is discussed, considering it as an anticipation of family dynamics after the birth of the baby. While the psychoanalytical perspective tries to explore the parental representational dimension and its connection with interactions, the system theory approach emphasizes the role of interactions in coparenting.

During pregnancy the obstetric ultrasound exam, which visualizes the fetus, has a profound impact on parents and facilitates coparenting interactions, as is documented by an interactional procedure created on the basis of the Prenatal Lausanne Trilogue Play (Carneiro, Corboz-Warnery, & Fivaz-Depeursinge, 2006). An interview with an expecting couple that shows their reciprocal relationship and support is also reported.

Considering the development of intersubjectivity in infants, this capacity can be stimulated by triadic interactions, as has been evidenced by research.

Chapter 5 provides a review of the research on mothers' brain transformations which implies the activation of care circuits. During pregnancy, there is an increase of hormones (estrogen and progesterone), which decrease at the end of pregnancy, while neuropeptide hormones like prolactin and oxytocin rise consistently. Research in animals and humans has documented the central role of oxytocin in the development of maternal caregiving behaviors.

During pregnancy and the postnatal period, neurobiological transformations occur in mammalians and humans, with the activation of the maternal circuit, which stimulates maternal love and pleasure in caring for the offspring; these have an overlapping neurobiological substratum with romantic love. An affective stimulus for maternal care is represented by the baby's face, as has been documented by neurobiological research, with the activation of different neurobiological areas, including the mirror neurons mechanism.

On the perspective of parents–infant interactions, chapter 6 deals further with the rise of the primary matrix of intersubjectivity, which starts immediately after the birth with a reciprocal orientation, attraction, and research of contact between caregiver and infant. The building of the primary matrix of intersubjectivity is stimulated by the human capacity of orienting toward faces and eye-to-eye contact as is demonstrated by the early activation of a specific neural network in infants. The mutual regulation creates a realm of nonconsciously regulated intuitive behavior and implicit relational knowledge. In this context, attachment to caregivers plays a central role not only because it guarantees a felt security through the physical closeness, as was suggested by Bowlby (1969, 1982), but also because it favors the exchange of affective cues, which create a feeling of sharing. An interesting issue is the relationship between psychoanalysis and attachment theory and whether there is a possible convergence or a marginal overlapping. While attachment theory emphasizes the felt security provided by caregivers, the intersubjective approach maintains that infants, from the beginning, are social beings who constantly seek other persons in order to engage in reciprocal imitation and in mutual emotional regulation. An intriguing question is whether the intersubjective motivational system is separate and complementary to attachment or whether it is a superordinate system which goes through all other motivational systems.

In chapter 7 the negative impact of parental stress on the infant's development, starting from pregnancy, is discussed. Although the concept of stress is quite elusive, research has evidenced that couple conflicts are significantly associated with a child's later difficulties in temperament and behavior. Of course, research about stress in humans has important limitations, but natural and human-made disasters act as natural experiments that can offer the possibility to study the mechanisms and the effects of stress. Findings of research raise important questions about the mechanisms of stress transmission to offspring, which suggest the mediation of the hypothalamus-pituitary-adrenal axis (HPA). The study of the consequences of trauma during pregnancy and of underlying mechanisms of action on the offspring introduces an interesting perspective related to nature–nurture interaction. While in the past the effect of environment on genetic mechanisms was denied, in recent years research has shown that epigenetic mechanisms, influenced by different factors, including environmental features, intervene on gene expression, modulating genetic effects.

In the last three decades, studies in highly stressed and conflictual families have shown that infants raised in these contexts present difficulties in the attachment process. This framework has been expanded by also considering the negative effect of the absence of caregiver intervention and protection. A particular emphasis has been put on the impact of frightened parental behaviors and contradictory communication of parents.

Stressful experiences represent risk factors for infantile development and predict a higher rate of negative consequences, which can be modulated by protective factors. In studying the effects of stress, a relevant concept is the individual differential susceptibility; this is rooted in differences in the functioning of neurobiological circuitry, but the number of risks in early childhood does predict behavioral problems in adolescence, thus supporting a cumulative risk model: The more risk is present, the worse the child's outcome.

Chapter 8, the concluding chapter, applies the discoveries generated by parents–infant studies and laboratory research to the development of best practices in the community, such as interventions in the parents–child interaction systems, as suggested by translational research.

To illustrate research data and studies reported in the text, we present figures, graphics, and schemata. In particular, we have decided to show some paintings from the Renaissance that describe, like microanalytic sequences, maternal attitude during pregnancy and parents–infant interactions in a vivid and evocative way.

The Birth of Intersubjectivity

CHAPTER 1

A New Take on Intersubjectivity

We live our life from its very beginning with the other. As mammals, for a short but crucial part of our prenatal life, we literally inhabit the body of the other, our mother. Sometimes, as twins, we even share our mother's body with someone else. Congruently, our brain-body system begins taking shape and, immediately after, starts developing its lifelong encounter with the world through the mutual relationship with another living human being. As we will see later on in the book, this presupposes the development of specific patterns of brain-body functional organization. Such patterns will continue to dynamically affect and be affected by our encounters with the world.

The fetus/neonate–mother relationship and all the following interpersonal encounters characterizing our life can be addressed from different perspectives. This first chapter starts by focusing on the topic of intersubjectivity and its development by relying on a multidisciplinary approach, combining, integrating, and critically discussing relevant contributions from cognitive neuroscience, as well as from philosophy, psychoanalysis, and developmental psychology. Such a multidisciplinary stance is a key feature of our approach in this book. The study of the brain cannot be decoupled by and thus should not neglect the rich and multifarious levels characterizing our social encounters with others. Thus, cognitive neuroscience can shed new light on intersubjectivity and its development, provided that it is capable of making sense of the way we experience others.

Historically speaking, cognitive neuroscience is no doubt a newcomer in the quest for understanding human nature. A common misconception of cognitive neuroscience consists in perceiving its reductionism as a sort of necessary totalitarian identity theory between brain and behavior, brain and psychology, or brain and cognition. Perhaps neuroscience occasionally endorses such identity theories. However, this should not necessarily be the case, and certainly it is not *our* case. Cognitive neuroscience should investigate human nature first and foremost by clarifying what human experience is made of. What does being someone mean to us, what does it mean to love or hate, feel loved or hated, feel safe or insecure, sharp or flat, moved or petrified, open to others or exclusively self-focused? These are some of the interesting questions cognitive science should be asking.

Much of this book deals with neuroscience in relation to intersubjectivity, not because we believe that the bonds reciprocally relating human beings, their absence or deficit, can today be univocally and causally explained by a subpersonal level of description that speaks of neurotransmitters, receptors, neurons, and brain neural networks. The idea that intersubjectivity is just the function of brain circuits is as satisfying as believing that the sun is just a ball of fire.

That said, however, one should add that knowing that some specific neurotransmitters, receptors, neurons, and brain neural networks are or are not active when we experience ourselves in relation to objects and to others gives us a totally different perspective on human nature. It enables the deconstruction of many of the words and sentences we normally employ when referring to that very same human nature.

Action, perception, cognition, subject, object, intersubjectivity, and language may be very differently conceived when addressed by a subpersonal neurocognitive level of investigation. Are we really born autistic? Are we really capable of a fully competent intersubjectivity only after having built our own personal identity? Does becoming a subject really precede the possibility of entertaining meaningful intersubjective relationships? Is intersubjectivity a purely theoretical and abstract enterprise? Can the most intimate and pivotal aspect of human language be reduced to its syntactic and recursive nature, neglecting its dialogic essence? All of these questions are tightly interlaced and should not be addressed as if they were totally independent from each other. Ideally, such questions should be addressed one by one while having them all in the background.

But even doing so does not suffice. The issue of intersubjectivity, like all other issues related to human nature, should also be framed within both phylogenetic and ontogenetic perspectives. We must study whether and how human intersubjectivity relates to the interindividual relations of other species of animals and to their underpinning neural mechanisms. We must study whether and how the way human beings develop their intersubjective skills relates to the way other animals develop theirs.

Cognitive neuroscience reveals that even at the innermost level of description, intersubjectivity speaks of the quintessential nature of human beings as situated, feeling, and acting bodies. Being, feeling, acting, and knowing describe different modalities of our bodily relations to the world. These modalities all share a constitutive underpinning bodily root that maps into distinct and specific ways of functioning of brain circuits and neural mechanisms. Action, perception, and cognition are, at the level of the brain-body system, made of the same stuff, although differently wired and differently functionally organized. Donald Winnicott employed almost the same words when he wrote: "It is not logical, however, to oppose the mental and the physical as these are not of the same stuff. Mental phenomena are complications of variable importance in psyche-soma continuity of being, in that which adds up to the individual's self" (1975, p. 254).

For the first time, by means of cognitive neuroscience we can look at subjectivity and intersubjectivity from a different and complementary perspective. Does that mean that subjectivity and intersubjectivity should give way to an objective, third-person computational account? Not necessarily. Cognitive neuroscience's research agenda should consist of applying its methodological reductionism to the study of these issues, without sacrificing or eliminating the rich experience we make when encountering others. The standard solipsistic and theoretical account of intersubjectivity offered by classic cognitive science (from now onward referred to as "classic approach") can be challenged. Strikingly copious and converging evidence attests to the intrinsic relational nature of human beings. The news is that such relational nature also transpires at the neural, subpersonal level investigated by cognitive neuroscience.

Before diving into these matters, we briefly show how the classic approach dealt with intersubjectivity during the second half of the 20th century.

THE SO-CALLED PROBLEM OF OTHER MINDS

Humans have been told about their social nature at least since the time of Aristotle. However, this knowledge has not prevented the development of a solipsistic account of human nature. Solipsism, when referring to a philosophy of mind, implies that in order to define what a mind is and how it works, one only needs to focus on the single individual's mind. Such an account, originating in modern times from Descartes, dominated the way human social cognition was addressed and explained for decades. It also influenced the initial, almost exclusive emphasis that psychoanalysis historically placed on the intrapsychic dimension of human nature.

According to the classic approach, human intersubjectivity would ontogenetically develop following universal maturational steps, reaching its final stage in coincidence with the acquisition of full-blown linguistic competence. This account basically equates human social cognition with social metacognition, that is, with the possibility of explicitly reflecting upon and theorizing about one's mental life in relation to the mental life of others.

According to the same view, when applied to phylogenesis, all other social species, including nonhuman primates, in order to navigate in their social world exclusively rely upon the visible aspects of behavior and its statistical recurrence in a certain context. This view implies a radical cognitive discontinuity between humans and all other species of animals, epitomized by the "mental Rubicon" metaphor. Human beings would inhabit the mind readers' side of the river, while all other species, including nonhuman primates, would be confined to the behavior readers' side. Such an account privileges a highly sophisticated cognitive interpretation of intersubjectivity, emphasizing its supposed main if not exclusive theoretical nature. The solution proposed by the classic approach to the so-called problem of other minds consists in building a theory of others' minds. This solution presupposes that overt behavior is intrinsically opaque, thus incapable of disclosing anything relevant about the "what" and "why" of others' actions, attitudes, and thoughts. To understand what the other is doing, feeling, thinking, and why, we should ascribe the witnessed other's behavior to inner and thus not directly accessible mental states.

Such a solution also conditioned developmental psychology, leading to the staging of children's social cognitive development almost exclusively by relying on children's verbal reports and language-mediated performances.

The essence of social cognition is related to the comprehension of others' behavior. In our daily life, we constantly, thus not always consciously, make sense of the behavior of our social partners. Behavior, however, according to the classic view, can be fully understood only once one can ascribe it to some hidden mental state causing it.

Let us use an example from daily life. Suppose you are sitting in a coffee shop. You turn your gaze to your right, where you see a customer sitting at a table beside yours, aiming with her hand at a cup of coffee in front of her. Most likely you would immediately grasp that she is about to sip some coffee. Now, the problem is this: How did you accomplish such an understanding? According to the classic approach, you had to translate your neighbor's biological motions, in principle intentionally opaque, into the mental representations about her *desire* to drink coffee and her *belief* about the fact that the dark brown liquid filling the cup is indeed coffee. The still almost pervasive view on intersubjectivity holds that understanding others squares with manipulating symbolic representations.

The picture of the mind conveyed by classic cognitive science and by many quarters in analytic philosophy is that of a functional system whose processes can be described in terms of manipulations of informational symbols according to a set of formal syntactic rules. Similarly, concepts are considered to be abstract, amodal, and arbitrary propositions represented in some "language of thought," which shares with language at least two distinctive features: generativity and compositionality (Fodor, 1975, 1981, 1983; Pylyshyn, 1984). Thinking is thus reduced to computation. Consequently, the understanding of other minds is conceived solely as a predicative, inferential, theory-like process, and mental states are theoretical states of a commonsense psychological theory called folk psychology.

Indeed, according to folk psychology, thought is referential and the content of mental representations is described in terms of desires, beliefs, and intentions. When perceiving others, as in the coffee shop example, we would translate the perception of their actions into the desires and beliefs likely originating from them. Such propositional attitudes are taken to be contentful representational mental states. Understanding others would be a metarepresentational enterprise, in the sense that when explicitly ascribing mental content to others, one would represent to oneself their mental representations.

A neurobiologically plausible naturalization of social cognition would thus entail the search for neural states mapping desires and beliefs. Indeed, many cognitive neuroscientists did exactly that. If one believes that a gap separates individual human beings, conceived of as mentalizing monads, whose only mean-ingful connections can be traced in their theoretically driven mentalizing skills, an obvious consequence will be that of looking for the neural correlates of beliefs and desires as such. The reification of propositional attitudes inevitably led many cognitive neuroscientists to look for the brain areas/circuits housing desires and beliefs.

This epistemic strategy, though, clearly suffers of circularity. On the one hand, it is postulated that intersubjectivity is basically overlapping with the pos-sibility to entertain a theory of other minds. To study such a Theory of Mind (ToM), researchers normally ask volunteers to use propositional attitudes (e.g., by ascribing false beliefs to fictional characters), while scanning their brains by means of functional magnetic resonance imaging (fMRI). The brain areas acti-vated during the mentalizing task are hence considered to be the house in the brain of the ToM module(s). We doubt that by applying this analysis to the study of social cognition we will ever be able to integrate the folk psychological and the neuroscientific levels of description within a coherent and biologically plausible naturalized framework. Let us see why.

Most of the brain imaging studies investigating ToM (for recent reviews, see Frith & Frith, 2012; Van Overwalle, 2009) have repeatedly claimed the ToM specificity of several brain areas, like the temporo-parietal junction (TPJ) area and medial prefrontal cortex (mPFC). A similar ToM relatedness was also at-tributed to the anterior cingulate cortex (ACC), whose activation during mind-reading tasks was repeatedly attested to by a number of brain imaging studies (for a summary of this literature, see Bird, Castelli, Malik, Frith, & Husain, 2004). The bilateral damage of medial frontal areas, however, does not produce any sort of mind-reading deficit, as shown by the neuropsychological case described by Bird and colleagues (2004). The authors of this study described a stroke patient who suffered a bilateral anterior cerebral artery infarction producing extensive bilateral damage to the medial part of the frontal lobes. After a thorough and meticulous investigation of the patient's ToM competence, the authors conclud-ed that she did not have any significant impairment in tasks probing her ability to construct a ToM. In the words of Bird et al., this demonstrates that "the extensive medial frontal regions destroyed by her stroke are not necessary for this func-tion. . . . We conclude that our findings urge caution against using functional imaging as the sole method of establishing cognitive neuroanatomy" (Bird et al., 2004, p. 926).

As exemplified by the previous clinical case, the classic approach to mind reading is unable to convincingly explain why medial frontal areas and TPJ ac-tivate during explicit mentalizing tasks, besides referring to the tautological no-tion that mind reading is implemented there. To make things worse, the mind reading specificity of the activation of these brain areas is seriously questioned. Mitchell (2008), for example, convincingly showed that TPJ, long held to be specifically activated by mind reading activities, like ascribing false beliefs to oth-ers (Saxe & Kanwisher, 2003; Saxe & Powell, 2006; Saxe & Wexler, 2005), can be equally modulated by nonsocial attentional tasks. Even more interestingly, TPJ has been shown to contribute to multisensory integration of bodily information underlying the conscious and coherent experience of the bodily self (see Berlucchi & Aglioti, 1997; Blanke et al., 2005; Committeri et al., 2007). Transcranial magnetic stimulation (TMS) studies investigating the "rubber hand illusion" (Botvinick & Cohen, 1998), the phenomenal incorporation of an observed prosthetic rubber hand stroked in synchrony with one's own unseen hand, showed that transient interference with the activity of the right hemisphere TPJ reduced the illusion (Kammers, de Vignemont, Verhagen, & Dijkerman, 2009; Tsakiris, Costantini, & Haggard, 2008).

As suggested by Tsakiris and colleagues (2008), right TPJ could provide a coherent sense of one's body. It must be added that by means of its functional connectivity, TPJ is part of a network (including the anterior insular cortex, the posterior parietal cortex, and the premotor cortex) implicated in multisensory integration during self-related and other-related events and experiences. Thus, one could hypothesize that TPJ systematic involvement with mind-reading tasks does not depend upon the fact that it contains false-belief ascription-specific neurons, but because self-other differentiation at a bodily level is a necessary ingredient of such mentalizing activity.

From a cursory review of contemporary mind reading–related neuroscientific literature, one has the impression that the standard notion of mind reading should be thoroughly discussed. The contemporary classic approach to intersubjectivity is predominantly split into two major camps. The first one is championed by simulation theory (ST; see Goldman, 2006). ST privileges the self as the model of the other. Understanding others means putting oneself into others' mental shoes. Antecedents of this model, although less sophisticated, can be traced back to John Stuart Mill and his argument of inference by analogy. According to Mill's argument, we attribute mental states to others—who are just moving bodies—because their behavior evokes memories of our previous situation-related experiences. ST, at least in Goldman's version, stresses the relevance of one's direct access to one's own conscious phenomenal and mental states.

The second camp is exemplified by theory-theory (TT). As noted earlier, this rationalistic model basically describes intersubjectivity as a nonprivileged theoretical epistemic approach to an otherwise unintelligible other, whose mental content can be read from the outside by applying reasoning. Folk psychology dictates the rules governing mind reading. The developmental psychologist Vasudevi Reddy pointed out that despite their differences, both ST and TT approaches posit a gap between minds; both "see the knowledge of other minds as an attributional process—something which requires more than just perceiving the psychological. But there is an alternative which starts from questioning the very assumption of a profound gap between minds. . . . I will suggest that this alternative—the second-person approach—changes the way we think about the 'gap' and even suggests that psychology's methods for understanding people need to be changed" (2008, p. 25).

The second-person approach (also known as second-person perspective) differs from third-person approach because it defines a radically different and deflationary epistemic approach to the problem of other minds, by substantially reducing the mental gap supposedly separating them. Michael Pauen (2012, pp. 38–39) recently outlined three minimal requirements an epistemic approach should meet in order to be recognized as second person. First, it has to draw on a replication or imagination of the mental state to be recognized; second, it must include a self/other distinction, so that the epistemic subject is aware that the state being replicated belongs to the other; third, it must enable the epistemic subject to recognize his or her epistemic situation as different from that of the other person. Even more interestingly, such requirements do not presuppose the epistemic subject being explicitly aware of them. Actually, as pointed out by Pauen, "it seems that they are automatic and subconscious to a large extent" (2012, p. 43). As will become clearer in the following sections, all three requirements are compatible with the neuroscientific account of intersubjectivity and its development that we propose in this book.

THE SECOND-PERSON APPROACH

We do not only mentally entertain an "objective" third-person account of what others are and do to us and with us. When encountering others, we can experience them as bodily selves, similarly to how we experience ourselves as the owners of our bodies and the authors of our actions. When we are exposed to others' expressive behaviors, reactions, and inclinations, we simultaneously experience their goal directedness or intentional character, as we experience ourselves as the agents of *our* actions; the subjects of *our* affects, feelings, and emotions; and the owners of *our* thoughts, fantasies, imaginations, and dreams. Words can hardly describe how the intimate intentional attunement potentially evoked by the encounter with the other coexists with the sharp bodily boundaries that constantly define our being a Self, our being ourselves.

The Jewish philosopher and theologian Martin Buber (1878–1965) is a precursor of the second-person approach to intersubjectivity. In his seminal book *I and Thou* (*Ich und Du*, 1923, English translation by W. Kaufman, 1970), fully imbued with the Hasidic tradition, Buber singles out the fundamental relational character of human beings. Such relational character is at least twofold. It can be a third-person relation, an *I-It* (and I-She, I-He) or a second-person relation, an *I-You*. Buber calls them the two *basic words*. What distinguishes these relations is not their object but the relation style or, to put it in more technical words, the epistemic status adopted by the I. One can relate to another human being in the same way as one relates to inanimate objects. Similarly, one can relate to inanimate objects like a landscape, a tree, or a work of art as one relates to another human being.

All of the various types of relationships human beings entertain with one another can be lived and experienced in different ways. What changes is not the object of our relation with others but our attitude toward them. We can relate with the same person by treating her like a thing among other things, or like our beloved one. Even our beloved one can be an "It," a "She," or a "He." The other can be, for example, an instrument informing us about some state of affairs in the world; can help us through those affairs; can be someone we talk about; or can be an enigmatic case to mentally decipher, most likely employing an inferential mentalizing routine.

Thus, as Buber implicitly suggests, the solution to the problematic issue of intersubjectivity cannot be a forced choice between a third-person and a second-person perspective. We live our lives constantly switching between these two modes of interpersonal relation.

Granted that this is true, we are still facing another choice: whether to adopt an ecumenical holism or to discuss the notion of mind reading as classically conceived, challenging the idea that a theoretical metarepresentational approach to the other is the sole or main key to intersubjectivity. We think it would be potentially more interesting to explore the second alternative. Mind reading, as conceived of in a broad sense (Mbs), could designate our understanding of what is going on when relating to someone else in a variety of modalities of relations, not necessarily metarepresentational, that nevertheless share a fundamental functional feature: the mapping of the other onto the self, reciprocated by the mapping of the self onto the other. Mind reading in a narrow sense (Mns) should qualify as intersubjectivity only when a more explicit need for explanations requires less engaged, more third-person-like types of relations.

Before and below both types of mind reading is the fundamental relational nature of action (see Gallese, 2000, 2003a, 2007). The rhythm, synchronicity, and asynchronous engagements that humans systematically—and from the very beginning—experience in every interhuman relationship mark the birth of intersubjectivity. Indeed, a very stimulating aspect of Buber's book lays in the suggestion that the I-You relation is primal to the I-It, since the latter presupposes the existence of an I. According to Buber (1923/1970), the full-blown I only emerges once one perceives oneself as a You, when interpersonal dialogue turns into a self-centered inner dialogue. "In the beginning is the relation," wrote Buber, "as the category of being, as readiness, as a form that reaches out to be filled, as a model of the soul; the a priori of relation; *the innate You*" (English translation by W. Kaufman, p. 78). Many years later, the pediatrician and psychoanalyst Donald Winnicott wrote: "What does the baby see when he or she looks at the mother's face? I am suggesting that, ordinarily, what the baby sees is himself or herself. In other words, the mother is looking at the baby and *what she looks like is related to what she sees there*" (1971a, p. 151, italics in original).

To contextualize Buber's thought within a contemporary cognitive neuroscience perspective, one could hypothesize that since "the longing of relation is primary" (Winnicott, 1971a, p. 78), the You could be initially viewed as the crystallization of the outcome of the appetitive motivational (or seeking) system (see Panksepp, 1998; Solms & Panksepp, 2012) coupled with a relationally programmed motor system (Gallese, 2000; Rizzolatti & Gallese, 1997; Rizzolatti & Sinigaglia, 2007, 2010). Such a basic "package" would enable the parallel genesis of the I and of the thing (see next section).

In interpersonal relationships Buber's *innate You* is realized in the encountered You. Here Buber prefigures Stein Bråten's (1988, 1992, 2007) notion of alter-centric participation, that is, the innate capacity to experience what the other is experiencing as being centered in the other (see also chapter 6).

When encountering others, we can relate to them in the detached way typical of an external observer. We can "objectively" explain others, reflect, and formulate judgments, elaborate parameterizations and categorizations on their actions, emotions, and sensations by adopting a third-person perspective, aimed at objectifying the content of our perceptions and predictions. The purpose of these cognitive operations is the deliberate categorization of an external state of affairs. The same others, though, can also be experienced according to a total shift of the object of our intentional relations. When engaged with others in a second-person perspective, we are no longer directed to the content of a perception in order to categorize it. We are just attuned to the intentional relation displayed by someone else (Gallese, 2003a,b, 2005). Intersubjectivity is not exclusively confined to a declarative, metarepresentational third-person perspective. We are not alienated from the actions, emotions, and sensations of others because we own those same actions, emotions, and sensations.

A new understanding of intersubjectivity could therefore benefit from a bottom-up study and characterization of the nondeclarative and nonmetarepresentational aspects of social cognition (see Gallese, 2003a, 2007). One key issue of the new approach to intersubjectivity we propose here is the investigation of the neural bases of our capacity to be attuned to the intentional relations of others. By means of intentional attunement, "the other" is much more than a different representational system; it becomes a bodily self, like us. This new epistemological approach to intersubjectivity has the merit of generating predictions about the intrinsic functional nature of our social cognitive operations, cutting across, and not being subordinated to a specific mind ontology, like that purported by the classic approach.

THE EMBODIMENT OF MOTOR GOALS
AND MOTOR INTENTIONS

For several decades the neurophysiological investigation of the cortical motor system of nonhuman primates mainly focused on the study of elementary physical features of movement such as force, direction, and amplitude. However, the neurophysiological study of the ventral premotor cortex and the posterior parietal cortex of macaque monkeys revealed that the cortical motor system plays an important role in cognition. In particular, it showed that the cortical motor system is functionally organized in terms of *motor goals*.

The most anterior region of the ventral premotor cortex of the macaque monkey, area F5 (Matelli, Luppino, & Rizzolatti, 1985), controls hand and mouth movements (Hepp-Reymond, Hüsler, Maier, & Qi, 1994; Kurata & Tanji, 1986; Rizzolatti, Scandolara, Matelli, & Gentilucci, 1981; Rizzolatti et al., 1988). Most F5 neurons, similar to neurons of other regions of the cortical motor system (Alexander & Crutcher, 1990; Crutcher & Alexander, 1990; Kakei, Hoffman, & Strick, 1999, 2001; Shen & Alexander, 1997), do not discharge in association with the activation of specific muscle groups or during the execution of elementary movements, but they are active during motor acts—movements executed to accomplish a specific motor goal—such as grasping, tearing, holding, or manipulating objects (Rizzolatti et al., 1988; Rizzolatti & Gallese, 1997; Rizzolatti, Fogassi, & Gallese, 2000).

Area F5 motor neurons do not code physical parameters of movement such as force or movement direction, but rather the pragmatic relationship between agent and target of the motor act. F5 neurons indeed are activated only when a particular type of effector-object relation (e.g., hand-object, mouth-object) is executed until such relation leads to a different state (e.g., to take possession of a piece of food, to throw it away, to break it, to bring it to the mouth, to chew it, etc.).

MIRRORING OTHERS' MOTOR GOALS AND MOTOR INTENTIONS: MIRROR NEURONS

A second category of motor neurons in area F5 is made by multimodal neurons that discharge when the monkey observes an action made by another individual and when it executes the same or a similar action. These neurons were designated "mirror neurons" (Gallese, Fadiga, Fogassi, & Rizzolatti, 1996; Rizzolatti, Fadiga, Gallese, & Fogassi, 1996; Rizzolatti & Gallese, 1997; see also Kraskov et al., 2010).

Neurons with similar properties were later discovered in a sector of the posterior parietal cortex reciprocally connected with area F5 (Bonini et al., 2010; Fogassi et al., 2005; Gallese, Fogassi, Fadiga, & Rizzolatti, 2002) and in the primary motor cortex (Dushanova & Donoghue, 2010; Tkach, Reimer, & Hatsopoulos, 2007). The main triggering element to elicit the mirror neurons' response during action execution and observation is the interaction between the agent's body effectors like the hand or the mouth and the object: Mirror neurons in monkeys respond neither to the observation of an object alone nor to the sight of a hand mimicking an action without a target (Gallese et al., 1996).

F5 mirror neurons respond to the execution/observation of a grasping motor act, regardless of the executed/observed movements required to accomplish that goal (Rochat et al., 2010). The intensity of the discharge of F5 mirror neurons is significantly stronger during action execution than during action observation. This suggests that the mirror mechanism is not opaque to the issue of agency, that is, the issue of *who* is the agent and *who* is the observer within the dyadic social relationship.

A few years after their discovery, mirror neurons were interpreted as the expression of a direct form of action understanding. This led to the proposal of their relevance for social cognition (Gallese et al., 1996; Rizzolatti et al., 1996; Rizzolatti & Gallese, 1997). Mirror neurons, it was hypothesized, would enable a motor, goal-related description of the perceived action, richer than the mere visual account of its features. This was demonstrated later on by two studies. In the first study, Umiltà and colleagues (2001) found that nearly 50% of F5 mirror neurons respond to the action outcome even in the absence of complete visual information about it, since the observed experimenter's hand grasps the object behind an opaque occluding surface, thus outside of the monkey's sight.

These data do not downplay the coexistence within the brain "visual" system of a visual analysis of others' behavior. The point being made is that what turns such behavior into intentional, goal-related motor acts, what turns someone else's *moving hand* into a *grasping hand* is the reuse in the observer's brain of the neural resources enabling the use of one's hand as a grasping hand. The purely visual "pictorial" analysis is most likely per se insufficient to understand someone else as grasping something to do something with it. Without reference to the observer's internal "motor knowledge," mapped in parieto-premotor cortical circuits, the purely observational, third-person pictorial description is devoid of experiential meaning for the observing individual (Gallese, 2000; Gallese, Rochat, Cossu, & Sinigaglia, 2009).

In a second study, Köhler and colleagues (2002) demonstrated that F5 mirror neurons also respond to the sound produced by the consequences of someone else's purposeful hand-object interaction, like breaking a peanut. This particular class of F5 mirror neurons ("audiovisual mirror neurons") respond not only when the monkey *executes* and *observes* a given hand motor act but also when *listening to* the sound typically produced by the same motor act. These neurons not only selectively respond to the sound of actions but also discriminate between the sounds of different actions. The functional properties of mirror neurons reveal the existence of a neurophysiological mechanism—the mirror mechanism (MM)—by means of which perceived events as different as action sounds and action images are mapped and integrated by the same motor neurons, enabling the execution of the very same actions (for review, see Gallese, 2003a,b, 2006; Gallese, Keysers, & Rizzolatti, 2004; Gallese et al., 2009; Rizzolatti et al., 2001; Rizzolatti & Sinigaglia, 2008, 2010).

A further step was accomplished by discovering that F5 and parietal mirror neurons respond differently to identical motor acts (e.g., grasping) according to the final goal of the action in which those acts are embedded (e.g., grasping an object to bring it to the mouth or into a container; see Bonini et al., 2010; Fogassi et al., 2005). This shows that the MM actively controls and responds to the observation of sequences of goal-related motor acts (grasping, holding, bringing, placing) properly assembled to accomplish a more distal motor goal state. These results demonstrate—at least at the level of basic actions—that the MM also codes motor intentions like grasping to eat or grasping to place.

Another recent study (Caggiano, Fogassi, Rizzolatti, Thier, & Casile, 2009) demonstrated that the distance at which the observed action takes place modulates F5 mirror neuron activity. About 50% of recorded mirror neurons responded only when the observed agent acted either inside or outside the monkey's arm-reaching distance.

Such modulation, however, did not simply measure the physical distance between agent and observer. Many mirror neurons not responding to the experimenter's grasping actions carried out near to the monkey resumed their discharge when a physical transparent barrier was interposed between the object and the observing monkey. Blocking the monkey's *potentiality* for interaction with the observed agent (e.g., stealing the food) remapped the agent's near spatial location as far.

What is the relevance of the MM for macaque monkeys' social cognition? The studies reviewed earlier demonstrate that the MM expresses functional properties that could enable monkeys to understand what others are doing and for what basic purpose. Macaque monkeys are capable of shared attention behaviors (Ferrari, Kohler, Fogassi, & Gallese, 2000; Ferrari, Coudé, Gallese, & Fogassi, 2008). Shepherd, Klein, Deaner, and Platt (2009) discovered a class of mirror neurons in the lateral intraparietal (LIP) area involved in oculomotor control, signaling both when the monkey looked in a given direction and when it observed another monkey looking in the same direction. Shepherd and colleagues (2009) suggested that LIP mirror neurons for gaze might contribute to sharing of observed attention, thus playing a role in imitative behavior.

MIRRORING OTHERS' MOTOR GOALS
AND MOTOR INTENTIONS:
THE MIRROR MECHANISM IN HUMANS

The existence of the MM is now also firmly established in the human brain. Action observation activates premotor and posterior parietal areas, likely human homologs of macaque areas in which mirror neurons were originally described. The MM for action in humans is coarsely somatotopically organized; the same premotor and posterior parietal regions normally activated when we execute mouth-, hand-, and foot-related acts are also activated when we observe the same motor acts executed by others (Buccino et al. 2001; see also Cattaneo & Rizzolatti, 2009). Watching someone grasping a cup of coffee, biting an apple, or kicking a football activates in our brain the same cortical regions that would be activated if we were doing the same.

The MM in humans has been shown to be involved in imitation of simple movements (Iacoboni et al., 1999, 2001) and in imitation learning of complex skills, like learning how to play a guitar (Buccino et al., 2004; Vogt et al., 2007). Furthermore, the MM can offer a neurophysiological explanation of many interesting phenomena described by social psychologists, like the "chameleon effect"—observers' nonconscious mimicry of bodily postures, expressions, and behaviors of their social partners (Chartrand & Bargh, 1999). It is worth noting that such examples of nonconscious intersubjective mimesis all share a prosocial character, since their occurrence increases during social interactions with affiliative purposes.

Coherently with the goal relatedness of mirror neurons in monkeys recently demonstrated by Rochat and colleagues (2010), a transcranial magnetic stimulation (TMS) study on humans showed that observers' motor system excitability was modulated by the goal of the observed motor act, regardless of the movements required to accomplish it (Cattaneo, Caruana, Jezzini, & Rizzolatti, 2009).

Posterior parietal and ventral premotor areas, part of the network exhibiting the MM, are activated by the observation of hand actions, even when accomplished by a nonanthropomorphic robotic arm (Gazzola, Rizzolatti, Wicker, & Keysers, 2007), or when observers are congenitally upper limb deficient and thus could never practice hand grasping (Gazzola, van der Worp, et al., 2007). In the latter case, the observed hand grasping activated the motor representations of mouth and foot grasping in the brain of the two patients. The parieto-premotor MM generalizes motor goals also when relying—like macaques do—on action sounds through the auditory channel (Gazzola, Aziz-Zadeh, & Keysers, 2006). Similar functional properties were found in congenitally blind patients (Ricciardi et al., 2009).

Finally, a recent TMS adaptation study confirms the specific role of the motor system in the mapping of motor goal relatedness in a context-independent way. Visual areas sensitive to the observation of biological motion are devoid of this property (Cattaneo, Sandrini, & Schwarzbach, 2010). This shows once more and in humans, too, that the visual description of motor behavior falls short of accounting for its goal relatedness. The relational character of behavior as it is mapped by the cortical motor system enables a direct appreciation of purpose without relying on explicit inference. Is this behavior reading, mind reading, or neither? We leave it to the reader to decide.

Few brain imaging and neurophysiological studies provide preliminary evidence of a possible role of the human MM in mapping basic motor intentions, like eating, drinking, and putting objects away (Cattaneo et al., 2008; Iacoboni et al., 2005). Iacoboni and colleagues (2005) demonstrated that the ventral premotor cortex responds differently to the observation of different motor intentions associated with grasping, like drinking or cleaning up. Brass, Schmitt, Spengler, and Gergely (2007) showed activation of the MM when observing unusual actions like switching on the light with a knee, both when plausible (agent's hands are occupied) or not (agent's hands are free) to observers.

This very concise review of part of the scientific literature on mirror neurons and the MM shows that behavior can be described at a high level of abstraction, without implying an explicit language-mediated conceptualization. The motor system, together with its connections to viscero-motor and sensory cortical areas, structures action execution and action perception, and action imitation and imagination. When the action is executed or imitated, the cortico-spinal pathway is activated, leading to movement. When the action is observed or imagined, its actual execution is inhibited. The cortical motor network is activated, though, not in all of its components and not with the same intensity; and action is not produced but only simulated.

The presence of the MM both in nonhuman and human brains opens a new evolutionary scenario with "motor cognition" as a leading element for the emergence of human intersubjectivity (Gallese, 2000; Gallese et al., 2009; Gallese & Rochat, 2009). We do not necessarily need to metarepresent in propositional format the intentions of others to understand them. Motor goals and intentions are part of the vocabulary being spoken by the motor system. Most of the time we do not explicitly ascribe intentions to others; we simply detect them. When witnessing others' behaviors, we can directly grasp their motor intentional contents without needing to metarepresent them.

THE SHARED WORLD OF EMOTIONS
AND SENSATIONS

The discovery of the MM for actions led to the hypothesis that mirror neurons could be just the tip of a much bigger iceberg, still to be uncovered in the domain of emotions and sensations (Gallese, 2003a,b; Goldman & Gallese, 2000). Empirical evidence lent support to this hypothesis. Other mirroring mechanisms seem to be involved with our capacity to share emotions and sensations with others (de Vignemont & Singer, 2006; Decety & Sommerville, 2003; Gallese, 2001, 2003a,b, 2006). When perceiving others expressing a given basic emotion by means of their facial mimicry, the observer's facial muscles activate in a congruent manner (Dimberg, 1982; Dimberg & Thunberg, 1998; Dimberg, Thunberg, & Elmehed, 2000; Lundqvist & Dimberg, 1995), with an intensity proportional to their empathic nature (Sonnby-Borgstrom, 2002).

Systematic reciprocal correlation between the bodily expression of emotion and the way in which emotions are understood was repeatedly observed. When individuals enact emotion-specific body postures or facial expressions, they experience emotional states and evaluate external events in a congruent fashion (for review, see Niedenthal, 2007). The integrated activity of sensory-motor and affective neural systems simplifies and to a certain degree automatizes the behavioral responses living organisms are supposed to produce in order to survive in their social environment.

The perception and production of emotion-related facial expressions could impinge on common neural structures whose function can be hypothesized to be similar to the MM. Indeed, both observation and imitation of the facial expression of basic emotions activate the same restricted group of brain structures, including the ventral premotor cortex, the insula, and the amygdala (Carr, Iacoboni, Dubeau, Mazziotta, & Lenzi, 2003). Voluntary imitation of the expression of emotions, however, does not necessarily produce the subjective experience of the emotion one is imitating. An fMRI study specifically addressed this issue by scanning brain activity of healthy participants both during the phenomenal experience of disgust, induced by inhalation of disgusting odorants, and the observation of video clips showing other people expressing the same emotion with their facial expression. Witnessing the facial expression of disgust in others activates the left anterior insula at the same location activated by the first-person subjective experience of disgust (Wicker et al., 2003). This result is also consistent with the clinical observation that damage to the anterior insula disrupts both the possibility of subjectively experiencing disgust and recognizing the same emotion when expressed by others (Adolphs, Tranel, & Damasio, 2003; Calder, Keane, Manes, Antoun, & Young, 2000). It appears therefore that there is a we-centric (see Gallese, 2001, 2003a,b) dimension in the experience of a given affective state. When observing someone else's facial expression, we do not understand its meaning only through explicit inference from analogy. The other's emotion is first and foremost constituted and directly understood by reusing part of the same neural circuits underpinning our first-person experience of the same emotion.

Similar mechanisms were described for the perception of pain (Botvinick et al., 2005; Hutchison, Davis, Lozano, Tasker, & Dostrovsky, 1999; Jackson, Meltzoff, & Decety, 2005; Singer et al., 2004) and touch (Blakemore, Bristow, Bird, Frith, & Ward, 2005; Ebisch et al., 2008, 2011, 2012; Keysers et al., 2004). When looking at the body of someone else being touched, caressed, slapped, or injured, part of our own somatosensory system, normally mapping our own subjectively experienced tactile and painful sensations, is also activated. Altogether these results suggest that an important aspect of intersubjectivity, when witnessing the expression of others' emotions and sensations, can be described in terms of reuse of the same neural circuits underpinning our own emotional and sensory experiences (see Gallese, 2003a,b, 2006, 2007; Gallese et al., 2004). It has been proposed that a common functional mechanism, embodied simulation (ES), can account for this variety of intersubjective phenomena in an integrated and neurobiologically plausible way.

INTERSUBJECTIVITY AND EMBODIED SIMULATION THEORY

The notion of simulation can be employed in many different domains, often with different, not necessarily overlapping, meanings. Simulation is a functional process that possesses certain content, typically focusing on possible states of its target object. In philosophy of mind, the notion of simulation has been used by proponents of the ST of mind reading (Goldman, 2006; see earlier) to characterize the pretend state adopted by the attributer to understand another person's behavior. Basically, according to this view, we use our mind to put ourselves into the mental shoes of others.

At difference with standard accounts of ST, ES is characterized as a mandatory, nonmetarepresentational, nonintrospectionist process (Gallese, 2003a, 2005, 2006; Gallese & Sinigaglia, 2011b). ES theory, in fact, challenges the notion that the sole account of intersubjectivity consists in explicitly attributing to others propositional attitudes like beliefs and desires, mapped as symbolic representations. Before and below mind reading is *intercorporeality* as the main source of knowledge we directly gather about others (Gallese, 2007). As recently emphasized by De Preester following Merleau-Ponty, the body of intercorporeality is primarily perceived as a systematic means to go toward objects. This is the reason why, De Preester argued, "the other is seen as a behavior and the 'I' is primarily a 'motor I'" (2008, p. 137).

A direct form of understanding others from within, as it were—intentional attunement (see Gallese, 2003a, 2006)—is achieved by the activation of neural systems underpinning what we and others do and feel. Parallel to the detached third-person sensory description of the observed social stimuli, internal nonpropositional "representations" in bodily format of the body states associated with actions, emotions, and sensations are evoked in the observer, as if he or she were performing a similar action or experiencing a similar emotion or sensation.

ES theory provides a unitary account of basic aspects of intersubjectivity showing that people reuse their own mental states or processes represented in bodily format to functionally attribute them to others. ES theory does not provide a general theory of mental simulation covering all types of simulation-based mind reading. ES aims at explaining the MM and related phenomena, like spatial awareness, object vision, mental imagery, and several aspects of language (see Gallese & Sinigaglia, 2011b). By accounting for the MM in terms of mental states reuse, ES makes reference to the *intrapersonal* resemblance or matching between one's mental state when acting or experiencing an emotion or a sensation and when observing others' actions, emotions, and sensations. *Interpersonal* similarity between the simulator's and target's mental state or process does not make for mental simulation unless arising from *intrapersonal* reuse of the simulator's own mental state or process (see Gallese, 2011; Gallese & Sinigaglia, 2011b). Being neurally implemented inside the brain, of course, is not what makes a mental representation embodied. A representational format is typically associated with characteristic processing profiles. Motor, viscero-motor, and somatosensory profiles characterize a bodily formatted representation, distinguishing it from a propositional representation, even in the presence of (partially) overlapping content.

Mental states or processes are embodied primarily because of their bodily format. As argued by Gallese and Sinigaglia (2011b), like a map and a series of sentences might represent the same route with a different format, so mental representations might have partly overlapping contents (e.g., a motor goal, an emotion, or a sensation), while differing from one another in their representational format (e.g., bodily instead of propositional). This is crucial because the format of a mental representation constrains what a mental representation can represent. When planning and executing a motor act, bodily factors (e.g., biomechanical, dynamical, and postural) constrain what can be represented. The bodily representational format thus constrains the way a single motor goal or a hierarchy of motor goals are represented, a way that is different from a propositional representation of those same goals or hierarchy of goals. Similar constraints thus apply both to the representations of one's own actions, emotions, or sensations involved in actually acting and experiencing and also to the corresponding representations involved in observing someone else performing a given action or experiencing a given emotion or sensation. The constraints are similar because the representations share a common bodily format.

MM-driven ES plays a constitutive role in the basic form of mind reading, not requiring the involvement of propositional attitudes, mapped onto mental representations with a bodily format (i.e., motor representations of goals and intentions, as well as viscero-motor and somatosensory representations of emotions and sensations). ES theory does not necessarily imply that we experience the specific contents of others' experiences. It implies that we experience others as having experiences similar to ours.

As posited by the father of phenomenology Edmund Husserl (1977, 1989), and recently reemphasized by Dan Zahavi (2001), it is the alterity of the other to guarantee the objectivity we normally attribute to reality. Although one could add, siding with Merleau-Ponty, "In the absence of reciprocity there is no alter Ego" (1962, p. 357). Perhaps it is not possible to conceive of oneself as a Self without rooting such appraisal in an earlier stage in which sharing prevails. As we have seen, in adulthood a shared manifold of intersubjectivity (Gallese, 2001) also underpins, scaffolds, and enables our social transactions.

Anyway, the character of alterity, of *other selves* we implicitly attribute to others as we experience them, also maps at the subpersonal neural level. The cortical motor circuits at work when we act neither completely overlap nor show the same activation intensity (see earlier; Rochat et al., 2010) as when others are the agents and we are the observers of their actions. Furthermore, as shown in previous sections, a variety of inhibitory mechanisms usually prevent the motor system when observing others' behavior from producing overt contagious behavior or, more generally, a systematic actual reenactment of what is being observed.

The same logic applies to emotions (see Jabbi, Bastiaansen, & Keysers, 2008) and sensations (see Blakemore et al., 2005; Ebisch et al., 2008, 2011, 2012). Jabbi and colleagues (2008) showed that experiences as different as being subjectively disgusted, imagining someone else being disgusted, and seeing disgust portrayed in the facial expression of others not only all lead to the activation of the same network of brain areas (the anterior insula and the anterior cingulate cortex) but also to the activation of different brain areas according to the specific modality in which disgust is experienced (my real disgust, someone else's imagined disgust, or your observed disgust).

MOTOR COGNITION AND THE ORIGIN
OF THE MIRROR MECHANISM

ES theory challenges the traditional purely mentalistic and disembodied view of intersubjectivity and social cognition heralded by the classic approach, by positing that the capacity to understand others' intentional behavior—both from a phylogenetic and ontogenetic point of view—relies on a more basic functional mechanism, which exploits the intrinsic organization of the primate motor system. As reviewed in the preceding sections, abilities like goal detection, action anticipation, and hierarchical representation of action with respect to a distal goal can all be viewed as the direct consequence of the peculiar functional architecture of the motor system, organized in terms of goal-directed motor acts (Rizzolatti & Gallese, 1997; Rizzolatti et al., 1988, 2000). Such abilities were qualified as *motor cognition* (Gallese & Rochat, 2009; Gallese et al., 2009). The Czech philosopher Jan Patočka in his book *Body, Community, Language, World* wrote: "Our primary experience of ourselves is an experience of primordial dynamism that manifests itself in our awareness of our existence as a moving, active being. This dynamism appears as distinctively linked to that which orients us in our movements . . . in such a way that our energy is always focused on something, on what we are doing" (1998, p. 40). An important corollary of the motor cognition hypothesis is that the correct development of motor cognition is required to scaffold more cognitively sophisticated social mental abilities.

Motor goal coding is a distinctive functional feature of the organization of the cortical motor system of primates, humans included. This functional principle can also shed light on the debate on the relative importance of motor and perceptual experience to grasp the meaning of an observed action. When the observed action performed by others becomes part of the observer's motor experience, it leads to a more anticipated and stronger response of mirror neurons. Indeed, coherently with these data, several brain-imaging studies conducted on human beings have shown that the intensity of the MM activation during action observation depends on the similarity between the observed actions and the participants' action repertoire (Aglioti, Cesari, Romani, & Urgesi, 2008; Buccino et al., 2004; Calvo-Merino, Glaser, Grèzes, Passingham, & Haggard, 2005; Cross, Hamilton, & Grafton, 2006; Haslinger et al., 2006). In particular, one fMRI study (Calvo-Merino, Grèzes, Glaser, Passingham, & Haggard, 2006) focused on the distinction between the relative contribution of visual and motor experience in processing an observed action. The results revealed stronger activation of the MM when the observed actions were frequently performed by observers with respect to those that were only perceptually familiar but never practiced by them.

These discoveries emphasize the crucial role played by the motor system in providing the building blocks upon which more sophisticated social cognitive abilities can be built. But when does the MM originate? The earliest indirect evidence available to date on the MM in human infants comes from a study by

Shimada and Hiraki (2006), who showed with near infrared spectroscopy (NIRS) the presence of an action execution/observation mapping system in 6-month-old human infants. Southgate, Johnson, and Csibra (2008) showed with high-density electroencephalography (EEG) that 9-month-old infants exhibit alpha-band attenuation over central electrodes (a sign of motor activation) both during hand action execution and observation. Moreover, Southgate, Johnson, El Karoui, and Csibra (2010) showed a similar motor activation effect in 13-month-old infants during prediction of others' motor goals, with an experimental paradigm modeled on that of Umiltà and colleagues (2001) in which monkeys' mirror neurons were tested during the observation of a hand grasping behind an occluding surface. Finally, van Elk, van Schieb, Hunnius, Vesperc, and Bekkering (2008) recorded 14- to 16-month-old infants' EEG during observation of action videos. Their findings indicated stronger motor activation during observation of crawling compared to walking videos. The size of the effect was strongly related to the infants' own crawling experience. Like the authors of this study conclude, data suggest that already early in life one's own action experience is closely related to how the actions of others are perceived.

We do not yet know when and how the MM appears. We do not know whether mirror neurons are innate and how they are shaped and modeled during development. It has been proposed that mirror neurons are the outcome of a simple associative mechanism binding the motor commands enabling action execution with the visual perception of the same action (Heyes, 2010; Keysers & Perrett, 2004). This hypothesis, however, does not account for mirroring mechanisms pertaining to motor acts performed with body parts to which neither monkeys nor humans have direct visual access, like the mouth and the face. Second, this hypothesis, for the same reasons, is forced to downplay or even deny plausibility of compelling evidence about neonatal imitation both in nonhuman primates (Ferrari et al., 2006; Myowa-Yamakoshi, Tomonaga, Tanaka, & Matsuzawa, 2004) and humans (Meltzoff & Moore, 1977). Third, this hypothesis falls short of explaining empirical evidence showing that motor experience without any visual feedback boosts perceptual ability when directed to human biological motion (see Casile & Giese, 2006).

An alternative account of the ontogenesis of the MM was provided (Gallese, 2009b; Gallese et al., 2009). The recently discovered sophisticated prenatal development of the motor system (Castiello et al., 2010; Myowa-Yamakoshi & Takeshita, 2006; Zoia et al., 2007) led Gallese to hypothesize that before birth, specific connections may develop between the motor centers controlling mouth and hand movements and brain regions recipient of visual inputs after birth. Such connectivity could neurophysiologically "instruct" and train areas of the brain that, once reached by visual information, would be ready to respond to the observation of hand or facial gestures, thus enabling neonatal imitation.

Neonates and infants, by means of specific neural connectivity developed during the late phase of gestation between motor and "to-become-visual" regions of the brain, would be ready to imitate the gestures performed by adult caregivers in front of them and would be endowed with the neural resources enabling the reciprocal behaviors characterizing our postnatal life since its very beginning (see chapter 6). A similar motor conditioning of visual processing could also account for the perceptual advantages offered by motor experience with respect to visual familiarity observed in a variety of perceptual tasks performed by adults.

An innate rudimentary MM is most likely already present at birth, to be subsequently and flexibly modulated by motor experience and gradually enriched by visuomotor learning. Indeed, fully consistent with Gallese's hypothesis are very recent preliminary results in newborn macaque monkeys showing EEG desynchronization within the 5–6 Hz range during both facial gesture execution and observation, but not during the observation of nonbiological motion (Ferrari et al., 2012). According to Lepage and Théoret (2007), the development of the MM can be conceptualized as a process whereby the child learns to refrain from acting out the automatic mapping mechanism linking action perception and execution. This scenario found recent support from data obtained both in monkeys (Kraskov et al., 2010) and humans (Mukamel, Ekstrom, Kaplan, Iacoboni, & Fried, 2010). In fact, as outlined earlier, both studies presented neurophysiological evidence of mirror neurons activated during action execution but inhibited during the observation of actions done by others. The development of cortical inhibitory mechanisms likely leads the gradual transition from mandatory reenactment to mandatory embodied motor simulation.

The discovery of the MM provided a neurofunctional basis to interpret the ever-growing evidence coming from developmental psychology research on the role played by experience-based motor knowledge in shaping the ontogenetic development of intersubjectivity. These issues will be concisely addressed in the next section.

THE ONTOGENY OF INTERSUBJECTIVITY IN HUMANS

Human beings are social creatures, and action represents the earliest mean to express their social inclination. Very early in life human social cognition is anchored to action at an interindividual level (von Hofsten, 2007). At birth, humans already engage in interpersonal mimetic relations, by means of neonatal imitation. Since the seminal study of Meltzoff and Moore (1977), the innate presence of imitative abilities in human infants is a well-known transitory phenomenon, extensively investigated and confirmed by different studies. Newborns are able to reproduce facial gestures (Legerstee, 2005; Meltzoff & Moore, 1992), facial expressions (Field, Woodson, Greenberg, & Cohen, 1982), and, to a certain extent, hand gestures (Fontaine, 1984; Nagy et al., 2005). Five- to eight-week-old infants imitate the tongue protrusion behavior of a human model only, and not the one of a nonbiological agent (Legerstee, 1991). This finding shows that neonatal imitation behavior is selective for conspecifics. Neonates are innately prepared to link to their caregivers through imitation and affective attunement, clarifying yet another of the various capacities that locate human infants in the social world from the very beginning of life.

Infants very early on participate in social interaction sequences. As aptly put by Legerstee, "infants communicate with eye contact, facial expression, vocalizations, and gestures while assimilating the rhythm of their interactions to that of their caretakers" (2009, p. 2). They actively solicit their caregivers' attention and engage themselves in body activity displaying a "protoconversational" turn-taking structure, that is, characterized by a structure similar to adult conversations (see Bråten,1988, 1992, 2007; Meltzoff & Brooks, 2001; Meltzoff & Moore, 1977, 1998; Stern, 1985; Trevarthen, 1979, 1993; Tronick, 1989). Furthermore, as shown by Reddy (2008), few-months-old preverbal infants when participating in social interactions even show signs of so-called self-conscious emotions like embarrassment, pride, and coyness. They display these behaviors at a developmental age preceding the onset of self-reflective consciousness, definitely well before being capable of self-recognition when looking at their reflection in a mirror. Reddy wrote, "[Self-conscious-emotions,] rather than derive from conceptual development in the second year of human infancy, exist in simple forms as ways of managing the exposure of self to other from early in the first year and are crucial for shaping the infant's emerging conception of self and other" (2008, p. 41).

It was proposed that from a functional perspective one important aspect of cognitive development has to do with expanding the prospective control of action (Gallese et al., 2009). Indeed, in humans motor skills mature much earlier on than previously thought. At birth the primary somatosensory and motor cortex show an advanced maturation compared with other brain areas (Chiron et al., 1992). Newborns are already endowed with a rudimentary form of eye-hand coordination (von Hofsten, 1982) and can purposely control their arm movements to meet external demands (van der Meer, 1997).

Even more interestingly, recent evidence shows that motor control is remarkably sophisticated well before birth. Fetuses at the 22nd week of gestation show anticipatory opening movement of the mouth preceding the arrival of the hand (Myowa-Yamakoshi & Takeshita, 2006) and display hand movements with different kinematic patterns depending on where they are aimed (Zoia et al., 2007; see figure 1.1A). The kinematic study of prenatal twin fetuses' behavior offers a unique opportunity to investigate the dawning of intersubjectivity in our species.

A recent study (Castiello et al., 2010) showed that fetal twins already at the 14th week of gestation display upper-limb movements with different kinematic profiles according to whether they target their own body or the body of the other twin (see figure 1.1B). Furthermore, between the 14th and the 18th week of gestation the proportion of self-directed movements decreases, while that of the movements targeting the sibling increases. The human motor system, well before birth, is already instantiating functional properties enabling social interactions. Such social interactions are expressed obeying different motor potentialities. The dawning of the *interpersonal self* (Neisser, 1988) thus appears to

FIGURE 1.1.   Motor behavior of the fetus. (A) Video frame showing the self-directed movement toward the mouth of a 22-week-old fetus. (B) Video frame showing a 14-week-old fetus touching the back of the sibling. (Modified from © 2010 Castiello et al.)

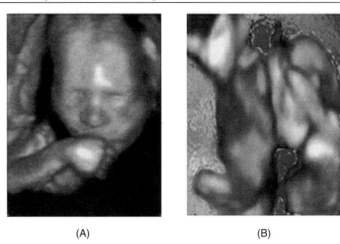

(A)   (B)

occur before birth. When the context enables it, as in the case of twin pregnancies, bodily otherness is mapped on one's own motor potentialities, similarly to the basic social interactions taking place after birth.

Is motor cognition relevant for the development of intersubjectivity? According to a widely held opinion, its role is taken to be marginal. As we argued earlier, the dominant view is still equating intersubjectivity and social cognition with explicit mind reading. Mind reading, in turn, is viewed by many as a mainly theoretical enterprise—Theory of Mind (ToM; Premack & Woodruff, 1978)—grounded on metarepresentational abilities consisting of the ascription to others of belief/desire propositional attitudes of folk psychology.

It was maintained for a long time that the achievement of a full-blown ToM occurs when infants pass the false-belief task (Baron-Cohen, Leslie, & Frith, 1985), that is, when they understand others' behavior as being driven by their own representation of the world, which might not necessarily reflect reality in accurate ways (Baron-Cohen et al., 1985; Wimmer & Perner, 1983).

Solid experimental evidence, though, shows that during the first year of life, infants' action understanding is already fairly well developed. These early forms of action understanding do not imply any metarepresentational capacity, nor can they be interpreted in terms of mind reading, at least not in terms of mind reading in the narrow sense (see earlier). Gergely and Csibra's teleological stance hypothesis (Csibra, Birò, Koòs, & Gergely, 2003; Csibra, Gergely, Birò, Koòs, & Brockbank, 1999) posits that by 9 months of age, infants are equipped with an inferential system applied to factual reality (action, goal state, and current situational constraints) for generating nonmentalistic goal-directed action representations. According to these authors, an action is represented as teleological only if it satisfies a "principle of rational action," stating that an action can be explained by its goal state if the agent reaches its goal through the most efficient means, given the contextual constraints.

However, a different theoretical view on the emergence of infants' goal-directed action interpretation stresses the intrinsic link between action understanding and motor experience. Several scholars emphasize the constructional effect of self-agentive experience on infants' understanding of actions' goal relatedness (see Sommerville & Woodward, 2005). Infant research by means of habituation/dishabituation paradigms showed that previous motor experience facilitates 3-month-old infants' perception of goal-directed actions performed by others (Sommerville, Woodward, & Needham, 2005). Moreover, 10-month-old infants' ability to construe an action representation as hierarchically organized toward a distal goal strictly depends on their ability to perform similarly structured action sequences (Sommerville & Woodward, 2005).

It must be stressed that the congruency between the observed action and the observer's motor repertoire is crucial for goal prediction. Infants produce proactive goal-directed eye movements when observing an agent placing balls into a bucket, only to the extent they can perform the same action (Falck-Ytter, Gredeback, & von Hofsten, 2006). Furthermore, infants' early goal discrimination is initially confined to actions executed by conspecifics. Six-month-old infants are sensitive to the action's goal of others only when performed by a human agent (Woodward, 1998). Meltzoff (1995) showed that older infants imitate the unseen motor goal of a human model but not of an inanimate object.

Goal detection forms the core ability of action understanding and social learning through imitation. Both adults (Baird & Baldwin, 2001) and children represent actions as constituted by units hierarchically organized with respect to an overarching goal. Ten-month-old children similarly to adults can parse actions in units whose boundaries correspond to the completion of a motor goal (Baldwin, Baird, Saylor, & Clark, 2001). Imitation tasks reflect children's ability to represent actions' units as organized toward a distal goal. Preschoolers when asked to imitate the action of another person reproduce the higher order goal of the action (Bekkering, Wohlschläger, & Gattis, 2000). Eighteen-month-old infants reproduce the goal they inferred from the failed attempts of a human demonstrator (Meltzoff, 1995). Carpenter, Call, and Tomasello (2005) showed that infants flexibly interpret the goal of an observed sequence of movements according to the context and therefore reenact either the goal of the observed action or the means by which it had been produced. Underlying this cognitive flexibility is the fundamental ability to discriminate between means and ends. Altogether, we believe that this evidence lends support to a deflationary account of the development of important aspects of intersubjectivity in humans.

Of course, this is only a partial picture. We emphasized almost exclusively the role of the cortical motor system in intersubjectivity, and for sake of concision we only briefly mentioned sensations, emotions, and affects. Our actions, however, are almost never divorced by the sense of emotionally charged personal involvement with the situation. However, emotions and affects can be fully understood only when considering the role of the cortical motor system in making sense of our and others' behavior. Indeed, as recently pointed out by Daniel Stern (2010),' the pervasive affective quality of mother–infant interactions can be captured by the notion of "forms of vitality." According to Stern, forms of vitality consist of a gestalt of movement, force, temporal flow, and intentionality. Such action-related gestalt leads to a subjective globality carrying along a sense of vitality or aliveness. As Stern wrote, "Vitality forms are associated with a content. More accurately, they carry content along with them. Vitality forms are not empty forms. They give a temporal and intensity contour to the content, and with it a sense of an alive performance. The content can be a shift in emotion, a train of thoughts, physical or mental movements, a memory, a fantasy, a means-end action. . . . The vitality dynamic gives the content its form as a dynamic experience" (2010, p. 23). Dynamic forms of vitality would developmentally precede the domain of feelings and emotions and represent the primary manner in which infants experience the human world. It will be very interesting to investigate how these different dimensions interact at the level of the brain.

CONCLUSION

The late Mauro Mancia, a neuroscientist and psychoanalyst who pioneered the establishment of a dialogue between psychoanalysis and neuroscience, repeatedly emphasized the importance for psychoanalysis, both from a theoretical and clinical point of view, of implicit memory and of unrepressed unconscious (Mancia, 2004, 2006). The plasticity of the MM could play an important role in the constitution of the implicit memories that constantly accompany our relations with internal and external objects, as a sort of background *basso continuo*. By internalizing specific patterns of interpersonal relations we develop our own characteristic attitude toward others and toward how we internally live and experience these relations. It can be hypothesized that our personal identity is—at least partly—the outcome of how our embodied simulation of others develops and takes shape.

Back to intersubjectivity, the conclusion we may provisionally draw is the following: We should abandon the Cartesian view of the primacy of the ego and adopt a perspective emphasizing that the other is co-originally given as the self. Both self and other appear to be intertwined because of the intercorporeality linking them. Intercorporeality describes a crucial aspect of intersubjectivity not because the latter is phylogenetically and ontogenetically grounded on a mere similarity between our body and the body of others due to superficial, perceptual similarity, but because we and others all share—to a certain degree—the same intentional objects and our situated motor systems are similarly wired to accomplish similar goals. It is the sharing of the same situatedness and the sharing of the same intentional goals that make intercorporeality a privileged access to the world of the other.

After having sketched a new possible take on intersubjectivity, from now onward we will focus on a peculiar intersubjective relationship, that between mother and child. In the next chapter we address the notion of motherhood.

CHAPTER 2

On Becoming Mother

When speaking about mothers, we must necessarily trace the evolution of the human species, which is conventionally dated to about 200,000 years ago, although its history actually started much earlier. According to Sara Hrdy (2009), more than 1 million years ago, hominins confronted a decisive change in their social organization and in their way of raising children, engaging in a cooperative breeding that, we might suggest, had great and unpredictable psychological and neurobiological consequences for the human species. Cooperative breeding can be defined when different members of the social group other than biological parents (alloparents), such as grandparents, aunts, uncles, and older siblings, help and support one or both parents in the upbringing of offspring. This special human cooperation was underlined by Tomasello and colleagues: "The crucial difference between human cognition and that of other species is the ability to participate with others in collaborative activities with shared goals and intentions" (2005, p. 675). This point of view has been recently reinforced by Zaki and Ochsner: "Compared to many other animals on the planet, human beings are small, slow and weak. And yet, we have unequivocally won the cross-species competition for global domination. . . . Although many answers may be offered to this question, psychologists increasingly believe that it is our interpersonal faculties, especially our ability to cooperate with and understand others, that have supported our species' success" (2012, p. 675).

A probable outcome of this cooperation was an increase of the human clan: Mothers and fathers could generate more closely spaced children and for this reason had a higher probability of bringing up more numerous offspring, despite high infant mortality, which heavily endangered the survival of infants, especially during the first years of life. Considering that hominin mothers could raise various children of young ages, all needy and requiring a lot of care and food, the mothers who were aided by their extended families and by members of their social group could make sure that their still immature and dependent children could be fed, cared for, and protected.

In the influential article "The Origin of Man" (1981), the American paleo-anthropologist Owen Lovejoy suggested that men have become bipedal so they could provide and carry food back to women and children waiting for them in their shelters. To this regard, Hrdy (2009) argued that mothers producing these dependent offspring also expected help from other members of the extended family clan because fathers alone could not satisfy the children's needs.

At the same time, as with other mammals, human mothers learned to care for the newborn baby, immature and helpless, by becoming psychologically and neurobiologically attuned to the baby's affective expression and behavior and being able to decode his or her bodily needs and states of distress.

Acquiring these sensitive attitudes and capacities, mothers could physically take care of their baby, recognizing and understanding their baby's expressions through visual and hearing competence and intervening adequately in order to protect or feed him or her. Therefore, when hominin mothers evolved to acquire a more sensitive attitude and attunement to their children, this recently acquired competence could be transferred to relationships with other members of the family and social group. At the same time, this maternal attentive and sensitive context stimulated the development in infants of this special competence to be attuned to and understand the mental state of caregivers, through a special "contagious" mimicking (Perner, Ruffman, & Leekam, 1994). From the evolutionistic point of view, infants more in touch with adults were favored by natural selection with a better chance of survival, even in negative situations. In fact, when more attuned babies were in trouble or were distant from their mothers or from other familial members, they were able to communicate and express their distress to others, having learned that they could obtain protection from caregivers utilizing this communicative competence.

In this evolutionistic pathway many questions are still without answer: Has alloparenting previously changed maternal attitude and sensitivity stimulating a specific attunement, or has it modified infants' attitude as they were obliged to adjust and interact with different persons, not always familiar? This advantage acquired during infancy could have been used later during the subsequent experience of parenting.

The actual process of parental attunement has been clarified by Fonagy: "It is our belief that the caregiver's capacity to observe the moment-to-moment changes in the child's mental state is critical in the development of mentalizing capacity. The caregiver's perception of the child as an intentional being lies at the root of sensitive caregiving, which is viewed by attachment theorists to be the cornerstone of secure attachment (Ainsworth, Blehar, Waters, & Wall, 1978; Isabella, 1993). . . . What I believe is far more important for the development of mentalizing is that exploration of the mental state of the sensitive caregiver enables the child to find in the caregiver's mind an image of himself as motivated by beliefs, feelings and intentions, in other words, as mentalizing" (1998, pp. 141–142).

Humans' behavior differs from that of apes: If we observe a chimpanzee baby we realize that it is able to watch and scan with attention the faces of other members of its group and even imitate their behavior, but its attention is focused primarily on its mother, which is its exclusive social reference. The development of human infants follows a different pathway: The mother, as is known, is the central caregiver in the life of an infant who becomes attached to her and constantly tries to catch her intentions and emotions. However, the infant can have at the same time relationships with other adults by checking their expressions and trying to grasp their intentions and availability to interact with him or her.

Building multiple attachments, human babies have learned to read the emotions and intentions of a number of persons from the first months of life, expressing a different phenotype produced by the interaction of genetic endowment and the pressures of environment. This is also confirmed by Bowlby (1969, 1982), who proposed that a child develops a hierarchy of attachment relationships, with the mother as the primary caregiver. Observing infants in East Africa, Mary Ainsworth (1967) wrote: "Nearly all the babies in this sample who became attached to their mothers during the period spanned by our observations became attached also to some other familiar figure—father, grandmother, or other adult in the household, or to an older sibling" (p. 315). This observation was further confirmed by Ainsworth and colleagues (1978) in a sample of infants in Baltimore; this suggests that the infant's attitude is common in different countries, despite the different models of rearing performed.

This is the realm of intersubjectivity, the central theme of the book, which will focus on the specific competence of mind reading (as narrowly defined in the first chapter) in human mothers, especially in interaction with children who learn to be in touch with their mother and other people from the beginning. As Hrdy (2009) suggests, the emergence of mind reading certainly happened before the spread of human groups in different continents, approximately 70,000 years ago. In this context, as Brockway (2003) underlines, the most intuitive mothers were able to use an empathic awareness of the infant's behavior, both physical and psychological, thus promoting the survival of offspring. We can easily presume that women have evolved to be more intuitive and empathic than men because mothers, in upbringing their baby, need to read the baby's behavior, but a question is still open regarding why this special attitude has evolved in humans and not in our close cousins, the great apes which share 98% of our genetic endowment.

If this question is still without an answer, we can suggest that during mammalian evolution the neocortex of the brain, which represents the planning, executive, and control center of the nervous system, emerged. Particularly in humans, the evolution of the neocortex has been promoted by human ecological dominance and social competition (Flinn, Geary, & Ward, 2005) and also by the higher level cooperation among hominins (Tomasello et al., 2005). Under the selective pressure of the search for food and the complex organization of social life, the brain has evolved toward a larger size associated with greater cognitive and emotional competence. The neocortex is specifically enlarged in primates with a social life and is even bigger in primates which participate in larger groups (Dumbar, 1992).

Specific regions of the primate's executive brain, the cortical and striatal regions, have expanded while other areas connected to primary and immediate behaviors (hunger, sex, aggression, maternal care) have on the contrary decreased in size (Keverne, 2005). A particular role is performed by the frontal cortex, which has shown progressive enlargement through mammalian evolution. In the brain's maturation process, the medial prefrontal cortex, which contributes to the recognition of different emotions (Shamay-Tsoory, Tomer,& Aharon-Peretz, 2005) and to forming a personal impression of other persons, continues developing until late adolescence (Sowell, Thompson, Tessner, & Toga, 2001).

It is worthwhile to emphasize that there is a difference in parenting between small-brained mammals and large-brained primates (Keverne, 2005). In small-brained mammals, the mother is the nurturant figure and the father sometimes participates in the rearing. In this case, maternal behavior is consistently activated by the biological influence of gonadal hormones on the limbic brain, confirming that maternal functioning depends upon physiological mechanisms, primarily through olfactory communication. On the contrary, primates with a large cortical brain are less influenced by hormones because "evolutionary events have had a large impact on all primary motivated behavior, including parental care where pregnancy and parturition are not an essential prerequisite for good parenting or indeed for bonding with infants" (Keverne, 2005, p. 109).

Primates and above all humans, who live in a complex familial and social organization, become good parents in relation to their personal and familiar experience and to the social context's influence in relationship with the child, who in turn interacts with and confirms parents through his or her attachment behaviors. The olfactory connection to areas of the social reward regions of the brain is replaced in humans by neocortical activation with multimodal sensory cues that intervene in planning and emotional regulation (Chiba, Kayahara, & Nakano, 2001). It has been suggested that the endogenous opioid system could have a great relevance, especially during parturition and suckling, the latter promoting the positive attitude that characterizes the maternal behavior (Broad, Curley, & Keverne, 2006).

Considering human parental experience, the cognitive and emotional functioning of parents, especially internalized working models of attachment of self and others and the ability to be attuned with the child, plays an important role. The human mother is influenced by emotional experience, by personal attachment, by family, by social relationships, and by biology that facilitate her bonding to the child. However, the long dependence of children, who need complex and multiple interactions, implies that the mother should be aided by the father and relatives, whose active participation has been facilitated by the evolutionary emancipation of infant care from hormonal influence. The human genotype has given rise to different phenotypes influenced by environmental conditions, which could induce different developmental pathways, especially if they intervene during sensitive periods (Bateson et al., 2004), as it happens during pregnancy and motherhood.

The long evolutionary process has favored, as we have seen, a cooperative rearing system, in which the mother represents the main figure but is supported by other figures such as the father, the grandparents, and other family members. However, this rearing system has itself deeply modified human neurocognitive functioning, favoring a long apprenticeship, so infants could learn the complex codes of relationships and exchange in the human community. If in the past it was family members who took care of education and upbringing, during the recent centuries specific organizations such as day care centers and schools have been developed to integrate the parents' role. And for thousands of years, motherhood itself was a human social group's primary means of increasing its numbers, thereby making its clan stronger and better equipped to meet its goals in terms of exploration and of dominating and exploiting its territory. Over time, motherhood has acquired a great symbolic significance that is recognized by most societies and even sanctified in major religions.

THE ARCHETYPE OF MOTHERHOOD

Throughout the history of the human species, maternity has had a great value, on a symbolic level as well, as it has allowed human groups and communities to reproduce and multiply their numbers, heightening the chances of prevailing over other groups and dominating nature. Among the first artistic products of the Paleolithic Era are the Steatopygian Venus statues, small female figures featuring accumulation of fat on the hips and gluteus and large breasts, as if to underline woman's fertility and her maternal characteristics. It is difficult to say whether these statues were meant as symbolic images or if they reflected an actual specific female body conformation; however, it is interesting that these objects were found from Siberia to Europe, demonstrating a widespread and shared symbol of beauty and fertility.

Motherhood and maternity have different meanings in many cultures and religious traditions, which lead to frequent idealized images of maternal or feminine spirituality. Christian, Judaic, and Hindu religious scriptures have placed motherhood in an exalted realm; this is true not only for the figure of the Madonna in the Christian tradition but also for the Devi-Ma (Goddess Mother) in the Hindu tradition. This quasi-sacred concept of women and maternity has been fiercely criticized in the past decades, especially by the feminist movement, which stressed the strong pressures exerted by traditional societies on women to conform to this social role, thus effectively excluding them from the productive world.

In the Western world, influenced by Catholic culture and tradition, the image of motherhood is connected to the Madonna, who represents an archetype of mother, which has inspired the great Renaissance artists. The generating act that starts Mary's motherhood is the Annunciation: The Archangel Gabriel announces to Mary that she has been chosen to give birth to the Son of God. The Annunciation, a highly symbolic moment for Christianity, inspired many artists during the Middle Ages and the Renaissance, each one of them bringing his own religious concept and artistic talent but following the commissioners' often ecclesiastic requests.

In the painted representations of the Annunciation, certain constant features are present: The Archangel is at the center, in a prominent position, as if to indicate that the divine word is the most important aspect of this great event, while Mary in her modesty is relegated to her procreating role. The angel is a divine ambassador; his enormous wings indicate the long flight he has undertaken to reach Mary on Earth and tell her the Good News. The long trumpet present in some paintings, which the angel uses to amplify God's message, acquires a specific relevance in view of the importance of the mission the angel has been entrusted with. Other interpretations see Mary as the true actress, the true protagonist of the Annunciation: With modesty and intimate inner joy and pride, she accepts being chosen by God to give birth to a divine child whom the world's destiny depends on. Mary is sometimes represented in a hieratic way, the accent being on the devotional and saintly aspects of the event rather than on the motherly or, even less, on the feminine ones.

The artistic rendering of the Annunciation by Pinturicchio (figure 2.1) is particularly pregnant with meaning: The encounter between the Archangel and the Madonna happens within a sumptuous architectural setting; above is an image of God from which the Holy Spirit is descending as a dove. In the background, a great window opens onto a countryside and an inhabited hamlet, as if to remind us of the existence of the human world.

But the Archangel's Annunciation and the Immaculate Conception dogma, which decrees the sacredness of Mary's motherhood, have affected the way motherhood is conceived in Western civilization. Mary's fecundation was not the consequence of a sexual, carnal act, but a fruit of spirituality, an expression of God's will. This image of the Virgin Mother has contributed to imposing a maternal and female archetype in the Western world. The Virgin Mother has also influenced society's concept of motherhood by engendering a sanctified image of the mother, who, by virtue of her being mother, is distinct from all other women.

Psychoanalysis has confronted the symbolic significance of the Annunciation in an essay by Ernest Jones, one of Freud's most brilliant pupils ("The Madonna's Conception Through the Ear," 1914). According to Jones, the Annunciation evoked to the infantile unconscious, especially men's, the conviction that our own birth is not the consequence of a sexual act but of a maternal conception in which the father has not taken part. This infantile theory would actually mask

FIGURE 2.1.   Pinturicchio: "The Annunciation," Cappella Baglioni, Spello. (© Elio Ciol/ Corbis)

the child's incestuous fantasies about his mother, which tend to dismiss the father figure.

Jones's psychoanalytical interpretation takes into consideration an ancient tradition of the Catholic Church, according to which Jesus was conceived by the penetration of the Holy Spirit's breath into the Virgin Mary's ear, as Saint Augustine has written. By referring to church texts and artistic representations, Ernest Jones unveils a number of unconscious symbols of sublimated sexuality in the Annunciation. From this point of view, the Archangel's words penetrating into the Madonna's ear could be, on an unconscious level, a sexual penetration, the words fecundating Mary like semen and starting a pregnancy. The flower, the lily, we see Gabriel offering Mary in Pinturicchio's painting represents the Madonna's purity and is a symbol of female sexuality; and, as Jones points out, the loss of virginity is also defined as defloration. Lastly, the ear, in Jones's symbolic interpretation, represents the vagina.

We have not spoken of Joseph, the human father. Joseph is the putative father, the one who gives the child his name, guaranteeing social recognition. But the true filiation is maternal, as if the child were only Mary's. In the life of nearly every child, the mother is almost inevitably the central figure, as happens in many cultures. However, the cross-cultural research (Bornstein, 2002, 2004) has found that mothers belonging to different cultures are more alike in their caregiving behaviors that minister to the most basic physical needs of babies, than in their discretionary behaviors, for example, playing with their children. Of course, this is partly due to infants' needs that elicit a limited number of basic responses from parents, independent of the context in which they are born. Motherhood's sacredness is one of the themes that can appear during pregnancy, on an explicit level when spoken about by the woman, by her family, or in a social context; or on an implicit level, not conscious and not verbalized, and in this case it may find expression in the mother's fantasies and daydreams.

Fava Vizziello, Antonioli, Cocci, and Invernizzi (1993) have confirmed that Italian mothers in the seventh month of pregnancy express narrative themes or myths concerning motherhood and the baby that may be verbalized. These themes may concern a reparative and compensatory function in order to maintain a stable ideal of the self (for example, the child from heaven for maternal grandparents), a defensive attitude in order to maintain personal self-esteem (for example, the child is like the mother, who is competent), and lastly a fear connected to anxieties and worries about pregnancy or the child.

The fears and anxieties experienced during pregnancy have been told in a terrifying way by Roman Polanski's 1968 movie *Rosemary's Baby*. As Pines (1972) pointed out, pregnancy reactivates oedipal dynamics, and in this film these fall into pathological conflict: The pregnancy is no longer a fulfillment of the mother's wish; on the contrary, she is a victim of a malignant set of parents. Indeed, Rosemary, the protagonist, is raped by her husband and is invaded by a foreign and alien being, a demonic presence that drags her into an alarming and paranoid world, where all is uncertain and dangerous. The film probably would have struck Freud as an illustration of his concept of the "uncanny," which is "frightening because it is not known and familiar" (1919/1955, p. 219).

WISH FOR A BABY

For the purposes of the following discussion, we shall revise the area of motherhood, beginning from pregnancy and running through the infant's first year, which is when the mother–infant intersubjective matrix is built. The matrix sustains the child in acquiring the social and intersubjective competence necessary for joining the human community. The psychoanalytical relational model suggests that the subjectivity is interpersonal from the beginning and substitutes the intrapsychic conception of the mind, which has been sustained by psychoanalysis (Mitchell, 1988). In this perspective a contradiction is highlighted between subjectivity and intersubjectivity, within which personal meanings are embedded (Mitchell, 2000) rather than drives rooted in biology.

Like other primates, infants are relatively immature in locomotion but precocious in communicative development. For this reason, human parents must prepare themselves to become competent mothers and fathers in order to interact with their own children and communicate with them from birth. This takes a long training in humans, which starts during infancy (doll games) and reaches maturation during late adolescence through identification with parental figures (Bornstein, 2004).

Parental caregiving probably evolved in humans alongside the achievement of bipedality, although some anthropologists, such as Lovejoy (1981), have suggested that bipedality itself originally resulted from a variation in genetic reproduction and developed because of advantages related to the care of immature offspring. The specificity of maternal bonding may be influenced by the necessity to protect the progeny against predators, as has been suggested by the attachment theory (Bowlby, 1969, 1982), but also by birth spacing and demographic propagation. From this point of view, the selection of parent–infant bonding may have been related to the particular capacities in human community necessary for social communication and learning.

In exploring the link between parental attitude and the infant's development, psychoanalytical theory has fundamentally highlighted the role of the maternal and paternal intrapsychic world, substantially influenced by unconscious processes. This theoretical construct about motherhood has its antecedents in Freud's theoretical thinking, represented by the hypothesis that any relation experienced both on the conscious and unconscious level with one's own parents during infancy will have a decisive influence on the development of the baby's personality. In his paper "On Narcissism: An Introduction," Freud dealt with parental roles during the intergenerational process, focusing on the function of parents' "compulsion to ascribe every perfection to the child" (1914/1957, p. 91). In the subsequent lines he added that "the child shall fulfill those wishful dreams of the parents which they never carried out—the boy shall become a great man and a hero in his father's place, and the girl shall marry a prince as a tardy compensation for her mother. . . . Parental love, which is so moving and at bottom so childish, is nothing but the parents' narcissism born again, which, transformed into object-love, unmistakably reveals its former nature" (1914/1957, p. 91).

It is interesting to notice that within the concept of compulsion to ascribe, one may foresee Klein's later discovery of projective identification (1946). This mechanism is not only intrapsychic but also intersubjective and may entail the modification of the object upon which the projection takes place, not only in fantasy but in reality as well. The concept of projective identification is an important bridge between psychoanalysis and the recent intersubjective approach because it considers not only the personal projection of thoughts, beliefs, and parts of the self onto another person but also the change that takes place in the latter person by the projection, where he or she actualizes, without any awareness, the attributions in his or her behavior or thinking. This is particularly relevant in the parent–infant relationship, as Seligman (1999) accurately illustrated with detailed observations, because the asymmetry in the relationship favors maternal and paternal attributions to the child, who is very sensitive to the parents' projections. This process takes place during a mutual interaction in which the parent actively pressures the child to behave, feel, and think in accordance with the projection. In addition to projective identification, the list of such concepts includes empathy, mirroring, and, even more broadly, internalization (Seligman, 1991).

Freud's observations are particularly interesting because in a way they unmask parental love, which is not only generosity, abnegation, protection, and care of the infant but also narcissism because a child might be born to accomplish his or her parents' unfulfilled dreams. The child often personifies the parents' Ego Ideal, and this explains why parents see themselves in their children and often have binding expectations, because of which they cannot accept the fact that their children choose another path than the one they have pointed out. Psychoanalysis highlights the conflict dynamics and the unconscious functioning of the relationship between parents and children that have often been undervalued in infant research, which tends mostly to emphasize the intersubjective and communicative dimension of relationships between parents and children. In this regard, Winnicott wrote an illuminating paper, "Hate in the Countertransference," which explored maternal hate toward one's own baby: "The mother, however, hates her infant from the word go. I believe Freud thought it possible that a mother may in certain circumstances have only love for her boy baby; but we may doubt this" (1947/1958, p. 201). Taking into consideration the possible reasons why a mother could hate her child, Winnicott listed the baby as "a danger to her body in pregnancy and at birth. The baby is an interference with her private life, a challenge to preoccupation" (1947/1958, p. 201).

This preoccupation could be expressed during pregnancy in the mother's unconscious dreams, as Ferenczi highlighted in a brief paper, through "the sheltering of little living things in and on the body . . . the same holds for intestinal worms = child" (1914/1926, p. 361). In the same paper, Winnicott explained how a mother deals with this: "The most remarkable thing about a mother is her ability to be hurt so much by her baby and to hate so much without paying the child out, and her ability to wait for rewards that may or may not come at a later day" (1947/1958, p. 202).

Another contribution toward the comprehension of intersubjective mechanisms has been given by Sandler, who spoke of the concept of actualization or rather of "a wished-for role interaction, with the wished-for or imagined response of the object being as much a part of the wishful fantasy as the activity of the subject in that wish or fantasy" (1976, p. 64). Sandler's concept of actualization highlights the mainly unconscious attempt to manipulate or provoke intersubjective situations so as to reproduce aspects of past experiences and relationships in the present context. Applying this to parents and their infants, Selma Fraiberg wrote, "In every nursery there are ghosts . . . visitors of the unremembered past of the parents. . . . These unfriendly and unbidden spirits are banished from the nursery . . . the bonds of love protect the child and his parents against the intruders" (1980, p. 164). In some cases it may happen that the family appears to be possessed by its ghosts and the parents and their child may find themselves reenacting a moment or a scene from another time that had different protagonists. In this situation the baby is already in peril and would show the early signs of emotional starvation or malignant attribution because he or she is burdened by the oppressive past of his or her parents.

In a later essay, "Group Psychology and the Analysis of the Ego," Freud considered the other aspect of this mother–infant process: He explored the identification mechanism of the child, which represents "the earliest expression of an emotional tie with another person" (1921/1955, p. 105). Although Freud referred to the identification with the father of one's "personal pre-history" through which one "should like to grow like him and be like him" (p. 105), he described this kind of link in a baby as the first relationship it has with its mother.

Psychoanalytical theory has fundamentally highlighted the maternal intrapsychic and representational constellation, which is deeply influenced by the mother's infantile experiences and by her vicissitudes with parental figures. In this context, relational events and unconscious resonance are reciprocally connected.

In this approach, emphasis has been placed on the narcissistic character of parental love and drive investment of the baby, which influence the maternal affective state, especially during the infant's first months. In fact, according to psychoanalysis, the infant's development is strongly influenced by his or her drives, which must be gratified by the mother in order to establish a basic infantile homeostasis. Nevertheless, psychoanalysis suggests that infants' basic needs are in contrast with the environmental organization, provoking from the beginning a conflict between individual wishes and parental attitudes.

WAITING FOR A BABY

What does a women feel upon discovering she is pregnant? The first question or dilemma that a woman has to work out is whether to have the child. In the midst of joy, happiness, impotence, and fear, deep psychological and physical transformations start taking place and lead the woman toward a maturation of her identity with the acquisition of a maternal identity. Pregnancy is characterized by a complex interaction of biological, psychological, and social factors that have a profound resonance in the maternal unconscious and conscious world. It is a period of transition, transformation, and personal reorganization that can give rise to a developmental crisis, with possible mental disorganization. During pregnancy, hormonal, neurochemical, and neurobiological changes occur within the mother, in addition to changes in her psychic world and identity. The perception of the fetal movements implies a sensorial, coenesthetic, and visceral experience for the mother, which stimulates the building of the representation of the baby, strictly rooted in the body. Complex mental representations of the self as a mother and of the baby occur, along with the building of the attachment bond and providing care for the baby.

The chance to integrate these developmental shifts in a coherent way (Slade, Cohen, Sadler, & Miller, 2009) is related to the personal mental resources that the woman has collected and elaborated during infancy, adolescence, and young adulthood, particularly in relation to her parents and specifically to her own mother. The personal history of the woman's attachments plays an important role, of course, because there is a close and reciprocal connection between the personal attachment experience during childhood and the subsequent parental caregiving system (Bowlby, 1969/1982). As George and Solomon (2008) have underlined, the parent's caregiving system activates a repertoire of behaviors that have a protective function toward the baby.

According to Winnicott (1953), the capacity to identify with a "good enough mother" helps a woman face the experience of motherhood with her own mother as a reference model. The woman can refer to this model mentally in everyday life when she feels anxious, depressed, or in trouble. At the same time, a woman who has a good and balanced relationship with her own mother does not fear that her mother may be competitive over her pregnancy or may interfere with it.

The complex interactions intervening during pregnancy imply that the woman is not the only protagonist of this period of life, but so are her partner, her family, and the social and cultural context that confers a symbolic meaning to motherhood. Considering maternal mental dynamics, Daniel Stern conceptualized the emergence of a "new psychic organization" (1995, p. 192), "the motherhood constellation," that characterizes not only the period of childbirth but also pregnancy. Motherhood constellation is the dominant organizing axis of the mother's psychic life while other motivational systems, like the oedipal one, are set aside. Stern (1995) has suggested that this mental organization is transient and intensely addresses three different preoccupations and discourses that are internally and externally relevant, one about herself as a mother, a second one about her own mother, and lastly about the child. In this context, thoughts and emotions are polarized on specific themes: (a) life and growth concerning the survival and the development of the child (e.g., Am I capable as a mother in bringing up the baby?), (b) primary relatedness and emotional engagement (e.g., Am I a loving and interacting mother in my relationship with my child?), (c) supporting matrix (e.g., Am I a supporting and protecting mother with my child?), and (d) identity reorganization (e.g., How will this experience shape my life?). While the concept of motherhood constellation is based on clinical observations, more recently it has been validated also by empirical research (Innamorati, Sarracino, & Dazzi, 2010).

We have discussed the main themes that appear during the experience of motherhood; however, different maternal pathways, which are relevant because they may also predict mother–infant interactions after childbirth, may be visualized. As Raphael-Leff (2010) has evidenced, different maternal orientations can reflect the woman's subjective experience. The first orientation is that of the Facilitator Mother, who considers pregnancy as the culmination of her feminine experience. She experiences motherhood with great emotional involvement, and she considers the fetus as a child to be addressed and spoken to, as though he or she were an intimate partner. She plans a birth as natural as possible, trying to avoid a traumatic separation from the child.

For the Regulator Mother, pregnancy is an unavoidable and unexciting way of getting a baby. She tries to maintain her usual life and to avoid being influenced by pregnancy and the baby, which she considers a fetus and not yet a child. Childbirth is imagined as a dreadful and painful event, possibly to be treated with medical assistance.

The third group is that of the Reciprocator Mother, who is able to tolerate uncertainty and mixed feelings about herself and the baby. She accepts the inevitable ambivalence implicit in every relationship; she accepts feelings of resentment connected to pregnancy and to caring for the baby.

The last group is that of the Conflicted Mother, who oscillates between an ideal image of self and a rebellion against it. This woman, still involved in painful infantile experiences and in a conflictual relationship with her own mother, manifests ambivalent feelings toward the motherhood and the baby.

A woman's first pregnancy, as Pines (1982) has highlighted, may be one of the most enriching and lively stages of her life cycle. For a young woman who had a "good enough" (Winnicott, 1953) relationship with her own mother, we can imagine that the temporary regression to a primary identification with the omnipotent, fertile, life-giving mother may be a satisfying developmental phase in which further integration of the self may be achieved. For other women, the regression stimulated by pregnancy and motherhood may be an anxiety-producing and frightening experience. The infantile wish of women to merge with their mother and, at the same time, the fear of losing one's personal identity with a partial failure of self-object differentiation may be revived, creating a difficult integration with adult reality.

A first pregnancy favors a further stage of identification, strongly rooted in a biological basis. "The woman becomes like her own mother, a 'physiological' mature woman, impregnated by her sexual partner—and in fantasy with mother's—powerful enough to create life herself" (Pines, 1982, p. 312). The physical changes of pregnancy facilitate a woman's bodily reexperience of primary unity with her mother and at the same time a distancing through differentiation from her mother's body. A further stage of separation-individuation can be attained by the woman.

PHANTASMATIC AND IMAGINARY BABY

Bodily changes during pregnancy are inevitably accompanied by a reenactment of infantile emotional development, with libidinal, aggressive, and narcissistic drives in the relationship to the self and to the object relationships. Deep conflicts relating to past developmental stages reemerge, and the woman may become aware of primitive, previously repressed fantasies arising from sexual theories built during childhood, about her own conception, intrauterine life, and birth (Pines, 1972). It follows that positive and negative aspects of the self and of the object may be projected onto the fetus inside the maternal body.

In this regard, Lebovici (1983), adopting a psychoanalytical approach, made an important distinction between the phantasmatic baby and the imaginary baby. While the phantasmatic baby appears in maternal dreams, expression of her unconscious world derived primarily from oedipal conflicts with her own parents, the imaginary baby is the conscious and frequently shared construction that the parents create from their perception of the child or from their wishes for him or her. These images of the baby, which are present during pregnancy, will interact after childbirth with the actual baby, creating a more realistic representation of the baby.

To illustrate the meaning of this conceptualization, we present a clinical vignette of a pregnant woman. Angela is a 28-year-old mother interviewed during the eighth month of her pregnancy. Angela is facing her first pregnancy alone because her family of origin resides in another city. About the choice of having a baby, she says: "Well, I really wanted it. I have always adored children; we've been married for about two years and it seemed the right moment for me — it really was, I wanted it. I don't know how much my husband really did." She also has decided to give up working to dedicate herself completely to the child, even though this choice has been criticized by her in-laws. She was "terrified" at the idea of letting her in-laws know about her pregnancy, whereas it was different with her mother because their relationship has always been very open. Her husband "was pleased," she says, "but I think I probably forced him." Every now and then she has nightmares and she fears the birth, giving birth to a baby who is malformed, but she cannot talk about this to anyone, not even her husband, who is very close to her. She began feeling fetal movements at about the fourth month; she does not want to know the sex of the baby and she sometimes imagines it as a boy and sometimes as a girl. She and her husband have not been able to choose a name yet. She cannot imagine or dream what the baby is going to be like. When she imagines the baby after birth, she asks herself many questions, she thinks about the schooling, about when he or she will be grown up, but then she feels that she is daydreaming too much. She would like a calm and contented baby, "a little being who is also passive"; she is a bit worried about having no experience with newborn babies, having seen a newborn baby for the first time only a week ago. She has met 5- or 6-month-old children who were quite lively and this frightens her. About her infancy, she reports that her parents divorced and there was no relationship with her father, but things were different with her mother. She was always running around, busy in the house, and she and her brothers always had to be good and quiet. With her child she thinks it will be different, that she will have much more time; this is why she gave up working: "I definitely want to be available to my child, perhaps because that's what I missed as a child." It appears that Angela has faced this pregnancy as her own choice, maybe a mission, that she has undertaken by herself against her husband's and in-laws' wishes. Caring for her baby will serve as compensation for her deprivations and pains during her own childhood; it is a secret baby ideal, who lives inside her but who has no face, sex, or name.

This "imaginary baby" (Lebovici, 1983) is inevitably a "passive little being" that Angela creates in her mind through her conscious fantasies. The baby is the object of the mother's narcissistic desire, capable of giving the mother a personal completeness and enabling her to defeat her feeling of inadequacy and failure. However, Angela seems scared by the baby who is going to be born; she fears he might be too lively and aggressive, the "phantasmatic baby" (Lebovici, 1983) who reenacts her own infantile self, unrecognized and full of anger and resentment at not having been sufficiently looked after and loved. In a subsequent interview, more focused on her attachment experiences during childhood, she talks about her life in a small provincial town, with her very stern father who worked at home. She and her brothers had very little room for themselves and could not move about. With her parents "there was no relationship" and, she adds, "perhaps that's exactly why I made the decision to devote myself to the child, because my father was practically never there . . . he was on a pedestal and you couldn't go near him." Her mother was very much available, but she had a lot of work, too. As a child Angela knew she was not allowed to ask for anything or expect anything from anyone, "so the mere fact of just telling her about something I wanted was already a sign of a good relationship to me."

During the interview, talking about her father gradually upsets her more and more: "It's still difficult for me to talk about it, my father left home . . . goodness, it makes me so cross that I still find it impossible to talk about it." She cries and says that when she was 13 years old her father left home to move in with a young woman who lived in the same building, and he started a new family with her. She stopped seeing her father then. She says she has never forgiven him for leaving her, but then immediately corrects herself and says: "for leaving my mother."

During pregnancy, she contacts him to tell him about the baby; when the child is born, she calls him from the clinic, but he does not come to see her.

During the interview, her adolescent disappointment at having her womanhood refused by her father comes to light; her father, in fact, chose another young woman who was only a little older than herself. Keeping these vicissitudes in mind, we may suppose that Angela has tried through her own pregnancy to give her own father a baby in the unconscious intent of bringing him back to his family, and thus succeeding where her own mother failed. Angela may have tried to work out her fantasies through her baby, and her pregnancy may have been started with the secret desire to reconquer her father, giving him a baby just as the young woman he went away with did. Angela gets her expectations severely frustrated because her real baby, after childbirth, does not personify and actualize her own fantasies.

This clinical vignette illustrates the significance of the phantasmatic baby for an expectant mother's mental world, as the baby inevitably reenacts mental dynamics and oedipal conflicts connected to the parental figures (Lebovici, 1983).

MATERNAL REPRESENTATIONS

The concept of mental representation has played a key role in the development of psychoanalysis, clinical research, and theoretical speculation. This is already clear in Freud's early writings, but a more complete explanation of this theoretical concept has been formulated by Sandler and Rosenblatt (1962). According to them, the term "representation" implies two separate concepts: a stable internal mental organization, an internal map that collects and integrates all mental images and relational dispositions between the self and others; and second, the contents and the cognitive-affective characteristics of these images, which dwell within every personal experience. A more controversial aspect is the way in which the process of internalization takes place.

This involves the construction of an internal mental world, quite separate from external reality, to give a meaning to one's personal experiences, to make predictions, and to make decisions about future behaviors. In the formation of representation, establishing how much weight must be given to experiences directly connected to reality rather than to unconscious fantasies is difficult.

When specifically considering pregnancy, the female identity of a woman has to confront a process of psychological transformation and reorganization that leads to the acquisition of a maternal identity sustained by mental representations of self as a mother and of the future baby, although he or she is still unborn (Ammaniti, Candelori, Pola, & Tambelli, 1999; Raphael-Leff, 2010; Slade et al., 2009). During pregnancy the woman's central task is the reworking of the relationship with her own mother, while developing a feeling of connection to the child and at the same time recognizing her separateness. The representation of the baby is both part of the mother's identity and separate from her at the same time.

According to Sandler and Sandler (1998), representations of self and others in interaction are built on everyday relational experiences with other people, which are internalized as a mutual representation. Mental representations are colored by affects that give them a depth and a profile as happens in a landscape. This point of view has been emphasized by contemporary relational and intersubjective psychoanalysis, which tries to highlight the complex interactions between outside and inside relational experience.

In recent years, interviews and coding systems that assess and rate maternal representations of the child have been proposed (Aber, Slade, Berger, Bresgi, & Kaplan, 1985; Benoit, Parker, & Zeanah, 1997; George & Solomon, 1996; Zeanah & Benoit, 1995). However, most of them explore parental attitudes after birth. Few studies have focused on maternal representations during pregnancy in order to assess the mental dynamics of mothers and to identify predictive markers of the mother–baby postnatal relationship (Ammaniti & Tambelli, 2010; Fava Vizziello et al., 1993; Lis, Zennaro, Mazzeschi, & Pinto, 2004; Raphael-Leff, 2010; Stern, 1995).

The interest in studying and exploring psychological dynamics during pregnancy is connected to the possibility of recognizing parental styles that could predict parental postnatal attitudes and behaviors (Bürgin & Von Klitzing, 1995; Carneiro, Corboz-Warnery, & Fivaz-Depeursinge, 2006; Fonagy, Steele, Moran, Steele, & Higgitt, 1991; Raphael-Leff, 2010) as well as of uncovering vulnerabilities and risk factors during pregnancy that may negatively interfere with the postnatal caregiving system (Börjesson, Ruppert, Wager, & Bågedahl-Strundlund, 2007; Ross & McLean, 2006; van Bussel, Spitz, & Demyttenaere, 2009).

Semistructured interviews such as the Interview of Maternal Representations during Pregnancy, revised version (IRMAG-R, Ammaniti & Tambelli, 2010), explore the mental world of mothers. The interview, performed between the sixth and the seventh months of pregnancy, explores the pregnant woman's mental representations, focusing on the woman's past experiences, on how she copes with pregnancy and maternity, and how she progressively creates an image of the fetus and of the future child. The narrative structure of the interview is coded to consider the mother's representation of herself as a mother and the representation of the baby on the basis of seven mental dimensions.

The exploration of maternal representations during pregnancy using IRMAG-R on the basis of maternal narratives has empirically confirmed the theoretical models built on clinical observations (Bibring, 1961; Pines, 1972; Raphael-Leff, 1993, 2010): the integrated/balanced representational model, which is the most common in normal samples, the restricted/disinvested one, and, finally, the nonintegrated/ambivalent one.

The interview stimulates the woman's narrative of her experience of pregnancy and of becoming a mother, exploring the mental representations of herself as a mother and of her unborn child. The narration is not assessed with respect to contents, but with respect to the narrative's organization.

In the interview, questions about the following areas of personal experience are asked: (1) the woman's and the couple's desire for a baby; (2) emotional reactions of the woman, of the couple, and of the other family members to pregnancy; (3) emotions and changes in the woman's life, in the life of the couple, and in relation to the families of origin during pregnancy; (4) perceptions, positive and negative emotions, maternal and paternal fantasies, and the internal child's psychological space; (5) future expectations and possible life modifications; and (6) a personal history perspective.

The research has evidenced different maternal representations (Ammaniti, Tambelli, & Odorisio, 2013) that will be illustrated with different clinical vignettes collected during interviews with mothers at the seventh month of pregnancy.

AN EXPECTANT MOTHER WITH AN INTEGRATED REPRESENTATION OF HERSELF

The integrated/balanced maternal representation is a coherent narration of the personal experience a woman is living, rich in episodes and fantasies that convey an intense emotional involvement in an atmosphere of flexibility and openness toward the physical, psychological, and emotional transformations the mother is confronting. The relationship with the child is already present during pregnancy, and the child is considered as a person with his or her own motives and moods.

Martina's story is a perfect example of an Integrated Mother. In her answers, we feel the importance she gives to her pregnancy on which she has concentrated all her forces and investments. A great capability of recognizing her mental states as well as her husband's emerges from her words, as if she is used to examining herself and the people who surround her.

Q: Would you tell me about your pregnancy?

A: This was a desired pregnancy, completely, because I'm over thirty years old. I was once married, then separated, and now I live with this new man who gives me a great sense of tranquillity. I have always wanted a child, so I thought I had to have it now or decide I'd have a life without children. So I did all the tests, a year before, I got prepared; it definitely was a planned pregnancy. When I became pregnant, I had just switched to a new job, since I was planning to have a child I had switched from a full-time to a part-time job. I have many interests, I do artistic gymnastics and many other things; I don't believe you have to quit everything when you have a baby. Of course, you will be dedicating most of your time to the baby, but you have to keep doing your own things.

Q: How did you face this pregnancy?

A: I had some problems, from a physical point of view. Psychologically I faced it very well. Of course you are a bit shocked, I think that happens to everyone because there's something new, something you don't quite understand, especially when you have your first ultrasonography, when it's still tiny, you see this little spider. And then this child is growing inside of you. It kicks you, and you feel something weird and think, "Oh God, there's a baby growing inside of me." I know, it's not really strange, but it just surprises you.

I actually accepted it from the start; I wanted a child so much; of course it's also important that the man I live with now gives me such tranquility.

In these few sentences, Martina's storytelling provides a coherent picture of her personal life and of her desire to have a child, which can now be fulfilled within her new relationship. Her narrative also communicates a strong affective involvement that confirms the picture of the Facilitator Mother described by Raphael-Leff: "Immediately on assuming she is pregnant, she gives herself over to the heightened emotionality of pregnancy, steering clear of situations and substances she fears may be harmful" (1993, p. 66).

Q: Would you tell me how you felt when you first found out you were pregnant?

A: When I first found out, because of the practical problems with my job, I wasn't actually sure if I should be happy or not. Then I thought that everything could be arranged, because even when confronting problems of schedules, of work, when you know you're going to have a baby it all becomes relative before the baby.

At first you're a bit surprised, even because they tell you you're pregnant but you can't feel it yet. You feel as usual, normal, at least until you start growing a belly.

Q: When did you notice the first changes in your body?

A: Everybody asks that. In the first few months, only around the fourth month when the belly starts becoming noticeable. At that stage, when it's still small, you actually feel as if you are only overweight and feel ugly. Now that I have a big belly, I have no problems; if I pass before a mirror, I see it.

With these words, Martina underlines the importance of body changes during pregnancy; these are changes she had problems adjusting to in the beginning, but which then become the tangible and reassuring proof that her child is growing inside of her.

Q: Have there been specific moments of great emotion during the pregnancy, until now?

A: Sometimes I feel very sad; I don't know if this is normal, or connected to the pregnancy. For example, I am more easily upset and seem to feel things more intensely.

Q: Do you have specific fears?

A: I'm afraid the baby might have some problems, defects, but it's not a great fear; I'm actually convinced I will deliver a beautiful girl. I don't know why, but I'm convinced.

Q: Have you had dreams related to the pregnancy?

A: One dream I remember, because it was only a couple of nights ago, I was losing blood from my mouth, I don't know why. In general when I dream I see myself pregnant, yes, I'm always pregnant in my dreams now, even if I don't remember them clearly.

With these answers, Martina demonstrates the emotional oscillations that are typical during pregnancy (Pines, 1972) and the fears of possible defects or malformations, which are also typical preoccupations described by Winnicott (1956) and related to the last months of pregnancy. The dream expresses the fear that the pregnancy might be interrupted, by expelling the fetus from the mouth.

Q: When you realized there was a baby girl inside of you, what did you feel?

A: As I said before, a lot of amazement. And in this period, I feel very creative. Alessandro (the partner) said: "Of course, this is the most creative of periods!" And I answered, "Actually, if you think about it, you and I have created a girl, created her from scratch, because before there was nothing."

Q: And the awareness of this new being came with her first movements?

A: With the first movements, yes, but even more in this last month. I really feel her, I feel she's in here.

Q: What do you imagine her like?

A: Beautiful. I imagine her beautiful. And then obviously she sleeps. She has to sleep for months. And then I imagine her calm, friendly, and always smiling.

Q: And physically?

A: I imagine her tall, skinny. And blond with blue eyes. Simply beautiful.

Q: Would you say that there already is a relationship between you and the baby?

A: I don't know. I sing lullabies to her, inventing them. I talk to her, simple things like "How are you?" I talk to her in my head more than with my voice. In the morning I tell her, "Now I will sing a lullaby for you, calm down."

Martina, like many other women, can already—at this stage of pregnancy—picture her child's face and attributes specific psychological features to her unborn child. At the same time, Martina talks to her daughter as if they were sharing a conversation, which anticipates their future exchanges.

Q: What do you think she will need in the first months?

A: Most of all love, lots of love, attention, in the first months especially. She needs to feel she is in a warm atmosphere, full of care, where she is taken care of, welcomed.

Q: What kind of mother do you think you will be in the first months?

A: In the first months I would like to be tolerant, open. I hope to be very stimulating for the baby, and very caring.

Martina's narration shows how pregnancy is for her a maturation of her female identity; she has prepared herself for it with a strong longing for motherhood. Her storytelling appears fluid and coherent and demonstrates a good capacity for reading her feelings and her partner's, with a certain degree of irony as well. Her world of fantasies and dreams appears quite rich; she expresses her miscarriage fears in the dream where her mouth is bleeding. However, she seems capable of analyzing her fears and depressive anxieties. She has a definite image of her child and demonstrates she has been able to set up a dialogue with him or her, as if he or she were an imaginary companion to play and sing with. There are many overlapping elements with Raphael-Leff's depiction (2010) of the Facilitator Mother.

AN EXPECTANT MOTHER WHO TRIES TO LIMIT THE IMPACT OF PREGNANCY

The maternal restricted/disinvested representation emerges from narratives in which a strong emotional control prevails, with mechanisms of rationalization toward the fact of becoming a mother and toward the child. These women talk of their pregnancy, of motherhood, and of the child in poor terms, without many references to emotional events and changes. The storytelling has an impersonal quality, is frequently abstract, and does not communicate emotions or specific images or fantasies.

Flaminia is a young woman who shows a restricted representation of herself as a mother and of her child. Even though she gives value to her motherhood experience, Flaminia wants to maintain her independence and self-control and does not want to be too conditioned by the child who is about to be born.

Q: Would you tell me about your pregnancy?

A: I must say I was very lucky, I never had any problems. Even in the first three months, I had no nausea, vomiting, etcetera. I did some things which you're supposed to avoid, like skiing, going on a motorcycle . . . but I felt ok, I felt I could do it. But my first three months were characterized by a certain nervousness, a state of tension. After the first three months I started getting used to the idea and calmed down. I still had no physical problems. Then slowly, with great difficulty, I started getting used to the idea of my body transforming.

Q: Why a baby in this moment of your life?

A: I thought about it a lot because I didn't feel ready, even if I'm not a kid anymore. I always had this idea I wouldn't have kids. I'm not crazy about kids, I've never been drawn to them much. Then, maybe because you feel the need after a number of years in a marriage, or maybe because my husband who wasn't convinced either, changed his mind . . . it was a series of things which pushed me towards this decision.

Flaminia seems to have accepted the idea of a pregnancy after a number of years of marriage more as a need, as an answer to certain social expectations, than because of her desire for a child, since she does not really love children. She tries not to be influenced by her new condition and continues to practice sports that, as she admits herself, are not suited to pregnancy. Flaminia's attitude seems to correspond to that described by Raphael-Leff for the Regulator Mother "who wishes to regulate her life" (1993, p. 67).

Q: What did you feel when you found out you were pregnant?
A: I am quite cold, as a person. I don't get carried away easily, so even in this case I wouldn't have told anyone, I'd have kept it to myself. I first needed to get used to the idea.
Q: Have there been specific moments of great emotion during the pregnancy, until now?
A: Maybe when I did the ultrasonography towards the fourth month. That's the first time you actually see this little growing being and you see it whole. But mostly my feeling was a reflection of the great emotion I could see on my husband's face. Seeing his reaction, I let myself be influenced by his state of mind, mood, and felt it as if it were my feeling.
Q: During the pregnancy, have there been times when you felt worried or mad about something? Have you ever felt any particular needs?
A: I can't think of anything now. The preoccupation everyone has, about the baby's health.
Q: Have you had dreams during the pregnancy?
A: Yes, but I never remember my dreams. I remember I was eating yogurt in the last one, but I have no idea what it might mean.

Regarding affective involvement, Flaminia describes herself as a cold person, who does not get carried away by emotions; if she has had some worries, they are nothing but the worries every pregnant woman has, and this shows her attempt to rationalize and depersonalize her experience.

Q: How do you imagine the baby?
A: I actually don't imagine it.
Q: Do you imagine its physical features, its character?
A: No.
Q: And its sex?
A: Not even its sex, I didn't want to know and I don't want to think about it. It will be a surprise.

Q: Do you and your husband talk to the baby or use nicknames?

A: Yes, but it's mostly my husband who talks to it, not me. Even if I feel there is a bond between the baby and me, I still can't bring myself to talk to it.

Flaminia's narration shows her effort to not be too influenced or involved in the pregnancy, carrying on with her usual life and rhythms in order to escape the regression process typical of this phase (Pines, 1972). She does not seem capable of creating an image of the child; she does not even want to know the sex, as if to keep him or her in a neutral space, a limbo. At the ultrasonography, her emotional reaction was conditioned by her husband's, as if she were not capable of having a feeling of her own. This picture overlaps with the Regulator Mother described by Raphael-Leff (2010).

A CONFLICTED EXPECTANT MOTHER
TORN BETWEEN DESIRE AND FEAR

The nonintegrated/ambivalent maternal representation is the one found in confused narrations, characterized by digressions and by the woman's difficulty with answering questions in a clear and articulate way. The coherence of the story is poor, and an ambivalent involvement of the mother toward the experience she is living, toward her partner and toward her family, is present. These women often express contrasting attitudes toward their motherhood or toward the child. The son or daughter is frequently awaited to satisfy the caregiver's needs.

Roberta, a 29-year-old woman, is an example of a Nonintegrated Mother. The idea of having a child has made its way to her along with many ambivalences and uncertainties, revealing all the difficulties that a nonintegrated mother manifests in fully accepting a maternal identity.

Q: Would you tell me about your pregnancy?

A: In the beginning we had many things, those egoistic projects of settling everything first, because we started out with nothing, and we thought "we'll think about a baby later on." So let's say it wasn't a thought, like we both had no clear desire of a baby in the beginning. Then when things started working out, everything, we looked each other in the eyes and said, "What do you think about it? I am thirty already." And he didn't want to, he had decided that he was already old when we married; he had already settled, so he had some difficulties, he said he didn't want to be a grandfather. . . . He had these problems, fears, which I didn't have, mine were completely different, like how will I help my child in twenty years' time, finding a job, or school, for example.

Now I'm completely terrified on how to do things, and the kindergarten, the people he will hang out with because we know what it's like, and my mentality is not "live by the day"; maybe I worry too much about everything around me.

That's why I used to say, "Let's wait," then one fine day this decision just arrived. "What do you think about it?" "And maybe, yes, it's time," we made a joke about it, "Time to take on responsibilities. . . ." That's when I started thinking, I started asking around, how many children, how long did it take, etcetera.

Roberta's narration displays the ambivalence and conflict with which she has faced pregnancy: On one hand, she wanted a child, but on the other she seems to resist the idea because she is afraid of facing motherhood. For this reason she looks to other women for reassurance, as if she were still not completely sure of her choice.

Q: During pregnancy were there times when you felt worried or mad about something?

A: In the beginning, after a month and a half, I started having nausea problems, upset stomach, lots of saliva, so that after two months I was thinking, "Why on earth did I do it?" Because I was really sick . . . I was thinking, "What a terrible pregnancy I'm going to have" because some would say, "It's all going to end soon" and others, "I threw up all the way to the ninth month." . . .

And my doctor said, "It's mostly psychological." On one hand we wanted it, but on the other maybe that was partly true, because I was very embarrassed to tell my boss; I didn't know how to tell him.

Q: How did you feel when you found out you were pregnant?

A: I found out after only a week, and there I was, telling the nurse, "Are you really sure?" because maybe it could be like with those pharmacy tests, which are uncertain. They told me in the pharmacy that if it's sure, when it appears clearly it's positive; when it's uncertain it could be positive or negative. I was so excited because it's not . . . I was saying, "No, it's not possible." . . .

In the laboratory, the doctor said, "Look, the stick doesn't become pink if it's not positive"; so nothing, this thing was pink, "If you say so it must be, you guarantee, when I walk out of here I can tell my husband."

The news of her pregnancy creates uncertainty and ambivalent feelings in Roberta, as if she were not aware of what was happening inside her body and once again needed confirmation from someone else.

Q: Have there been specific moments of great emotion during the pregnancy?

A: Yes, when I did my ultrasonography in the fourth month, when they said, "This is the heart beating" and on the screen monitor there was this confused image, but when we saw the head, I absolutely didn't imagine that I could see a profile. It really gave me a strange impression, seeing it. . . .

Q: Are there dreams you remember of this pregnancy period?

A: Yes, I realize I have been dreaming more, but mostly it's bad dreams. Sometimes sad dreams, sometimes bad ones, really bad.

Q: What did you feel when you first realized there was a baby inside you?

A: Happy, because I thought it's there, so I have to be careful of what I do, to do things to not. . . The first period for example I was very anxious and I had terrible pains in the stomach and I was afraid the baby felt pain, too.

Q: How do you imagine this baby?

A: Wishing is different from imagining. How I imagine it, I don't know, I imagine the baby ugly and dark, with dark hair; how I wish it to be instead is different, obviously beautiful and with clear eyes, beautiful; well, I'd like one thing, one wish, that it doesn't look like me.

Q: Do you imagine the baby as a boy or a girl?

A: I imagine it as a boy, but I hope it's a girl.

Roberta appears very ambivalent toward her pregnancy and her child. On the one hand, she wishes for him or her, but on the other hand, she is very anxious about the child's future. She still cannot define her expectations; she pictures him as a boy, but she would like a girl. Her ambivalent feelings are very strong, and she cannot integrate them, showing strong oscillations. The picture corresponds to Raphael-Leff's (2010) clinical description of the Conflicted Mother.

After these clinical examples, we must refer to the research on mental representations during pregnancy (Ammaniti et al., 2013), which has shown that in a normal sample of pregnant mothers the most represented category is the Integrated one (56.7%), while the Restricted one reaches a 24.3%, and the Ambivalent one 19%. In risk samples (depressive and social risk), the distribution is different: The most represented is the Ambivalent one (36.9%), which is characterized by a conflictual approach toward pregnancy, then the Restricted one (32.9%), and lastly the Integrated one (30.2%).

The maternal categories have different psychic constellations, using the term proposed by Stern (1995) "maternal constellation," which represents different mental strategies and dynamics for organizing the personal experience of motherhood. As has been evidenced, the Integrated/Balanced style represents the most coherent maternal strategy, while the other two manifest less flexibility in facing the new experience of motherhood. Many factors influence the maternal style: the woman's personal history as well as her model of attachment, the marital relationship, and the family and social support.

The quality of maternal categories will have a profound impact on the mother–child relationship (Aber, Belsky, Slade, & Crnic, 1999; Slade, Belsky, Aber, & Phelps, 1999) and will play a significant role in ultimately determining the security and safety of the child's experience with his or her mother (George & Solomon, 1996; Zeanah, Benoit, Hirshberg, Barton, & Regan, 1994). Of course, a conflictual attitude during pregnancy can predict a higher probability of difficulties in maternal caregiving after birth and risks for the interaction between mother and infant.

Recognizing mothers' vulnerabilities during pregnancy is important because it is possible to start a supportive intervention during this period, which can modify the mother's attitude and help her contain her anxieties and fears, especially in the last trimester.

BY FORCE OF MATERNAL FANTASY

By Force of Fantasy is the title of an extraordinary book by Ethel S. Person, which explores the area of "fantasies-daydreams, castles in the air, mental scripts, and scenarios" (1995, p. 1), a mental filter that gives depth and color to the mental life. It is a private and quite secret subjective life that creates imaginative stories about one's own personal life, one's family, and other people. In other words, it could be defined as an internal dialogue that creates a fantastic internal theater with the wishful aim of gratifying sexual, aggressive, or self-aggrandizing wishes or giving a form to personal hopes.

The secrecy of fantasies is an intrinsic feature that Freud highlighted: "The adult . . . is ashamed of his phantasies and hides from other people. He cherishes his phantasies as his most intimate possessions, as a rule he would rather confess his misdeeds than tell anyone his phantasies. It may come about that, for that reason, he believes he is the only person who invents such phantasies and has no idea that creations of this kind are widespread among other people" (1908/1959, p. 145).

Throughout pregnancy and the child's first months, a woman lives with myriad conscious and fantastic thoughts. These occur because the physiological and psychological changes brought on by pregnancy and motherhood generate perceptions, ideative processes, feelings, and conscious and unconscious fantasies about the self, the couple's relationship, the family she comes from, and obviously the child.

These fantasies can be expressed in daydreams, which might appear in her waiting moments, during which the woman tries to imagine the face and a configuration for her child. These are open-eyed fantasies that are often then discussed with the partner and that are centered on the choice of a name for the child, on his or her sex if not known, on the likeness or differences from the mother's and father's families, and on preparing outfits and equipment in the house. Paraphrasing Winnicott's expression, Soulé proposed, in one of his essays (1991), the image of a "knitting-enough mother," a mother who gives free rein to her fantasies, measuring them, while knitting, against the coming baby's body. As Soulé wrote, the mother not only gives life to the child but also builds his or her "containment," which must be prepared in advance as if to prefigure and anticipate the child's personal reality.

We must point out that fantasies have an important role not only because they help to prefigure the future—one example is the mother who, during pregnancy, pictures herself taking care of and breastfeeding her child and imagines the child's face, thus readying herself for their encounter. As shown by Singer (1966) in his book *Daydreaming*, an imagination that manipulates symbols implies the mental capacity to create possibilities beyond the evidence of the actual perception and to suggest, for the future especially, alternatives to the real world of people, places, and things.

It may happen that fantasies concentrate on the fear of bearing a defected or sick child and these will be overcome at the child's birth; others may concentrate on one's inadequacy at taking care of the child and these fears, as well, will be overcome when the mother actually starts taking care of the child.

This psychological dialectic between maternal fantasies and the reality of pregnancy and of the postpartum period, as between personal and shared fantasies, creates a deep and intimate dimension that characterizes the motherhood experience. The specificity of this experience was expressed by Winnicott (1971b) with the fecund but elusive concept of "potential space." As Winnicott wrote: "That place, potential space, is not inside by any use of the word. . . . Nor is it outside, that is to say, it is not part of the repudiated world, the not-me, that which the individual has decided to recognize (with whatever difficulty and even pain) as truly external, which is outside magical control" (1971b, p. 41). Potential space is an intermediate area of experiencing that lies between (a) the inner world, "inner psychic reality" (1971b, p. 106) and (b) "actual or external reality" (1971b, p. 41). It lies "between the subjective object and the object objectively perceived, between me-extensions and not-me" (1971b, p. 100). . . . [This] area is a product of the experiences of the individual person (baby, child, adolescent, adult) in the environment that obtains" (1971b, p. 107).

And within this potential space, the thinking processes and fantasies of pregnancy develop and may be thwarted, if a difficulty or a breakdown occurs in maintaining this dialectic. If a good balance between these two aspects of the experience is attained, personal fantasies fit into a shared reality that is only enriched by the fantasies. In this space, the representations of the self as a mother and of the future child develop and differentiate, acquiring depth.

This is the case with Luisa, 30 years old, who speaks of her pregnancy saying: "It upset all my rhythms and I felt stuck." She tells of how, during the last months of the pregnancy, she cannot think of anything except the baby; before falling asleep she tries imagining him and visualizing what he will be like. Watching the ultrasonography, she had the impression the baby was suffocated by the womb because he lives in such a completely different situation from herself: "not out in the open, he can't see the light, can't move around like I do." It is interesting to note that Luisa has claustrophobic fantasies about the child, probably connected to her own childhood history, during which her mother overwhelmed her with attention and care.

When the dialectic between subjective world and the reality experienced fails, an inflation of the fantastic world can take place. This can obscure the real child, and the child is thus attributed with salvific powers, attributions that will later interfere with the development of identity through ego-alien factors (Winnicott, 1969).

THINKING FOR TWO

The interviews have clearly demonstrated that Integrated Mothers are capable of keeping their yet unborn baby in mind. They are able to have a differentiated psychic image of the baby, with whom they have a dialogue as if he or she were present outside the womb, attributing emotions and intentions to him or her, trying to give a sense to and interpret the child's movements. The Restricted Mothers' approach is quite different: They seem incapable of having an image of their child, and they treat him or her like a fetus and not like a baby they can relate to and dialogue with.

This specific maternal competence could be attributed to mentalization, which in the early conceptualization has emphasized cognitive aspects (Frith & Happé, 1994; Harris, 1989; Jurist, 2008), underlining the awareness of thoughts and beliefs more than desires. Mentalization refers to a personal explicit and implicit ability to recognize our own and others' mental states, and to see these mental states as separate from behavior. Later on, with Fonagy's contribution (2001b), mentalization, which has also been defined as "reflective functioning," encompassed being able to recognize one's own personal thoughts, emotions, wishes, desires, and needs in other people as well, and to see that these internal events may have an impact on personal actions and on others but that they are separate from those actions.

In this theoretical context, reflective functioning has been described as the capacity to reflect upon the mental states of others inside the actual relationship (Fonagy, Gergely, Jurist, & Target, 2002; Slade, 2005). In the case of mothers, during pregnancy they can imagine the baby inside them as having intentions, feelings, and desires and at the same time recognize their own personal states of mind and emotions. The reflective function is a crucial aspect of the interpersonal interpretive mechanism, a unique human quality necessary to process and interpret interpersonal experience and make sense of it (Fonagy et al., 2002). An important aspect of reflective function is the empathic stance and emotional resonance with the child's emotions and needs and thus the capacity to appropriately mirror the infant's internal states after birth.

The term *reflective function* must be differentiated from *metacognition* because it not only considers metacognitive processes, such as perspective taking and appearance-reality distinction (Hesse, 2008), but the emotional experience inside a relationship as well.[1] The attention to the concept of maternal reflective function has been promoted by research (Fonagy, Steele, Moran, et al., 1991) that studies the models of attachment in a sample of mothers and fathers. This research evidenced a great variability in mothers' reflective function. While some parents could reflect on the relation between their parents' mental state and their personal behavior, clearly separating their parents' experience from their own, other parents manifested little understanding of the feelings and motivations of their own parents.

This capacity has a great relevance for the mother, as well as for the relationship with her own child. As Slade wrote: "A mother's capacity to hold in her

---

[1]This topic will be discussed in depth in subsequent chapters in order to clarify the significance and the context of different mental representations and also their neurobiological basis.

mind a representation of her child as having feelings, desires, and intentions allows the child to discover his own internal experience via his mother's representation of it" (2008, p. 314).

In the area of mentalization, different concepts overlap and for this reason it would be helpful to trace theoretical and empirical distinctions. As Arnott and Meins (2008) have discussed, it is helpful to distinguish parents' representations of the child from the representation of themselves as mind-minded caregivers. The mind-mindedness has been operationalized (Meins, 1997) in terms of mothers' tendency to focus on their children's mental qualities, rather than their physical characteristics or behavior. While maternal mind-mindedness has previously been evaluated considering this quality after the baby's birth, recent research (Arnott & Meins, 2008) has explored this quality before the baby is born. During pregnancy parents can view the unborn child as a separate being, believing that the fetus can act independently of the mother and interpreting his or her movements as the expression of his or her intentions and desires. In the research, parents have been asked during pregnancy to describe the child at 6 months of age after birth. The expectation was that the parents who were more able to recognize the child as a separate being during pregnancy would give a better prediction of the behavior of the child at 6 months. On the contrary, parents less able to recognize the child as a separate person would be less capable in predicting the child at 6 months.

The research has evidenced a positive correlation between mothers' total number of comments in the antenatal demand "describe your child" prediction and their scores for appropriate mind-related comments during the infant–mother interactions at 6 months postpartum. A similar result has been evidenced in fathers, although they are less able to discriminate the mental state of the child. At the same time the findings suggest that parents' emotional involvement with the fetus does not imply their ability to imagine the unborn child's future characteristics or to interact with their child in a mind-minded way. The conclusion of the study emphasizes the importance of the maternal capacity during pregnancy to represent the fetus as a potential and intentional child for future parental mind-mindedness.

There is a link between reflective function and affect regulation. In fact, a mother with this capacity can develop a mental model for the child's emotional experience, who shall attain a capacity for self-regulation.

CHAPTER 3

Maternal Caring, Concern, and Preoccupations

Psychoanalysis and social learning theories have suggested that an infant's relationship with the mother develops because she feeds the infant (Freud, 1910/1957; Sears, Maccoby, & Levin, 1957), and the infant's pleasure connected with the satisfaction of this need is associated with the mother's presence. Bowlby (1980) found a new explanation by observing how children become attached to people who do not feed them. Bowlby's (1980) theoretical framework gives a different explanation based on evolutionistic theories: The child's bond is not linked to social learning but stems rather from a biologically based desire to maintain a physical proximity to an attachment figure. The intrinsic motivation of the attachment motivational system drives the child to maintain proximity to the mother in a goal-corrected manner. According to Bowlby (1979), emotions are strongly associated with attachment:

> Many of the most intense emotions arise during the formation, the maintenance, the disruption, and the renewal of attachment relationships. The formation of a bond is described as falling in love, maintaining a bond as loving someone, and losing a partner as grieving over someone. Similarly threat of loss arouses anxiety and actual loss gives rise to sorrow; whilst each of these situations is likely to arouse anger. The unchallenged maintenance of a bond is experienced as a source of joy. (p. 130)

The attachment motivational system has a complex interplay with other behavioral systems. Among other motivational systems, Bowlby highlighted the value of the caregiving system, which is "like attachment behavior . . . in some degree preprogrammed" (1956, p. 271). The caregiving system is connected to caring for and protecting children but does not cover the entire range of parental behaviors. Cassidy (2008) considered only the parental behaviors, part of the caregiving system, which promote proximity and comfort when parents perceive that the child is in trouble.

A more precise definition of the caregiving system was given by Mayseless (2006), according to whom mental models of caregiving

> (a) are based on actual experiences in caregiving-related circumstances; (b) serve to regulate, interpret, and predict the care-receiver and the caregiver's caregiving-related behaviors, thoughts, and feelings; (c) reflect reality but also regulate and create it; (d) are flexible to some extent and can be updated by new experiences and self-reflections; (e) involve several distinct memory systems: procedural, semantic, and episodic, at various levels of consciousness and with varying degrees of affective load; and (f) reflect the operation of various defensive processes that serve to protect the caregiver from unbearable anxiety and psychological suffering. (pp. 28–29)

Of course, a parent may have different models of caregiving for every child, reflecting the specific history of the relationship, the birth order, and the characteristics of the child.

The activation of the caregiving system in mothers is urged by different cues, connected to their biological and hormonal conditions especially during motherhood, personal infantile history with their own parents, self-representation as a parent, quality of emotional regulation, and relationship with the partner and the family. The personal condition of the child and his or her attachment can also stimulate the caregiving system, considering that the babyish features of the child have evolved in order to activate parental involvement.

It is not simple to distinguish psychological and hormonal factors during pregnancy that interact and reinforce reciprocally. Fleming, Ruble, Krieger, and Wong (1997) studied hormonal and experiential correlates of maternal responsiveness during pregnancy and puerperium. The first goal of their research tried to verify whether during pregnancy human mothers present a change in maternal responsiveness before the birth of the baby, as highlighted in other mammalian species. The second goal was to establish whether a relation exists between changes in maternal feelings and attitudes and hormonal changes. The child-caring dispositions of mothers were explored with a questionnaire regarding attitudes toward pregnancy and birth, self-esteem, and other interpersonal relationships which was submitted during the first, second, and third trimesters, at the end of pregnancy, and then again in the first and third month postpartum.

During pregnancy significant changes were evidenced in different maternal areas like infant care or mothering, while they were limited in the area of relationship with own partner and own mother. A significant and relevant stage effect for feelings for the fetus between the first and the second trimester of pregnancy was highlighted, while the psychological attitude toward the child increased linearly throughout the pregnancy. An interesting conclusion of the research pointed out that no correlation between maternal hormones and maternal attitudes during pregnancy especially referred to maternal feelings of attachment to the fetus. Only postpartum maternal attachment feelings are correlated to pregnancy hormones. On the basis of these results it could be suggested that the changes of maternal attitude during pregnancy can be explained rather by changes in emotional and cognitive functioning and in maternal attitudes than by hormonal changes. These data differentiate the growth of human maternal responsiveness compared to primates and other animals, which are strongly influenced by hormones (Corter & Fleming, 1995).

A further confirmation comes from observation of the increase of maternal positive feelings toward the fetus in the second trimester of pregnancy, when mothers begin to perceive the first fetal movements. In this research (Fleming et al., 1997) maternal attachment to the fetus was explored; however, it was difficult to define the feeling for the fetus as equivalent to attachment, according to the theoretical framework proposed by Bowlby (1969, 1982).

In any case, there has been an increased recognition over the past 20 years that the relationship between a mother and her child starts to develop before the child is born. However, the significance of maternal-fetal attachment (MFA) is still not well conceptualized and studied.

It is interesting to note that the concept of MFA is not being studied by researchers and clinical professionals in the attachment field. This is confirmed by the fact that the 2008 second edition of the *Handbook of Attachment*, edited by Cassidy and Shaver, does not have the term *prenatal attachment* in its Subject Index. The concept of MFA appears rather in obstetrics, where operators and researchers have the chance to observe maternal affective attitude and concern toward the fetus, who throughout the pregnancy increasingly becomes an important presence within the mother's mental world. Revising the recent literature and research in this field (Alhusen, 2008; Brandon, Pitts, Denton, Stringer, & Evans, 2009; Cannella, 2005), we will now try to run through the quite contradictory path that has characterized the theorization and research on MFA.

Retracing the steps of the theoretical definition of MFA, we should first take into consideration the Kennell, Slyter, and Klaus study (1970), which gave an indirect confirmation of the prenatal attachment by observing intense grief in mothers of infants who died during birth, demonstrating that a prenatal emotional bond already exists between a mother and her unborn child.

In the same period, Lumley, an Australian perinatal epidemiologist, started interviewing primipara mothers throughout the three trimesters of pregnancy, observing that mothers are able to mentally represent their babies and that they have an increasingly defined child image during pregnancy (Lumley, 1972). The introduction of ultrasound scanning during pregnancy stimulated Lumley to examine the impact of the ecographic image of the fetus on mother–infant bonding (Lumley, 1980). Lumley's observations confirmed that this early image of the fetus enhances a mother's ability to recognize it as a "little person" (Lumley, 1980, p. 215). Subsequently, Lumley performed the first empirical longitudinal study on prenatal attachment, using interviews before and after childbirth and evidenced first-time parents' attitudes toward their baby, defining maternal attachment as an "established relationship with the fetus in imagination," perceived as a "real person" (Lumley, 1982, p. 107) in 30% of mothers in the first trimester, 63% in the second trimester, and in 92% by the 36th week of gestation. The observation of lagging attachment in mothers was interpreted as being related to unpleasant symptoms of pregnancy and lack of affective support on the part of husbands. These first findings undoubtedly had the merit of defining the mothers' psychological attitude and dispositions toward her baby during pregnancy, which would later lead to the establishment of the conceptualization of prenatal attachment.

A further step was made by Rubin (1967a,b, 1975), a nurse working in maternity care, who explored women's attainment of the maternal identity, thus contributing to the basis for the theoretical definition of attachment. Maternal bond begins before birth and profoundly influences the subsequent bond between mother and neonate.

Rubin identified four developmental tasks that women face before childbirth: (1) seeking safe pathway for self and baby; (2) ensuring that the baby is accepted by other familiar people into their life; (3) binding in; and (4) giving of herself. Although Rubin did not mention any specific concept about attachment theory, the four tasks underline maternal attitudes considered relevant during the experience of motherhood partially overlapping with the constellation of attachment. A brief comment about the last concept: The mother's giving of herself includes the mental process through which a woman includes the representation of her child in her own representation of herself as a mother, developing a sense of "we-ness" (Rubin, 1975, p. 149). It is interesting to notice that the concept of we-ness was previously discussed in a different context by the psychoanalyst George Klein (1967), during the same years, according to whom psychoanalysis needs a theory of a "we-go" to integrate its theory of an ego. And during pregnancy the sense of we-ness is a specific quality of the maternal mental world.

Although Rubin did not explicitly use the term "attachment," she wrote: "By the end of the second trimester, the pregnant woman becomes so aware of the child within her and attaches so much value to him that she possesses something very dear, very important to her, something that gives her considerable pleasure and pride" (Rubin, 1975, p. 145).

In the same period Leifer, an American psychologist who adopted a psychological approach, prepared an interesting and documented monograph reporting observations from a study on the psychological changes observed during the course of pregnancy (Leifer, 1977). The major theoretical assumption of the study is that pregnancy and early motherhood may be viewed as different developmental tasks, which are faced in different ways predictive of adaptation after birth to the maternal identity. Leifer's study had different aims: (a) to identify the psychological changes in women during their first pregnancy by assessing the potential psychological crisis during pregnancy and motherhood; (b) to describe the unfolding of maternal feelings; and (c) to assess, during the first stage of pregnancy, the quality of the maternal attitudes early in pregnancy that could be predictive of behaviors and adjustment to later stages of pregnancy and the capacity to assume a parental role.

The complex and articulated longitudinal study of Leifer was performed in a relatively small sample of white, middle-class primigravidas, with an age range of 22–33 years, with no previous gynecological or psychiatric difficulties, currently living with their husbands. These women were interviewed at each trimester of pregnancy, on the third postpartum day, and at 2 months postpartum and then a follow-up questionnaire. The rich data, obtained from extensive interview schedules and personality measures, provide evidence that deep changes are characteristic during pregnancy, with emotional upheaval and rapid identity oscillations, but at the same time women experience a growing sense of internal coherence, satisfaction, and personal integration. The research evidenced that the degree of personality integration achieved by early pregnancy is predictive of the later psychological personal maturing throughout pregnancy and early parenthood.

Later on Cranley (1981), a nursing researcher, tried to elaborate and define the theoretical construct of MFA as "the extent to which women engage in behaviors that represent an affiliation and interaction with their unborn child" (Cranley, 1981, p. 282). She wrote: "Integral to that development is the consideration of the woman's identity, her role identity, the identity of her developing fetus, and perhaps most important, the relationship between herself and her fetus" (1981, p. 281), underlining the centrality of identity transformation during pregnancy. The nature and the development of this maternal relationship, defined as prenatal attachment, are important markers that could be correlated with postnatal attachment.

With this in mind, Cranley (1981) developed the first antenatal attachment scale, the Maternal-Fetal Attachment Scale (MFAS), using the six aspects she had conceptualized (Differentiation of Self from Fetus, Giving of Self, Role Taking, and Nesting, for example), which is still used most frequently by researchers interested in prenatal studies.

The conceptual path was sufficiently set, and it stimulated a great interest in a prenatal nurse researcher, Müller (1990), who was not satisfied with Cranley's approach. She found that it was too focused on behaviors without adequately considering maternal thoughts and fantasies, which forge the emerging and the dynamics of the affiliation process between mother and fetus. In her work Müller gave another definition of prenatal attachment as "the unique, affectionate relationship that develops between a woman and her fetus. These feelings are not dependent on the feelings the woman has about herself as a pregnant person or her perception of herself as a mother" (1990, p. 11). A different model of attachment in pregnancy was proposed by Müller who suggested that an expectant mother is deeply influenced by her early experiences with her own mother (or her primary caregiver), which profoundly affect the development of maternal representations, extremely relevant for the adjustment to pregnancy and the attachment to her fetus. Also, Müller designed and proposed her own instrument, the Prenatal Attachment Inventory (PAI), that measures prenatal attachment in order to investigate the specific and unique relationship that develops between a mother and her fetus, an affectionate attachment (Müller, 1993).

The process of defining prenatal attachment is not yet concluded, probably because the conceptualization was not sufficiently convincing. Another researcher, John Condon (1993), considered Cranley's work unsatisfying in its description of MFA. For this reason he decided to build his approach on the attachment theory directly, accepting Bretherton's broad view of attachment as an "emotional tie" or "psychological bond" to a specific object, which gives MFA a greater coherent theoretical construct (Bretherton & Waters, 1985; Condon, 1993). Condon suggested that mothers develop during pregnancy a specific attachment, characterized by a deep emotional tie or bond of love, and in this relationship the mother seeks "to know, to be with, to avoid separation or loss, to protect, and to identify and gratify the needs of her fetus" (Condon & Corkindale, 1997, p. 359).

A new instrument to assess prenatal attachment was developed by Condon (1993), who considered the previous instruments inadequate in differentiating the maternal attitude toward the fetus from the attitude toward the condition of pregnancy and motherhood. For this reason, his Maternal Antenatal Attachment Scale (MAAS) tended to focus exclusively on maternal thoughts and feelings about the baby.

The conceptualization of prenatal attachment is obviously not satisfying yet and the definition provided by Doan and Zimmerman, which combined different behavioral, cognitive, and emotional approaches, did not solve the issue: "Prenatal attachment is an abstract concept, representing the affiliative relationship between a parent and fetus, which is potentially present before pregnancy, and is related to cognitive and emotional abilities to conceptualize another human being, and develops within an ecological system" (2003, p. 110).

A possible explanation for this long path that we have described is the lack of theoretical conceptualization of MFA, which has not been supported by the research with consistent evidence. In a review of research on maternal–fetal attachment, Alhusen (2008) recently concluded that most of the studies in this area have methodological or design limitations, such as inadequate operational definition of the construct, insufficient homogenous samples in the research, and inadequate consideration of context, which limit a more comprehensive understanding and confirmation of MFA. Studies performed in maternal–fetal attachment area, using the mentioned scales, do not consider important aspects, as for example the planning of pregnancy, the dynamics of marital relationship, and gestational age (Shieh, Kravitz, & Wang, 2001), which could be specifically relevant to MFA.

CAREGIVING SYSTEM FROM THE
ATTACHMENT THEORY'S POINT OF VIEW

Although the term *maternal attachment* has been used by various researchers in reference to the prenatal period (Condon, 1993; Cranley, 1981; Müller, 1993), this concept in the pregnancy context has a wide psychological meaning not so specific, like the one used in the framework of attachment theory.

In this regard it would be more useful to reconsider the original formulation of attachment behavior as it was conceptualized by Bowlby (1969, 1982), which promotes proximity to the attachment figure, a bond of one individual with another individual, who is perceived as protective and stronger, for example, the bond of an infant to the mother. In this perspective it would be better to use the concept of the caregiving system for parents during pregnancy: "a behavioral system in its own right—that is, as an organized set of behaviors guided by a representation of the current parent-child relationship" (George & Solomon, 2008, p. 834). So a substantial shift from the aim of seeking protection and care from attachment figures to providing protection, comfort, and care for an immature child would be more appropriate. Of course, an important principle is the reciprocity and close connection between the caregiving system and the attachment system, as the former develops in the context of the latter.

As we have previously discussed, the activation of the caregiving system depends on internal and external cues that stimulate the protective function. But while in attachment behavior the motivation is clear, connected with safety, Bell and Richard (2000) considered which is the motivation for caregiving that could be based, according to them, on the affective state of caring, which colors the relationship with the child. More precisely, caring is a dyadic emotion that develops over time and is directed toward a specific partner, in this case a baby, and his or her needs. In this context, empathy plays a decisive role and implements caring because it implies the emotional acceptance and resonance toward the other person, especially if he or she is in a needy state.

Perhaps this definition of caregiving undervalues the personal pleasure and emotional satisfaction in caring for another person and above all for a small child. An independent confirmation comes from neurobiological studies that demonstrate the role of the orbitofrontal cortex (Kringelbach, 2005), which is involved in emotional processing and specifically in a hedonic pleasant experience, stimulated by a particular rewarding experience such as caring. The baby can be a rewarding stimulus that arouses in mothers a subjective experience of pleasantness. Also Schore (2000, 2002) has discussed the role of the orbitofrontal cortex, especially of the right hemisphere, which intervenes in regulating the affective mechanism of attachment. This neurobiological system is also connected with empathy, which implies the recognition of "another individual's emotional state by internally generating somatosensory representations that simulate how the individual would feel" (Adolphs, Damasio, Tranel, Cooper, & Damasio, 2000, p. 2683). In other chapters the topic of empathy is discussed more deeply by focusing on the role of mirror neurons mechanism and of the insula, which imply also visceral-motoric representations.

During pregnancy the caregiving system is activated when the baby is still inside the mother's body and will be stabilized completely after the baby's birth. The mother's caregiving behaviors could be guided by maternal representations of the baby inside her, already organized during the third trimester of pregnancy with a specific represented identity of the child. The baby in this period is perceived as very needy and immature, so he or she should be protected and cared for with attention and concern by maternal sensitivity, in order to avoid any hurt or trauma.

The relevance of maternal representations during pregnancy could be confirmed by maternal behaviors after childbirth. It has been evidenced that prenatal representations have a great influence on the subsequent postnatal maternal behaviors (Benoit et al., 1997; Huth-Bocks, Levendosky, & Bogat, 2002; Huth-Bocks, Levendosky, Theran, & Bogat, 2004). Theran, Levendosky, Bogat, and Huth-Bocks (2005) have examined the influence of postnatal change or stability of internal working models of attachment over time (from prenatal to postnatal period) on postnatal parenting behaviors. It has been observed that mothers who presented nonbalanced representations prenatally, but whose representations shifted to balanced ones in the postnatal period, are less likely to provide sensitive caregiving to their children than mothers with balanced representations at both times. Also balanced mothers in pregnancy with a postnatal shifting to nonbalanced ones are more sensitive with the child if confronted with nonbalanced mothers at both times.

While prior meta-analyses have demonstrated that a mother's internal representation of her own childhood attachment experiences are related to her parental behaviors with her own child (van IJzendoorn, 1995), the question about how maternal representations during pregnancy could affect subsequent maternal behavior is still open. Recent research (Dayton, Levendosky, Davidson, & Bogat, 2010) attempted to explore this direct connection, emphasizing the power of maternal internal representations to guide postnatal maternal behaviors at an unconscious level. The findings of the research confirm that maternal representations during pregnancy influence parenting behavior with the child. More specifically, mothers with balanced representations during pregnancy tend to exhibit higher levels of positive parental behaviors, while mothers with distorted representations of their child show a higher level of hostility and anger in the interaction with the child. Lastly, mothers with disengaged representations later manifest a more controlling behavior with the child. What is revealing in this study is that the regulation style connected to maternal working models during pregnancy is significantly related to maternal regulation style (sensitive, controlling, hostile) when the child is 1 year old. Dayton and colleagues (2010) hypothesized that the relationship between prenatal representations and postnatal parental behaviors might be not only correlational but causal as well because the former are measured during pregnancy before mothers could have any interaction with the infant.

While the reported studies focus on the relationship between maternal representations during pregnancy and postnatal maternal behaviors, another perspective in studying attachment during pregnancy was explored in a classic article by Peter Fonagy, Howard Steele, and Miriam Steele (1991). In this article they reported longitudinal research about maternal representations of attachment during pregnancy and the infant–mother attachment at 1 year of age. The mothers are interviewed during the third trimester of pregnancy with the Adult Attachment Interview (AAI; George, Kaplan, & Main, 1985), while the children at 1 year performed the procedure of the Strange Situation (Ainsworth et al., 1978), which assesses the quality of child–mother attachments. The results demonstrate an intergenerational concordance: 75% of secure mothers have securely attached children, while 73% of dismissing or preoccupied mothers with respect to attachment have insecurely attached children.

During this research, analyzing the AAI data and trying to understand the process underlying the intergenerational transmission of attachment and particularly Main's (1991) notion of metacognitive monitoring, Fonagy and colleagues (1991) began to develop the concept of reflective functioning, evidencing in the group of mothers great variations in individual reflective capacities. While some parents could reflect on the relation between their parents' mental state and their own behavior and could differentiate parental mental states from their own, other parents manifested a limited understanding of the feelings and mental states behind their parents' behavior. Parents who present a high reflective function are themselves classified in most cases as secure/autonomous in attachment and have children who are themselves securely attached at 1 year of age. In a similar way, parents who manifest a low reflective function are likely to be insecure in relation to attachment and their children are highly likely to be insecure.

As Bowlby outlined (1969, 1973, 1980), the attachment system is strictly connected with the representational process and, we could add, with the development of the reflective function of the self. At the same time a shared conceptualization has been reached, that the self develops and exists in relationship with others (Sroufe, 1990), and this is true for mothers, who during pregnancy create a sense of we-ness that prepares them to interact with their children after birth.

FOCUSING ON THE BABY

As Dinora Pines (1972) highlighted, the expectant woman experiences bodily uneasiness and fatigue during the third trimester of pregnancy, as the baby grows inside her. During pregnancy characteristic mood swings occur, oscillating from joy and satisfaction about the imminent arrival of the child to conscious and unconscious anxiety about the baby's possible abnormality and about labor. Maternal fantasies about the damage the fetus may inflict can appear, and the fetus may be perceived as an intruder or a parasitic being (Ferenczi, 1914/1926) that is going to devour her.

A particular state of mind defined by Winnicott (1963/1965) will develop in this period: the capacity for concern for the baby and the pregnancy. In "The Development of the Capacity for Concern" from the book *The Maturational Processes and the Facilitating Environment: Studies in the Theory of Emotional Development* (1965), Winnicott gave a precise definition:

The word "concern" is used to cover in a positive way a phenomenon that is covered in a negative way by the word "guilt." A sense of guilt is anxiety linked with the concept of ambivalence, and implies a degree of integration in the individual ego that allows for the retention of good object-imago along with the idea of a destruction of it. Concern implies further integration, and further growth, and relates in a positive way to the individual's sense of responsibility, especially in respect of relationships into which the instinctual drives have entered. Concern refers to the fact that the individual cares, or minds, and both feels and accepts responsibility. At the genital level in the statement of the theory of development, concern could be said to be the basis of the family, where both partners in intercourse—beyond their pleasure—take responsibility for the result. But in the total imaginative life of the individual, the subject of concern raises even wider issues, and a capacity for concern is at the back of all constructive play and work. It belongs to normal, healthy living, and deserves the attention of the psycho-analyst. (p. 73)

As Winnicott pointed out, a capacity for concern develops during pregnancy: The mother grows more and more capable of taking care, paying attention, and feeling and accepting the responsibility of her own maternity, avoiding from the first months the stress factors or traumatic experiences that might have a negative impact on the pregnancy. This is the case for a young woman who, after being told she was pregnant by a nurse, walked home, in her own words, "trying to avoid rough movements or jostling, as if I were tiptoeing on eggs." The capacity for concern intensifies throughout the pregnancy, so mothers will focus all their attention on the child, trying to pick up every signal or movement and striving to guarantee a comfortable and protective environment within their bodies. Another mother, for example, failed to perceive movements from the fetus for many hours during her last month of pregnancy and was alarmed; she tried establishing a mental contact with her daughter, so she could confirm that everything was OK with her. After an intense concentration, so the woman tells, her daughter sent her a message with a strong kick.

But not all mothers have the same capacity for concern. There are mothers, like the aforementioned, who are capable of taking on responsibility for their maternity. These are the mothers who have a balanced and integrated representation of themselves (Ammaniti & Tambelli, 2010) and for whom pregnancy is the expression of a profound desire for motherhood. The situation differs meaningfully with mothers who have a restricted and disinvested representation of themselves and of their child and who do not seem capable of expressing a capacity for concern, as is demonstrated by the fact that they do not want to be conditioned by their pregnant state and continue engaging in strenuous activities without showing preoccupation for the possible consequences on the pregnancy or the child.

Maternal capacity for concern is undoubtedly connected to the fact that females are more empathic than males (Hoffman, 1977) and that they sometimes do not even develop self-empathy "because the pull of empathy for the other is so strong, because females are conditioned to attend to the needs of others first, and because women often experience so much guilt about claiming attention *for* the self, even *from* the self" (Jordan, 1991, p. 30). This specific woman competence could be related to cultural factors and style of upbringing but also to genetic factors, the latter based on preference for social stimuli. A recent study (Sander, Frome, & Scheich, 2007) has evidenced how infant laughter and crying elicit stronger activation of the amygdala and of the anterior cingulate cortex in women than men, just as visually evoked responses to infant faces are larger and earlier in women than men (Proverbio, Zani, & Adorni, 2008). Further studies (Singer et al., 2006) have confirmed that women respond more empathically than men when confronted with images of suffering people. There is an agreement that the right hemisphere may be more involved in empathy than the left hemisphere (Ruby & Decety, 2003, 2004), and the increased activation of the right hemisphere in women may explain gender differences in empathy (Rueckert & Naybar, 2008).

There are many definitions of empathy, each one highlighting different aspects. In the psychoanalytical field, a proper definition has been proposed by Schafer: "The inner experience of sharing in and comprehending the momentary psychological state of another person" (1959, p. 345), which relies on a high psychological functioning and ego strength. In the area of infant research, Stern, referring to mothers' empathy, recognizes four distinct and probably sequential processes: "1) the resonance of feeling state; 2) the abstraction of empathic knowledge from the experience of emotional resonance; 3) the integration of abstracted empathic knowledge into an empathic response; and 4) a transient role identification" (1985, p. 145). This last definition by Stern partially overlaps with what Decety and Meyer (2008) wrote about empathy from a neurobiological point of view, distinguishing automatic emotion sharing, which permits the synchronization of the mother with the infant's emotional expression, from her self-other awareness, which has the aim of separating the maternal self from the child and having some minimal mentalization ability.

Maternal empathy has a great influence on the psychological development of the child, as Winnicott highlighted in this other passage from the aforementioned chapter: "The capacity for concern belongs to the two-body relationship between the infant and the mother or mother-substitute. In favorable circumstances, the mother by continuing to be alive and available is both the mother who receives all the fullness of the baby's id-drives, and also the mother who can be loved as a person and to whom reparation can be made" (1963, p. 82).

MATERNAL PREOCCUPATIONS AND FEARS

Always very attentive of mothers' mental states, Donald Winnicott proposed a further observation of the woman's mental state during the last phase of pregnancy. In a brief statement, Winnicott (1956/1958) explored this particular maternal attitude:

> It is my thesis that in the earliest phase we are dealing with a very special state of the mother, a psychological condition which deserves a name, *Primary Maternal Pre-occupation*. . . . It gradually develops and becomes a state of heightened sensitivity during, and especially towards the end of, the pregnancy. It lasts for a few weeks after the birth of the child. It is not easily remembered by mothers once they have recovered from it. . . . This organized state (that would be an illness were it not for the fact of pregnancy) could be compared with a withdrawn state, or a dissociated state. . . . I do not believe that it is possible to understand the functioning of the mother at the very beginning of the infant's life without seeing that she must able to reach this state of heightened sensitivity, almost an illness and to recover from it. (pp. 301–302)

With a few illuminating and weighty sentences, Winnicott focused on a potentially very fecund concept for comprehending a mother's psychological state during pregnancy and during the child's first development. During this period, a mother develops a heightened sensitivity and is deeply focused on the infant, paying little attention to other people and their social context. This preoccupation has a particular value since it heightens the maternal ability to anticipate the infant's needs, to read his or her unique signals, contributing to developing a sense of self for the infant. Winnicott emphasized the crucial importance of such a stage for the infant's self-development and the possible developmental risk for infants when mothers are unable to tolerate these intense and lively preoccupations.

Although this concept has been accepted and re-elaborated in subsequent clinical observations regarding conflictual mother–infant interactions, it has received relatively limited attention in empirical research, especially in studies about typical developmental pathways of parenting (Fraiberg, Edelson, & Shapiro, 1975; Leckman et al., 1999; Stern, 1995; Zeanah et al., 1994).

Mothers and fathers are both mentally focused on the child, checking his or her physical well-being, physical growth, and emotional state repeatedly, trying to prevent potential imagined or real dangers in the environment. Of course, during pregnancy the maternal checking is more focused on fetal movements, for example, if they are too rapid or too slow or if they are absent.

To confirm the concept of primary maternal preoccupation empirically, Leckman and his colleagues (1999) interviewed mothers and fathers using a semistructured interview, the Yale Inventory of Parental Thoughts and Actions (YIPTA), during and after pregnancy, from the eight month of pregnancy to the third month after childbirth. The Inventory has been designed to explore parental thoughts and preoccupations about the baby (his or her well-being or physical appearance, for example), parental behaviors concerning the care of the baby (checking the baby, for example), building the relationship with the baby, intrusive thoughts and harm-avoidant behaviors (thoughts about harming the baby, for example), and the time occupied by preoccupations and actions. In the sample of interviewed parents, none had a personal history of obsessive-compulsive disorder episodes, while a small percentage of them has reported episodes of major depression.

The results evidence a time course of parental preoccupations, with the highest level 2 or 3 weeks postpartum (figure 3.1). Mothers consistently manifest a higher level of preoccupation for the baby than fathers, thus confirming Winnicott's clinical conceptualization. Around the second or third week postpartum, mothers report that their thoughts about the baby are intense and tend to occupy nearly 14 hours per day, while fathers report nearly 7 hours. In the case of parents of firstborns, the time of preoccupations is longer.

Almost all the parents report persistent worries about the well-being of their child, and more than 95% of the mothers and 80% of fathers worry about the possibility that something negative might happen to the child. Among the intrusive thoughts, many parents report the preoccupation of not being a good parent. Thoughts of harming the unborn child are also present in 37% of parents. To reassure themselves, 73% of the mothers and 49% of the fathers report having checked the baby's movements in utero or made an effort to distract themselves (20%).

Together with these preoccupations, parents may also feel positive thoughts of reciprocity and unity with the infant as well as thoughts about the perfection of the infant. For example, 73% of the mothers and 66% of the fathers report having the thought that their baby is "perfect" at 3 months of age.

In another longitudinal study during the first pregnancy and later at 6 months after birth, with a sample of 120 couples, women report increasing levels of worries toward the end of their pregnancy and 25%–30% describe being preoccu-

FIGURE 3.1. Preoccupations in mothers and fathers from the eighth month of pregnancy to the third month after birth. (Reprinted from *Acta Psychiatrica Scandinavica*, Volume 100, Issue Supplement S396, Leckman et al., "Early parental preoccupations and behaviors and their possible relationship to the symptoms of obsessive-compulsive disorder," p. 9, 1999, with permission from John Wiley & Sons Ltd.)

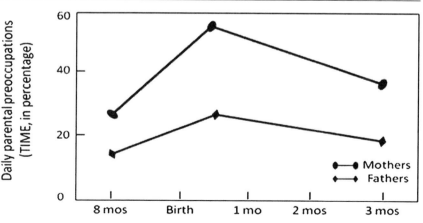

pied with worries about how to care for the infant postpartum (Entwisle & Doering, 1981). Immediately before and after birth, worries may be substantially higher.

Less commonly, intrusive thoughts of injuring the child assail the mother (or father) with a possible outcome of postpartum obsessive-compulsive disorder, depression, or both (Winter, 1970). Parents also experience fantasies or worries that they may in some way inadvertently harm their infant, for example, by dropping the baby, or by more actively damaging the baby in a moment of resentment and frustration.

We have reported Leckman and colleagues' research (1999) extensively not only because it is a brilliant and significant empirical confirmation of Winnicott's conceptualization about primary maternal preoccupation (1956/1958) but also because of the multiple implications in the area of parents–infant interaction. In the last months of pregnancy and in the first months after childbirth, almost every mother and father experience a specific and finalized state of mind, which is distinct from the mood fluctuations and anxiety that are quite common to this period. Parents are focused on the child in a period of extreme vulnerability for him or her, which requires specific attention to the needs of the baby.

Such worries may sometimes predict postnatal difficulties in parent–infant interaction but in most cases, as normative studies have shown, these preoccupations and anxieties are quite common and limited to the end of pregnancy and to the immediate postnatal period. Only their persistence after the first 3–6 months may be the sign of a difficult parent–infant interaction (Mayes, Swain, & Leckman, 2005).

From the evolutionistic point of view these parental preoccupations have been selected in order to enhance the parental capacity and sensitivity and reduce the possible risks for the baby. In fact, the rate of infant mortality has only recently been drastically reduced, while in the past, pregnancy, labor, and the baby's first year of life were periods of great danger for the survival of the mother and of the baby.

These data confirm not only Winnicott's conceptualization (1956/1958) but also the clinical formulation of maternal constellation by Daniel Stern (1995), both focused on the survival and well-being of the baby.

Another important aspect regards what Winnicott wrote about this maternal mental state of preoccupation as "almost an illness," which has many overlapping features with obsessive-compulsive disorder (OCD) symptoms. Parents manifest, as we have seen, intrusive and unceasing thoughts about the baby and themselves, desire to do the right thing, and repetitive behaviors in order to reduce or prevent anxiety. In the case of people with OCD, typical symptoms are characterized by a high sense of responsibility, perfectionism, avoidance of unceasing thoughts, and an ego-dystonic attitude.

Discussing the difference between normal and abnormal obsessions, Rachman and de Silva (1978) underlined that this difference lies in the frequency and intensity of the thoughts rather than their content. In our experience, maternal and paternal thoughts during pregnancy are more ego-syntonic because they are justified in the parents' minds by the particular situation of expecting a baby, which naturally provokes preoccupations and concern.

Leckman and Herman (2002) have hypothesized that these anxious intrusive thoughts and harm-avoidant behaviors are related to OCD and that some forms of OCD are the result of a dysregulation of the neural circuits that are normally activated during the initial phases of parenthood (Leckman et al., 1999). With few exceptions, however, the evidence is supported by neuroimaging studies and neurosurgical findings that have consistently evidenced the role of the orbito-frontal and amygdalal regions and their connections with the thalamus and the ventral striatum in OCD (Saxena & Rauch, 2000). In addition, some patients with OCD have high levels of cerebral spinal fluid oxytocin (Leckman et al., 1994). It is well known that oxytocin, a nanopeptide hormone, plays a role in the emergence of maternal behavior. In a recent study by Levine, Zagoory-Sharon, Feldman, and Weller (2007) healthy women were followed at three points: first trimester and third trimester of pregnancy, and first postpartum month. Plasma oxytocin levels show high individual stability, but while a third of the sample show consistent oxytocin levels, others show increasing or decreasing trends or a peak in late pregnancy. An increase in oxytocin from early to late pregnancy is correlated to higher maternal–fetal bonding.

It has been supposed that the origin of OCD is connected to a dysfunction of serotonin metabolism, combined with the rapid fall of estrogens and progesterone at the end of pregnancy (Williams & Koran, 1997). Another hypothesis (McDougle, Barr, Goodman, & Price, 1999) stresses the role of oxytocin instead: This reaches high levels at the end of the pregnancy and in the postpartum period and could favor the rise or the worsening of OCD. However, the experience of delivery itself or of the immediate following period must not be underestimated as possible triggering factors for OCD (Maina, Albert, Bogetto, Vaschetto, & Ravizza, 1999).

Perhaps the most compelling evidence of the association between pregnancy and OCD is the rate (11% to 47%) of women who have their first onset of OCD in the peripartum period (Leckman & Mayes, 1999; Williams & Koran, 1997) or at the end of the pregnancy. Leckman and his colleagues (1999) further documented that normally during this period there is a heightened sensitivity to threat and that both fathers and mothers experience anxious intrusive thoughts and engage in compulsive-like harm-avoidant behaviors, which bear a striking resemblance to several of the symptom dimensions of OCD.

The review of this literature suggests that the expression of maternal behavior is governed by early experiences and events which imply a likely reorganization of hypothalamic and limbic circuits that are involved in physiologic and hedonic homeostasis as well as in stress response.

On a clinical level, an important symptom during this phase of life is the fear of harming one's own child. Many researchers (Kofman, 2002) have shown that pregnancies with a high level of stress can lead to a preterm delivery or a reduced development of the fetus or temperamental deficits, although not all the data confirm this assessment (DiPietro, Novak, Costigan, Atella, & Reusing, 2006; Wadhwa, Sandman, & Garite, 2001).

Returning to our observation of at-risk mothers, we have noted the presence of persistent preoccupations during pregnancy that are much more intense and invasive than those described by Winnicott and appear even before the eighth month. At the same time these preoccupations differ from the repetitive thoughts that cause anxiety typical of OCD; therefore, we prefer calling them intrusive preoccupations as they appear in a phase of life's cycle in which they have an adaptive function, even though they cause a state of affective dysregulation. On a phenomenological level, they recall obsessive preoccupations for the persistence with which they appear and a certain psychological defensive attitude, although it is limited because these are basically ego-syntonic thoughts that are exclusively associated with the maternity experience. In a sample of mothers at risk of depression and psychosocial risk, we have highlighted intrusive preoccupations concerning the pregnancy, possible diseases or malformations of the fetus, delivery, the postnatal period, their maternal capacities, and the possible repercussions of the child's birth on the couple's relationship. Often there are previous traumatic experiences in the mother's personal history, often in the obstetric field such as recurrent miscarriages, previous dystocial delivery involving intense pain, or death of the fetus in the final stage of pregnancy or immediately after birth. These events have undoubtedly made the woman more sensitive and lead her to experience a new pregnancy with strong worries and preoccupations.

The intrusive preoccupations must be distinguished from anxiety states that are common during pregnancy and are connected to more contextual aspects and the experience itself. Alongside these intrusive preoccupations, we have noticed in these mothers phobic fears that focus on specific real aspects such as the mother's older age or on the fetus's specific characteristics discovered during the ultrasound, such as a poor ponderal development or large dimensions of the cranium.

Preoccupations and fears may be stimulated by specific questions of the IRMAG-R (Ammaniti & Tambelli, 2010), which has been recently modified from the previous version in order to explore these areas in a more systemic way. Studying the interviews of pregnant women who show preoccupations and fears, we have found different representational pictures. A first representational picture is characterized by phobic fears and pervasive intrusive preoccupations that surface throughout the whole interview, even when the questions do not specifically refer to these contents. The main feature of these interviews is the woman's state of alarm; she faces the experience of pregnancy and the arrival of a child with apprehension and fear.

In other interviews, the intrusive preoccupations and phobic fears may appear in a defensive context, characterized by an affective flattening similar to that of the restricted/disinvested representations (Ammaniti & Tambelli, 2010), sometimes accompanied by a concrete description with sensorial details as it happens in dissociative mental states.

AN EXPECTANT MOTHER TORN BY INTRUSIVE
PREOCCUPATIONS AND PHOBIC FEARS

Next we present excerpts of an interview that documents the intense preoccupations and fears that may appear during pregnancy. Piera is around 40 years old;
in her personal history she has suffered from panic attacks, and these have appeared again during pregnancy. Piera had a first pregnancy that led to the birth
of her son Mario and a second pregnancy that ended with a miscarriage after her
amniocentesis test. In the text of the interview, passages with preoccupations and
fears are italicized.

Q: Tell me about your pregnancy, what your feelings were, how you faced it.

A: It went . . . it was very close, in time, to the other one, when I lost the baby
during the fourth month, after the amniocentesis. This pregnancy was partly
planned and partly not, I mean that . . . I was always a bit in crisis, my husband
and I would sometimes talk about it . . . like "Let's try again, soon, to send this
fear and tension away." He was maybe a bit more convinced than I was. I was
kind of yes and no, yes, then no again. Anyway, it happened, I skipped my period
one month, and I really wasn't thinking about it that month. . . . I took a pregnancy test, I am always very regular with my period, so the day after, the first day
I was late I did it and knew that, yes, I was pregnant. *What can I say (laughs), I
actually didn't take it. . . . I felt anxious*, I . . . it's not the first time . . . when I did
the test I didn't even wake my husband, *I spent the whole night . . . I thought it
over and over . . . the fear I guess, the not being . . . not being ready*, physically but
also psychologically for a new pregnancy.

Q: So this was the first phase, how did it go on from there?

A: (laughs) Then it happened that I had miscarriage threats in the first . . . at
the end of the month, whatever, I had miscarriage threats, it was only a slight
bleeding but . . . I had to rest for three months. I had had miscarriage threats during the other pregnancy as well, I had spent twenty days in the hospital so . . .
and . . . so *I had to rest and then I'd happen to see blood spots and I'd call the
hospital to know if everything was ok . . . anyway, I got over it, I was always so anxious, just the fear.* Then there was the question about doing the amniocentesis or
not, should I, shouldn't I . . . is it a problem, I don't think . . . for me it was the
worst moment, the height of my anxiety, *I really felt . . . I couldn't sleep, couldn't
breathe properly, I had sudden panic attacks because of . . . then I took the test and
after that I spent the whole Christmas holidays anxious.* And even during the test,
my heart was, I did it privately . . . *that's how it went. And the after period as well,
having to rest, the fear because of the miscarriage risk*, it all was the same as . . .
But slowly, slowly we made it to the eighth month. *The anxiety, the fears, they're
all still there. Anyway, I'm living this pregnancy differently, . . . now what I feel is
not fear but tension because* . . . what I went through before, I think it has left its
mark, in the sense that I'm afraid of the ultrasound tests, *I'm afraid of . . . of everything that concerns the . . . just anything can make me . . . make me anxious and
if there's any problem I'm frozen there, fearing I won't be able to . . . no, even just*

to understand if there's true reason for alarm, a danger, everything is foggy for me when that happens.

Piera's fears and doubts about a new pregnancy—after her previous miscarriage caused by the amniocentesis—appear clearly in her answers. She repeatedly asks herself whether she should become a mother (Abelin-Sas, 1992). Having experienced a traumatic event, Piera now fears the same might happen in this new pregnancy and insistently seeks reassurance, though this cannot protect her from a new miscarriage threat, which probably is a consequence of the impingement of her mental state over the body, connected to the fact that the traumatic terror has been stored in implicit memory. This critical situation probably determines a disorganization of her defensive system, causing panic attacks (Masi, 2004).

Q: So even the slightest hitch agitates you.
A: No, because I somatize a lot and so this happens . . . when there are actual pregnancy symptoms, there are . . . I mean that the hormones and all the rest, there are times in which I feel them, a few dizzy spells . . . *I think it's because I have low blood pressure when it actually is the fear and the tension.* So maybe some of the symptoms are altered.
Q: How did your sisters take the news of your new pregnancy?
A: Well, my sister, you see . . . D., who is the youngest, has three children and she isn't thirty years old yet. C., the other sister, has just had a baby boy. No, it's ok, but for them, more or less . . . yes, they were happy. . . . And sincerely, I'm not really gifted with children; in fact, the first child was programmed, but I'm not really you know I'm not really that young anymore, so my patience isn't great (laughs). I have a thousand doubts, a thousand fears and anxieties. And at a certain age women . . . maybe *it's fear of the passing of time,* of letting the right moment pass you by . . . *That is, pregnancy makes me anxious; of course it is more so now because of what happened . . . but for me, the situations in which I don't have control over my own body, birth, all that happens within my body and I don't have . . . control of the situation . . . it's a physiological situation in the sense that . . . it all happens month after month, and I'm there thinking it all over, it's all ok . . . I think it's a way of . . . it happens to other women as well, I have experience of other women in pregnancy, all these fears and anxieties appear.*

Piera underlines the role of her body in the experience she is living. Changes she has no control over are taking place, just like the miscarriage threats that she can do nothing about and which make her feel completely impotent (Masi, 2004).

Q: And how has your life changed during pregnancy?
A: It has changed a lot in the sense that ... I really would have liked to live it with a bit more peace of mind. . . but it was inevitable that this would happen. I

didn't have the time to process everything . . . or maybe I reacted well at first but then I cracked up . . . I don't know this. I, well, didn't even enjoy my baby girl's ultrasounds, *everything appears black now, black, black* . . . and I could have avoided it but there's this thing . . . it's just stronger than me.

Q: Has the imminent arrival of your baby girl brought changes in your life and habits as a couple?

A: Yes, surely. But there have been lots of changes, I mean, I don't have a lot of dialogue with him and so . . . or he is not capable of perceiving these things, like when he would say, "Nothing's wrong, everything's fine." So if I sometimes try to explain these things to him . . . there was one evening when I was . . . I cried, I let off steam and he understands me but he says, "What can we do? We just have to go on . . . I understand how you feel but there's Mario to think of." This was his reaction.

Q: How did you feel when you first started wearing pregnancy clothes?

A: Look, for sure I told you, I didn't buy anything for this pregnancy. . . . Now my sisters have given me wide overalls, something wintery. I've reached the eighth month, but I *haven't felt the need to buy any of that stuff, just as I strangely haven't felt the need to buy clothes for the baby, there are many things I avoided doing.* I mean, now I'll start . . . because now the time has come, even the stuff for the hospital, I've prepared the suitcase, *the baby's layette with the things necessary for the first days, but I'm not . . . I told you, I don't feel that tendency.*

Q: Your baby is moving a lot now?

A: She's always moving now, they say that at the eighth month they have less space to move around, but she's still doing it a lot. *And I always get alarmed if I don't feel her . . . but you can't live in constant worry.*

Q: When does she move mostly?

A: She moves a lot more . . . during the evening, when I lie down and am more relaxed, then she moves a lot. I feel her during the day as well, especially when I eat, she moves a lot, I think she's eating as well . . . I feel really feeble, I think it's my diet, it's not that I don't eat, I eat a bit of everything, my diet is varied but . . . nothing . . . I just feel tired.

Q: And how do you interpret these movements? Do you connect them to your moods?

A: No, as I said, I feel a lot . . . she's already pushing . . . contractions, and here in the high part of my belly I feel her feet, her legs when she moves . . . and sometimes she pushes on my diaphragm, I can't breathe, *you feel as if you were dying, I tell you.* And these are nice . . . I told you, I react, I feel her, search for her with my hands . . . *but I'm afraid of doing something to her, of touching her or pushing too hard,* you know for me, I always thought . . . that nature, this is why I say God exists, there is something supernatural in life otherwise it wouldn't be possible. I'd say, how powerful nature is, that inside our bodies we can . . . *what frightens me, gets me . . . I'll say let's hope everything is alright, works out, the greater problem has passed but . . . maybe it's my personality, too sensitive, very . . . but since I was a child, very predisposed to this.*

As we have seen, Piera shows anxieties and preoccupations about this pregnancy, probably connected to her obstetric history (a miscarriage after the amniocentesis) but partly connected to the personal frailties she has manifested since childhood with an affective dysregulation, as demonstrated by the panic attacks. Her main preoccupation is the threat of a new miscarriage occurring during the current pregnancy, which is characterized by anxieties, fears, and panic episodes. Piera, like other women who have had past traumatic experiences, has not invested much in this new pregnancy. She does not prepare things for the baby's arrival, in the fear that it will all end with a new miscarriage. As happens often in traumatic situations, she is reexperiencing her trauma, which she fears might repeat itself, so she maintains herself in a waiting position, almost detached, to avoid having to face disappointment and loss once again.

CHAPTER 4

Coparenting During Pregnancy and the Postnatal Period

While previous studies about infancy and parenting have mostly emphasized a two-person psychology, focusing on the relationship between the mother and the infant, there has recently been a shift toward a three-person psychology, which explores the interactions of mother, father, and child.

We must remember that the parenting model conceptualized by Belsky (1984) already highlighted the complexity and multidetermination of parenting, which is influenced not only by the parents' individual characteristics but by the child's as well, as by the social context and the parents' conjugal relationship. Especially this last relationship represents one of the fundamental subsystems that interact with and support parenthood and can have a positive or negative impact on parental functioning.

Given the reciprocal influence among the conjugal relationship, parenthood, and the child's development, in the past years the couple's functioning with respect to parental roles has been explored, in order to understand this interaction better. The quality of the conjugal relationship must be first taken into account, considering the level of reciprocal satisfaction within the couple and its ability to face dyadic conflicts. In analyzing parenthood subsequently, the individual functioning of the mother or the father with the child must be distinguished from coparenting, which specifically refers to the reciprocal support and interaction between the two parents and their involvement and interaction with the child (Belsky, Crnic, & Gable, 1995; McHale & Rasmussen, 1998).

Research on coparenting has brought about a deeper knowledge of the characteristics and dynamics of the relational subsystem between the parents and the child that exert a great influence on the infant's development, just like the individual relationship between each parent and his or her child.

Before moving on to different definitions of coparenting, outlining the theoretical reference context might be worthwhile. As von Klitzing, Simoni, and Burgin have pointed out, "configurations of three (mother, father, and child) have been central" (1999, p. 71) in psychoanalysis. In fact, threesome dynamics characterize the oedipal period, which manifests itself in the psychic world of children after infancy and toddlerhood. According to Freud (1923/1961), when the child acquires the recognition of the difference between sexes he or she enters into a triangular relationship with parents. In psychoanalytic theory, however, there are other references with different emphasis to triangular dynamics between child and parents, in the work of Melanie Klein (1928), Lacan (1953), and Mahler, Pine, and Bergman (1975), for example.

Some authors believe that a triangulation connected to oedipal fantasies can appear in future parents' mental experience quite before the child's conception, transmitting therefore the triadic perspective to children from the early years of life. Von Klitzing and colleagues have proposed an important distinction between "triadification" (1999, p. 74), the interpersonal process of forming a triad, and "triangulation" (1999, p. 74), which describes the intrapsychic process connected to the mental relationship between mother, father, and child, for example, in oedipal dynamics. In this chapter, we shall use the expression "triangular relation" for the intrapsychic aspects underlined by psychoanalysis and the expression triadic interactions for the three-way communications and interactions that appear in observational studies.

Within another theoretical model, coparenting has been studied in a systemic-evolutionary perspective that conceptualizes the interactions and behaviors between the two parents and the child as a unit that can assume different configurations depending on the fact that all three interact at the same time or that two members of the group interact mostly, while the third remains marginal (Fivaz-Depeursinge & Corboz-Warnery, 1999). In this regard, Patricia Minuchin sustained that "studies of the parent-child dyad . . . do not represent the child's significant reality, especially after infancy" (1985, p. 296).

The various definitions of coparenting emphasize different characteristics, depending on their reference theoretical model. In a psychoanalytic perspective, von Klitzing and Burgin (2005) define the dynamics of parental partnership in terms of parents' capacity for a reciprocal and flexible exchange and dialogue, and triangular mental representations of their child in the couple's experience.

In a systemic perspective, the way two partners work together in their roles as parents is emphasized, with characteristic coparental dimensions: support versus undermining of the partner's parental role; differences in childrearing choices and values; distribution of parental commitment, tasks, and responsibilities in the everyday routine; and finally, the coordination of interactive patterns within the family, characterized by conflicts, coalitions, and reciprocal balance expressed when both partners are involved with the child (Feinberg, 2002). Developing the systemic perspective further, van Egeren and Hawkins (2004) and McHale and colleagues (2004) have elaborated the theoretical construct of coparenting by integrating and furthering the previous definitions found in scientific literature.

According to van Egeren and Hawkins, "a coparenting relationship exists when at least two individuals are expected by mutual agreement or societal norms to have conjoint responsibility for a particular child's well-being" (2004, p. 166). McHale and colleagues focused on the reciprocal behaviors more and described coparenting as the "coordination among adults responsible for the care and upbringing of children" (2004, p. 222).

As we have seen, coparenting is defined by the parents' commitment toward the child within the family context, and it is connected not only to the way they take care of the child but also to the mental representations of the child they share and to the image of the partner in his or her parental role. Coparenting is thus a bidirectional process, an interactive and intersubjective one we might say, in which the actions and attitudes of one partner influence and are influenced by the other's.

We may talk about coparenting even when referring to one parent and the child. The second parent does not necessarily need to be physically present; in fact, even the absence of a parent can define a coparenting configuration (McHale, Kuersten-Hogan, & Rao, 2004; van Egeren & Hawkins, 2004) because his or her parental presence is symbolic as well, and he or she is inevitably recalled or denied by the parent who is present.

From this point of view, the mental representations support the interactions, and this holds true for the image of the child that is in the parents' minds before birth as well. As van Egeren and Hawkins (2004) have pointed out, during pregnancy and even before conception, couples tend to develop mental representations of themselves as parents and may discuss their future as parents (discussing how to organize their lives with the child, how to divide the caregiving commitments, or how to make decisions regarding the child in everyday life, for example). This exchange between expectant parents is a good predictor of their future coparenting interaction, which will be actualized only when the child is born.

The dynamics and exchanges between parents may be studied from different perspectives; for example, some of the dimensions considered relevant are solidarity within the couple, reciprocal support, antagonism, and sharing (Feinberg, 2002; McHale et al., 2004; van Egeren & Hawkins, 2004). In this perspective, affective interaction and sharing is stressed more than behavior: With coparenting solidarity, the parents express positive and affectionate feelings to each other while interacting with the child. Other aspects to be considered are the level of sharing responsibilities and efforts in the child's care and the mutual involvement, when both parents are involved with the child. On the contrary, parents may encounter conflict and undermine each other when taking care of the child.

These parental attitudes are directly observable in the family's everyday life or are perceived by one of the parents by understanding his or her partner's mental state and interpreting his or her parental behavior. A number of factors may negatively influence the dynamics between parents and serve as obstacles in their relationship: disagreement and conflict on educational decisions for the child (Belsky et al., 1995) or greater involvement with the child and undervaluing of the couple relationship (van Egeren, 2003). It is particularly conflictual when the mother assumes the primary responsibility toward the child and feels hurt by the father's interventions and behaviors when he is taking care of the child. It is quite common that the mother may try to interfere and devalue the father, by assuming a "gatekeeping" function (van Egeren, 2003, p. 290), when he is taking care of the child. Another negative consequence on the coparenting experience may come from mothers who feel frustrated in their expectations because they perceive that the partner is not recognizing and supporting them enough in taking care of the child (van Egeren, 2004).

AN ILLUSTRATION OF COPARENTING

Even though research and clinical studies have contributed greatly to the comprehension of interactive dynamics between parents and children, we should also remember Freud's words in "Delusions and Dreams in Jensen's Gradiva": "[Poets and artists] in their knowledge of the mind, are far in advance of us everyday people, for they draw upon sources which we have not yet opened up for science"(1907/1959, p. 8).

Throughout the centuries many painters have created meaningful, pathos-filled images of mothers in the act of breastfeeding or taking care of their children, above all referring to the images of Mary and Jesus. If these religious images emphasize the sacred, almost hieratic aspect of the encounter between Mary and Jesus, there are paintings that describe a true encounter between mother, father, and newborn child with great insight, representing the matrix of the everyday experience. One of these is "The Tempest," painted by Giorgione (figure 4.1) during the first years of the 16th century and now exhibited in the Accademia Galleries in Venice.

In Giorgione's painting, the protagonist is a naked young woman who is facing the viewer. Within a countryside setting, she is sitting on a mound that acts as a stage and emphasizes her role as the protagonist. In her right arm is a few-months-old child. She is suckling him and her body's posture suggests she is showing him off to the viewer, with intimate complacency. A white veil wraps both her shoulders and the baby. In front of the woman, but on a lower ground and across a stream, is a young man wearing a red jacket and colored trousers; he is standing, leaning on a wood staff. He is looking at the mother and child, protectively. In the background is a hamlet of houses and above it a lightning-ridden stormy sky.

This mysterious painting has given way to many interpretations (Settis, 1990), some of which have uncovered allegoric meanings (Force, represented by the young soldier, and Charity, represented by the mother) and alchemic symbols as well (air, water, earth, and fire). However, from the point of view of someone who is no expert in art but is used to studying the behavior of parents and chil-

FIGURE 4.1.   Giorgione: "The Tempest," Museo dell'Accademia, Venice. (© Arte & Immagini srl/Corbis)

dren during the first months, other aspects stand out in this painting, and are illustrated in our book.

First of all, the triadic interaction among mother, father, and child, which has been studied thoroughly by the Lausanne school (Fivaz-Depeursinge et al., 1999), is here represented. Mother and child are within an intimate space, signaled by the white veil, which recalls a placental membrane wrapping them both. This is not a closed space, a symbiotic one which excludes others, because the mother, while breastfeeding, is looking out toward the viewer, who represents society. The mother and child are the protagonists of the scene; they occupy the center of life's stage. Not far but separated by a stream is the young man, a soldier according to some critics. He is not armed, he is not clad in shiny armor, and he carries no threatening weapons; his attire reminds us more of a young man of his time, the bright colors recalling the gaiety of his heart. Today we could picture him as a young father who is looking out for the mother–child couple, while acknowledging the difference of his role as a father from the mother's. His position on a lower ground underlines this difference. The wood staff is not an offensive weapon; rather, it looks more like a stick to lean on, possibly useful for defense. The protective and defensive function of the young man may emblematically be aroused by the coming storm, perceived as a threat to the mother and child. The theme of protection and defense is central in attachment theories (Bowlby, 1969, 1982) because both parents must ward off the dangers that threaten the fragile and defenseless child's survival.

We should here recall what Lacan (1957–1958/1998) wrote about the imaginary, almost fusional relationship between mother and child, in which "the child seeks to be the object of the mother" and within which the respective boundaries could be lost if not for the intervention of "the father's speech which must lay down the law for the mother" (Diatkine, 2000, p. 1028). This is a principle of reality that restores the mother–child relation to a common semantic context, that is, the world of shared meanings that sets rules and boundaries.

Second, the interaction between the mother and the young man, who embodies fatherly vigilance, brings to mind the concept of coparenting: the relationship between the two parents, "the coordination among adults responsible for the care and upbringing of children" (McHale et al. 2004, p. 222).

Third, the mother's and child's nudity emphasizes the importance of bodily contact and its fundamental role in establishing attachment bonds, as well as in regulating the child's psychological and biological rhythms, because of the "hidden regulators" (Hofer, 1995) that step in to regulate blood pressure, heart rate, and neurohormonal rhythms, as has been demonstrated in animal testing.

COPARENTING BETWEEN DYAD AND TRIAD

While research originally focused mainly on those factors within the couple that affect the coparenting dynamics in a dyadic perspective, later on the research widened the coparenting perspective, recognizing the influence of the child's temperament and characteristics on coparenting dynamics. The child's psychological characteristics influence both the dyadic functioning of the parents and the triadic interactions, including the child as well.

Fivaz-Depeursinge and Corboz-Warnery (1999), considering the context of the triadic family unit of mother-father-child, identified two subsystems within this context. The first subsystem is the parenting couple (defined as the structuring subunit), whose task and commitment is to guide and support the child's development, while the second is represented by the child himself (defined as evolutionary subunit), who in turn, growing and developing his or her own autonomy and competence, stimulates and influences the quality of the coparenting dynamics and functioning. The two subsystems can interact and work together, influencing the capacity of the family to organize itself as a working group, defined also as a "family alliance" (Fivaz-Depeursinge & Corboz-Warnery, 1999, p. 1).

The dyadic and triadic coparental dimensions inevitably tend to overlap, and there are different opinions on which is the most relevant. Van Egeren and Hawkins (2004), for example, give greater relevance to the dyadic relationship between parents, which, according to them, is the parenting analysis unit even within a triadic analysis context (with the child), a subsystem of the wider family context.

In any case, to explore the specific characteristics and dimensions of the relational subsystem, such as incoherence and conflict in parental engagement, coparental antagonism, cohesion and harmony, and child versus adult centeredness (McHale, 2007), is more important than to evaluate the greater theoretical relevance of the triadic or dyadic context. Considering the aforementioned dimensions, McHale has identified five distinct family types. First of all, there are "child-at-center families," who focus on the baby, whose needs and requests lead the family interaction, which is characterized by parental engagement with the child, but not with each other. Second, "competitive coparenting families" are characterized by parental engagement with the child, but, in this case, interactions are colored with antagonism and the absence of warmth and cooperation. Subsequently, "cohesive child-centered families and cohesive parent-in-charge families" (2007, p. 375) are characterized by warmth and cooperative interactions between parents. Finally, "excluding families" are characterized by discrepancies and disconnections between parents, so while one parent is engaged the other one is disengaged.

The same elements that influence parental functioning (Belsky, 1984) intervene in establishing the coparenting relationship. Among these are the social and cultural backgrounds of the parents, their personalities, the specific dynamics of their interpersonal relation, and their decisions in the education and upbringing of the children (Belsky et al., 1995).

In this ambit, the parents' attachment model seems to affect the quality of the coparenting relation after the child's birth (Talbot, Baker, & McHale, 2009), especially when the mother with a secure attachment tries to protect the child while facing a coparenting conflict; on the contrary, the father with a secure attachment seems to favor cohesion of the parental couple.

COPARENTING AND
THE INFANT'S DEVELOPMENT

As we have seen, coparenting starts taking shape during pregnancy, but the interaction between parents can change after the child's birth and during his or her first years (Carneiro et al., 2006; van Egeren, 2003). At the same time, the impact the child and his characteristics have on the coparental relationship has been examined (McHale & Rotman, 2007; McHale et al., 2004; Schoppe-Sullivan, Mangelsdorf, Brown, & Sokolowski, 2007). Of course, there is an obvious asymmetry between the coparenting subsystem and the developmental one represented by the child, which is characterized by an exchange and a reciprocal adaptation between the child's characteristics and the parents' relational patterns.

McHale and colleagues (2004) suggested that a difficult temperament of the child can have an impact on the quality of the parents' relationship. During the child's first months, the parents initially try to adapt by compensating for the child's difficulties, but it is possible that later their involvement with the child might lessen, with less responsiveness and detachment.

Difficulties in the parents' relationship that arise during pregnancy might stabilize and worsen after the child's birth, if the child manifests a difficult temperament, or modify into a more positive relationship, if the child manifests an easy temperament (McHale et al., 2004).

These observations have not been confirmed by Schoppe-Sullivan and collaborators (2007), who did not find a significant association between interactive patterns of the parental couple and child's temperament, evaluated at 3½ months after birth. However, in the case of a good prenatal alliance and less reciprocal antagonism, the parents are more capable of cooperating in caring for a child with a difficult temperament.

Considering now the influence of the coparental relationship in the behavioral and socioemotional development of children, research has evidenced the strong association between coparental cooperation, competition, and affective involvement and the behavioral, interpersonal, and emotional development of the child in his or her first years (Feinberg, 2002; McHale et al., 2004). In this regard, Fivaz-Depeursinge, Favez, and Lavanchy (2005) have evidenced that the infant's early triadic capacity promotes his or her primary intersubjectivity. At the same time, Fivaz's observations reveal that children have an active role in contributing to family life from the beginning, even earlier than most developmental theories have suggested.

Exploring the relationship between dysfunction in the coparental interaction and the infant's development, McHale's longitudinal study (2007) has shown that coparental dysfunctions, when children are between 8 and 11 months, are predictive of a higher level of anxiety and aggressiveness in these children during preschool age. At the same time an association between the quality of coparental dynamics and the adaptive functioning of children, considering internalizing and externalizing manifestations, school competences, understanding of emotions, and self-regulation in preschool and school years, seems to be confirmed (McHale, 2007).

But the parenting couple's dysfunctions can have a differential impact according to the developmental phase the infant is going through. In this regard, Belsky and collaborators (1995) hypothesized that the child's developmental phase at

15 months of age, characterized by specific developmental tasks (as emerging communication, development of autonomy, and growing opposition to parents), represents a stress situation for the parents, as they have to engage more in a shared commitment. Differences in dimensions of the parents' personalities (extroversion, sociability, and empathy) may have a negative influence on the quality of their parental relationship, which would be amplified by the impact due to the child's specific developmental period.

In a following study, Belsky and Fearon (2004) widened the ambit by exploring the possible interaction between characteristics of the couple's dynamics, their parental relationship, and the infant's development. On this basis five familial configurations have been identified, considering the greater or lesser balance between the conjugal and parental relationship, which can be thus summarized: "(1) consistently supportive, (2) consistently moderate, (3) good parenting/poor marriage, (4) poor parenting/good marriage, and (5) consistently risky" (p. 511). The first three configurations are characterized by a balance between the quality of the conjugal relation and the quality of the parental relation, but they manifest differences in the degree of intimacy between partners and of sensitivity toward the infant, which can be high (consistently supportive), medium (consistently moderate), or low (consistently risky). The other two categories, on the contrary, show a discrepancy between the quality of the conjugal subsystem and that of the parenting one (good parenting/poor marriage and poor parenting/good marriage). Evaluating the outcome of families' different configurations in the children's development (in terms of social competence and relationships, school abilities, behavioral issues), the best results are found in children of the group 1 and 2 families (consistently supportive and consistently moderate), compared to those of the last group (consistently risky). In the case of a discrepancy between the conjugal subsystem and the parenting one, performances in school and cognitive abilities are best in children of group 3. At the same time, it has been confirmed that the parental subsystem has a greater influence than the conjugal one on the child's development; in fact, few differences have been found between performances of children from groups 1 and 3, where the parental dimension is high, even if not necessarily accompanied by a good conjugal dimension (Belsky & Fearon, 2004). In other words, children are more influenced by the quality of coparental behaviors than by the conjugal dynamics of their parents, even if the latter are more conflictual.

As we have seen, coparenting is undoubtedly influenced by the couple's relationship and by the characteristics of the infant. A reciprocal adaptation takes place between parents and children that starts during pregnancy and develops through the different phases of the vital cycle. What happens is a spillover process (Katz & Gottman, 1996), according to which some affective and relational dynamics of the couple subsystem can influence and interfere with the functioning of other subsystems, for example, the parental relationship.

From the perspective of a confirmed substantial stability of the coparenting alliance during the phases of the child's development, a remodulation and renegotiation of reciprocal roles take place between the parents during different phases of the life cycle, stimulated also by the infant's new acquisitions, which push them to look for a new adaptation and balance (van Egeren, 2004).

PREGNANCY AND TRANSITION
TO COPARENTING

We must first of all mention the study by von Klitzing and colleagues (1999) on the interactive-affective dynamics of the parental couple during pregnancy, the triadic capacity, that is the mother's and father's capacity to anticipate future family relations without excluding oneself or the other partner from the relationship with the child. Their hypothesis is that the parents' intrapsychic and interpersonal triadic abilities assessed during pregnancy are associated with the quality of the dyadic and triadic relationship within the family as assessed 4 months after the child's birth. In this research, the couples are evaluated during the last trimester of pregnancy with a semistructured interview, the Triadic Interview (von Klitzing et al.,1999), which is submitted to the couple together and allows for the assessment not only of the individual mental representations of each partner but also the observable interactions and dialogues between the future parents. Later, the triadic interaction with the child is assessed 4 months after birth with the Lausanne Trilogue Play (Fivaz-Depeursinge & Corboz-Warnery, 1999), a standardized observational procedure that measures early triadic interactions between mother, father, and child jointly.

The results show a strong relation between the parental representational dimension during pregnancy and the interactive one observed subsequently. Furthermore, the quality of the parents' triadic interactions with the child is significantly correlated to parental representations of their future relationship with the child, during pregnancy, and specifically to their capability of having in mind the relationship with the child as part of a triadic relationship, recognizing the important participation of the father (von Klitzing et al., 1999).

Predictive factors of coparenting during pregnancy have been explored by van Egeren (2003) as well, who has developed a multidimensional model to analyze the main individual factors that can affect coparenting, submitting questionnaires to parents expecting their first child, during the third trimester of pregnancy, and then again at 1, 3, and 6 months after birth. This model is based on many variables connected with the parents' individual experience in their family of origin (perception of conflict), to certain traits of the parents' personalities (ego development and reactance), to the relationship with the partner (perception of cooperation and support), to the level of engagement in the parental role and each partner's opinions about the child's education.

The research (van Egeren, 2003) has shown that, among the predictive factors of coparenting, the mother's individual characteristics play a major role. For example, the mother's strong motivation to have a child can negatively affect her perception of the father, manifesting a devaluing attitude toward him that could generate in him a sense of exclusion. In this way the conflict within the couple could increase.

Considering the father's influence on the coparenting relationship, this is mostly connected to his schooling level and his work occupation, in addition to his experience within his family of origin (van Egeren, 2003).

McHale and collaborators (2004) have also studied the transition to coparenting during pregnancy by investigating the quality of the couple's interaction and the individual representational systems before the infant's birth, hypothesizing the existence of a relation between the interactive patterns of the couple and their mental representations during the third trimester of pregnancy. Couples expecting their firstborn have been evaluated, during the third trimester and then again 3 months after birth. During pregnancy, the couple's interaction was studied throughout observation of a problem-solving task, a discussion on a theme chosen by each partner on what they would like to change in their relationship. Furthermore, the semistructured Coparenting Interview (McHale et al., 2004) was submitted to each partner individually, in order to explore the mental representations related to his or her family of origin experience and to the other partner's family of origin, to the aspirations, wishes, and preoccupations related to the future family. The results have been confronted with the family alliance 3 months after the child's birth, assessed with the Lausanne Trilogue Play (Fivaz-Depeursinge & Corboz-Warnery, 1999), taking into consideration negative reactivity to the child's temperament. The parents have also performed (before and after the child's birth) questionnaires to assess their conjugal satisfaction, the expectations of each other's future involvement in the child's care, and their orientations about the child's education.

Results have evidenced that prenatal conjugal quality and the parents' expectations of future family life are predictive of the family's interaction 3 months after birth (McHale et al., 2004).

The observation of coparenting interaction during pregnancy with an observational procedure such as the Lausanne Trilogue Play, in both its prenatal version (Carneiro et al., 2006) and its postnatal version (Fivaz-Depeursinge & Corboz-Warnery, 1999), has also confirmed a correlation between prenatal coparenting alliance and postnatal family alliance observed at 3, 9, and 18 months after the infant's birth (Carneiro et al., 2006; Fivaz-Depeursinge, Frascarolo, & Corboz-Warnery, 2010).

Taking into consideration the conjugal satisfaction and the couple's interaction, it has been noted (Carneiro et al., 2006) that fathers are more able to cooperate with the mother in caring for the child if there is a good couple relationship. On the contrary, mothers are capable and focused on the child even during conflictual conjugal relationships, as mothers feel more involved in their maternal role because they experience the filiation process more internally and physically.

A first conclusion: During pregnancy, the couple is already defining parental roles and developing expectations for the future. The transition toward parenting is a period of reorganization in the couple's life, which entails many changes: The relationship needs to be remodulated and renegotiated, the family role must be reviewed, and new competences must be acquired. In fact, with the child's arrival new parental relational systems develop, such as the individual relationship between each parent and child and the relationship between partners in their role as parents (Cohen & Slade, 2000; van Egeren, 2004). The results of major research on coparenting in pregnancy confirm the importance of an early assessment of the coparenting relationship, useful in identifying at-risk situations and programming support action (Carneiro et al., 2006; McHale et al., 2004).

THE PSYCHOLOGICAL IMPACT OF ECHOGRAPHY IN THE COUPLE DURING PREGNANCY

During pregnancy, in the phase of transition toward parenthood, the child-to-be assumes a major role. Literature on the psychological dynamics of pregnancy highlights how throughout pregnancy the parents' perception of the infant gradually changes. While in the beginning the perception of the infant is strongly influenced by parental fantasies, it slowly becomes more realistic because of fetal movements and of the images of the ultrasound examinations that are repeatedly done throughout pregnancy. As is well known, obstetric ultrasound is a procedure of diagnostic visualization, which, done routinely during pregnancy, has an important role in the psychological expecting process, determining a change in the conscious and unconscious fantasies of the parents when confronted with the true images of the infant. Ultrasound images intervene in the construction process of the parents' mental representations, not only those of the mother but also those of the father, who often is present during the test as well.

Scientific literature on the psychological impact of obstetric ultrasound on parents, and especially on mothers, has shown that the ultrasound test is considered a positive experience (Beck Black, 1992; Cox et al., 1987; Garcia et al., 2002; Ji et al., 2005; Larsen, Nguyen, Munk, Svendsen, & Teisner, 2000). The echographic experience is undoubtedly influenced by the mother's personality, by the social context, by the perception of the ultrasound experience itself (Lumley, 1990), and by the technicians' attitude, which can favor the parental couple's psychological elaboration of the event (Missonnier, 1999).

An Italian research study (Fava Vizziello, Righetti, & Cristiani, 1997/2003) has analyzed the emotional resonance and the mental representations of pregnant women after their first ultrasound. The positive perception of the ultrasound experience, which helps the mother acquire a more realistic perception of the infant, also shared with the father, has been confirmed.

Missonnier (1999) defined the ultrasound scan as the "initiation ritual towards parenthood," which allows for exploring the formation of precocious parents–infant ties. The ultrasound makes the infant's presence visible to both parents and can favor the passage toward fatherhood, since the expecting father is not directly involved in the partner's physical changes (Campbell, 2006;

Draper, 2002; Ekelin, Crang Svalenius, & Dykes, 2004; Finnbogadòttir, Crang Svalenius, & Persson, 2003; Freeman, 2000).

In scientific literature, there is common accord on the positive role of an obstetric ultrasound for the development of the mother–fetus bond. It can ease the formation of the coparenting relationship, contributing to the sharing of conscious fantasies about the infant and to the construction of the parenting identity of mothers and fathers (Ekelin et al., 2004).

One of the elements to consider is the gestational age at which the ultrasound scan is done; Kurjak and collaborators (2007) believe that the image of the child's face shown by a three-dimensional (3D) or four-dimensional (4D) ultrasound in the first trimester may be counterproductive and create a distorted representation of the child. The best time to look for the child's face is between weeks 23 and 30 (Kurjak et al., 2007). In this gestational period, 3D and 4D ultrasounds show fetus features that have by this stage reached the "infantile prototype" of babyness (figure 4.2). This is a universal characteristic that distinguishes the young of the human species from other species and has an irresistible pull on adults; by means of an innate mechanism, it induces adults to take care of the infant (Stern, 1977). Babyness is characterized by a large head, oversized if compared to the rest of the body; a wide forehead protruding from the face; large eyes; and chubby cheeks.

Besides the fetus's features, the 4D ultrasound shows his or her movements as well. Starting from the 14th week of pregnancy, there are partial movements, which look like intentional gestures: For example, a fetus might touch the um-

FIGURE 4.2. Fetus in a three-dimensional ultrasound echography. (Printed with permission)

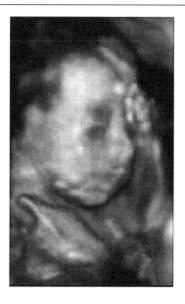

bilical cord, his or her own face, or other parts of the body; turn his or her head; and open the mouth (Piontelli, 2010). These movements can excite strong feelings in the parents because they communicate a sense of vitality and allow the parents to imagine a mental activity behind these movements (Stern, 2010). The direct observation of parents' behavior during the ultrasound is still little used, but it may contribute to widening our knowledge of the parents' interaction in this phase. In a preliminary study, Stadimayr and collaborators (2009) individuate a number of typical attitudes of parents during an ultrasound; for example, recognizing the fetus's somatic characteristics, looking for resemblance to one parent or the other. During the ultrasound, certain interactive behaviors take place between the two parents, such as eye contact and reciprocal responsiveness. Following these observations, we might assume that the quality of the couple's relationship during a 4D ultrasound in pregnancy might be predictive of the quality of the coparenting relationship after the infant's birth.

With these considerations as a starting point, our research team (Ammaniti, Mazzoni, & Menozzi, 2010) has performed an exploratory study of the transition to parenthood for primiparous couples and specifically the observation of coparenting interactive patterns during the 4D echography.

For this purpose, we have designed an observational tool adapted from the Prenatal Lausanne Trilogue Play, the well-known procedure for studying the coparental subsystem in formation at the prenatal stage (Carneiro et al., 2006). Different questions have steered our work: Do couples show coparental patterns during the interaction with the baby-to-be in the 4D echography? Does the 4D obstetric ecography activate intuitive parenting behaviors during pregnancy?

According to the Lausanne paradigm (Carneiro et al., 2006), the use of an observational method to assess coparenting during pregnancy could also enact parental representations (Fivaz-Depeursinge, Frascarolo, & Corboz-Warnery, 2010). In the Prenatal Lausanne Trilogue Play, parents interact by simulating the encounter with their baby, role-playing with a doll. This experience requires a playful attitude and the ability to anticipate the triadic subsystem with the baby.

During an ultrasound test, parents are confronted with a real picture of the fetus instead of a doll, which should represent the future baby. This being a common experience for expectant parents, we have hypothesized that the observation of parents while they are watching the 4D ultrasound together might evidence their actual parental interchange during pregnancy. Furthermore, the 4D obstetric ultrasound could open a window on the early contribution of the baby-to-be in shaping parental representations and interactions.

Our sample has included 18 primiparous volunteer couples. All of them have performed a check-up 4D ultrasound between the 24th and 28th week of pregnancy. Average age has been 32.2 years for mothers and 33.1 years for fathers; the educational level was a bachelor's degree for 63.9% of parents and a high school degree for 36.1% of parents.

All fathers were present when mothers underwent the 4D ultrasound. The observations were performed about 1 week after the ultrasound. All fetuses were healthy and there was no evidence of psychopathological symptoms in parents, as assessed by Symptom Checklist-90-Revised (SCL-90-R; Derogatis, 1977) and Center for Epidemiologic Studies Depression Scale (CES-D; Radloff, 1977). To evaluate the interactions between the two parents, we have used the coding of the prenatal coparenting alliance (Carneiro et al., 2006) based on coparent playfulness, structure of the play, couple's cooperation, and family warmth. We have also considered parental behaviors, specifically intuitive ones (Papousek & Papousek, 1987), and parental dialogues explored through an analysis of content of maternal and paternal dialogues while talking with the fetus on video.

Couples first undergo an extensive conjoint interview, which explores the couple's representation and experience about the transition to parenthood; then they are asked to watch the last 4D ultrasound on a computer screen. As in the Prenatal Lausanne Trilogue Play procedure, parents are seated in a triangular configuration, with a computer screen on a round table (figure 4.3). On the screen, connected to a personal computer, the last 4D obstetric ultrasound is played.

Parents are asked to "talk to the baby," imagining that he or she can listen to them. We have hypothesized that the 4D ultrasound would show the image of the present baby, instead of the "future" baby represented by the doll, and would be strictly embedded into the parental experience during pregnancy. We have also hypothesized that the instruction to "talk with the baby" instead of to "interact with the baby" could fit the stimulus of the video better. As in the Prenatal

FIGURE 4.3.   Parents watching the fetus on the screen. (Printed with permission)

Lausanne Trilogue Play procedure, parents are asked to follow four configurations: (a) one of them talks to the baby, then (b) the other parent does, then (c) both parents talk to the baby together, and finally (d) they both talk about the experience they just went through (Carneiro et al., 2006).

The analysis of parental behaviors has evidenced that mothers smile at the baby more than fathers do and that both parents smile at the baby more than at each other. No difference has been evidenced in the quality of the mother's and father's dialogues with the baby on screen, although the fathers seem to talk with the baby less.

During the microanalysis of the video, an unexpected behavior has been noticed: 50% of mothers and 27% of fathers have shown imitative behaviors; more precisely, parents imitate movements performed by the fetus with hands, arms, mouth, and lips.

Considering the parents' dialogues while watching the baby on screen, mothers and fathers tend to name themselves "Mom" or "Dad" in 50% of cases or to name the partner "Mom" or "Dad" in 36% of cases; 50% of parents find a likeness between the fetus and the partner, especially mothers (55%), and 52% of parents call the baby by name. These dialogues show the rising of an affiliation process as well as of parental identity.

These results show that the obstetric ultrasound elicits in parents recognition of the fetus as their own child. And it suggests that the baby can become as early as pregnancy a "secret sharer," borrowing the title of a story by the fiction writer Joseph Conrad (1909/1950). This secret sharing is testified by the unconscious, almost automatic imitation of the fetus's movements, by mothers especially. Just as there is an imitation mechanism in newborns, that creates—with a "like me" mechanism—an equivalence between self and other (Meltzoff & Prinz, 2002), in the same way equivalence mechanisms—we might say mirroring mechanisms (Papousek, & Papousek, 1987)—activate in the parents as early as pregnancy, and help them identify with their child and familiarize with him or her. As has been discussed in other chapters, we can hypothesize that in the brain the mirror neurons system is activated as early as pregnancy and allows an embodied simulation (Gallese, 2009a) with which parents activate within themselves facial expressions and movements of their child, in order to become like him or her and favor the affiliation process. At the same time, parents help the child in their minds to become like them, in a reciprocal equivalence. This process during pregnancy is fundamental because it readies both parents to encounter the child after birth.

In our observations, the family warmth is correlated to the total duration of smiles at the baby, confirming that the alliance and the sharing of the two partners support the focus on the child and the positive emotional resonance.

The fathers in our study are involved with the child, experience a paternal identity, and are able to have a dialogue with their child, although the baby is still in the mother's belly. There are of course some differences between mothers and fathers: Mothers smile more and talk more with the baby, as they are more used to having an internal dialogue with him or her, sharing the expectant period with him or her.

It must be said that the context of pregnancy in the West has changed deeply in the last decades of the 20th century, not only because of the growing medicalization of pregnancy itself but also because of the fact that the father is much more present and participates more in the interaction with the child-to-be. Fathers share the crucial moments of the expectancy period and also, thanks to the ultrasound exam, get to meet their own children and participate in what is happening inside the mother's body.

AN EXPECTANT COUPLE

We here report part of an interview of a young couple, carried out within the research on parental representations during pregnancy (Ammaniti et al., 2010). This dialogue demonstrates well the exchanges that take place in this phase of a couple's life. The future mother is 33 years old and works in a medical laboratory, while the future father is 35 years old and is a factory worker. They married after a long engagement, and soon after the woman became pregnant and is expecting a girl. The pregnancy is progressing well; the future mother reports some depressive symptoms, but below risk level. Regarding couple dynamics, the woman appears not to be very satisfied with her relationship with her partner, while the man is satisfied with the couple relationship. No particular problematic situations emerge from family histories, but both partners show a certain distance from their own parents, confirmed by the absence of memories in the attachment field.

Interviewer: First of all, how is the pregnancy going?
Mother: Well.
Father: Well.
M: Very well. I can't complain (laughs). Not at all.
I: How did you feel, throughout these first months of pregnancy?
M: Well, sometimes I don't even . . . A bit more now, because she moves around, and it's different now. But, at first, I almost didn't realize I was pregnant, apart from the slight sickness in the beginning. Even now, I sometimes still have to realize (laughs), I don't know, it's just that I feel so well. I may be more tired in the evening, but sometimes, as I said, I just don't realize it.
F: It's more or less the same for me. Even because I work in an almost exclusively male environment, so we talk about other things and when I call her, maybe I'll ask her about Maria, that's what we're going to call her.
I: Why did you decide to have a child, in this moment of your lives?
M: This is something I really, I just don't know how to explain.
F: It's the fulfillment of the couple.

M: Yes, you mean . . .

F: I always said to her that when we got married it wasn't just to play the "romantic couple" but to have a child, then maybe. . .

M: A family.

F: A family, a family of my own.

I: Do you remember when you found out you were expecting?

F: We were sleeping together and I heard that she got up at night, but she is used to getting up so I didn't think much about it. The next morning I went off to work and when I came back I found a pair of baby socks on the table.

M: Baby shoes.

F: With a "Welcome home Dad" note. So I understood.

M: I suspected, but I didn't want to say anything because I wanted to surprise him. At 5 A.M., I woke up, mostly because of the anxiety and I took the test . . . it was nice but traumatic at the same time, discovering it this way, not really traumatic, but "Oh my God" and then I went back to bed and didn't say anything in the morning, obviously as soon as I got to work I told all my girlfriends (laughs).

I: And how were you feeling? Do you remember?

M: Strange . . . strange. A strange feeling, nice but also a bit scary at first, because you think "Oh my God," I don't know . . . a strange feeling. A bit scared also because it is a major change, so, well anyway happy, because I knew he wanted it . . .

I: And how did you feel?

F: Definitely happy, but like her, also a bit strange, it was something different from what . . . it's one thing to say "I'm a father" when you really are, now I'm not . . . (laughs).

It is interesting to notice how the partners interact during the interview, each one giving his or her point of view. The father-to-be, who has intensely wished for a child, tends to emphasize the positive aspects of the period they are going through, while the mother certainly appears happy but also expresses her difficulties in accepting the change that has taken place in her, on a psychological level but most of all on a somatic level (Raphael-Leff, 2010).

I: Do you remember when you first felt her move?

M: Yes, I do, because . . . I don't know if you were there, I don't remember. In the beginning I felt something, but I wasn't sure what it was. Because it also hurt a bit, and I don't know, a strange feeling, and he told me, "That's because she's moving."

I: When was that?

M: When do you start feeling the baby? Maybe around the fifth, sixth month. I don't remember exactly, but I think it was more or less around that time.

I: And how was it? What did you think about it?

M: Nice, really nice! (laughs) It was nice, and now you see the whole belly moving (laughs). She kicks, it hurts a bit because she's getting bigger, but it's nice. Nice, yes, you feel the foot.

I: And do you remember the first time you felt her move?

F: There was a series of unlucky episodes, she would say "she's moving" and when I got there she'd stopped. In the end, I finally managed to feel . . . some movement, I managed to feel it. Then, two or three weeks ago I felt a real contact. I think it was the heel and I touched it. I could feel it, right here.

I: And how was it?

F: Wonderful!

I: And now do you happen to feel her movements together, with your hands?

M: Yes, yes (laughs). But as soon as he comes close, she stops.

F: There must be something with my hands, every time I . . .

M: I think it's just that you don't have enough patience because you just have to put your hands here, and then she . . .

F: I think it's because of my cold hands. Maybe if I touch her with cold hands. I'm always out and when I come back my hands are cold, even if I wash them or take a shower, when you touch the belly, I don't know, maybe it's not true, but I do have cold hands.

I: Do you remember when you saw her on the ultrasound for the first time?

M: Yes, I do. I realized . . . That's when I really realized she was there because in the beginning you don't really have a belly, you might be a bit rounder but you don't have a belly yet, you don't feel her move, and I was feeling well anyway and it was nice. What really moved me was to see the brain (laughs), everyone has his own part, it wasn't the heart for me it was the brain, I clearly remember that. I really realized. A wonderful feeling.

I: And were you together?

F: Yes. In that same ultrasound, what touched me was the heart, seeing the heart beat, so fast, I realized.

I: What did you feel?

F: Ehm, it's a thing, I don't know how to explain it.

M: A lump in the throat . . .

F: A bit, a sort of happiness, something I'd never felt before. I wouldn't know how to describe it.

I: How did you feel at the last 4D ultrasound you did, instead?

F: An idiot! (they laugh) I looked at her and would say "It's you! It's you," then every time she turned, I mean, I don't know how the ultrasound really works, but when it got closer, they zoomed in, I was always finding resemblances. "Here, she's me!" (laughs).

M: For me it was a wonderful feeling, but I always had the feeling she was a girl, even before they told me. (. . .) But what they say about the umbilical cord (laughs), that there's a connection . . . I feel it, so ok, seeing her had a certain effect, it's really nice because you see the features, you see the face . . . I was afraid before doing it, yes.

Both parents' answers reveal a good capability to support the other and share the experience they are living without interference or competitiveness. The father appears to be respectful of the mother's boundaries and avoids interjecting in the answers which are specifically about her. We might say there is a turn-taking in which each one is attentive and acknowledges and values the other's experience.

I: Did you have any specific concern?

M: Ehm, no, well there's always a bit of terror, to know if she's ok, or if she's not, I think that's normal (laughs). So, well, nothing much, I was a bit scared, but then seeing her, well it was great.

I: You already know the child's sex. Did you have preferences?

M: Well, this is it, I already knew. At the first ultrasound, the one I said really touched us, they had given us an approximate idea because it was too early, "It's just a guess, don't rely on it." Then at the morphology ultrasound they told us, they confirmed it. So that's when we had the . . .

F: The certainty.

I: Have you chosen a name for the baby?

M: Well, in the beginning we had chosen another name, but then I didn't like it anymore, because he kept on using it and it didn't sound right. So we changed. We had three names to choose from, and in the end he said "I like Maria!" so OK.

F: A completely democratic choice, anyway! (they laugh)

I: Do you talk about her often?

M: Yes! Yes, yes.

F: About everything. From the bedroom furniture we need to buy, and "I bought this, we need to go buy this."

M: We'll send her to kindergarten, we'll raise her like this, she mustn't be spoiled, she mustn't become too girlish. A bit of everything, that is.

I: Have you had any dreams about the pregnancy, the delivery, or the baby?

M: Yes, I have.

F: She did.

M: In the beginning, I once dreamt it was a boy, but when I woke up I didn't have a special feeling . . . The following night I dreamt it was a girl and I woke up feeling it really was a girl. That was the first dream I had . . .

And lately, I dreamt about the delivery, but I don't remember much. Very little. Because I'm terrified of giving birth (laughs), so I think it's that, even if I am doing this preparation (course) which is helping me a lot, because it makes you think of the delivery as something very natural, very, but I'm afraid. So I think this is going to continue for the nine months, until I give birth.

I: Have you already noticed similarities or differences between yourselves and the child?

M: Well, one thing which is different from both of us, the two of us just collapse at a certain hour, I before him, at nine. We both wake up early, move around the whole day, and when it's nine o'clock we fall asleep, nine thirty, ten maximum. So, we are people who go to bed really early. Instead, she (laughs) is really awake, so she'll be different from us in this. I don't know what else.

F: Physically, I recognized some gestures which are hers. While she sleeps, she often touches, covers her face, does . . . and the chubby cheeks, those are hers, too.

M: I have big cheeks, and now they seem even bigger. Well, I was born this way. Not exactly at birth, because I was very small, but soon after I was round as an apple. So that's how I imagine she'll be, round but with his mouth.

F: And you see how far fantasy can take you (they laugh). No, no, but the eyes' shape, yes.

M: How can you see that . . .

F: Yes, yes, but it's true, because in the moment when this thing is true, when as I said they zoom in, it changed, in a second she would seem different and your mind wanders, you think "maybe this part looks like. . . and that part comes from . . ." So it's true, all that fantasizing seems foolish, but it is true as well.

I: How do you imagine your child will be, once she is born?

M: (laughs) Like she is now, I imagine she won't sleep at night, she'll have a strong character, I don't think she'll be a calm baby, that's the feeling I have. Ehm, yes. I hope she won't be too big at birth, she has time to grow later on, no problem (laughs). And you?

F: I'll tell you an anecdote which tells it all. We were sleeping, it was three o'clock at night. At a certain point (laughs) she turns on the lights, leans against the bed's head and goes "Oh God, oh God, it hurts, it hurts," so I think . . .

M: Well, it really was hurting.

F: She'll be a pest, this is the feeling I have, I hope not, but. . .

I: In what ways would you like her to be like you or not like you?

M: Well, I would like her to have my determination in life, and I think we agree on that (laughs).

F: Yes.

M: To have the will to fight and demand respect from others, ehm, then, well this . . .

F: Well, from my side, that she have my character because hers . . .

M: But what aspect of my character?

F: About socializing or also of the fact that when we argue, after an hour or an hour and a half, I'm over it.

I: Which are your greatest fears now?

M: . . .You go! (to her husband)

F: About Maria? Oh God, right now, I don't want to sound superficial, but nothing comes to my mind. I might not be ready, I hope I'm ready, even when maybe I think about a certain situation now. . . I'm afraid that when she'll ask something from me, if I set limits now, then when that day comes it really might be a limit.

I: For example?

F: I don't know, if she should ask me, I can say that my parents were always there for me when I asked. I would like it to be the same for her, I don't want to fix myself on certain certainties now as "I'll be ready for this, I'll be ready for that," because I might live things badly, so I prefer to be. . . well, maybe to get to that situation and then see if I'm ready, without having decided first.

I: How has each one of you changed, since you've been expecting the child?

F: The changes are everywhere; I do sports, off-road cycling with my mountain bike and sometimes even jumps, I used to go alone and no. . . I still do it often, but much more. . . I don't do jumps anymore, unfortunately, unfortunately (laughs), I even take my mobile with me, something I never. . .

M: He never used to. He would go alone, wouldn't tell you where. "Will he come back?"

F: Everything's changed, everything. This thing has and it's a minor thing, but so have the important things. To think about life as if it weren't yours anymore, but hers.

M: Yes, that of course. But maybe a bit more mature, then sometimes I think "oh God, I'm pregnant, how strange" because I still feel like I'm the girl who was looking for a job, so it's as if time has flown by, I mean, I don't realize I'm thirty. I still feel young for some things but grown up for others.

I: How do you think your wife has changed?

(they laugh)

F: Aside from the physical changes which are obvious, she has become motherly, a mother, now she worries, which she didn't before.

M: I worried before as well.

F: It was a side of you I didn't know.

M: So what, I'm a bit more apprehensive?

F: You are much more apprehensive. And it's something I notice in all mothers, in my mother, in hers.

I: How would you describe your current couple relationship?

F: Oh, I'm not sure I understand the question (they laugh), what aspect do you . . .

M: Well, our life as a couple is more or less the same; of course, there is less intimacy than before, sure.

I: So about your being present at delivery, you've already decided, you've discussed it?

M: Yes, we always said he would be present.

F: Yes, if I don't faint (they laugh).

I: From the beginning of the pregnancy, what was the hardest moment between the two of you?

M: Last weekend (laughs) when we fought because he did something . . . you did something which really upset me. We had spoken about it, argued, I'm sorry, I'm sorry, and then the next morning, no, that same afternoon he did it again. That was the hardest moment. I got over it, mostly because of Maria (laughs), yes, because if it were for me. . . I don't think I would have left him but . . . not really, but I would have gotten over it much later and with many more reservations. You realize that having a child you can't just act out. So that.

F: I sincerely do not remember!

M: That's how I felt it! (laughs).

I: What kind of parents do you imagine you'll be once the baby is born?

M: I have many good intentions, if I can follow them through (laughs). I don't know, I don't want to spoil her, I don't want to keep her in my arms the whole time, I don't . . . I don't know. I don't want to be too apprehensive, I want to be able to manage her, I don't know, I don't even know how to explain it actually, but . . . I would like her to do certain things, to not take advantage of her parents as in "mommy or daddy will clean up" or "I want it because I want it!" as you often hear. No, that's not how things are. As if it was all due. Many good intentions but then . . .

I: How would you like to be as a mother?

M: I would like to breastfeed, as long as possible. But even there, you never know what will happen.

I: And you?

F: I agree with her. I hope it will work.

I: What kind of father would you like to be?

F: I hope, I really do, that I'll manage not to cave in every time she cries, because I already know that every time she cries I'll go down those stairs, I just know. But for now I pretend . . .

M: Pretends he's tough . . .

F: Not tough, because you really can't, I dare anyone.

M: . . . not to spoil her.

F: Yes, not to spoil her.

I: How do you imagine your wife will be as a mother?

F: She will be a mother. . . a firm mother, I see her authoritarian, and it's difficult that, if she asks for something, she certainly won't spoil her.

M: Let's hope (laughs).

F: That's how I see her!

I: How do you imagine your husband as a father?

M: All the contrary! (laughs) He will give in immediately, especially because she's a girl, so I think he'll give in. He will be very affectionate because that is how he is, his character, which I am not. So I think he will be very affectionate, he won't leave her in peace for a second! (laughs) And he'll spoil her.

Throughout the interview, dynamics within the couple highlight a good capacity of both partners to confront this important phase in their conjugal life. A positive couple space emerges from the interview, within which both are capable of emotionally sharing their common life and of confronting and recovering from critical moments and relationship difficulties.

At the same time, we observe the rising of a parental dimension in both, as they interact and sustain each other in this waiting period and in prefiguring their role as parents after the child's birth. A process of affiliation is noticeable in both: Their daughter has come to occupy a relevant space in their individual psychic world as in the couple's. It must be noted that the father sustains his partner's maternal identity, recognizing the centrality of her role and knowing how to be near her without interfering, stepping in, or backing out from the commitment.

TRIANGULAR INTERACTION AND DEVELOPMENT OF THE INFANT'S INTERSUBJECTIVITY

The notion of primary intersubjectivity during infancy (Trevarthen, 2009) has received important confirmations since 1960. Microanalytic studies of the movements of face, hands, and voice expressed by infants in their engagements with mothers and fathers have deeply changed the developmental theory of the infant mind. Infants have an inborn capacity to share others' feelings and mental states (Stern, 2004). Primary intersubjectivity, characterized by interactions of the baby with the caregiver affectively resonating to one another, gives a grounding for understanding the feelings of relatedness to one another.

Research has focused fundamentally on the mother–infant dyad, which is now challenged by the discovery of early triadic interactions in infants. As Fivaz-Depeursinge, Lavanchy-Scaiola, and Favez (2010) have discussed, there is an open question: Are triadic interactions based on a dyadic program, which implies a separate communication with each partner, or on a triangular program? In a dyadic program, the infant would communicate separately with each of his partners, while in a triangular program the infant is able to communicate simultaneously with more than one partner at a time.

Considering what was discussed in chapter 2 about cooperative breeding, it is possible to suggest that human infants have been exposed for thousands of years to different members of the social group their parents were a part of. This complex experience has deeply changed the mind and the brain of infants who had to learn to face multiple interactions. As Stern (2004) has stressed, intersubjective capacity must operate for groups as well as dyads, thus conferring a survival advantage. Humans are a relatively defenseless species who survive because of their capability to coordinate group activity within the family or tribe. Stern wrote, "Many different capacities and motivations act together to form and maintain groups: attachment ties, sexual attraction, dominance hierarchies, love, sociability. Intersubjectivity must be added to the list" (2004, p. 98).

The observations of Fivaz and the Lausanne Group (Fivaz-Depeursinge, 2001; Fivaz-Depeursing & Corboz-Warnery, 1999) have evidenced that 3- and 6-month-old babies show the beginnings of intersubjectivity with the mother and father in order to build a reciprocal triad. Infants have shown a sense of triangularity, following one parent's gaze toward the other parent (Tremblay & Rovira, 2007), with a precocious awareness of three-person interactions. Recent research (Fivaz-Depeursinge, Frascarolo et al., 2010) has further confirmed the infant's capacity for triadic interactions, activated not only while playing with parents but also while watching them dialogue or, lastly, during the still face evaluation (Tronick, Als, Adamson, Wise, & Brazelton, 1978) when the infant is confronted with contradictory signals. Triadic interactions may have the function of collectively sharing affects and may be connected to a triangular program. An interesting question raised by Fivaz-Depeursinge, Frascarolo et al. (2010) addresses the role of the attachment system in triadic interactions or of the intersubjective motivational system as suggested by Stern (2004). It is difficult, especially during infancy, to divide the attachment motivational system from the intersubjective one because both serve a survival strategy by maintaining a physical closeness to the attachment figures and guaranteeing communication and affective sharing with both parents. This is also confirmed by Tremblay and Rovira (2007), who have documented the infant's richer expressions in person-person-person interactions rather than in person-person-object interactions. To this regard, Nadel and Tremblay-Leveau (1999) hypothesized that triadic interaction could represent an important connection between primary and secondary intersubjectivity, as it widens the attention and the interaction from an early focus on one person to a third pole of attention. While at 9 months infants regularly consult the faces of their parents in order to have a social referencing about what is happening in the environment, at 3 months infants are already conscious (Tronick, 1998) of the presence of their parents and of their interaction.

As we have discussed at the beginning of this chapter, psychoanalysis has consistently conceptualized and discussed the intrapsychic meaning of oedipal triangulation in the development of children and in the origin of neurosis. However, this conceptualization should be confronted and discussed, considering recent observations on early triadic interaction.

It is useful to distinguish two different research fields and the consequent conceptualizations:

1. The oedipal period, as conceptualized by Freud (1923/1961) and later developed by Melanie Klein (1928), specifically refers to intrapsychic conflict dynamics that the child faces in relation to his or her parental figures. The appearance of the oedipal period takes place, according to Freud, after the third year, while Melanie Klein believed oedipal phantasies start during the infant's first year of life. It must be noted that, differently from triadic interactions, the child has fantasies about the intimate relationship between parents from which he or she feels excluded, feeling jealousy, anger, resentment, and competition.

2. Regarding triadic interactions, these are noticeable from the infants' first months of life, as research has demonstrated, while we cannot infer their

psychic state. The communication between the child and the two parents comes to the foreground; it has a specific value on an adaptive level since it facilitates the affective sharing and protection.

However, notwithstanding the different context and methods of research, there are possible intersections, as pointed out by Emde (1994a), who distinguished the intrapsychic level represented by the figure of "Oedipus as Provocateur" (p. 98), an individual story that implies a conflict of wishes and intentions. The second level of the story is familial, "Oedipus as Victim" (p. 99), in which conflicts arise between Oedipus and the parents who neglected and seduced him. In this perspective, interpersonal and intergenerational dynamics of the struggle are emphasized. The third level is intersystemic, "Oedipus as Seeker" (p. 101): In this case Oedipus is trying to uncover the secret knowledge about himself and his past.

Returning to our question, we can state that the triangular approach of psychoanalysis emphasizes the child's fantasies and drives directed toward the parents and their intimate relationship; on the contrary, triadic studies underline the child's research of parents' availability and interaction with them in order to obtain their protection and sharing. Of course, triadic and triangular communication provoke a sense of exclusion in the infant (Emde, 1994b), who witnesses his or her parents' dialogue and perceives he or she is not within their attentional field. Later on, the exclusion is more connected to parents' intimacy, which is the central focus of psychoanalysis.

CHAPTER 5

Neurobiological Basis
of Motherhood

A long with the psychological transformations that take place during pregnancy and in the first year of the baby's life, striking changes occur in the mother's brain with the activation of maternal care circuits (Panksepp, 1998). The
fundamental modifications that characterize the transformation from female
brain into maternal brain are initiated by pregnancy hormones–gene interactions. The activated brain circuits promote nurturant and caregiving behavior
toward offspring in mothers and less frequently and in a reduced way in fathers;
this is understandable because the mammalian female brain is preadapted to
care for the offspring.

As has been illustrated by Panksepp (1998), during pregnancy estrogens remain at modest levels and rapidly increase as delivery nears, while progesterone
is high and decreases at the end of pregnancy and prolactin rises consistently
(figure 5.1). In addition to these hormones secreted during pregnancy, other biochemical factors affecting the nervous system can intervene in triggering the
mother's attitudes.

In this regard, Gintzler (1980) has reported an activation of the endorphin
system, the intrinsic mechanism that modulates responsiveness to aversive and
painful stimuli connected with the pituitary gland and the hypothalamus over
the course of a rat's pregnancy, especially just before birth. In addition to preparing the mother for the pains of delivery, the endorphins may initiate maternal
behavior. It is now sufficiently documented that the rise and the regulation of the
maternal behavior requires the coordination of many hormonal and neurochemical systems and that the female brain is particularly sensitive to the biochemical
changes that occur during pregnancy.

A special role in maternal caregiving onset is performed by oxytocin (OT), the
neuropeptide hormone whose increased secretion emerges in the context of
physiological and hormonal modifications related to pregnancy. OT not only

FIGURE 5.1.   During pregnancy, hormones like estrogens and progesterone and neuro-modulators like oxytocin, prolactin, and endorphins are produced in large amounts. Hormones and neuromodulators activate the maternal circuit represented by the cingulated cortex, the prefrontal and orbitofrontal cortices, the nucleus accumbens, the amygdala, the lateral habenula, and the periaqueductal gray. (© Cristina Trentini; printed with permission)

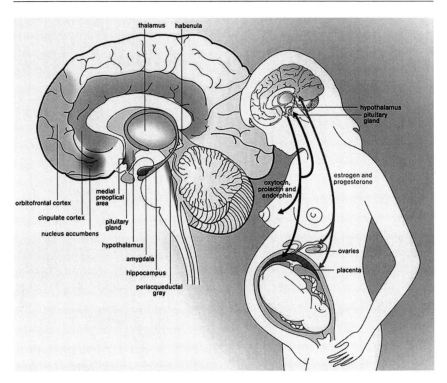

stimulates uterine contractions during delivery and milk let-down but also promotes maternal and protective caregiving behavior (Insel & Young, 2001).

In animal models the connection among OT, early maternal environment, and the emergence of parenting behavior has been studied. It has been evidenced that OT greatly influences processes of parent–infant bonding in a range of mammalian species, including rats, prairie voles, and primates (Kendrick, Keverne, & Baldwin, 1987; Maestripieri, Hoffman, Anderson, Carter, & Higley, 2009; Neumann, 2008). Several specific brain areas are involved in the initiation and maintenance of maternal pup–directed behavior. Lesion studies have documented and indirectly confirmed that the medial preoptic areas (MPOAs), located in the rostral hypothalamus, and their connections with the mesolimbic dopamine system for reward processing, play a critical role in maternal attitude (Numan & Insel, 2003; Swain et al., 2004). The thalamus, parietal cortex, and brain stem also perform an important role in the processing of infant-related somatosensory information, such as smell, touch, and vocalizations (Xerri, Stern, & Merzenich, 1994). In this context the prefrontal cortex has a special role in integrating this information and monitoring parental behavior (Afonso, Sison, Lovic, & Fleming, 2007).

A study performed in female voles (Wang, Liu, Young, & Insel, 2000) has evidenced that hypothalamic OT gene expression and receptor binding increase during the postpartum period. And another study has confirmed that OT may be secreted in rats from parvocellular paraventricular nucleus neurons and the medial preoptic area, both hypothalamic regions mediating maternal behavior (Douglas & Meddle, 2008).

Early social experiences influence the oxytocinergic system, connected with maternal behavior and the formation of affiliative bonds (Champagne et al., 2008; Meaney, 2001); in this regard individual differences have been evidenced in the OT receptors of female pups. These receptors are influenced by different early maternal behaviors (like licking or grooming, etc.) that the pups receive during infancy, and that they later reproduce as mothers to their offspring (Meaney, 2001).

These data highlight the role of OT in the intergenerational transmission of attachment, further confirmed by another study (Francis, Diorio, Liu, & Meaney, 1999; Francis, Young, Meaney, & Insel, 2002) that has evidenced that female rat pups more cared for by their mothers, in the form of high degree of licking and grooming (HLG), are more likely to manifest HLG behavior to their own pups. On the contrary, the female offspring of mothers who have provided low levels of licking and grooming (LLG) manifest a similar pattern of LLG behavior when they too become mothers. Furthermore, the adult offspring of the LLG mothers have shown lower levels of glucocorticoid receptor gene expression and decreased synaptic density in the hippocampus (Kaffman & Meaney, 2007).

In mammalian monogamous species characterized by biparental care, OT also influences paternal behavior (Bales, Kim, Lewis-Reese, & Sue Carter, 2004; Cho, DeVries, Williams, & Carter, 1999; Gubernick, Winslow, Jensen, Jeanotte, & Bowen, 1995; Wynne-Edwards, 2001). These animal studies evidence that OT is associated with more adequate parental behavior (Gordon, Zagoor-Sharon, Leckman, & Feldman, 2010), while on the contrary the secretion of cortisol is associated with lower levels of maternal behavior.

It has been demonstrated in humans as well that OT, tested only peripherically, is associated with empathy, intimacy, trust (Grewen, Girdler, Amico, & Light, 2005), and capacity to read mental states of others (Domes, Heinrichs, Michel, Berger, & Herpertz, 2007), while an alteration of OT metabolism has been evidenced in neglecting parents (Fries, Ziegler, Kurian, Jcoris, & Pollak, 2005). Maternal touch of the infant and breast contact with his or her mouth in the postnatal period can stimulate OT release in mothers (Matthiesen, Ransjo-Arvidson, Nissen, & Uvnas-Moberg, 2001). In a study by Feldman, Weller, Zagoory-Sharon, and Levine (2007), plasma levels of OT and cortisol were measured in women during the first trimester and last trimester of pregnancy and first postpartum months. At the same time maternal bonding was assessed by studying both maternal behavior and mental representations. The study evidenced that maternal OT across pregnancy and the postpartum period is associated with more competent maternal behavior and adequate mental representations. OT levels are consistent across pregnancy, and initial levels of OT predict postpartum bonding behavior, as well as maternal mental representations of bonding. OT is also associated with a pleasurable maternal feeling of bonding and attachment representations, but not with anxious and preoccupied thoughts. Such observations could further confirm the hypothesis that OT could intervene, reducing anxiety and favoring quiet states and pleasurable and highly regarded recognition of attachment (Uvnas-Moberg, 1998).

An interesting article by Swain and colleagues (2008) illustrates a research study that has compared mothers who had a vaginal delivery (VD) with mothers who had a caesarean delivery (CD) in order to test the hypothesis that VD mothers are significantly more responsive to their own baby's cry at 2–4 weeks after the delivery. The results of the research confirm the hypothesis that VD mothers are more sensitive to their own baby's cry than CD mothers during early postpartum in sensory processing, empathy, and motivation.

It is important to note that at 2–4 weeks postpartum, the effects of mode of delivery on brain reaction to a mother's own baby's cry are significant. The complex biopsychosocial differences observed in VD versus CD may be explained through different mechanisms, suggesting, as has been already evidenced in animal models, an increased release of oxytocin connected with the vagino-cervical stimulation by the baby during VD (Kendrick, 2000). These observations are relevant because they confirm the importance of the natural VD for maternal functioning, whereas in the current US health care system, there is an overuse of caesarean delivery.

Although fathers do not experience pregnancy, birth, or lactation, a similar neuroendocrine trend has been found in the development of fathering and mothering attitudes in mammals (Wynne-Edwards & Timonin, 2007). The links between OT and the mesolimbic dopaminergic pathways in animal monogamous fathers suggest that OT influences paternal reward system through attachment-related stimuli from partner and child (Young, Lim, Gingrich, & Insel, 2001). In several biparental species, fathers exhibit parenting behavior similar to mothers (Ahern & Young, 2009; Bredy, Lee, Meaney, & Brown, 2004; Frazier, Trainor, Cravens, Whitney, & Marler, 2006), yet they manifest a specific parental interaction. In fact, monogamous mothers and fathers, after separation from their pups, manifest an increase of their parenting behavior in a different way: Mothers engage in licking and physical contact with pups, while fathers provide tactile stimulation and support exploratory behavior (Lonstein & De Vries, 1999). Thus, whereas hormones associated with birth, lactation, and affectionate closeness may induce hormonal changes in mothers, the neuroendocrine basis of fathering is influenced by tactile stimulation of the pup and active promotion of pup behavior such as exploration. Fathers have shown an increase in plasma OT during pregnancy (Gubernick et al., 1995), and the amount of paternal care is associated with OT (Ziegler, 2000).

Studies on the oxytocinergic system of fathering in humans are quite limited, and the mechanisms connected with paternal behavior are not yet clarified. Father–child interactions in humans are also characterized by a more physical stimulatory play, which is highly rewarding and increases the father and child's positive activation (Feldman, 2003). A recent study by Feldman, Gordon, Schneiderman, Weisman, and Zagoory-Sharon (2010), has evidenced the involvement of the oxytocinergic system in human mothering and fathering with a quite similar pattern which has been observed in other mammals.

OT is not the only neurotransmitter that plays a role in the initiation of parental affiliative bonds; other neurotransmitters have been found to be involved in maternal responsiveness. In animal studies, serotonergic gene expression and dopamine-related and GABA-related genes are upregulated in mother rats compared to nonmothers (Kinsley & Armory-Meyer, 2011).

NEUROBIOLOGICAL TRANSFORMATIONS DURING PREGNANCY AND THE POSTNATAL PERIOD

Animal studies, as the ones performed in rats, have evidenced that hormones during pregnancy not only affect brain areas involved with maternal behavior but also regions that regulate memory and learning. These brain stimulations during pregnancy influence stress/anxiety systems as well as learning, memory, and aggression promotion. This expression of neuroplasticity is of major importance, also because it has both deep and enduring effects in the life cycle (Love et al., 2005). Considering modifications in basic brain regions that facilitate maternal behavior, research has documented hormonal and structural modfications connected with the hypothalamus and preoptic area (POA), which influence maternal behavior (Kinsley & Amory-Meyer, 2011). As Theodosis, Shachner, and Neumann (2004) have shown, neuronal and glial connections in hypothalamic centers intervene, reorganizing the neural network and reaching more flexibility. Additionally, the pituitary gland exhibits chemo-architectural changes in response to maternal experience. Therefore, considering regions that support the rising of maternal behavior, researchers have found an increase in gray matter volume of the prefrontal cortex, parietal lobes, and midbrain areas (Kim et al., 2010).

It is evident that an efficient and adaptable maternal brain sustains maternal changes that optimize maternal behavior and enable the successful rearing of the offspring. In this regard, the hippocampus has a special role in maternal behavior by regulating the search and acquisition of food and favoring general spatial orientation (Champagne et al., 2008). In conclusion, the mother's brain is characterized by an inherent plasticity that is necessary to respond to the continuously changing demands of motherhood and of raising the offspring.

The mammalian mother's dedication to her demanding and immature pup is the most motivated of all animal behavior, exceeding even sexual and feeding behavior. In studying the appetitive or motivational processes underlying the performance of maternal behavior (Mattson, Williams, Rosenblatt, & Morrell, 2001; Seip & Morrell, 2007), a set of experiments based on the place preference paradigm have been performed. These experiments explore the more rewarding property of an injection of cocaine or three pups for maternal lactating dams. At postpartum days 10 and 16, the dams prefer the cocaine cue-associated chamber, whereas the dams tested at postpartum day 8 prefer the pup cue-associated chamber. These observations have highlighted an interaction between the timing in the postpartum period and the exhibited preference for cocaine or pups, evidencing that the offspring may be the reward that stimulates maternal behavior of mammalian mothers.

The satisfaction of nursing for both mother and infant, which sustains maternal behavior and bonding, has been confirmed by a further study (Ferris et al., 2005). To test the rewarding nature of nursing, functional magnetic resonance imaging (fMRI) has been used to map brain activity in lactating dams exposed to their suckling pups versus cocaine. Suckling stimulation in lactating dams and cocaine exposure in virgin females have activated the dopamine reward system. In contrast, lactating dams exposed to cocaine instead of pups have shown a deactivation of brain activity in the reward regions. In conclusion, pup stimulation is more reinforcing than cocaine for lactating dams.

It has been hypothesized (Kinsley & Lambert, 2006) that suckling pups attached to their mother's nipples may release tiny amounts of endorphins, natural neuromodulators, in the mother's body, which may act somewhat like an opiate drug, inducing the mother to be constantly in contact with her pups and to care for them because the mother finds it pleasurable. Also humans, like all animals, act in order to survive and procreate and are influenced by the hedonic feeling of the subjective experience, but only humans express a self-awareness of the parental role and are able to report the subjective feeling associated with parental experience verbally.

Early theories of motivation have proposed that hedonic feeling is fundamentally controlled by need states, but these theories do not give an adequate explanation for why mothers constantly try to be in contact with their child. Thus, the incentive value or the reward valence of a stimulus is considered an important motivation, subjectively experienced as pleasantness and pleasure (Kringelbach, 2005). Pleasure is associated with happiness, performing an important evolutionary function (Kringelbach & Berridge, 2009).

In the reward experience two different aspects should be distinguished: the hedonic sensation, which refers to the liking or pleasure related to the reward; and incentive salience, which refers to the wanting or desire for the reward. From this point of view, early interactions and attachment bonds between parents and infants take on a particular importance in the experience of pleasure shared with others.

Significant associations with subjective pleasantness and pleasure have been found almost exclusively in the medial orbitofrontal cortex. In humans and higher nonhuman primates, the orbitofrontal cortex receives multimodal information and has a special role in incentive salience and subjective hedonic experience. Considering the neuroanatomical connectivity of the orbitofrontal cortex, it has been evidenced that this area specifically intervenes integrating sensory and visceromotor information and modulating behavior through both visceral and motor systems. The orbitofrontal cortex displays neuroanatomical connections not only with the basolateral amygdala but also with cingulate cortex, insula/operculum, hypothalamus, hippocampus, striatum, periaqueductal gray, and dorsolateral prefrontal cortex (Kringelbach, 2005), suggesting that the orbitofrontal cortex plays an important role in the networks involved in emotional processing.

The reward value of the stimulus is connected with anterior parts of the orbitofrontal cortex, where it can be modulated by other internal states and can be used to influence subsequent behavior, stored for monitoring, learning, and memory, and made available for subjective hedonic experience (Dehaene, Kerszberg, & Changeux, 1998). Of course, the hedonic experience depends not only on the orbitofrontal cortex but also on a complex neurobiological network, which consents its access to consciousness and implies the explicit evaluation of a stimulus's affective valence.

MATERNAL LOVE AND PLEASURE

Parental love, especially maternal love, is closely linked to romantic love because it provides one of the most powerful motivations for human action. This love for a child has been represented throughout the ages in literature, painting, fiction, and music as one of the richest and most inspiring expressions of human life. A wonderful illustration of maternal love can be found in the painting by the Italian Renaissance painter Filippino Lippi "Madonna in adorazione del bambino" (figure 5.2). In this painting the Madonna is deeply focused on her child, and her face expresses a sense of pleasantness, intimate satisfaction, and serenity.

Maternal love and romantic love have a common evolutionary purpose: the maintenance and the perpetuation of the species. At the same time, they are characterized by an intimate, profound bond. As Daniel Stern (1993) has written, expressions of love begin early in an astonishing way. Mother and child behavior overlaps with the behavior of two lovers. For example, mother and child look at each other without speaking, hold a physical closeness with faces and bodies in constant contact, display alterations in vocal expressions or synchrony of movements, and perform particular gestures like kissing each other, hugging, touching, and taking the face or the hands of the other. Mother and baby after the second month of life together can maintain a reciprocal prolonged gaze with an enchanted facial expression. Also, language assumes a special mark. When parents speak to their child, or lovers talk to one another, they can violate the

FIGURE 5.2.   Filippino Lippi: "Madonna in adorazione del bambino" ("Madonna in adoration of the child"), Galleria degli Uffizi, Florence. (© Summerfield Press/Corbis)

rules of the language. They emphasize the musicality of the words instead of the meaning, they use baby talk, and they express a wide range of nonverbal vocalizations, even altering the common pronunciation of words.

Facial expressions assume a special register also, altering and emphasizing the facial mimic. There is also a choreography in the movements of mother and baby, like those of two lovers; they move in synchrony, getting closer or more distant on the basis of a common rhythm.

Neuroimaging research has evidenced interesting overlapping neural activation regions between romantic and maternal love, as they are both highly rewarding experiences (Bartels & Zeki, 2004). In a previous fMRI study, Bartels and Zeki (2000) investigated the activity of the subjects' brains who were deeply in love while they viewed pictures of their romantic partners, compared with the activity produced by viewing pictures of friends of a similar age, sex, and duration of friendship. Using fMRI, the same researchers (Bartels & Zeki, 2004) later studied the activity of mothers' brains viewing the pictures of their own child, compared with the activations produced by viewing pictures of another child of the same age with whom they were familiar for about the same length of time, of their best friend, and of another person they were acquainted with.

In the maternal brain, activations have been found in the medial insula, in the cingulate gyrus dorsal and ventral to the genu. All of these activation foci overlap with those activated by romantic love. Specific activations in the study with mothers have included regions in the lateral orbitofrontal cortex and in the lateral prefrontal cortex. Activity has been found also in other cortical foci like a region near the frontal eye fields, the occipital cortex, and the lateral fusiform cortex. Subcortical bilateral activity, also overlapping with that found with romantic love, has been described in the striatum, in the substantia nigra, and in subthalamic regions. Additionally, activity has been found in the posteroventral part of the thalamus and in a region overlapping the periaqueductal gray of the midbrain, none of which are active with romantic love. The activity in the midbrain also overlaps with the reticular formation, the locus ceruleus and raphe nucleus. It is likely to originate from activity in periaqueductal gray, as this region not only has a high concentration of oxytocin receptors, but it is also known to be involved in maternal behavior.

Both maternal and romantic love elicit overlapping deactivation profiles in different areas connected to cognition, negative emotions, and mentalization. Although weaker, the deactivation pattern evoked by maternal love is remarkably similar to that observed with romantic love. The typical pattern is bilateral, although it affects the right hemisphere in a more substantial way: specifically the middle prefrontal cortex, the parieto-occipital junction/superior temporal sulcus, the medial prefrontal/paracingulate cortex, and the temporal poles. It also involves the posterior cingulate gyrus, the medial cuneus, and the amygdaloid region.

The similarity of the maternal results compared to those obtained in the study on romantic love is striking (Bartels & Zeki, 2000, 2004). Several regions overlap precisely, while others are specific to each form of relationship. Activity entirely specific to maternal love includes the lateral orbitofrontal cortex, and, subcortically, the periaqueductal gray, both of which are not active with romantic love.

The activated regions belong to the reward system and contain a high density of receptors for oxytocin and vasopressin, suggesting the neurohormonal involvement in these strong forms of attachment in humans as it has been observed in animals. At the same time both forms of affective relationship suppress activity in regions associated with negative emotions, as well as regions associated with "mentalizing" and social judgment. This suggests that strong emotional ties to another person inhibit not only negative emotions but also social judgments about that person.

In conclusion, Bartels and Zeki (2004) have shown that maternal and romantic relationships activate specific regions in the reward system and lead to the suppression of neural activity associated with the critical social judgment of other persons and with negative emotions, which explain the sentence "love is blind." In this regard a Neapolitan saying illustrates well the intimate, involving, and blind relationship between a mother and her child: "Every black beetle is beautiful to its mother."

NEUROBIOLOGICAL STUDIES

Maternal transformations of the brain have been highlighted by recent neurobiological research, employing new research instruments such as fMRI which measures hemodynamic changes in response to neural activity and offers excellent spatial resolution, but poor temporal resolution. Neuroscientific research indicates that the intense hormonal fluctuations that occur during pregnancy, birth, and lactation may remodel the female brain, increasing the size of neurons in some regions and producing structural changes in others. Recent experiments have shown that mother rats outperform virgin rats in navigating mazes and capturing prey (Kinsley et al., 1999).

As Mayes and colleagues (2005) have underlined, the initiation and maintenance of human maternal behavior involves a specific neural circuit. Pregnancy and continuous interactions with the child determine structural and molecular changes, which have not been completely clarified, in specific limbic, hypothalamic, and midbrain regions, reflecting the adaptive mental dynamics associated with maternal attitude. Maternal behavior is strongly influenced by different brain regions identified by several researches: The medial preoptic area of the hypothalamus (mPOA) is largely responsible for development of maternal responses, as well as the hippocampus, which intervenes in memory and learning as we have already discussed in animal studies. These modifications of the brain are activated by the increased secretion of estrogens and progesterone produced by the ovaries and placenta during pregnancy. Current brain imaging data have evidenced that the right orbitofrontal cortex actively intervenes not only in the experience of hedonic pleasure, but also in modulating the mother's abilities to decode her infant's emotional expressions, in order to respond to them in a sensitive way (Nitschke et al., 2004). This brain region is actively implicated in the socioemotional behavior and affect-regulating functions that are specifically involved in the attachment system (Schore, 2003).

Also, recent studies have shown that the human brain may undergo changes in sensory regulatory systems. For this reason, human mothers are capable of recognizing the many odors and sounds of their infants (Fleming, O'Day, &

Kraemer, 1999). Mothers who show high postbirth levels of the hormone cortisol are more attracted to and motivated by their infants' odors and more able to recognize their infants' cries. Research findings show that with the rise of cortisol levels, the stressing experience of parenting may promote attention, vigilance, and sensitivity in parents, confirming the hypothesis that the activation of stress response systems stimulates an adaptively increased vigilance during the period of heightened maternal sensitivity with the arrival of a new infant.

After the birth of the baby, the emotional regulation of maternal behavior seems to be controlled by highly stable biological systems that govern expressions of both mothers' and infants' behavior and emotions. A special role is performed by the right hemisphere, defined as "the emotive brain," which presents its greatest growth especially during the first 18 months of life with a dominant role throughout the first 3 years of life (Chiron et al., 1997; Schore, 1996, 2003). During this period, the right hemisphere works as a unitary system, preparing the organism to react to developmental challenges (Wittling, 1997) and to distressing situations.

Affectionate contact between the infant and the caregiver activates the limbic and mesofrontal regions that undergo developmental changes in the first years of life, starting with an early maturation phase that regards the right hemisphere (Joseph, 1996; Schore, 1996, 2003). Several neuroscientific research studies confirm that the right hemisphere is also significantly involved in maternal nurturant behavior with interconnections among the amygdala, orbitofrontal cortex, and cingulate, which perform the necessary integration between feelings and impulses to act.

Human mothers—both right- and left-handed ones—and many primates hold their newborns with the left part of the body (Sieratzki & Woll, 1996), utilizing left arms and left hands more frequently than fathers and nonmothers (Horton, 1995). This lateralized attitude allows the position of the child in the left maternal visual field, directly communicating with the right hemisphere, which is in turn involved in processing affective and nonverbal communications and in producing intuitive comforting gestures (Schore, 2003; Sieratzki & Woll, 1996). Manning and colleagues (1997) have suggested that these predispositions allow for the flow of dyadic affective communications toward right hemispheres, considered the cerebral region of human social attachment processes (Ammaniti & Trentini, 2009; Henry, 1993; Horton, 1995; Trentini, 2008).

Overall, then, psychobiological studies are revealing that mother–infant systems are intercorrelated within a superordinate organization that allows mutual regulation of cerebral, biochemical, and autonomic processes. Through these "hidden" mechanisms (Hofer, 1990), the adult brain works as an external regulatory and organizing system, which favors the development of the infant's immature homeostatic functioning. In this context, attachment is not only an overt behavior but is also an internal organization, "being built into the nervous system, in the course and as a result of the infant's experience of his transactions with the mother" (Ainsworth, 1967, p. 429).

In the last decades important studies using fMRI have explored brain activity in response to infant auditory, visual, and related stimuli. As we have already discussed, fMRI explores brain activity by indirect measure of changes of regional blood oxygenation and captures brain activity over a period of a few seconds (Swain & Lorberbaum, 2008), yet it misses major changes, like prolonged emotions or states of mind.

We shall present a summary of the studies in this area, having as reference a complete review of Swain and Lorberbaum (2008) on maternal neurobiological regions. In these studies parental brains have been studied frequently using infant cries or pictures as a stimulus in order to activate different regions of the maternal brain. The main focus of these studies is maternal and paternal empathy, which imply perception, emotional resonance, and response to the child's different emotional expressions.

We have previously discussed developmental, neurobiological, and clinical conceptualization of empathy, and now we would like to report an interesting neurobiological definition of empathy that has been proposed by Decety and Jackson (2004), implying the dynamic interaction between three major functional components. The first component is the affective sharing between the self and the other, which may be conceptualized as the ability to detect and resonate with the immediate affective state of another person (Trevarthen & Aitken, 2001). This ability is based on mechanisms of perception/action coupling that lead to shared representations between the self and the other (Gallese, 2006, 2009a).

Secondly the self-other awareness, without which the only affective sharing would lead to the phenomenon of emotional contagion, that is, the "total identification without the discrimination between one's feelings and those of the other" (Decety & Jackson, 2004, p. 75).The last component of empathy is the mental flexibility to adopt the subjective point of view of the other. This ability is linked to reflective functioning, which allows individuals to ascribe mental states to others (i.e., feelings, wishes, thoughts, intentions, and desires) and to interpret them in a meaningful way (Fonagy et al., 2002).

Two neural areas mainly involved in empathic resonance are the cingulate and the insula, as Singer and colleagues (2004) have shown in an experiment based on the empathic experience of pain of a loved person. Another study of Carr and colleagues (2003) has recognized the central role of the insula in integrating emotional information, with cortical areas displaying mirror properties.

Reviewing studies about the maternal neurobiological basis, the first studies have been performed by Lorberbaum and colleagues (1999), who measured brain activity in mothers while they listened to infant cries compared with a white noise. The cry stimulus activated the subgenual anterior cingulate and right inferior mesial prefrontal/orbifrontal cortex. In a more controlled and wide study by the same team (Lorberbaum et al., 1999), activated regions included the anterior and the posterior cingulate, thalamus, midbrain, hypothalamus, septal region, dorsal and ventral striatum, medial prefrontal cortex, right orbitofrontal/insula/temporal polar cortex region and right temporal cortex, and fusiform gyrus. It should be emphasized that fusiform gyrus is activated by human face and voice recognition (Swain & Lorberbaum, 2008), but it was unclear in Lorberbaum's research (1999) whether the activation of brain regions could be connected with unspecific attentional process or with the focusing on the specific infant cry stimulus. The second hypothesis about the specific stimulus of the infant cry has been confirmed by another study in which women have responded more in above described areas to a baby cry than to an emotionally neutral vocalization (Purhonen, Paakkonen, Ypparila, Lehtonen, & Karhu, 2001). Also in a further study confronting the response of mothers and control women to infant cries, a higher activation was evidenced in the mothers (Purhonen, Kilpelainen-Leeset et al., 2001).

These initial studies have confirmed the special mental state of mothers' attunement with their child, whose expressions (face, cry, etc.) are powerful emotional stimuli. In a subsequent study (Seifritz et al., 2003) fathers have also been considered and compared with mothers, as well as with nonparent males and females. In this research, stimuli consisted of sounds of infant crying and laughing compared to neutral sounds. An increased activation was found in parents' bilateral temporal regions with infant crying and laughing. Sander and colleagues (2007) reported a striking gender effect with infant laughing and crying stimuli versus control sound with an activation of the amygdala and of the anterior cingulated regions in women, while the control stimuli activated men more intensely.

An interesting question is whether the parental brain could respond in a different way to the infant stimulus across gender, suggesting that women are more predisposed for responses to preverbal infant vocalizations. A further study (Swain et al., 2004) compared the response of mothers and fathers with a "standard" cry and control noises in the postpartum period at 2–4 weeks and 12–16 weeks. Mothers have manifested more preoccupation than fathers, with a maternal increased activation in the amygdala and basal ganglia, confirming the typical alarm and concern in the postpartum period.

BABY'S FACE AS AN AFFECTIVE STIMULUS

As Darwin (1872) pointed out, the infant face affectively stimulates human adults, so they will respond to and care for the child, increasing infant adaptation, that is, reproductive success, and facilitating survivorship of one's own offspring. Subsequently, Konrad Lorenz (1943) highlighted that infantile facial features serve as an infant schema with innate releasing mechanisms for affective bond and nurturing in adult humans. Infantile facial features are characterized by a relatively large head, predominance of the brain, large and low-lying eyes, and bulging cheek region. In this regard Bowlby (1969) hypothesized that these "babyish" features would increase the infant's chance of survival by stimulating parental responses.

However, the neural basis for the responses to the infant face compared to that of the adult face has not yet been clarified. Human fMRI experiments have found activity specific to faces in an area of right posterior fusiform cortex corresponding to the fusiform face area (Kanwisher & Yovel, 2006; Tsao, Freiwald, Tootell, & Livingston, 2006). Several research groups have employed the baby face expressions to activate parental brain areas (Bartels & Zeki, 2004; Leibenluft, Gobbini, Harrison, & Haxby, 2004; Lenzi et al., 2009; Nitschke et al., 2004; Noriuchi, Kikuchi, & Senoo, 2008; Ranote et al., 2004; Strathearn, Li, & Montague, 2005; Swain et al., 2003; Swain, Leckman, Mayes, Feldman, & Schultz, 2006).

In the work of Swain and colleagues (2003, 2006), mothers and fathers watched photographs of their baby (0–2 weeks postpartum), which were chosen by them, and then they were confronted with the picture of another baby. In this study fMRI has evidenced, confronting responses to own-other baby, an increased activation of frontal and thalamocortical areas at 2–4 weeks postpartum.

The study by Leibenluft and colleagues (2004) has been performed with mothers using photographs of their own older children (5–12 years old), confronted with unfamiliar children's photographs. In this case fMRI has evidenced the activation of the anterior paracingulate, posterior cingulate, and superior temporal sulcus, important areas for empathy that are not so evident in other studies. A possible answer could be connected with the older age of children, with whom the maternal interaction could be different, based more on a mentalizing attitude. It is important to note that in the study by Leibenluft and colleagues the pictures of children included different facial expressions (happy vs. neutral vs. sad).

In the research of Nitschke and colleagues (2004), primiparous mothers, while watching pictures of their own smiling child and of an unfamiliar one, were studied using fMRI. In their conclusions, Nitschke and colleagues (2004) have stressed the importance of the orbitofrontal cortex for maternal attachment.

Ranote and colleagues (2004) have used video blocks of their child and an unknown infant instead of using a picture as a stimulus and have evidenced in mothers an increased neurobiological activation of the left amygdala and temporal pole in their own versus an unknown infant. The activated areas are involved in emotional regulation and in mentalizing.

Also, in the study by Noriuchi and colleagues (2008), video clips were used in a sample of mothers, with no sounds, of their own infant and other infants of approximately 16 months of age expressing two different attachment behaviors (i.e., smiling at the infant's mother and crying for her). Although a limited sample, this study showed that brain regions activated in mothers included the orbitofrontal cortex, periaqueductal gray, and dorsal and ventrolateral parts of putamen, with a specific brain response for the mother's own infant's distress.

In another study, Strathearn and colleagues (2005) have explored the neurobiological response of mothers while watching different emotional faces of their infants aged between 3 and 8 months (smiling, neutral, and crying) confronted with unknown infants' images. Viewing their own infants activated brain rewarding areas in mothers (ventral striatum, thalamus, and nucleus accumbens) and areas with oxytocin projections (amygdala, bed nucleus of the stria terminalis, and fusiform gyrus).

In conclusion, following Swain, Lorberbaum, Kose, and Strathearn (2007), who have reviewed fMRI studies examining parental responses to infant faces, comparing parental responses to their own infants and other infants, it appears that an increased response to one's own infant's face is evidenced in striate and extrastriate visual areas and in reward-related areas such as the nucleus accumbens, anterior cingulate, and amygdala. It should be added, however, that these studies do not clarify whether there is something specific about the infant face per se rather than one's own infant's face, partly because familiarity could confound the comparison.

The impact of the infant's face has been explored in a subsequent study (Kringelbach et al., 2008), which has investigated whether adults show specific brain responses to unfamiliar infant faces compared to adult faces, matching them in terms of attractiveness. Using magnetoencephalography, it was found that highly specific brain activity has occurred in response to unfamiliar infant faces but not to adult faces. This activity has involved the medial orbitofrontal cortex, an area implicated in reward behavior, as we have already discussed with a significant difference in power between infant and adult faces. These findings seem to confirm the existence in humans of an innate releasing mechanism described by Lorenz (1943), which favors affective bond and nurturing of young infants.

These observations expand previous research, showing that early orbitofrontal cortex activity not only facilitates visual recognition of masked stimuli, closely linked to the salience or attentional processing, but also of salient nonmasked infant faces but not of adult faces. These findings would suggest that the specific features of infant faces might stimulate a heightened attentional/emotional mechanism that predisposes humans to respond to infant faces as a special stimulus which elicits caring.

As we already discussed, the peculiar configuration of the infant's face is a powerful motivator of parental caregiving behavior (Darwin, 1872; Eibl-Eibesfeldt, 1989; Lorenz, 1943; Sprengelmeyer et al., 2009). This response of attraction to infants is also present in adults who are not yet parents (Glocker et al., 2009a, 2009b; Parsons et al., 2010; Stern, 1977) and may be linked to evolutionary mechanisms ensuring survival of the species.

MATERNAL EMPATHY AND THE
MIRROR NEURONS SYSTEM

It is thus clear that intersubjective experiences are mapped onto an individual's cerebral functioning from the first years of life. This aspect can be further illustrated by referring to the recent discovery of the mirror neurons system (MNS;

Gallese, 2001; Gallese et al., 1996), which was discussed in chapter 1. Mirror neurons map observed and executed actions, personally experienced and observed emotions, or sensations within the same neural substrate by means of "embodied simulation" (Gallese, 2006, p. 15) processes. This concept of embodiment is used to explain how neurobiological events are sought to account for mental events (Emde, 2007). By means of "embodied simulation," internal representations of the body states associated with actions, emotions, and sensations are evoked in the observer, as in the case of mothers, as though they would be doing a similar action or experiencing a similar emotion or sensation. These functional processes enhance individuals who are confronting the behavior of others, in experiencing a specific phenomenal state of intentional attunement. Such a condition generates a peculiar quality of familiarity with other individuals, produced by the collapse of the other's intentions and emotions into the observer's (Gallese, 2006). In this way, the MNS can be described as the neurobiological correlate of intersubjective system, since it represents the innate and embodied motivation to be in contact with others' emotions and to share subjective experience with them.

On the basis of these considerations, we have carried out research (Lenzi et al., 2009) to study maternal intersubjectivity by exploration of mothers' MNS during the presentation of infants' emotional stimuli. We report now, in a more extensive way, our group's study of different responses in mothers watching infant facial emotional expressions. The mothers have watched four facial emotional expressions—joy (J), distress (D), ambiguous (A), and neutral (N)—of their infants and of unfamiliar infants aged between 6 and 12 months. During fMRI scanning, mothers have been asked to perform two different tasks: to observe and empathize with the children' emotions in pictures or to imitate them.

fMRI scanning has evidenced that mothers when observing and imitating facial expressions of their baby and of the unfamiliar one have activated premotor cortical regions, specifically the ventral premotor cortex (vPMC) and the inferior frontal gyrus (IFG), which show mirror neurons properties as they are characterized by embodied simulation mechanism, by the activation of the same neural circuits underpinning emotional and sensorial experiences (Gallese, 2009a). MNS, by interacting with the limbic system (Ls), the key emotional center of the brain, through the anterior insula (I), may be critical for empathy (Carr et al., 2003), as has been confirmed in our study with mothers.

The results show that imitation of infant facial expressions (J/D/A) activates the MNS to a greater extent if confronted with a neutral face. Considering the response to different facial expressions, the imitation of joyous expression has activated a network that is distinct from that associated with other facial expressions. Mothers imitating children with happy expressions activate the right hemisphere, which is defined as the emotive brain. Several studies confirm that the right hemisphere is significantly involved in maternal nurturant behavior.

Furthermore, observation of one's own child as opposed to an unfamiliar child has evoked in mothers a greater lateralized response in the bilateral mirror areas (figure 5.3) (vPMC and the right IFG, right sulcus temporal superior [STS]) and right insula (RI). It is noteworthy that a positive correlation has been evidenced between right anterior insula during observations of all faces and maternal reflective functioning, which supports the hypothesis that the MNS-I-Ls (limbic system) is activated to a greater extent in mothers with greater mentalizing competence, a capacity particularly useful in the relationship with the child.

Interesting data have also emerged regarding maternal observation of ambiguous expressions of the infant when compared with all the other expressions. Studies have shown a significant activation of brain areas located in the frontal cortex, left presupplementary motor area, and right anterior cingulum and parietal cortices.

Let us summarize the results of our study, which has addressed the issue of maternal imitation and empathy in the preverbal period, before language becomes a major communicative channel between mother and infant. The activation of the maternal MMS-I-Ls by infants' emotional expressions supports the hypothesis that, as the mirror mechanism is critical for action representation and understanding, it is activated to a greater extent by expressions demanding mimicry, which serve a social goal (i.e., the transmission of an emotion). Furthermore, this system is also more active when a mother observes and empathizes with her own (as opposed to someone else's) child and is a function of maternal reflective function. This finding may be explained by the greater effort a mother makes to understand her own child's emotions, a proposal that is perfectly in keeping with the attachment theory (Bowlby, 1958). Single emotion exploration also has yielded clearly separate neural substrates for the joyous and ambiguous expres-

FIGURE 5.3.   Own child versus other child. The right ventral premotor cortex is one of the areas activated more during observation of the mother's own child than during that of someone else's child. A, ambiguous; D, distress; J, joy; N, neutral; R, right. (Reprinted from *Cereb. Cortex*, Vol. 19, Issue 5, Lenzi et al., "Neural Basis of Maternal Communication and Emotional Expression Processing during Infant Preverbal Stage," pp. 1124–1133, 2009, with permission from Oxford University Press.)

R Premotor cortex (48, 0, 36)

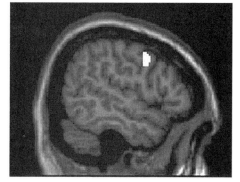

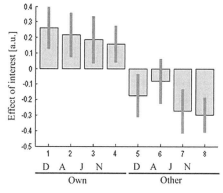

sions: Imitation of happiness prevalently has activated right subcortical and paralimbic temporal areas, whereas the observation of an ambiguous picture has activated high-order cognitive and motor areas. These findings support the theory that different emotions, which arouse very different feelings, must have, at least in part, a separate neural basis.

According to a model based on anatomical and functional studies on imitation and empathy, the MNS codes the goal of the action (Iacoboni et al., 1999; Rizzolatti et al., 2001) and reproduces it, whereas the anterior insula sends this information to the limbic system to give the action (in our case a facial expression) an emotional content (Gallese et al., 2004). Therefore, our results are in keeping with the simulation theory (or motor theory of empathy), according to which empathy is generated by inner imitation of others' actions (Gallese, 2003; Gallese & Sinigaglia, 2011a).

Data show that emotional expressions markedly activate the large-scale network composed of the MNS, anterior insula, and the amygdala, with greater activity when observing emotional stimuli as opposed to neutral ones. The greater activity observed in the MNS and insula in the imitation task may also be explained by the fact that emotional expressions require active imitation, whereas neutral expression does not (or at least to a far lesser extent). Moreover, results show a similar trend in the observation task. This partial overlapping of activations (both in the task requiring imitation and in the task requiring no movement) suggests that emotional expressions tend to activate the MNS-I-Ls more than neutral expressions. This increased activity may be explained by the goal contained in the emotional expressions, that is, "the action" required to create an expression is aimed at conveying emotional content to obtain a reaction from the external world.

Differences in brain activity between observation of one's own child and that of someone else's child show how healthy mothers, according to the attachment theory, make a greater effort to understand the emotions of their own child, as opposed to someone else's, to be able to successfully respond to the child's needs and to promote the child's survival. Increased activity in MNS may also be due to an effect of motor familiarity of the observed expressions. A recent study (Calvo-Merino et al., 2006) has found that the MNS is more strongly activated during the observation of stimuli (body movements) that are familiar to the observers from a motor point of view.

During the imitation task, we have found no differences in brain activity between a mother's own child and someone else's child, suggesting that imitating saturates the neural systems of action representation and emotional processing. Imitation may be a preferential and more natural way through which areas related to emotional processing are activated, as has been previously discussed considering parental intuitive behavior. This is suggested by the significance of mirror and limbic activations during imitation compared with observation (Carr et al., 2003).

Lastly, the study has found that activity within the system MNS-I-Ls is correlated to maternal reflective function, that is, the mother's capacity to ascribe to the baby emotions and to interpret them. This finding strongly suggests that the circuit we have explored is critical for empathy, just as the anterior insula, according to functional and anatomical data (Carr et al., 2003), is considered to be the relay between action representation (MNS) and emotion processing (limbic system). Moreover, the anterior insula is a center of visceromotor integration and is considered to be the primary cortical area for the interceptive state of the body (Gallese et al., 2004). The increased activity of the anterior insula in more empathic mothers may therefore also represent a greater ability to feel the emotions of others and especially of their own child.

The results show that imitation of joyous expressions compared with all other expressions activates certain right subcortical and cortical areas, supporting the theory that the right hemisphere is more involved than the left hemisphere in emotional processing and, thus, in maternal behavior (the right-hemisphere hypothesis) (Dalgleish, 2004).

Given its rich innervation of mesolimbic dopaminergic neurons, the striatum is well positioned to respond to incentive reward motivation and to pregoal attainment of positive effects arising from progression toward a desired goal (Davidson & Irwin, 1999). Activation of the bilateral amygdala may instead be related to a mechanism of maternal reward.

Studies have reported amygdala activation during positively valence and rewarding stimuli (Zald, 2003). Smiling back to a child is one of the most positive and common maternal imitative behaviors and is also very rewarding for the mother. When a mother is smiling back to her child, not only is she communicating that she knows what the child is feeling (happiness), but she also feels happy because the child is happy; that is, the process of mothering has been successful.

The increased temporal pole (TP) activation during the imitation of joyous stimuli may be related to the social and maternal value of imitating a child's smile. Studies on primate and humans have shown that TP pathology causes maternal aberrant behavior and lack of empathy (Carr et al., 2003; Olson, Plotzker, & Ezzyat, 2007).The anterior part of the temporal lobe and the hippocampus are critical for mood stability (Phillips, Drevets, Rauch, & Lane, 2003), socially appropriate behavior, and personality (Glosser, Zwil, Glosser, O'Connor, & Sperling, 2000).

During observation, we have found areas that have been significantly more active during ambiguous expressions than during other expressions. Activation has been located in frontoparietal areas, prevalently in the left hemisphere, as if the processing of such stimuli would depend on activation of emotion-related areas to a lesser extent, as mothers find difficulties in resonating with emotional expression of the child and need to use more cognitive processing to decode the unusual expression of the child.

It is interesting to note that the activation of the pre-supplementary area (SMA) is involved in high-order aspects of motor control, such as internal selection of an aspect of movement (Picard & Strick, 1996). It is possible that the activation of the pre-SMA is associated with the motor planning and control of maternal interventions; in fact, mothers not only manifest an empathic resonance toward their own baby, but they intervene by soothing their baby or continuing a joyful interaction.

Our study has addressed the issue of maternal empathy and communicative skills during an infant's first year of life before language develops, and it has been found that the MNS, the anterior insula, and the limbic system are the basis of these mother–infant interactions. This system is activated to a greater extent when the mother is observing her own child than someone else's child, and its activity is a function of the mother's capacity to interpret the child's internal states.

To verify the impact of infant facial image in young women before becoming mothers, we have explored in a subsequent study (Lenzi et al., 2012) the neurobiological activation, especially of MNS, stimulated by pictures representing different facial emotional expressions (joy, distress, and neutral) of unfamiliar infants aged from 6 to 12 months, used in the previous study (Lenzi et al., 2009). We have studied the different impact of infants' pictures in two groups of young-adult nulliparous women subdivided according to their state of mind with respect to attachment (secure subjects [F] and dismissing subjects [Ds]; Main & Goldwyn, 1997), who have undergone fMRI sessions. During each session they were instructed either to "watch and imitate the children's expressions" or to "observe and try to empathize with the children's expressions."

fMRI data show that empathizing and imitating all faces in both groups of young nulliparous women have activated motor and limbic areas, which are critical for imitation, empathy, and emotions, and the visual system. Emotions (emotional faces vs. neutral faces) also have activated limbic (striatum, amygdala, temporal poles [TP], and left ACC) and motor and mirror-related areas (SMC, right vPMC, right pre-SMA, right STS, bilateral left post-middle temporal gyrus, insula, and right cerebellum). These results are in line with data from the previous study on young mothers, based on the same tasks and stimuli (Lenzi et al., 2009), suggesting that similar circuits are engaged by nulliparous mothers when interacting with infant face stimuli.

Interesting data highlight the different neurobiological impact of infants' images depending on the attachment model of nulliparous mothers (figure 5.4). Unexpectedly, brain activations in dismissing women differ from those of secure subjects. While empathizing, dismissing subjects activate several areas to a greater extent than secure subjects, including MNS and the limbic system.

On the other hand, dismissing subjects deactivate frontomedial areas, that is, the perigenual anterior cingulated cortex (pACC) and the medial orbitofrontal cortex (mOFC). Within this context, hyperactivations of limbic and mirror areas may reflect an implicit and nonmodulated emotional involvement stimulated by an image of a child, whereas deactivations of the mOFC/pACC may reflect the emotional disinvestment toward attachment relationships, which is typical of dis-

FIGURE 5.4. Empathizing, all faces (vs. rest). Areas in light gray are those significantly more active during empathizing in Ds than in F. In black, we report areas more deactivated in Ds than in F. The plots show the mean effects in all six conditions (F-d, Fj, Fn, Ds-d, Dsj, and Ds-n). d, distress; J, joy; n, neutral; R, right; L, left; pre-SMA, presupplementary motor area; vPMC, ventral premotor cortex; IFG, inferior frontal gyrus; PPC, posterior parietal cortex; pAAC/mOFC, pregenual anterior cingulated cortex and medial orbitofrontal cortex. (Lenzi et al., 2012; Copyright © 2012 Wiley Periodicals, Inc.)

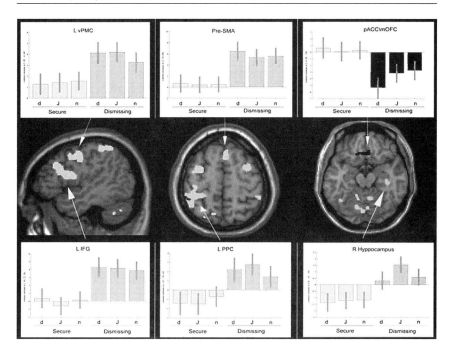

missing subjects and is an expression of a more cognitive level, which compensates for the nonmodulated emotional involvement.

It has also been observed that dismissing subjects have deactivated the pACC/mOFC to a greater extent than secure subjects when empathizing with all faces. In particular, plots of effects from these areas clearly show this deactivation pattern, which seems to be driven mainly by distressed faces. On the basis of the connections and architectonics of the OFC, some researchers (Ongur, Ferry, & Price, 2003; Ongur & Price, 2000) have proposed a frontomedial functional network that encompasses the pACC and the mOFC as well as the ventral medial prefrontal cortex. The pACC, which is strictly connected to the amygdala, is critical for emotional processing, and evidence has suggested that the pACC regulates amygdala response (Quirk & Beer, 2006; Quirk, Likhtik, Pelletier, & Pare, 2003). The mOFC projects also to the amygdala and massively to the ventral striatum; these projections are thought to subserve the reward or affective value of primary reinforcements, including face expression, taste, touch, and texture, and is also involved in the manifestation of positive emotion (Rolls & Grabenhorst, 2008).

This area has been found to be activated by positive affect displayed by mothers when viewing pictures of their infants (Nitschke et al., 2004) and vice-versa (Minagawa-Kawai et al., 2009). Thus, the OFC is not only critical for emotion modulation but also has a role in reinforcement and rewarding of positive behavior such as those during mother–infant interaction, thereby becoming critical for the construction of attachment.

The results of Lenzi and colleagues (2012) suggest that deactivation of part of this frontomedial network may represent the neural correlates of attachment avoidance behavior as typically seen in dismissing individuals. Moreover, the alexithymic profile appears to modulate neural activation in response to infants' images.

In particular, activity within medial orbitofrontal areas is not directly correlated with activity within the pre-SMA, and it is inversely correlated with the Toronto Alexithymia Scale-20 items (TAS-20, Taylor, Bagby, & Parker, 1992; Italian validation by Bressi et al., 1996) in dismissing subjects. The greater the difficulty in describing feelings, the greater the deactivation in these areas, suggesting a role of these areas in emotional awareness. Furthermore, greater activity in the pre-SMA, which contains mirror neurons (Mukamel et al., 2010; Nakata et al., 2008; Raos, Evangeliou, & Savaki, 2007; Rizzolatti et al., 1990; Rizzolatti, Luppino, & Matelli, 1996), and alexithymia, which is a sign of emotional dysregulation, appears to be correlated with a greater deactivation of brain areas related to attachment and reward (pACC/mOFC).

Now let us summarize the research that we have presented about the activation of the MNS in mothers and nulliparous young women, when watching pictures of different infantile emotional expressions. It is possible that intersubjective exchanges between women and babies are part of "an innate, primary system of motivation, essential for species survival, and has a status like sex or attachment" (Stern, 2004, p. 97). These intersubjective exchanges develop from birth between the baby and the mother, but also with the father, as we have shown in chapter 4, creating a triadic interactive context (Fivaz-Depeursinge & Corboz-Warnery, 1999). On the basis of neurobiological observations, it can be assumed that the parenting system is linked to the basic intersubjective motivation system, strictly connected to the attachment system, both essential to their transmission and reproduction over generations.

Research concerning neurobiological circuits has shown that specific brain regions are activated when different motivational systems involved in parental functioning are observed in the mother's behavior (Lichtenberg, 1989; Nitschke et al., 2004; Schore, 2003). The activity of the frontolimbic system intervenes in modulating social and emotional behavior and affect-regulating functions, which are specifically involved in the attachment system, as we have documented in our research (Lenzi et al., 2012). An important role in the attachment process is performed by the orbitofrontal cortex of the right hemisphere. In addition, in our research on maternal brain functioning we found that maternal mirroring and imitation of the affective facial expressions of the child activate the classical areas of mirror neurons and of the limbic system, key emotion centers of the brain. Parallel to the neural activation during motherhood, deep psychological changes intervene during pregnancy and after the birth of the baby, as we have documented in chapters 2 and 3. There is also a basic shift in the overall sense of self to include maternal identity, with the activation of the particular psychic configuration, specific to motherhood, the "motherhood constellation" (Stern, 1995).

CHAPTER 6

The Primary Matrix of Intersubjectivity

After delivery, mother and infant interact in order to satisfy and regulate basic and reciprocal needs. As Papousek and Papousek (1975, 1987) have highlighted, mother and infant create a preverbal communication context that forges a dynamic system based on an affective and phonetic lexicon and, later on, on a developing intersubjective understanding and sharing of affects, intentions, and motivations (Fogel & Thelen, 1987). This "is the realm of non-consciously regulated intuitive behavior and implicit relational knowledge" (Papousek, 2007, p. 258).

Mother and infant are intrinsically motivated "to be attracted and seek contact with one another" (Parson et al., 2010, p. 221). We have already discussed how mothers are attracted to the baby's face, which affectively stimulates them to focus on the baby, and to respond to and to care for him or her (Darwin, 1872). These babyish features serve as an infant schema that activates attention, affective bonding, and nurturing in adult humans who take care of the infant. As Kringelbach and colleagues (2008) have shown, a human-specific brain activation in the medial orbitofrontal cortex occurs in response to infant faces, even unfamiliar ones, but not to adult faces. This orienting system (Parson et al., 2010) is a prerequisite for interpersonal contact: When interacting with her baby, a mother tries to capture the baby's gaze and maintain eye contact, also by making facial expressions — "baby faces" (Stern, 1985, p. 73) — which are marked by exaggeration in fullness of display, longer duration, and slower facial movements. Gaze behaviors themselves are exaggerated, and mothers tend to maintain a close position to the infant so that the infant can focus on them in an exclusive way.

The infant, on the other hand, is oriented to and prefers human faces over nonhuman forms (Johnson, Dziurawiec, Ellis, & Morton, 1991), and at the same time the infant expresses his or her preference for speech over nonspeech sounds. This neonatal predisposition to orient oneself toward faces plays a decisive role in building a bond with the parents.

Empirical research (Morton & Johnson, 1991) has shown that infants manifest attraction for human face patterns immediately after childbirth, and later on, at 2 months, they are able to recognize their mother's face among others. Face-to-face interactions between parents and infants develop quite early and are bidirectional with high-intensity reciprocal mirroring, which creates a fusional experience, a cradle for the forging of affective attachment bonds.

Such visual experiences play a critical role in social and emotional development. In particular, the mother's emotionally expressive face is the most potent visual stimulus in the infant's experience. Gaze represents the most activating form of preverbal communication, and the perception of facial expressions is one of the most salient communicative channels.

Previously Winnicott suggested that the infant, when looking at his mother who is looking at him, sees himself in her eyes: "The mother is looking at the baby. . . . What she looks at is related to what she sees there" (1967/1971, p. 111). Later Kohut underlined that "the most relevant basic interaction between mother and child usually lies in the visual area: the child's bodily display is responded to by the gleam of the mother's eye" (1971, p. 117). According to Bowlby (1969, 1982), visual contact is a central element for the establishment of a primary attachment to the mother; in fact, mother and infant perform a protoconversation that is mediated by eye-to-eye contact, vocalizations, hand gestures, and movements of the arms and head (Trevarthen & Aitken, 2001). In a recent paper, Tomasello, Hare, Lehmann, and Call have evidenced that humans have especially visible eyes; in fact, they "are coloured in a way that helps advertise both their presence and their gaze direction much more saliently than in other primates" (2006, p. 315). One hypothesis is that human-type eyes evolved in the context of environmental pressures which sustained cooperative-communicative abilities that are typical of mutual and complex social interactions and imply joint attention and visually based communication such as pointing. It is important to underline that human eyes often express different emotional states (Baron-Cohen, Wheelwright, Hill, Raste, & Plumb, 2001).

After orienting to human faces and eye-to-eye communication, a second important step implies a selected and defined reciprocal recognition of infant and parents that happens within the first few days of life. Mothers can properly recognize their own child on the basis of the infant's smell, cry, and touch (Cismaresco & Montagner, 1990; Kaitz, Lapidot, Bronner, & Eidelman, 1992). On the part of the infant, he or she also demonstrates a clear preference for his or her mother compared with other persons. Infants prefer to view the mother's face than the face of an unfamiliar woman.

The neural basis of the infant's visual functioning has not completely clarified, although some researchers suggest that subcortical areas are involved in face attraction at birth, while the visual cortical area is necessary for reaching longer fixation time for face stimuli (Morton & Johnson, 1991).

A study carried out with 2-month-old infants (Tzourio-Mazoyer et al., 2002) has evidenced that, when looking at an unknown woman's face, infants activate a network of neural areas that belong to the core system for face perception as identified in adults (Haxby, Hoffman, & Gobbini, 2000) located in infants in the inferior temporo-occipital cortex, very close to adults' fusiform facial area (Kanwisher, McDermott, & Chun, 1997).

A special role in these early processes is undertaken by the right hemisphere. Quoting Schore: "Even more specifically, what is happening here is that the infant's early maturing right hemisphere, which is dominant for the child's processing of visual emotional information, the infant's recognition of the mother's face, and the perception of arousal-inducing maternal facial expressions, is psychobiologically attuned to the output of the mother's right hemisphere, which is involved in the expression and processing of emotional information and in nonverbal communication" (2003, p. 9). These early visual and affective exchanges are stored, as Schore (2011) has emphasized in a recent paper, inside the relational implicit knowledge embedded in the attachment bond, which is not only psychological but also neurobiological and bodily rooted.

On the basis of his research with rats, Hofer (2006) has evidenced a network of behavioral, physiological, and neural processes that underlie the psychological dimensions of attachment. Within the mother–infant interaction, multiple hidden regulators intervene on a physiological level that can shape the development of offspring. For example, warmth provided by the mother normally maintains the pup's activity level, and her milk maintains her pup's heart rate. In the case of maternal separation, there is a lack of these regulatory influences that provokes slowed behavior and low heart rate.

Applying these observations to early human development, it is possible to suggest that internal models of attachment can be constructed on early biological regulatory interactions. This could explain the visceral and bodily sensations that often accompany the vicissitudes of close human relationships, especially separations and losses.

During this early period the brain begins to form new synapses, so that the synaptic density (the number of synapses per unit volume of brain tissue) greatly exceeds the adult degree. This process of synaptic proliferation, called synaptogenesis, lasts up to several months, reaching maximum density in most brain regions (Blakemore & Choudhury, 2006). These early peaks in synaptic density are followed by a period of synaptic elimination (or pruning) which results in a strengthening of frequently used connections and the elimination of infrequently used ones. This experience-dependent process, which occurs over a period of years, reduces the overall synaptic density to adult levels.

These data derive mainly from studies of sensory regions of animal brains. Research carried out in rhesus monkeys (Rakic, 1995) has demonstrated that synaptic densities reach maximal levels 2–4 months after birth, after which the process of pruning starts and the left synaptic circuits become more efficient. However, synaptogenesis and synaptic pruning in the prefrontal cortex have a rather different time course. Synaptic pruning is thought to underlie sound categorization, for example, which intervenes in the process of learning one's own language. Sound organization is determined by the sounds in a baby's environment in the first 12 months of life and by the end of their first year, babies lose the ability to distinguish between sounds to which they are not exposed (Kuhl, 2004).

AGENCY AND MUTUAL REGULATION
BETWEEN CAREGIVER AND INFANT

Referring to the dyadic mother–infant system, the importance of mutual influences has been emphasized (Beebe & Lachmann, 1988; Gianino & Tronick, 1988). Using the system perspective (Sander, 1977, 1985), one of the essential features is the infant's primary activity in the process of engagement and exchange with human partners. Each partner with a personal endogenous organization is influencing the other partner and is simultaneously influenced by the other.

The experience of mutual regulation is translated into a sense of agency for the infant (Rustin, 1997). The infant has his or her own agency through which he or she influences the system. According to Sander (1985), the origins of human identity lie in the transformation of this influencing behavior of the infant inside the interactive system into a subjective sense of agency (Stern, 1985). This capacity enables infants to detect contingencies between their behavior and the response of the environment.

Closely related to the concept of agency is that of efficacy. Lichtenberg (1989) considers efficacy a central motivation in development, so when an infant is able to have his or her needs met (for example, to be satisfied with mother's milk after screaming), the infant experiences a sense of efficacy. Rustin (1997) proposes a useful distinction between agency, based on the innate capacities of infants, which enable them to organize experience and engage in the process of exchange, and efficacy, which is the capacity to reliably produce expected effects with those capacities. The sense of agency is connected with repeated experiences of having one's agency acknowledged along with repeated experiences of efficacy.

In the personal building of the sense of self, an important role is played by self-agency as it implies "volition, having control over self-generated action . . . and expecting consequences of one's action" (Stern, 1985, p. 71). A poignant illustration of self-agency is the 1609 painting (figure 6.1) by a female painter, Artemisia Gentileschi, when she was 16 years old. The painting "Madonna and Child," hosted in the Galleria Spada in Rome, describes the active movement of the left hand of the child who is trying to awake or to caress a sleeping Madonna during feeding. The painting captures a moment of intimacy between mother and child, who is trying to revive his mother, exactly as has been observed during the "Still Face" lab procedure (Tronick et al., 1978), in which the baby faces a

FIGURE 6.1.   Artemisia Gentileschi "Madonna and the Child," Galleria Spada, Rome.
(© Ministero per i Beni e le Attività Culturali)

still and detached mother. It is interesting to note that the painting, which portrays the Madonna in a moment of tiredness, was painted by a woman, who probably understood the weight of motherhood better, while male painters tend to idealize maternity, as we have previously discussed.

The infant and mother jointly learn to regulate affective and behavioral states, allowing the baby to learn in this context how to communicate and interact with others and become active within his or her environment (Sander, 1962). The process of mutual regulation unfolds throughout development, attaining a more complex organization.

Early infant studies have particularly emphasized matching, reciprocal concordances, and sharing between mother and infant, who appear to move like dancers (Beebe, 1982; Stern, 1977), while the conflictual dimension during interactions has been minimized. This dimension has, on the contrary, been conceptualized by developmental theories of psychoanalysis.

Subsequent research has depicted an interactional picture that is also characterized by discordances, mismatch, and interactional failures. Cohn and Tronick (1987) have shown that infants and mothers spend only about 30% of their time in synchronous or matching states. Gender differences also influence affective and regulatory behaviors, as differences in interactive coherence do (Weinberg, 1992). Infant boys are more emotionally reactive than girls: They express positive as well as negative affect more, focusing on the mother more intensely and displaying more signals of escape and distress as well as requests for contact, if compared to girls.

Tronick and his colleagues (Tronick & Cohn, 1989; Tronick & Gianino, 1986a) have depicted the typical mother–infant interaction as moving from coordinated to miscoordinated states and back again. It is quite frequent that a mother does not pay attention to her child's behavior or may even misunderstand it, thus generating an interactive error or a mismatch. This is also due to the immaturity of the child, who is not able to express and communicate his or her needs and to the caregiver's difficulty in decoding the infant's behavior. Interactive errors are quite common in mother–infant dyads and in most of the cases are easily repaired.

In studies of face-to-face interaction, when infants are 6 months old, repair is very frequent, every 3–5 seconds (Tronick & Gianino, 1986b). In the process of mutual regulation and repair, mother and infant both participate with their interactive capacities in order to maintain an internal regulation, which is a prerequisite for social exchange and communication as well as for acting in the world (Sander, 1962).

MUTUAL REGULATION DURING FEEDING

A good example of mutual regulation can be observed when a mother feeds her baby, as has been brilliantly illustrated by Kenneth Kaye (1982). During the first month of life, human infants suck in bursts of 4–10 sucks, about one per second, a peculiar human model not found in any other mammal. During pauses, mothers usually step in by jiggling the baby, a maternal intuitive response to the baby's pause during sucking. It has been observed that the effect of jiggling, then stopping, consists in eliciting the sucking. Both experienced and inexperienced mothers quickly learn to reduce the time of jiggling during the baby's first 2

weeks, from 3.1 seconds to 1.8 seconds (Kaye & Wells, 1980). This mutual behavior is a good example of turn-taking interaction and mutual contingency. A
possible explanation of the infant's pause may be in the effect it has upon the
mother, since the pause is not for breathing, swallowing, or resting. This behavior has the observable effect of involving mothers in the baby's pattern, creating
reciprocal turns.

While the sucking mechanism of the infant is initially intrinsic, based on neurobiological organization, the mother has a different perception: She feels that
her baby has become lazy or sated. For this reason she begins to jiggle the baby,
but she ignores the fact that her jiggling lengthens the pause and the only way to
hasten sucking is to jiggle and stop. Mothers learn the consequences of their behavior on the child in a short time, if they are sensitive and pay attention to the
child. The function of the pause could be interpreted as a chance for the caregiver to fit turns into babies' biological cycles. Turn-taking interaction is built by
the intervention of mother, who can adjust to the child and create an interactive
organization by sharing rhythms and regulations with the child.

We may suppose that throughout the evolution of the human species, the
rhythm of breastfeeding was modified in order to allow mothers to use feeding
interaction to teach their children the social rhythm of turn-taking. In fact, observing interactions during feeding, we notice that in moments when the baby is
actively sucking, the mother sustains the child's rhythm without interfering but
maintaining an attentive presence. During pauses in the suction, the mother
steps in, stimulating the child not only physically but by speaking to him or her.
The mother often confirms the child with her words, by saying, for example,
"You liked mummy's milk today" or "My baby was really hungry today."

We may conclude that during feeding, caregivers do not only feed the child
and help him or her develop a daily feeding rhythm but also stimulate the child
to create an interactive model of turn-taking which will serve, in future life, as an
example for social exchange and verbal dialogue with others. The complexity of
human functioning has modified the feeding context, which has become an important space of dyadic interaction and learning.

INTERNALIZATION, EXPECTATIONS,
AND REPAIR

Ongoing regulation between mother and baby gradually stabilizes, creating expectations that are internalized in the infant's mind (Beebe & Lachmann, 1994;
Stern, 1985). Stern (1985) has formulated a theory of representations of interactions generalized (RIGS), considering that repeated and predictable interactional regulations set the basis for a generalized abstraction of the RIG. In the
formation of infant's representations, Stern (1988) highlighted the importance of
affect. Affect is also emphasized by Beebe and Lachmann (1994), who underline
its salient organizing principles, which influences the establishment of expectan-

cies. For example, the hedonic pleasure experienced by the infant when he or she is being fed, spoken to with a gentle rhythm, or caressed creates intense expectancies in the baby, who later will expect or try to reexperience the pleasant affect.

The "heightened affective moments" (Beebe & Lachmann, 1994, p. 147), positive or negative, not only give interactional experiences a chromatic salience but also intervene in organizing them. As Stern (1985) has discussed, the vital dimension of affects in emotional communication is important during the early months of life. Affects are characterized by their intensity and profile with activation and deactivation inside specific categories, such as joy, distress, sadness, or anger.

In this regard, Panksepp considered "positive emotional systems . . . as attractor that capture cognitive spaces, leading to their broadening, cultivation, and development. Negative emotions tend to constrain cognitive activities to more narrow and obsessive channels" (2001, p. 132). The emotional environment experienced by the infant has lifelong consequences, creating emotional strengths and vulnerabilities.

From a neurobiological point of view, infants' psychological and emotional experiences are based on subcortical regions much more than on cortical ones (Chugani, 1996). Emotionality is an ancient competence in brain evolution, so the underlying brain systems could serve as an evolutionary basis for the emergence of social and cognitive abilities (Panksepp, 2001).

In infantile development, the infant's primary sense of self is probably more affective than cognitive, and the self structure (Panksepp, 2001), or core self (Damasio, 1999), is built around the affective experience. In this context, emotional feelings are generated by various emotional systems that have an influence on the primary neural representation of the body in the upper and middle brain stem.

The internalizing process of interactional and mutual regulation dynamics is an essential factor for internal representational formation (Loewald, 1960) of an intersubjective matrix (Stolorow, Brandchaft, & Atwood, 1987). As Beebe and Lachmann discussed, "basic to representation is the capacity to order and recognize patterns, to expect what is predictable and invariant, and to create categories of these invariants" (1994, p. 131).

Interactional experiences during the first year of life are organized and stored in an implicit coding that is "non-symbolic, non-verbal, procedural, and unconscious in the sense of not being reflectively conscious" (Stern, 2004, p. 113). Implicit coding regards the areas of nonverbal communication, body movements and sensations, affect and expectations. Fogel (2003) has highlighted that this experiential system is emotional, concrete, experienced passively, and mediated by sensations of the past rather than by explicit appraisals. The implicit memory, according to Fogel (2003), has a special regulatory function that acts in an automated and unconscious way, for example, when the infant is engaged in a relational experience. Another important aspect of implicit memory is the context dependence, so that the actual context of memory concerning interpersonal situations stimulates an implicit relational knowing (Beebe, 1998; Lyons-Ruth, 1998).

From the neurobiological point of view, the infant brain is experience dependent and learns during interactions to perceive the social environment as threatening or supporting (Panksepp, 2001); in this ambit, a particular role is performed by the right hemisphere, which provides the unconscious regulation of emotional interactions with others. Schore summarized this process in a cogent way: "The capacity involves the abilities to nonconsciously yet efficiently read faces and tones and therefore intentionalities . . . to empathically resonate with states of others, to communicate emotional states and regulate interpersonal affects, and thus to cope with the ambient interpersonal stressors of early childhood" (2001, p. 45).

Observing mother and child during breastfeeding, we can highlight the pleasure the child experiences while sucking and looking into his or her mother's eyes; the mother, on the other hand, during pauses, addresses the child with a musical rhythmic voice and words like "What a good baby you are." This interactional behavior acts as an encoder on the level of implicit memory, which reactivates every time the child is in his or her mother's arms and starts sucking. There is an implicit expectation of reliving positive experiences, which settle through time, contributing to a relational knowledge.

On the contrary, if the mother is late in satisfying the baby—in giving the baby milk when he or she is hungry, for example—the child experiences a state of distress and a higher tension, which can lead to a negative expectation. If this situation of mismatch happens not frequently, it can easily be repaired. This example introduces the important principle of "disruption and repair" (Beebe & Lachmann, 1994, p. 140), which describes interactive errors that are quite common in normal dyads and can be easily repaired (Tronick & Gianino, 1986a). The success or failure of interactive errors depends on the mother's capacity to read her infant's behavior and signals, and to understand the child's underlying mental states, feelings, and wishes, which allows her to predict the infant's actions (Fonagy & Target, 1998) and to regulate his or her distress.

Returning to the previous example of distress experienced by the child, if the mother understands the child's behavior and modulates his or her state of tension—by picking the child up in her arms and rocking him or her gently—the child will be able to latch on again and continue sucking calmly. But if, on the contrary, the mother perceives the child's crying as a reproach and attaches him or her to the breast abruptly, the mismatch can intensify, reactivating previous negative experiences that could cause a disjunction between them. In fact, if violations of expectancy felt as disruptive are not too frequent, the repair can be effective, while if disruptions happen too frequently, this may lead to a chronic disjunction between the two partners.

Reparative experiences have great relevance in the child's representational world; they create a trusting expectation toward the mother, favoring the development of a sense of we-go (Emde, 2009) that starts forming from the moment the infant begins visual checking with a significant other. Quoting Emde, "the processes of 'we-ness' begin in a profound manner, soon after birth, as instantiated by newborn and early infant imitations of parental expressions and actions" (2009, p. 559).

The experience of repair increases the sense of personal efficacy and supports the expectation that it is possible to repair a possible mismatch together. Beebe and Lachmann (1994) give a great value to reparative experience, which represents an important achievement of mutual and dyadic regulation. The dyadic regulation is introjected in the structure formation of the infant's self, contributing to his or her personal flexibility and resilience to adverse situations. An experimental design of disruption and possible repair is represented by the Still Face Paradigm (Tronick et al., 1978), in which a disruption of the infant's expectations is experimentally provoked in order to evaluate the infant's capacity of repair and coping.

Mutual regulation and repair is a co-constructed dynamic characterized by constant adjustments of each partner to the other's emotional expressions, body movements, touch, and verbal and nonverbal communication. Both partners contribute to mutual regulation and, although there is a clear asymmetry because the mother has more resources and capacity, the child is an active participant in this exchange.

Interactions and mutual regulation are strongly colored by affects. While regulated interactions arouse positive affects, such as joy, pleasure, and relaxation, dysregulated interactions arouse negative affects, such as distress, anger, and high tension. These emotional interactions, according to Tronick (1998), have the potential to expand each individual's state of consciousness with important consequences in development. This reciprocal experience supports "the transition to a more inclusive and hence coherent mutual regulatory system which hinges on a 'moment of meeting' between parent and child" (Lyons-Ruth,1998, p. 286).

THE BUILDING OF THE ATTACHMENT BOND

As we have illustrated, the newborn baby has an immediate propensity for human beings and shows a strong attraction to them from the beginning. In a complementary way, the baby's signals and behaviors elicit attention and caregiving from other humans, so that proximity, physical contact, and warmth are the most probable outcome (Marvin & Britner, 2008). From this perspective, the development of the infant's attachment bond cannot be understood outside the context of the mutual and complementary behavior of his or her caregiver. During the initial period, the infant and his or her caregiver are mutually engaged. The orienting system (Parsons et al., 2010) serves the infant to focus attention on the caregiver, thus facilitating interaction and proximity. In this phase, discrimination of the caregiver is still inadequate, but the sensory systems are structured so that the baby tends to respond to humans (Bowlby, 1969, 1982).

In the development of attachment behavior, a special role is played by the auditory and visual systems. In fact, soon after birth, infants are capable of visual orientation and tracking, and of attending to auditory stimuli, especially to human voices. Reaching, grasping, and clinging are also important attachment behaviors that appear later on. Lastly, smiling and crying are additional attachment behaviors. Such behaviors serve a survival aim for the infant, by promoting caregiving and protective behaviors in his or her caregivers (Carter & Keverne, 2002).

A gradual shift happens with the recognition system (Parson et al., 2010), which favors a more selective and individuated interaction of the infant with the caregiver. Gradually the infant manifests a clear preference for his or her caregiver over others, seeking contact—especially during stress situations—and reacting with distress when he or she is separated from the attachment figure. During early years, the closeness of the infant to the attachment figure guarantees the infant a sense of security, given that he or she is confident that the caregiver will be available when needed. The secure attachment also provides a basis for the child's independent exploration (Bowlby 1969, 1982).

The caregiver's availability and capacity to respond promptly and in a contingent way to infant cues is a decisive requisite for attachment security (Ainsworth & Bell, 1974; Bakermans-Kranenburg, van IJzendoorn, & Juffer, 2003). This parenting characteristic, so important to child–mother attachment, has been defined as sensitivity. Isabella (1993, 1998) has shown that sensitivity in parenting during the first months of life is a better predictor of attachment security than its presence in later parenting. Relevant associations between sensitive parenting and secure child–mother attachments have been demonstrated only for infants' first months of life. This could explain the moderate association discovered by de Wolff and van Ijzendoorn (1997) in a meta-analysis of over 1,000 cases between types of sensitivity and attachment security, which suggests that other aspects of parenting may have an important role in the development of a secure attachment.

While parental sensitivity is crucial in the first months of life, later on, when the infant's behavior becomes more complex and physical closeness is not sufficient to cover his or her needs, other parental competences intervene in maintaining attachments. In later years, it might be important for the child that parents share his or her experiences during interactions performing a social referencing.

Another important parental competence emphasized by Fonagy is the parent's capacity "to envision the child as a mental entity to parent-child relationship, evident soon after the birth of the child, which may be critical in the child's establishment of secure attachment and mind reading" (1998, p. 140). According to Fonagy (1998), the caregiver's competence to observe and read changes in the mental state of the child is fundamental not only for the development of the child's mentalizing capacity but also for his or her secure attachment.

An interesting question regards the connection between sensitivity and mentalization, which are closely associated, even though the concept of sensitivity stresses the emotional component more and mentalization emphasizes the cognitive component.

While the concept of attachment has a broad and general theoretical framework (Bowlby, 1969, 1982), in recent contributions some specific aspects have been explored, as the one proposed by Hofer (1994, 2006). On the basis of his observations with rats, Hofer has hypothesized the existence in humans of a cluster of behavioral and physiological subprocesses that maintain the organization of attachment.

Another perspective discussed by Beebe and colleagues (2010) supports a dyadic systems view of attachment, based on recent and documented research according to which mothers and infants construct the bond together, both partners actively contributing to the exchange. Whereas affect regulation has been considered critical for the attachment, in a previous study Jaffe, Beebe, Feldstein, Crown, and Jasnow (2001) have evidenced that interactive contingency of vocal rhythm is one of the transmission mechanisms of attachment security, while excessive or insufficient contingency at 4 months of life predicts insecure attachment.

Beebe and colleagues (2010) have also subsequently observed that facial-visual engagement and touch are the most salient modalities in predicting future secure and insecure dyads. Future secure infants are able to coordinate with mothers through gaze, facial affect, and vocal affect as separate channels, and mothers coordinate touch patterns with infant engagement. Also, in the outcome of attachment insecurity, maternal and infant touch has a great influence. In fact, a mother's intrusive or less affectionate touch is frequently connected with future insecurity.

Such a shift during the child's development from emotional regulation to shared social experience would correspond to mental and brain maturation during the first years of life. As MacDonald (1992) has suggested, two different attitudes coexist in parenting; one is based on the security-separation-distress system, which is activated by the attachment bond, and the other is based on the positive-social-reward system, which is activated when the child starts exploration. In the latter situation, parents share the discoveries of the child and confirm his or her capacity. The affects involved are also different. In the first situation parents express sensitivity and protection, whereas in the second situation parents express joy, confirmation, and sharing.

During the first trimester, infants begin to manifest differential attachment and social behavior with distinct developmental pathways toward the specific patterns of attachment discovered by Ainsworth and colleagues (1978), which remain relatively stable in the subsequent years. In fact, an important distinction exists between the attachment bond, which is present in nearly every infant, and the quality of attachment (Weinfield, Sroufe, Egeland, & Carlson, 2008). Individual differences of attachment bond are connected with the specific personal history with the attachment figures and are embedded in the interaction of the infant–caregiver dyad.

Infants are genetically predisposed to express attachment behaviors toward the human figure who looks after them, usually the mother; they use the caregiver as a "haven of safety" and as a "secure base" when exploring the environment (Ainsworth et al., 1978; Bowlby, 1969, 1982). In threatening situations, a child feels stressed and turns to the caregiver for protection and reassurance. The individual pathway of attachment relationship is characterized not so much by the quantity of attachment behaviors but by the organization and quality of attachment behaviors (Sroufe & Waters, 1977).

The general categories of "secure" and "insecure" attachment relationships describe manifest behaviors of the infant and, even more significantly, the infant's perception of the availability of the caregiver when he or she needs comfort and protection. While secure infants have experienced a protective presence of the caregiver during stressing situations, insecure infants are not confident of their caregivers because they have not received comfort and protection from these caregivers, who have been distant, indifferent, inconsistent, or rejecting toward the child. The experience of sensitive care from the caregiver stimulates mental expectations in the infant, which have been defined by Bowlby (1969, 1982) as internal working models of the caregiver available to respond to signs of distress in the infant or to his or her bids for contact.

The model of parent as responsive or unresponsive is closely embedded with a complementary model of the infantile self, depending on the infant's capacity to elicit or not a response from the parent. And, of course, this has important implications for self-efficacy, self-esteem, social relationships, and for personality formation (Thompson, 2008).

The attachment behaviors have been studied in a standardized context (Ainsworth et al., 1978), which shows how an infant organizes attachment behaviors when he or she needs protection or desires to explore the environment. At the same time, Ainsworth and colleagues (1978) have studied infants' home behaviors during the first year of life. It has been observed that insecure attached children (avoidant and resistant) express more anger and noncompliance with their mother and cry more, if confronted with secure children. Observing these children's mothers, who behave in an unfocused way during the Strange Situation, they are less sensitive, more interfering, and less responsive to children's requests than mothers of secure children. In the case of mothers of avoidant children, they have manifested refusal and aversion to physical contact with their infants, expressing restricted emotion during interactions with them.

Clear connections have been evidenced between Strange Situation observations and home observations, suggesting that this could depend more on the infant's temperament than on infant–mother interaction. However, a direct link between temperament and attachment security (Belsky & Rovine, 1987; Vaughn, Bost, & van IJzendoorn, 2008) has not been demonstrated.

NEW DEVELOPMENTS IN
ATTACHMENT THEORY

We have summarized the most salient aspects of the attachment theory, which has seen interesting developments in different directions (Bretherton, 1991) in the last decades. The first direction tried to explore the individual dynamics and developmental pathways of attachment, since the taxonomic approach chosen by Ainsworth and colleagues (1978) has been useful to describe observable behaviors but can lose the infants' conscious and unconscious mental dynamics that influence their responses within the attachment relationship. As Weinfield and colleagues have recently written, "expansions of our exploration of individual differences, however, do not negate or even lessen the importance of the research done with the existing classifications" (2008, p. 92). A possible course would be deepening the concept of the internal working model, as conceptualized by Bowlby (1969, 1982), which has a specific area of functioning connected with the infant's expectations about the availability and responsiveness of his or her caregivers. These expectations are integrated in a broader representational organization that includes representation of the self, representation of attachment figures, personal interpretations of own relational experiences, and decision strategies for interacting with others (Thompson, 2008).

In this regard, the concept of the internal working model has assumed such a wide explanatory breadth, acquiring a metaphorical quality more than a well-defined theoretical construct. In this perspective, it would be useful to understand better how during the first years of life the implicit knowledge of internal working models changes, with a transition to explicit knowledge and symbolic thinking, in the perspective of self and attachment figures. If behavioral evidence has been important to validate the construct of attachment during early years, a further step could be represented by the recognition of the senses of the self and of others inside attachment dynamics during the early years of life, as has been conceptualized by Daniel Stern (1985). Even before self-awareness and language, some sense of self exists and includes sense of agency, of physical cohesion, of continuity in time, and of having intentions in mind. A similar consideration has been formulated by Slade: "The focus on classification has reified and oversimplified the meaning and dynamic function of attachment processes, resulting in an overemphasis on classification within the research domain and failure to appreciate the complexity and depth of attachment processes as they are manifested within the clinical domain" (2004, p. 272).

A second direction has tried to explore the area of multiple attachments, which was initially highlighted by Ainsworth, who wrote that "nearly all the babies in this sample who became attached to their mothers . . . became attached also to some other familiar figure—father, grandmother, or other adult in the household, or to an older sibling" (1967, p. 315). Bowlby (1969, 1982) suggested that a child during infancy builds a hierarchy of attachment relationships, in other words, a network of attachment relationships. However, as Howes and Spieker (2008) have discussed, the existence of multiple attachment figures raises complex theoretical questions.

As we have discussed in chapter 4, the child begins to interact with different figures from birth and builds specific bonds with familiar figures, in most cases with the mother and father. Of course, relationships with attachment figures are not overlapping and are shaped by specific interactions (Fox, Kimmerly, & Shafer, 1991; van Ijzendoorn & De Wolff, 1997).

It is possible that a child not only builds primary attachments with familiar figures but may develop further attachments with nonparental caregivers. The theoretical issue of multiple attachments raises different hypotheses about the mental organization of attachment representations. The first hypothesis is integrative, which means the integration of different attachment representations into one single representation with a dominant one (van IJzendoorn, Sagi, & Lambermon, 1992). The second hypothesis suggests the existence of separate and defined representations, which have different influence and strength during development. In this case, the independent attachments can be activated inside relationships with different attachment figures. Another possible hypothesis sustains that the attachment representations may be independent during the first 2 years of life and later on be integrated in a representational network.

In clinically relevant situations, two or more working models of the same attachment figure can operate alongside two or more models of self. An interesting comment by Bowlby (1973) highlights that

> when multiple models of a single figure are operative they are likely to differ in regard to their origin, their dominance and the extent to which the subject is aware of them. In a person suffering from an emotional disturbance, it is common to find that the model that has greatest influence on his feelings and behavior, is one developed during his early years and is constructed along fairly primitive lines, but that the person may be relatively unaware of while simultaneously there is operating within him a second, and perhaps radically incompatible, model, that developed later, that is much more sophisticated, and that the person is more clearly aware of and he may mistakenly assume to be dominant. (p. 205)

Another direction is represented by the relationship between attachment and temperament, which concerns different ambits. Since attachment focuses on a co-constructed relationship between the baby and the caregiver, the quality of the bond and of the emotional regulation of the infant depend on the specific relational experience, also because the strategy of attachment has the property of a control system, based on a goal-corrected partnership.

If the attachment would depend on the infant's temperament, it could create a mismatch with the caregiver, and from an evolutionistic point of view this could represent an obstacle to survival. In a wide revision of studies about temperament and attachment (Vaughn et al., 2008), it has been concluded that individual differences in attachment (security vs. insecurity) cannot be explained by a temperament construct. The connection between attachment and temperament can also be studied through genetic studies. In the first molecular study on attachment, Lakatos and colleagues (2000) have found a relative risk in disorganized children who carry the receptor (*DRD4*) 7-repeat allele. But in further studies the association between *DRD4* and disorganized attachment or attachment security has not been found (Bakermans-Kranenburg & van IJzendoorn, 2007).

In conclusion, molecular and twin studies emphasize the central importance of shared environmental factors in attachment. Twins can be similar with respect to attachment security, but this depends not on the temperament but on the similar treatment by their parents.

A further direction explores the relationship between attachment and intersubjective attitude. Attachment has a specific domain based on the attachment motivational system, while mentalizing capacity describes the ability to interpret one's personal behavior as well as others' in terms of desires, feelings, beliefs, or motivations (Fonagy et al., 2002).

The attachment bond implies interpersonal mutuality and reciprocity (Diamond, Blatt, Stayner, & Kaslow, 1991), which are necessary to share affects and intentions with the attachment figures. This point of view has been deeply discussed by Fonagy (1998), who maintained, on the basis of research evidences, that the relationship between attachment security and mentalization could be a direct one or could be mediated by pretend play, mental state language, and peer interaction.

In a previous chapter, we discussed how the caregiver's capacity to recognize and understand mental states of his or her own parents may predict the security of attachment in the child. This particular capacity of the caregiver is critical also in his or her interactions with the infant in order to stimulate the development of the infant's mentalization. The perception of the infant as an intentional being is part of sensitive caregiving, which is considered extremely relevant for infantile secure attachment. Quoting Fonagy (1998), "secure attachment in its turn provides the psychosocial basis for acquiring an understanding of mind. The secure infant feels safe predicting the mental state of the caregiver and is thus more readily able to construct a mentalized account of the caregiver's behavior" (pp. 140–141). In other words, the infant feels more secure not only because the caregiver is close and reachable but also because he or she can predict the caregiver's behaviors that are relevant for attachment bids.

When Bowlby (1969) introduced the theoretical framework of attachment, he stressed the importance of the infant's behavioral system, the aim of which is guaranteeing the closeness to the caregiver. The physical proximity promotes the infant's safety and "felt security." At that time, research about caregiver–infant communication was just beginning, and this is probably why Bowlby gave stronger emphasis to behaviors of closeness and separation, which are quite similar in other primates.

Researchers like Tomasello (1999), Hobson (2002), and Lyons-Ruth (2006) have on the contrary sustained a discontinuity between humans and nonhuman primates based on the acquired capacity to attribute intentions, beliefs, and desires to others. Hobson (2002), in particular, considered human primary forms of emotional relatedness as the basis of the intersubjective capacity, although even in monkeys there is a complex emotional communication not based only on face-to-face interactions.

As Lyons-Ruth stated: "As the explicit sharing of intentional states became a more powerful force in human evolution . . . this shift also affected the infant-parent attachment system, moving the center of the attachment relationship from the more visible behaviors emphasized by Bowlby, such as clinging and following, to primary intersubjective processes, such as the exchange of affective cues" (2006, p. 598).

The human attachment system interacts with intersubjective processes that can be activated in the context of the relationship with the attachment figures in order to check their availability or capacity to intervene and to soothe the baby. Of course, in a situation of danger the search for closeness is more automatic and immediate, while the intersubjective evaluation requires a longer and complex process not always efficient in a situation which requires a quick reaction.

From this point of view, it is possible to consider the intersubjective process as it has been conceptualized by Stern: "a basic motivational system . . . a universal way to behave in a way characteristic of a species" (2004, p. 97). So the intersubjective motivational system is like a constant barometer that gives us information about our self and others in different contexts. For example, this psychological barometer supplies information when a child interacts with parents or when he or she plays with other children, or later when a boy tries to court a girl and assesses her availability. Intersubjective processes are like a blueprint underneath every motivational system and, in the case of the attachment system, they are activated when attachment needs emerge.

We must now consider the relationship between attachment theory and psychoanalysis, which both suggest that behavior and explicit thinking are closely linked to nonconscious mental processes. At this regard, the recent emerging of a relational psychoanalysis (Benjamin, 1998; Mitchell, 1988, 2000) reduces the gap with the attachment theory, mostly because the former tends to incorporate many aspects of the attachment theory.

In the 1960s, a deep contrast between psychoanalysis and attachment theory took place, partly because, as Mitchell stressed, the language of psychoanalysis puts in the foreground internal objects, self-states, representations of self and others, while Bowlby had "a more behavioral sensibility" (2000, p. 81). Quoting Mitchell further: "The disadvantage of Bowlby's behavioral emphasis has been the relative underdevelopment of psychodynamic dimensions" (2000, p. 83).

Another important difference is how Bowlby privileged real events and relationships, while psychoanalysis has emphasized the value of fantasies, linked to drives in the past but more recently linked to imagination, thus creating the conditions for a possible rapprochement.

An important conceptual differentiation has been evidenced from the beginning (Bowlby, 1969, 1982; Sroufe, Fox, & Pancake, 1983) between the concept of attachment and the one of dependency, the latter used in psychoanalytical theory. Since attachment behaviors and expressions of dependency are quite similar—crying, clinging, and research of closeness, for example—attachment has been erroneously considered a measure of dependency.

In psychoanalytical theory, infantile dependency stresses the mental representations and dynamics of the infant who lives the relationship with the mother in a fusional way (Mahler, Pine, & Bergman, 1975). On the contrary, attachment describes infantile behavior in connection with the attachment figures.

There is a debate about the relationship between attachment and psychoanalytic theory and the fact that they cannot be considered in the same domain. However, Fonagy affirms that "attachment theory is almost unique among psychoanalytic theories in bridging the gap between general psychology and clinical psychodynamic theory" (2001a, p. 5).

THE DEVELOPMENT OF THE INTERSUBJECTIVE MATRIX

Developmental research over the past 35 years has deeply revised the traditional view of the newborn baby as described by Freud: "a neat example of a psychical system shut off from the stimuli of the external world, and able to satisfy even its nutritional requirements autistically . . . is afforded by a bird's egg with its food supply enclosed in its shell" (1911/1958, p. 219). As Trevarthen (2009) has recently written, in the last decades research has highlighted that human beings are born not as single isolated individuals but as social persons who constantly seek other persons in order to engage in reciprocal imitation and in mutual emotional regulation.

With a challenging paper, Meltzoff and Moore (1977) demonstrated that neonates are able to imitate facial gestures, thus suggesting their preadaptedness to share codes for perception and action. Neonates' imitation (Meltzoff, 2002) evidences an innate link between observation and acts execution on one hand, and the existence of a connection from birth between infant and caregiver on the other, opening interesting implications for developmental interaction and intersubjectivity.

Imitation is particularly important in nonverbal communication through the code of facial expressions and gestures. As Meltzoff clarified, "infant facial imitation is a behavior that assesses the link between observation and execution of motor actions" (2002, p. 23). Observations of neonates' behavior have shown that infants can imitate facial expressions almost immediately after birth, before any other learning. In the original study (Meltzoff & Moore, 1977), infants were able to distinguish and reproduce lip protrusion from tongue protrusion, confirming the close connection between perception and execution.

A relevant question deals with the value and meaning of imitation in neonates. Imitation in infants is not simply repetition of another person's movements and expressions, but it assumes an interpersonal meaning (Kugiumutzakis, 1999). A possible reply is that infants may use the imitation in an interpersonal field in order to probe the identity of others by checking facial features. In other words, infants use an imitation game to verify the identity of the people they meet (Meltzoff, 2002). Another possible reply connects imitative responses with particular interactive moments, with the significance of affirmation, acceptance, or commentary to the displays of the other person. In subsequent periods, infants and toddlers tend to imitate others to confirm and reinforce friendship and affiliation, creating a mutual sense of sharing and being party to.

An interesting thesis about imitation suggests that this could be a possible precursor of later acquisition of the Theory of Mind (Meltzoff, 2002). The developmental process of imitation, according to Meltzoff (2002), could then be divided into three steps:

1. Innate equivalence between self and other confirmed by imitation and by recognition of equivalence between observed and executed acts.
2. Infant's registration of the repeated relation between own behavior and corresponding mental states.
3. Infant's recognition that others act similarly to him or her and have analogous mental states, starting to infer mental states of others.

The process we have delineated may appear too complex for the neonate's mental and brain organization; in any case, it focuses on the importance of early imitation, a social cognitive performance that establishes the important rule of "like-me-ness" (Meltzoff, 2002, p. 36) in social exchange.

Considering the neurobiological basis of imitation (see chapter 1), the role of MM in imitative actions has not yet been studied in human newborns, while it has been explored in 1-week-old macaques (Ferrari, Vanderwert et al., 2008). One-week-old macaques have shown a significant suppression of the alpha rhythm that could reflect the activation of areas recorded in the central-parietal motor regions connected with MM, which is sensitive to specific stimuli at an early age (Ferrari & Fogassi, 2012). It has been also evidenced that macaque infants respond to their mothers' lip smacking by lip smacking at them (Ferrari et al., 2009) with a possible correspondence with neonatal imitative responses. On this basis, the mirror mechanisms underlying imitative behaviors could be activated at birth for emotional communication.

Could this preparedness for social interaction evidenced immediately after birth already be present before birth as a propensity to interact with others (Gallese et al., 2009)? As introduced in chapter 1, the recent research of Castiello and colleagues (2010) has evidenced that twin fetuses between the 14th and 18th week of gestation studied by using four-dimensional (4D) ultrasonography display movements that are not only directed toward the uterine wall or self-directed but also specifically directed toward the cotwin. The proportion of movements directed toward the cotwin tends to increase from the 14th to the 18th week, and the duration of movements is longer as well as the deceleration when directed toward the cotwin.

These findings suggest that "social actions" tend to emerge in fetuses during the pregnancy itself, when the context enables it, as in the case of twins. This implies a congenital social propensity that the infant could express later, after birth.

Another aspect we must consider is the intersubjective embodiment, which concerns—as we have pointed out—motor actions first of all, both during the pregnancy and in the first postnatal period, which only later on acquire a character of mental experience in a process we might call "bottom up." This process has been confirmed by Dimberg and collaborators (2000), who, with small electrodes, have registered facial muscle movements in humans during the presentation of emotional faces on a computer screen. Empathic resonance with perceived emotions is brought about unconsciously and seems to run via bodies as well as minds (Niedenthal, 2007). As de Waal wrote, "this lets the subject get 'under the skin' of the other, bodily sharing its emotions and needs" (2012, p. 123). This perception-action mechanism, described by Preston and de Waal (2002), fits with Damasio's (1994) hypothesis about somatic markers of emotions. From this point of view, there is a correlation between imitation and empathy (de Waal, 2012), confirmed by the recognition that highly empathic persons tend to express an unconscious mimicry (Charman et al., 1997). A possible mechanism underlying both empathy and imitation highlighted by de Waal (1998) is identification, whose concept differs from the psychoanalytical one because it entails bodily mapping the self into the other. Another definition of this initial exchange regards protomimesis (Zlatev, Persson, & Gärdenfors, 2005), which involves a body matching without a differentiation between the subject and the body of the other that is matched. Bodily mimesis is based on the ability to match the largely proprioceptively defined body schema.

According to Singer and Hein (2012), intersubjective interactions are characterized by developmental sequences. The first, defined as emotional contagion, happens when emotions are transferred from one person to another without any awareness that emotions originate from another person. This is typical when an infant hears another infant cry and reacts by crying, too. The second step is empathy, which implies sharing the other's emotions with the awareness of self and other distinction. The third step is compassion, which implies a feeling of concern for the other and the wish to improve the condition of the other. The last, more cognitive step is the Theory of Mind or mentalizing, which implies cognitive inference about the other's mental state. Each one of these intersubjective experiences involves different brain regions (Singer & Hein, 2012).

CONTINGENCY, SYNCHRONY,
AND INTERSUBJECTIVITY

As we have already discussed, contingency (Beebe et al., 2010) is an important feature of parent–infant interaction. Also called synchrony, it "depicts the underlying temporal structure of highly aroused moments of interpersonal exchange" (2010, p. 329), and its importance has been stressed by Stern (1977), Tronick (1989), and Trevarthen (1979). Rhythmic behaviors, matching, correspondences, and sequential mirroring, which can be expressed in different sensory-motor modalities, emerge in the interactive flow of mother–infant exchange. The temporal sharing not only facilitates the infant's self-regulation through the experience of dyadic regulation (Feldman, 2003; Tronick, 1989) but also creates the basis for the infant's subsequent capacity for intimacy and empathy.

From the second month after birth, parents and infant begin to show a temporal structure in their interaction, in terms of behavior matching and sequential relations. Specific configurations of behavior become more frequent and more repetitive, assuming an automatic character. For example, if the mother speaks to her child with a rhythmic speech structure—"You really are a good boy"—the infant moves his head with the same temporal rhythm of the mother's speech, as occurs frequently during feeding (Sander, 1985).

In this period, the sharing of social gaze between parent and baby is the expression of coordinated interactions, which can occur between 30% and 50% of the time. At the same time, mutual gaze can be integrated with parents' and infant's affectionate touch, considering that mutual gazing and matching of facial expressions are typically human. At around 3 months, parents tend to touch their baby in an affectionate way and infants tend to respond with an intentional affectionate touch.

During the period from 3 to 9 months of life, synchrony between parent and baby changes so the frequency of gaze synchrony decreases while shared attention to objects (Landry, 1995) and mutual synchrony increases. As Feldman (2007) has documented, between 3 and 9 months synchrony undergoes a temporal transformation; at around 9 months, in fact, infants reach a more complex intersubjectivity (Trevarthen & Aitken, 2001). In the same period, the lead-lag structure, where one partner leads the interaction with the other, assumes a different character: While in the first months the parent leads and the child follows, later on, interactions are characterized by mutual synchrony and adaptation, so both partners become responsive to each other's rhythms.

These early synchronic experiences are fundamental for the development of the symbolic world, the empathy, the emotional resonance, and self-regulation that influence future capacity for intimacy. As Feldman wrote: "Synchrony, as a time-bound experience, offers a unique co-regulatory framework for perpetual dialogue of self and other, for the coordination of personal timing and shared moments, and for the ongoing integration of the emerging 'dancer' and the mutual 'dance'" (2007, pp. 346–347).

Synchrony is not exclusively dyadic, it can be observed also in the family between both parents and their child. In a study by Gordon and Feldman (2008), the synchrony in the parents and child triad has been studied and no differences have been found in infants' behavior toward mother and father. Mothers display more mutuality while their partners interact with the child and tend to support fathering in a consistent way.

While in normal samples the coordination tends to increase, in high-risk populations, regardless of whether the risk is the mother's or the child's, coordination decreases (Feldman, 2007).

Synchrony is also rooted in the body, and the rhythmic structure of interactions reflects the infant's biological rhythms. In a study by Feldman (2006) on three groups of infants (extremely low birthweight, low birthweight, and full term), it has been evidenced that in the last trimester of pregnancy emerges the organization of physiological oscillators, such as the biological clock, and the sympathetic control over heart rhythm; the maturational degree of every biological rhythm predicts mother–infant synchrony. Particularly interesting is the correspondence of the mother's and infant's heart rate with a synchrony in the acceleration or deceleration of heart rate within a lag of 3 seconds (Moshe & Feldman, 2006). A further confirmation has been given by the lack of heart concordance, when reduced gaze synchrony between mother and baby was observed.

Considering the infant's intersubjectivity more specifically, Trevarthen (1974, 1979, 1998) has suggested that the infant is born with a receptive competence to catch subjective states in other persons. Infant survival, in fact, depends not only on a bond with a caregiver who guarantees his or her protection but also on maintaining an intimate companionship with the caregiver, which changes in purposes and quality of exchanges.

This hypothesis has been confirmed by many researchers (Bateson, 1971, 1979; Stern, 1971, 1974, 1977; Tronick, Als, & Adamson, 1979), who have found important similarities between mother–infant protoconversations and informal conversations between adults, also using accurate timing measurements of interventions of adult and infant. The patterns of expressive movements in protoconversation are strongly influenced by rhythmic, melodic, and harmonic principles.

Further studies have evidenced that this inborn social capacity of infants has the aim of stimulating the interest and affective sharing of parents in order to motivate companionship and cooperative awareness (Trevarthen, 1982, 1987, 1988, 1989). The infant's communicative motivation, and the correspondent intuitive parenting, are expressions of a special human preadaptedness for social learning. In fact, by 2 months, infants start to express an immediate and implicit responsive appreciation of the adult's communicative intentions and feelings, which has been called primary intersubjectivity (Trevarthen, 1977). In the caregiver–infant relationship, musicality is important, and there is evidence that infants are selectively attracted to the emotional prosody and melody of maternal speech. Infants tend to engage with a synchronous rhythm of vocalizations, body movements, and gestures to match the musical expressions of the mother.

Infants are able to elicit and sustain an interchange of expressions with caregivers and in this way their states of mind become synchronized and mutually regulated in social engagement (Trevarthen, 2009). A newborn baby can look and listen for "sympathetic expressions of an intimately attentive caretaker or partner" (Trevarthen, 2009, p. 512) and respond with an imitative play (Kugiumutzakis, Kokkanaki, Markodimitraki, & Vitalaki, 2005). When routines and mutual behaviors are learned and stabilized, infants are able to reach a contextual distinction during play between familiar persons, with whom they share the coding that has been built together, and unfamiliar persons who do not know the rules of the game (Trevarthen, 2003).

Trevarthen's (1998) conclusions underline that primary intersubjectivity, expressed through neonatal imitation and protoconversation, is based on brain circuits designed to integrate expressive movements of eye, mouth, vocal apparatus, hand, and posture. According to Trevarthen (1998), the newborn brain catches corresponding movements and expressions in a conversational caregiver through temporal and morphological markers, a hypothesis also sustained by Meltzoff (1985, 1990). In this regard, Trevarthen (1998) suggested the existence of a coupled pacemaker or neural clocks, which are critical for infant and interpersonal coordination. A confirmation of neurobiological preadaptedness of infants emerges from research, which has confirmed that by 3 months of life normal and reversed speech activate similar cortical patterns in infants and in adults (Dehaene-Lambertz, Dehaene, & Hertz-Pannier, 2002).

SECONDARY INTERSUBJECTIVITY AND JOINT ATTENTION

In the second semester of their first year of life, babies develop an increasing interest in objects and in manipulating and playing with objects. Before the end of the first year, there is the acquisition of joint interest of mother and infant for the environment, stimulated by the infant's curiosity about the mother's focus of attention on objects and her intentions. Object awareness of the infant, as well as his or her personal awareness and communicating with persons, does not proceed in the same way, but around 9 months of life it reaches an integration of new forms of cooperative intersubjectivity (person-person-object awareness), which has been called secondary intersubjectivity (Trevarthen & Hubley, 1978). Secondary intersubjectivity represents a new acquisition that allows the infant to infer and grasp intentions of others from the way they manipulate and use objects.

An important social, affective, and cognitive acquisition of secondary intersubjectivity is the capacity to engage in joint attention exchanges (Bakeman & Adamson, 1984; Frith & Frith, 2003), which require a complex monitoring of the other person's focus of attention in relation to the self and toward an object. While Trevarthen (1977) and Meltzoff (2002) gave more emphasis to overt behaviors in intersubjectivity, Stern (1985) focused his attention on infantile inner states, characterized by the infant's perception of his or her own attentional focus and that of the partner, which may correspond or may differ, stimulating in this way the recognition of the self and of the other. To avoid an excessively broad concept of intersubjectivity, three intersubjective forms have been described by Stern (1985): joint attention, joint intention, and lastly joint affect, also called affect attunement. Of particular interest is affect attunement, which is the most relevant way of sharing subjective experiences. As Stern wrote: "The infant somehow makes a match between the feeling state as experienced within and seen 'on' or 'in' another, a match that we call interaffectivity" (1985, p. 132).

Observing mother–infant interactions, we notice that mothers' responses are characterized by verbal comments (33%), exact imitations of infant behavior (19%), and attunements (48%). An interesting overlap can be seen between the concept of attunement (Stern, 1985) and the concept of markedness proposed by Gergely and Watson (1996). Gergely (2007) has evidenced that parental emotion mirroring consists of specifically marked transformed versions of the infant's motor expressive pattern. The features of markedness are characterized, for example, by exaggerated, slowed-down, or only partial motor execution, which mirrors the baby's facial-vocal expressions. As Gergely and Watson (1996) have discussed, parental affect mirroring has a special role in the development of emotional self-awareness and control in infancy. Through the social biofeedback provided by parents' marked reflection, infants reach a sensitive focus to their categorical emotion states. Confronting attunement and markedness, the former implies a parental mirroring that is performed through different behavioral channels. For example, the mother catches her child's excitement expressed by a rhythmic beating on the table and translates her baby's affect through a synchronized rhythmic movement with her body, like a dance. In this way the mother transmits to her child her understanding of the child's mental state, which has been amplified and visualized through her posture. In the case of markedness, maternal mirroring maintains the same vocal and facial channels expressed by the baby, but infantile expressions are amplified and underlined, selectively mediating the infant's sensitization to his or her internal state cue.

According to the point of view of Tomasello and colleagues (2005), Trevarthen (1979) in elaborating the intersubjective dimensions during infancy has not given enough attention to intentional reading of the other, which on the contrary is stressed by the social-cognitive theory and could represent a unique human motivation to understand intentional actions of others. This specific interaction with others, according to Tomasello and colleagues (2005), could be acquired only after infants have experienced these intentional and mental states in their own activity and then use this personal experience to simulate those of others. While in the past Tomasello has emphasized the individual capacity to read and relate to the intentions of the others, in more recent contributions he has also recognized the value of emotional relatedness, adding it to the fundamental competence of understanding and sharing intentions and goals as well. In this regard, Hobson specified that "episodes of emotional engagement—and the processes of identification that configure human self-other connectedness and differentiation to make human emotional engagement specifically intense and moving—serve not only to establish sharing, but also to re-orientate an individual in attitude" (2005, p. 704). In Hobson's (2005) thinking, the motivation to interpret others' actions suggested by Tomasello and colleagues (2005) is not enough to explain in a satisfactory way the foundation of human relations, which are moved by personal and others' feelings more. As Hobson commented: "We have a basic human response to expressions of feelings in others—a response that is more basic than thought" (2002, p. 59). In this context, this exchange could imply a more deeply psychological identification, different from the process of identification described by de Waal (2012) based on bodily identification. Hobson also took into consideration the "universal body language, more basic than the language of words, that connects us with other people *mentally*" (2002, p. 48).

It may be hypothesized that the infant's experience, strongly rooted in the body through the imitation of facial expressions and the sharing of body rhythms, translates into a connection experience with the attachment figures, which comes with emotional states of pleasantness and inner satisfaction (see also chapter 1). While emotions are strictly connected with the scenery of the body, feelings play out in the scenery of the mind (Damasio, 2003), contributing to self-regulation at a higher level. Some centuries ago the philosopher Spinoza (1677/1955) anticipated this recent neuropsychological observation with his formulation: "The object of the idea constituting the human Mind is the Body," which appears in Proposition 13 of Part II of the "Ethics."

One might wonder how these specifically human capabilities of reading and predicting the intentions of others were acquired throughout evolution. Tomasello and colleagues (2005) suggested that humans not only have competed and coordinated with others, as most of primates, but they have learned to collaborate together in activities involving shared goals and joint intentions. From a phylogenetic point of view, selection processes have favored individuals who expressed a particular competence in reading others' intentions. An interesting question deals with the origin of this specific human cognitive competence, which is not only a genetic preadaptation but is stimulated by social interactions during early infancy. In particular, as Fonagy (1998) has discussed, the capacity of caregivers to observe and read mental states of the child is fundamental in the development of the child's mentalizing acquisition. There is a close connection between maternal attitude to envision the child as an intentional being and the infantile development of mentalization.

Drawing some conclusions, we could refer to what Daniel Stern has written about the intersubjective motivational system, which "can be considered separate from and complementary to the attachment motivational system—and equally fundamental" (2004, p. 100). While attachment focuses on the experience of felt security, especially in risk and critical situations which require protection, the intersubjective system regulates the experience of being part of and belonging to, which is central inside the family and the group. While in the context of attachment the self is in the foreground in connection with the protective and caring figure, in the intersubjective context the "we" is in the foreground with a common sharing and mental intimacy. Attachment and intersubjectivity are closely related: Being attached to somebody creates the chance to develop an intersubjective connection, and an intersubjective connection with somebody can be the first step toward forming an attachment with this person.

CHAPTER 7

Parental Stress and Outcomes During Infancy and Childhood

Although studies on maternal depression and anxiety are not always concordant and are sometimes contradictory, a significant finding that emerges is that the prenatal environment can have long-standing effects on the child's development. Maternal stress during pregnancy, although its definition is quite elusive, is frequently associated with an increased risk of subsequent emotional and behavioral problems in children, as well as with lower scores in cognitive competence in the first 2 years of life (Bergman, Sarkar, O'Connor, Modi, & Glover, 2007; Talge, Neal, & Glover, 2007). It has been suggested that stress during pregnancy may account for 10% to 15% of children's later difficulties (Talge et al., 2007), although we must bear in mind that prenatal stress has not been adequately defined yet and that stress may depend on personal, familiar, social, and economic factors.

Prenatal stress, as Talge and colleagues (2007) highlighted, not only interferes with gestational age and weight at birth, but with neurobehavioral organization of the fetus and of the newborn baby. This observation confirms what Field and colleagues (2003) reported: Newborns whose mothers have high levels of anxiety display greater right frontal brain activation, a physiological profile that has been associated with the expression of negative affect (Davidson, 1998). In a sample of African American pregnant women from a low-income environment (Jacob, Byrne, & Keenan, 2009), physiological functioning of the neonates has been influenced by maternal health history as well. Individual differences have been found in biobehavioral regulation, including resting heart rate and variability (HRV), with a significantly lower HRV in the newborns of mothers who reported past major depressive disorders. Maternal life stressors are frequently associated with lower HRV, reconfirming the fact that physiological dysregulation could also interfere with children's subsequent capacity to respond to stress.

Regarding the impact of stress factors, a study by Bergman and colleagues (2007) found that prenatal stressors associated with couple conflicts account for the majority of the variance in the child's later difficulties in temperament and developmental competences. In the case of couple conflict, support from the partner, which is very reassuring for women during pregnancy, is lacking.

Only a few studies have explored the effects of adversities experienced by a whole community on pregnancy outcomes. Exposure to a California earthquake has been associated with a modest shortening of gestation (Glynn, Wadhwa, Dunkel-Schetter, Chicz-Demet, & Sandman, 2001).

A recent paper by Ramchandani, Richter, Norris, and Stein (2010) reported results of the investigation on the influence of maternal prenatal stress on children's subsequent behavioral problems in an urban South African environment. In this research, different specific stressors have been specifically investigated in the contexts of marital stress (partner violence or relationship break), family stress (fight inside family, family member with a drug problem or with disability), economic stress (serious debt, insufficient income, having to support the family economically), and community stress and violence (danger of being killed or witness to a violent crime). The first result of the study highlights the association between maternal prenatal stress in the third trimester of pregnancy and behavioral difficulties of children at 4 years of age. These data are specifically connected with an African context—in which the stressors are particularly severe— but they overlap with findings from different studies across the Unites States and Europe. The second finding, which confirms the study by Bergman and colleagues (2007), shows that stress connected to the family and the partner is the most predictive of the child's later difficulties. As the authors emphasized, there are, however, some limitations to the study since the measuring of stress has been performed only in the third trimester of pregnancy, so the negative outcome could also be associated with different stress factors in other trimesters of pregnancy or in the postnatal period.

These findings raise important hypotheses about the mechanisms of stress transmission to offspring, which could be associated with a higher level of stress hormones in mothers that can damage the maturation of the brain of the fetus. It has been suggested that the specific type of damage to the fetal neural development may be less important than the timing of stress, which is critical in provoking risk of negative outcomes, since the timing can negatively affect maturational processes and phases of the fetus (Mednick, Machon, Huttunen, & Bonett, 1988). In other studies it has been confirmed that the most severe outcomes are associated with stressors which intervene during mid-gestation (Watson, Mednick, Huttunen, & Wang, 1999). One of the most reliable hypotheses suggests that the child's outcome is mediated through the hypothalamus-pituitary-adrenal axis (HPA), which is particularly activated in mid-gestation (Gitau, Fisk, Teixeira, Cameron, & Glover, 2004).

A confirmation derives from a study in animals by Huizink, Mulder, and Buitelaar (2004) which supports the theory that exposure to prenatal stress may result in a general neurobiological vulnerability to psychopathology, rather than provoking a direct effect on a specific form of psychopathology. Research about stress in humans has important limitations because stressful events cannot be controlled as they are in animal studies, in which it is possible to randomly assign stresses to different samples of animals.

In human life, natural and humanmade disasters act as "natural experiments," according to King and Laplante (2005, p. 46), since the distribution of stress exposure is randomized. During natural disasters, exposure to stress increases the rate of psychopathology in the community, represented by depression and post-traumatic stress disorder (PTSD), disorders particularly common among victims (North, Kawasaki, Spitznagel, & Hong, 2004; Rubonis & Bickman, 1991). In most cases, symptoms disappear with time; however, a certain percentage of the population will present long-lasting difficulties (Briere & Elliott, 2000). The person's own perception and experience of the stress associated with natural disaster influences his or her later mental state, especially if one fears that the danger could take place again or if one had a severe loss or has been injured.

The degree of risk for mental health outcomes is influenced by personal and gender characteristics of victims. For example, women are more vulnerable to disaster-related psychopathology than men, and married men appear to be at lower risk while married women may be at higher risk. Persons of low income or education are also generally at higher risk. New mothers, who frequently manifest several of these high-risk factors, may be especially vulnerable to the consequences of disasters (Armenian et al., 2002; Norris et al., 2002).

After an earthquake, women may be particularly susceptible to postpartum mental disorders. Up to 25% of postpartum women experience depressive symptoms (Adams et al., 2002; Chang, Chang, Lin, & Kuo, 2002), while 29% of pregnant women manifest minor psychiatric morbidity.

A natural controlled situation in the human field has been represented by the Quebec Ice Storm of January 1998, in which more than 3 million people faced electric power failures lasting from 6 hours to more than 5 weeks. Of course, a great number of pregnant women, in various periods of pregnancy, were randomly exposed to varying degrees of storm-related consequences. The research (King & Laplante, 2005) evaluated the impact of women's exposure to the ice storm and its different consequences (threat, loss, scope, and change), as well as their subjective response to the storm. These women's children were evaluated at 2 years of age, from a cognitive point of view: It has been evidenced that, in the cases of maternal moderate to high prenatal stress, the children have manifested decreased intellectual competence and language functioning. From a cognitive point of view, children have presented lower scores if mothers were exposed to the ice storm during their first or second trimester of pregnancy. Other results have also reported a negative effect on perinatal outcomes, on infant temperament, on behavioral and emotional functioning, and even on physical growth of children exposed to maternal stress during gestation.

More recently, another study (Harville, Xiong, Pridjian, Elkind-Hirsch, & Buekens, 2011) was performed after Hurricane Katrina, which struck the US Gulf Coast on August 2005. A group of pregnant women during the hurricane were interviewed at delivery and 2 months postpartum in order to assess depressive symptoms (with the Edinburgh Depression Scale) and posttraumatic symptoms (with the Posttraumatic Stress Checklist). Women have been interviewed about their experience of the hurricane with questions that explore threat, illness, loss, and damage. Results have shown that Black women and women with less education are more likely to have had a serious experience of the hurricane: 18% of the total sample have met the criteria for depression and 13% for PTSD at 2 months postpartum. The personal experience that one's life is in danger is associated with depression and PTSD, as it is for injuries to family members and severe damage on property. Such observations strongly support the hypothesis that prenatal development is characterized by sensitive periods of maturation of the fetus, which is particularly vulnerable to the persistent and severe effects of environmental stressors.

In the postpartum period, women who have experienced the impact of severe natural disasters are at an increased risk for mental health problems, but overall rates of depression and PTSD do not seem to be higher than in studies of the general population.

The effect of maternal antenatal stress on children, especially the state of fear, can be moderated by a positive postnatal upbringing and a secure bond with parents, as has been shown in the research by Bergman, Sarkar, Glover, and O'Connor (2008). These results—as the authors have discussed—raise developmental questions about the timing and efficacy of interventions to reduce the adverse effects of antenatal stress exposure.

To explain the impact of prenatal stress, the fetal programming, which is the fetus's physiological adaptation to the characteristics of the intrauterine environment, should be considered. Such physiological adaptation during pregnancy may then not be optimally suited for the postnatal environment, creating a health vulnerability of the offspring later in life. In animal studies, offspring of nutrient-restricted pregnant dams have atypically high percentages of body fat and weight at 9 months of age, if they are allowed to feed freely after birth (Desai, Gayle, Babu, & Ross, 2005).

As we have already discussed, research on prenatal stress has focused on the HPA in both mother and child as the primary biological mechanism underlying the long-term effects of prenatal stress. The HPA axis is a complex system that not only maintains a circadian rhythm but favors the adaptation of mammals to changes in their environment. The system is built in order to respond rapidly to stressful stimuli, and then it returns to the baseline state of homeostasis. Under stimulatory conditions, neurons in the paraventricular nucleus (PVN) of the hypothalamus secrete corticotropin-releasing hormone (CRH) into the circulation. In the anterior pituitary, CRH induces production of adrenocorticotropin (ACTH), which is released into the circulation to stimulate production of glucocorticoids from the adrenal cortex (cortisol in human and corticosterone in rat) (figure 7.1).

Elevated serum glucocorticoids provide the physiological appropriate context for an adaptive stress response but also immediately interact with corticoid recep-

FIGURE 7.1.   In chronic stress, levels of cortisol are low, levels of corticotropin-releasing factor (CRH) are high, and the sensitivity of the negative feedback system of the hypothalamic-pituitary-adrenal axis (HPA) is increased. (© Cristina Trentini; printed with permission)

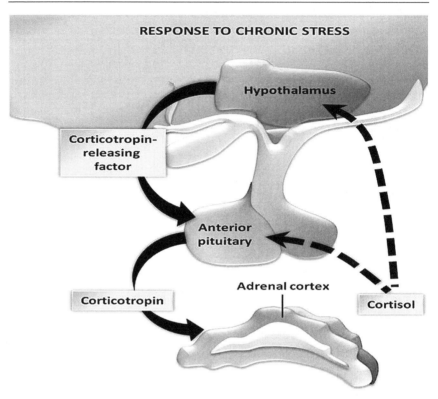

tors to inhibit the stress response via negative feedback. Negative consequences of chronic exposure to stress associated with high levels of glucocorticoids are well defined, such as structural damage to fundamental brain regions like the hippocampus.

The aim of HPA axis is to be rapidly activated to respond to stress but also to conclude the stress response as rapidly as possible. The response of the stress system is associated with relevant behavioral outcomes (Gunnar, 2001) and is susceptible—as animal studies have demonstrated (Levine, 2005)—to the long-term effects of early developmental experience. In several animal species, adverse conditions in early caregiving are associated with permanent dysfunction of the HPA axis, which has the aim of preserving physical health as well as mobilizing energy stores and promoting vigilance under stress and threat conditions (Gunnar, 2003). Lower cortisol levels have been observed among infants of mothers who developed PTSD in response to the September 11 attacks, compared to infants of mothers who did not develop PTSD (Yehuda et al., 2005). Lower cortisol levels are evident in infants born from mothers exposed to stress in their third trimesters, unlike in infants of mothers with milder stress or anxiety.

MECHANISMS OF TRANSMISSION OF STRESS DURING PREGNANCY

The study of the consequences of trauma during pregnancy and of underlying mechanisms of action on the offspring introduces an interesting perspective related to nature–nurture interaction. While in the past the effect of environment on genetic mechanisms was minimized, in recent years research has shown that epigenetic mechanisms, influenced by different factors, including environmental aspects (Jaenisch & Bird, 2003), intervene on gene expression, modulating genetic effects.

A notable definition of epigenetics has been proposed by Goldberg, Allis, and Bernstein (2007). According to them, epigenetics "in a broad sense, is a bridge between genotype and phenotype—a phenomenon that changes the final outcome of a locus or chromosome without changing the underlying DNA sequence" (2007, p. 635).

The unfolding of developmental processes from genotype to phenotype is context dependent and initiates during the maturation of the embryo/fetus, which is sensitive and responds to conditions of the internal or external environment during specific periods of cellular proliferation, differentiation, and maturation. It has been recognized that intrauterine environment may produce structural and functional modifications of the fetus, especially during critical periods of pregnancy when intrauterine environment performs a greater influence. The intrauterine environment affects the condition of the fetus through complex underlying physiological mechanisms, which can have long-term health effects, sometimes mediated by the physiology of birth and by subsequent postnatal conditions, which can increase or mitigate the effects of prenatal influences.

Illustrating epigenetic mechanisms, the recognition started with research on the effects of maternal diet on the coat color of the offspring of a particular species of mouse (Waterland & Jirtle, 2003). The findings of this research have shown that epigenetic mechanisms are connected to a biochemical process of methylation, which alters gene expression. The research has included evidence that the color of mouse hair is connected to variations in the methylation of a promoter on a particular gene and has found that methyl supplementation is associated with hair color changes that could be the consequence of the increased methylation at a particular gene locus. A quite different environmental stimulus has been studied by Cancedda and colleagues (2004), who have found that raising mice in an enriched sensory-motor environment stimulates the early maturation of the visual system with a precocious development of visual acuity, which is connected with altered gene expression leading to an increase of BDNF protein in the visual cortex of the brain. At the same time they have observed that more stimulated pups have experienced higher levels of licking behavior provided by adult females.

These animal studies have confirmed the great importance of environmental epigenetic mechanisms, whose effects are too complex to investigate in humans, as it is quite difficult to perform an experimental set in order to separate prenatal and postnatal environmental influences from genetic effects. A possible solution is represented by a research strategy in animals, more similar to human upbringing experiences, like the ones performed by Michael Meaney and his colleagues (Cameron et al., 2005; Champagne et al., 2004; Weaver et al., 2004). Their research is based on the observation that lactating mother rats express important differences in the degree of licking and grooming their offspring, independently from the amount of time spent with the pups. These individual differences in maternal nurturing behavior are associated with variations in the neurotransmitter dopamine in the brain of the offspring, demonstrating that changes in maternal behavior are associated with differences in the offspring's neuroendocrine response to stress and behavior.

Meaney and colleagues have also proposed a model that could explain the long-term effects of different early maternal caregiving patterns on the offspring later. Mothers that are more nurturing have adult offspring, which manifests less anxiety in behavior with reduced and shorter HPA responses to stressors (Caldji, Diorio, & Meaney, 2000; Zhang, Parent, Weaver, & Meaney, 2004). At the same time Weaver and colleagues (2004) have shown that this consistent maternal nurturing is associated with less methylation of the promoter region of the glucocorticoid receptor (GR) gene in the hippocampus of the offspring. Methylation blocks transcription of GR receptors and, on the contrary, decreased methylation increases the transcription, implying more feedback control of the HPA axis, less corticosterone response to stress, and less anxious behavior.

A relevant question is whether the endocrine responses in the behavior of the offspring are connected to their biological endowment or to their social rearing. The results of research clearly show that the effects are a consequence of the upbringing environment and not their biological inheritance.

Subsequently, the research team led by Michael Meaney (2004) has tried to determine how the specificity of rearing could modify the organism of the offspring so that behavioral consequences can be transmitted to the next generation until adult life. The research has shown that maternal behavior modifies the endocrine response to stress in a lasting way, through tissue-specific effects on gene expression (Weaver et al., 2004). An important question for future research was raised by Goldberg and colleagues, who highlighted that "many challenges remain, particularly with regard to the propagation of epigenetic information through cellular division and differentiation" (2007, p. 638).

As we have already discussed, during and after a traumatic experience, two steroid receptors mediate HPA negative feedback in the brain. The glucocorticoid receptor (GR) with low-affinity binding of glucocorticoids intervenes within the range of the stress response. The mineralocorticoid receptor (MR) has higher affinity to glucocorticoids and is vital in controlling basal HPA tone and the circadian rhythm. While the PVN predominantly expresses GR, both receptors are particularly present in the hippocampus, which is implicated in mediating the neuronal aspects of glucocorticoid feedback in the brain. Therefore, it is possible to suggest that dysfunction in either receptor system could severely affect the capacity of adaptation to the environment. In the model of epigenetic effects of prenatal stress on the hippocampal glucocorticoid receptors of the child, prenatal stress provokes increased methylation for the promoter region of the glucocorticoid receptor in the hippocampus. The consequences are less transcription, fewer receptors, less feedback control, and a greater cortisol response to stress (Talge et al., 2007).

In the early 21st century, the UC Irvine Development, Health and Disease Research Program, directed by Wadhwa, started to explore the interaction between biological, behavioral, and social context in human pregnancy, with the aim of studying the impact of maternal psychosocial stress on fetal maturation, on birth outcomes, and on subsequent newborn, infant, and child developmental outcomes. These studies suggested that maternal psychosocial stress exposure during pregnancy is significantly and independently associated with increased risk of adverse pregnancy and birth outcomes related to preterm birth and poor fetal growth, consequences partially mediated by stress-related alterations in maternal–placental–fetal (MPF) endocrine and immune processes.

More recent studies have further investigated the long-term effects of prenatal psychosocial stress exposure on adult physiology and health. A large number of studies of fetal programming have focused on the critical role of prenatal and perinatal nutrition, producing important findings (Langley-Evans & McMullen, 2010). On this basis it is possible to suggest that significant environmental conditions could have stimulated evolutionary selection, including not only a variation in nutrition but also stress conditions, which may impact the physical integrity and survival of human beings. For this reason a bidirectional interaction between nutrition and stress has emerged by research evidence supporting the idea that the consequences of stress on target tissues of either are moderated by eating (Epel, Lapidus, McEwen, & Brownell, 2001).

These studies adopted (Entringer, Buss, & Wadhwa, 2010) a prenatal stress perspective, a specific model for exploring interactions in early development since the maturing fetus receives and registers information about the maternal environment through most of the biological systems that later will mediate adaptation to endogenous and exogenous challenges. Subsequently the research has tried to investigate whether these long-term effects are independent from other intervening obstetric, newborn, and childhood risk factors. Another aim of the research has tried to explore whether these effects have a specific character or influence a range of outcomes, clarifying whether these effects are necessarily mediated by unfavorable birth outcomes.

In animals, experimental studies suggest that maternal exposure to psychosocial stress during pregnancy can independently provoke long-term effects on sev-

FIGURE 7.2.   Conceptual framework of a human biobehavioral model of prenatal stress and subsequent outcomes. (© Cristina Trentini; printed with permission)

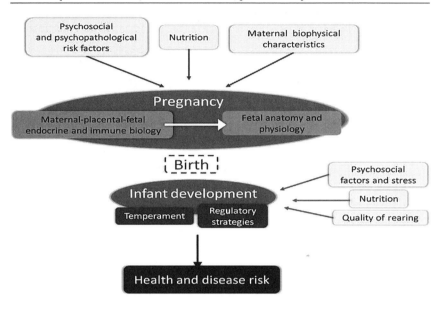

eral central and peripheral body systems in the offspring (Bowman et al., 2004). In humans, a study population (Entringer et al., 2010) has been carried out in younger as opposed to older adults, in order to focus on predisease markers of physiological dysregulation of metabolic, endocrine, and immune systems, as early predictors of disease susceptibility. Results have indicated that young adults exposed during intrauterine life to maternal psychosocial stress consistently exhibit significant dysregulation of all physiological parameters, with an increased risk of developing clinical disorders. It has also been shown that altered endocrine function, characterized by increased adrenocorticotrophic hormone (ACTH) and reduced cortisol levels during pharmacological and psychological stimulation, and impaired prefrontal cortex (PFC)–related cognitive performance (figure 7.2) are associated with stress exposure during intrauterine life. Consistent with the findings on cognitive competence are data from longitudinal studies on the long-term effects of prenatal stress (anxiety) on child brain morphology with gray matter reduction (Buss, Davis, Muftuler, Head, & Sandman, 2010).

These findings in humans suggest that the exposure to prenatal psychosocial stress during pregnancy may increase long-term risk of negative physiological and cognitive outcomes. Adopting the fetal programming perspective, underlying mechanisms have been explored, which explain the connection between different intrauterine adverse factors and multiple effects on physiological systems in the maturing fetus. It has been hypothesized that stress-related maternal–placental–fetal endocrine and immune processes during pregnancy may represent an underlying mechanism because they respond to many classes of intrauterine perturbations influencing multiple targets of fetal programming (Wadhwa, 2005). Thus, biological perturbations can occur in different periods of pregnancy and with different intensity, producing possible modifications of biological structure of the fetus, with consistent and increasing dysfunctions and alterations in the physiological systems. These modifications may have an impact on the physiological responsivity of these systems to environmental and endogenous influences, later on during infancy and childhood.

Glucocorticoid metabolism (cortisol in humans) (Harris & Seckl, 2010) is considered a critical endocrine mediator of fetal programming, with an emphasis on not only hormone production but also hormone action mediated by tissue-specific glucocorticoid receptor expression, sensitivity, and affinity and by maternal–fetal transfer. Other studies on maternal stress during pregnancy have evidenced an increase of cortisol and corticotropin-releasing hormone levels in the mother and the fetus (Field et al., 2004; Weinstock, 2008). Fetal cortisol concentrations are directly related to maternal concentrations, with a maternal: fetal ratio of 12:1 (Gitau, Cameron, Fisk, & Glover, 1998). It has been documented that 10%–20% of maternal cortisol passes through the placenta, and fetal cortisol levels are significantly correlated with maternal levels (Gitau et al., 2001).

In healthy adaptive responses to stress, normal circulating levels of cortisol are necessary, which is, as we have already illustrated, a corticosteroid hormone or glucocorticoid produced by the adrenal cortex that is often referred to as the stress hormone, involved in the physiological response to stress and anxiety. On the other hand, unusually high (or in rare cases, unusually low) levels of cortisol indicate a maladaptive response to stress that could provoke various pathologies.

As in animal studies, chronically high levels of cortisol can have negative effects on human brain structure and function (Hillshouse & Grammatopoulos, 2002), which influence infants' behavior. For example, infants of mothers with elevated prenatal cortisol have manifested increased infantile fussiness and difficult behavior (Davis et al., 2007; de Weerth, van Hees, & Buitelaar, 2003). Elevated prenatal maternal cortisol at 30–32 weeks gestation is significantly associated with maternal reports of infant negative temperamental reactivity (Davis et al., 2007). Higher levels of third-trimester maternal cortisol predict increased fussing, crying, and negative facial expressions, particularly during the first 2 months after delivery. And, in turn, infants with negative temperament are more likely to become behaviorally inhibited children, as highlighted by a longitudinal study (Pfeifer, Fisk, Teixerira, Cameron, & Glover, 2002).

Elevated prenatal cortisol has also been related to later emotional and cognitive consequences, including the increased risk of anxiety and depression as well as attentional deficits/hyperactivity and language delays (Talge et al., 2007). Although many of these findings are independent from the effects of postpartum depression and anxiety, the transmission mechanisms are quite complex because childhood problems may be mediated not only by prenatal modifications but also by elevated infant cortisol after birth. Among humans, nonexperimental research has shown that exposure to excessive amounts of cortisol in utero can affect the developing brain and spinal cord (Yu, Lee, Lee, & Son, 2004).

Confirmation derives from studies in rats and nonhuman primates about prenatal stress (Darnaudery & Maccari, 2008) artificially stimulating the HPA axis, and considering the timing of the stress, its intensity, duration, and the gender of the offspring. Structural changes have been evidenced in the hippocampus, the frontal cortex, the amygdala, and the nucleus accumbens of animals. Maternal stress not only increases corticosteroid levels in the pup fetal brain but also decreases fetal testosterone in males and alters catecholamine metabolism in female fetuses (Weinstock, 2007). Learning deficits related to neurogenesis and dendritic spine density in the prefrontal cortex and hippocampus are more readily evidenced in prenatally stressed pup males, while anxiety, depression, and an increased response of the HPA axis to stress are more prevalent in females.

A new and interesting perspective on the consequences of stress on the organism highlights the role of telomeres, which are specialized chromatin structures that protect the ends of linear chromosomes from DNA repair and degradation activities (Blasco, 2005). Critically short telomeres or telomeres lacking some telomere-binding proteins lose their functionality and are processed as DNA breaks, generating chromosome fusion. In the absence of a compensatory mechanism, dividing cells undergo gradual telomere erosion.

Telomere function has been studied, showing an accelerated telomere shortening in response to life stress (Epel et al., 2004). The team of Blackburn and colleagues at the University of California have shown through numerous and innovative studies that there are links between chronic stress and indices of poor health, including risk factors for cardiovascular disease and poorer immune function. Nevertheless, the exact mechanisms of how stress gets "under the skin" (Epel et al., 2004, p. 17312), as they write, remain difficult to explain. On this basis, these researchers have investigated the hypothesis that stress could have an impact on health by modulating the rate of cellular aging. They have provided evidence that psychological stress is significantly associated with higher oxidative stress, lower telomerase activity, and shorter telomere length, which influence cell senescence and longevity. Women with the highest levels of perceived stress have shorter telomeres compared to low-stress women. These findings have great implications for explaining how stress, at the cellular level, may influence an earlier onset of age-related diseases.

The association between stress during pregnancy and effects on telomeres in humans has only recently been explored (Entringer et al., 2011). The association in adults of psychosocial stress or stress biomarkers with leukocyte telomere length (LTL), which predicts age-related disease onset and mortality, suggests that telomere biology may represent a possible underlying mechanism which links stress and health outcomes. It is, however, still unclear whether stress exposure during intrauterine life can produce variations in LTL, thus promoting a susceptibility to pathology.

The research team lead by Blackburn has tested the hypothesis that stress exposure during intrauterine life could be associated with shorter telomeres later in adult life, after accounting for the effects of other factors on LTL. LTL has been assessed in a group of healthy young adults, half of whom were offspring of mothers who had experienced severe stress during pregnancy (prenatal stress group [PSG]), while the other half were offspring of mothers with a healthy pregnancy without stressing events (comparison group [CG]). Research has confirmed that prenatal stress exposure has significantly predicted subsequent adult telomere length in the offspring. This important study (Entringer et al., 2011) has provided clear evidence in humans of an association between prenatal stress exposure and subsequent shorter telomere length, describing an important biological mechanism which could explain the prenatal origins of adult health and disease risk.

From these observations it is possible to suggest that environment and particularly stress have different epigenetic pathways in influencing the genes, confirming that a rigid separation of nature and nurture does not correspond to the reality of human life. As Michael Rutter wrote: "Genes affect the liability to experience different forms of environments and they influence susceptibility to different environments but, equally, environments affect gene expression" (2006, p. 218).

STRESS AND PSYCHOSOCIAL RISK
IN INFANTILE DEVELOPMENT

Studies in highly stressed families have shown that infants raised in these contexts present difficulties in the attachment process, and they do not fit into the three categories of attachment patterns described by Mary Ainsworth and colleagues (1978). On the basis of these observations, Main and Solomon (1990) have developed a fourth category of infantile attachment defined as disorganized/disoriented: Infants manifest disoriented and conflicted behaviors in the presence of parent. The disorientation and disorganization of behavior is connected to the simultaneous need of infants to approach the parent for protection and to flee their parent for fear (Main & Hesse, 1990). While in a normal sample the percentage of disorganization in infants is 14% (van IJzendoorn, Schuengel, & Bakermans-Kranenburg, 1999), in low economic status samples the percentage is 24%. The presence of risk factors in the family can have consequences on infantile disorganized attachment depending on the specific risk. Studies have documented that 83% of abused and neglected infants manifest disorganized attachment toward the parent (Carlson, Cicchetti, Barnett, & Braunwald, 1989), and in a more recent study by Cicchetti, Rogosh, and Toth (2006), this percentage reached 90%.

This framework was further expanded by Lyons-Ruth (2006), who evidenced that absence of caregiver intervention and protection can also provoke infant disorganization. In this case, the absence of caregiving may lead to disorganization of attachment because the caregiver's regulation of the infant's fearful state is lacking. Other types of family risk have also been investigated: Maternal substance abuse, for example, is more frequently associated with infantile disorganization if compared with normal samples (Melnick, Finger, Hans, Pathrick, & Lyons-Ruth, 2008). The impact of mothers who have experienced a previous stillbirth has also been investigated, demonstrating a higher rate of disorganization in infantile attachment, compared with a normal sample (Hughes, Turton, Hopper, McGauley, & Fonagy, 2001).

The maternal state of mind affects the development of infantile attachment in a deep way and, from this perspective, the association between the hostile-helpless (HH) state of mind of mothers (Lyons-Ruth, Yellin, Melnick, & Atwood, 2005) or their unresolved patterns of attachment and infantile development of attachment has been studied. Parents who are still traumatized (Hesse & Main, 2006) may express, during the interaction with the child, an inexplicable frightened and frightening behavior. Hesse and Main (2006) have identified six parental behaviors connected with this parental frightened or frightening state, which can be observed while parents are engaged with the infant: threatening expression, frightened expression, dissociative manifestations, timid or deferential behavior, spousal or romantic attitude, and lastly, disorganized behavior.

As we have discussed, Hesse and Main (2006) specifically emphasized the impact of frightened parental behaviors, which produce a conflict in the infant who is unable to organize a coherent attachment strategy. This model was expanded by Lyons-Ruth, Bronfman, and Atwood (1999), who suggest that the infantile disorganization is not only associated with frightened parental behavior but also with contradictory and disrupted forms of affective interactive communication. According to the latter model, the contradictory and disrupted communication interferes with the organization of a coherent strategy of attachment because of parental negative-intrusive behavior, role confusion, withdrawal, affective communicative errors, and disorientation (Lyons-Ruth & Jacobvitz, 2008). The association between maternal disrupted affective communication and infantile attachment disorganization has been confirmed by many studies (Gervai et al., 2007; Goldberg, Benoit, Blokland, & Madigan, 2003; Grienenberger, Kelly, & Slade, 2005; Madigan, Moran, & Pederson, 2006). Maternal hypervigilance (Jaffe et al., 2001), which is a sign of maternal distress and anxiety, is also a predictor of attachment disorganization at 18 months and can be evidenced in mother–infant tight vocal rhythm tracking. While maternal disrupted affective communication is associated with infantile disorganization, this association has not been observed in the presence of maternal insensitivity (van IJzendoorn et al., 1999).

In a recent study by Beebe and colleagues (2010), a detailed microanalysis of mother–infant face-to-face communication was carried out, in order to evidence the dynamics of attachment transmission between mother and infant. In particular, the study explores mother and infant self-contingency (adjustment of maternal behavior correlated to her prior behavior), interactive contingency (contingent coordination), and other modalities of behavior (affect, visual attention, touch, spatial orientation) that may be involved in attachment formation and transmission, starting at 4 months of age and evaluating 12-month attachment, the latter assessed by the Strange Situation (Ainsworth et al., 1978). Considering dyads of future disorganized (D) infants, the study evidenced that 4-month-old infants are more likely males and show complex forms of emotional distress and dysregulation consisting in facial and vocal distress, discrepant facial and vocal affect, lowered engagement self-contingency, and less touching of one's own skin for self-regulation.

The behavior of mothers of future D babies is characterized by excessive gazing away (20% of the time) from the infant's face, increased looming head movements, frequent positive/surprise expressions while infants are distressed, lowered emotional coordination, heightened maternal facial self-contingency, and lowered maternal contingent touch coordination with the infant's touch. On the basis of Beebe and colleagues' data (2010), it has been evidenced that the dyad of future D children manifests an affective divergence and conflict, confirming also the theoretical framework of attachment as a dyadic system built by both mother and infant.

It is possible to infer that divergent behaviors of mothers may create a confusion in infants who, according to Beebe and collaborators (2010), could experience difficulty with feeling recognized by the mother and at the same time have difficulty understanding their mother's mind. The last consequence is the difficulty of infants with knowing themselves and having a possible sense of ownership of their own body.

These studies about the origin of attachment disorganization could further contribute to the understanding of the dynamics of ego-alien experiences, observed by Donald Winnicott in the clinical material, as a consequence of mother's "madness" (1969, p. 382). In his observation, Winnicott witnessed the child's "state of being possessed by a mother's madness when his own mother goes mad in front of him" (1969, p. 382). Winnicott described the communicative disruption in the interaction between mother and baby and the intrusiveness of maternal fears and anxieties, which are encoded into the nonconscious, implicit, procedural representations of the infant and may interfere with his or her development (Lyons-Ruth, 2006). When "maternal care is not good enough, then the infant does not really come into existence, since there is no continuity of being; instead the personality becomes built on the basis of reactions to environmental impingement" (Winnicott, 1960, p. 594), remaining an unmetabolized experience that is settled before the acquisition of explicit functioning associated with conscious images and symbols.

If the caregiver is distant and inaccessible, rejecting, communicating in a contradictory and confusing way, and lastly frightened and frightening, the infant experiences a psychobiological stress that interferes with the development of the attachment strategy and creates a disorganization based on the use of dissociative defenses rooted in the right brain. As Schore wrote: "The infant's psychobiological reaction to severe interpersonal stressors comprises two separate response patterns, hyperarousal and dissociation" (2010, p. 29).

The right hemisphere, which is dominant in human infants during the first year of life (Howard & Reggia, 2007) is activated when infants are exposed to a traumatic event (Bradley, Cuthberth, & Lang, 1996). As documented by research (Schore, 2010, 2011), the orbitofrontal cortex of the right hemisphere particularly intervenes in the attachment organization.

During their first months of life, infants activate the right hemisphere when they are exposed to a woman's face (Tzourio-Mazoyer et al., 2002). This was confirmed by Grossmann, Johnson, Farroni, and Csibra (2007) in an EEG study: In 4-month-old infants presented with a gazing female face, Grossmann's study has evidenced enhanced gamma electrical activity in the right prefrontal area.

According to Iacoboni and Dapretto (2006), the right hemisphere is also involved with the visual mirror neurons system, which is implicated in the infant's gazing. These observations about the central role of the right hemisphere during early periods of life have not been observed by a recent EEG study performed by Ferrari and colleagues (2012) on newborn macaques while they observe and produce facial gestures. However, a possible limitation in investigating the involvement of the two hemispheres in macaques could be associated with the restricted number of electrodes used in the experiment (personal communication by Ferrari).

Of course, every infant reacts to stress according to his or her own personal mental and neurobiological organization, which is conditioned also by gender. An interesting hypothesis about gender differences in reaction to threat has been proposed (Taylor et al., 2000): While "fight-flight" behaviors are stronger in males, "tend-befriend" responses are stronger in females. This hypothesis was further confirmed by David and Lyons-Ruth (2005), who observed that female infants confronted with maternal frightening and withdrawing behavior continue to seek a contact with the mother, while male infants show a disorganized conflict behavior and avoidance. This confirms Weinberg's observations (1992) about gender differences in infantile reaction to stressful situations with mothers.

While dissociation and hyperarousal are the most frequent infantile reactions to traumatic stress in the case of infant exposure to marital conflict of parents, a possible consequence is the role reversal of parents–infant interaction. While in typical families parents are focused on the child's needs, in role reversal interaction the parent is absorbed in his or her personal needs and for this reason he or she is insensitive and unresponsive to the child's needs (Macfie, Houts, Pressel, & Cox, 2008). As Sroufe, Egeland, Carlson, and Collins highlighted, "the parent is abdicating the parental role and the child is treated as a partner, agemate, or caregiver" (2005, p. 117).

The child's development is negatively influenced by parental role reversal because the parent, who has trouble with his or her partner, may shift his or her need of intimacy and protection to the child. The parent derives comfort and security from the child, who is perceived as an extension of the self who is necessary for parental self-regulation. From a psychodynamic point of view, the child is much too involved in the parent's life and has difficulties in maintaining a personal space, sometimes exposed to abnormal adultomorphic stimulations in the sexual area as well. A possible consequence is the development of a false self or of a confused self without clear boundaries.

A research study by Macfie and colleagues (2008) evidenced a differential pathway to role reversal for fathers and mothers. In the case of a mother's conflict behavior toward the father, the latter manifests a role reversal toward the child, while in the case of a father's conflict behavior toward the mother, the former manifests a withdrawal from her and the latter manifests a role reversal with the child. In the presence of a marital conflict, other dynamics could also be evidenced, like, for example, the spillover hypothesis. In this dynamic, the negative and aggressive affects connected with marital conflict could spill over to the parent–child relationship, creating tensions and conflicts (Coiro & Emery, 1998; Cox, Paley, & Harter, 2001). Another dynamic could be based on disengaged or distracted parenting stimulated by marital conflict, and in this case the parent is not able to use his or her psychological resources to care for the child (Katz & Gottman, 1996). Parental conflict during infancy may also affect developing physiological regulatory systems of the infant, like cardiac vagal tone, typically indexed by respiratory sinus arrhythmia (RSA), which is suggested to play a central role in the organization of behavior, emotion, and attention. RSA regulation (including measures of baseline RSA levels and RSA reactivity) has been found to be related to infants' soothability, attentional control, and emotion regulation (Stifter & Corey, 2001; Suess, Porges, & Plude, 1994), which perform an important influence on later behavioral and emotional adjustment. There are various mechanisms to explain how parental conflict could be related to the development of RSA regulation: Not only genetic factors but parental conflict as well may directly increase demands on infants to regulate arousal, also because higher conflict between parents may interfere with parental abilities to respond sensitively to infants' needs and support their regulation. Because vagal tone is suggested to have evolved to mediate social affiliation behaviors (Porges, 2007) and because the development of RSA is sensitive to socialization experiences from 3 to 12 months of age (Field, Fox, Pickens, & Nawrocki, 1995; Propper et al., 2008), the current research is guided by the theory that parent conflict is associated with RSA dysregulation as a function of the possible spillover that parental conflict may have on parenting behavior. Infants' self-regulation mechanisms are initially immature, and the development of effective RSA regulation may be a function of experiences of interactive protection by parents during early infancy (Feldman, Greenbaum, & Yirmiya, 1999; Propper & Moore, 2006). In recent research (Moore, 2010), the association between parent conflict and infants' vagal tone functioning has been investigated. In the study, mothers who reported levels of parent conflict and their 6-month-old male and female infants' respiratory sinus arrhythmia (RSA) have been measured in the Still-Face Paradigm (SFP). Higher parent conflict is associated with lower RSA at baseline and each episode of the SFP. Findings suggest atypical RSA regulation and reliance on self-regulation for infants in families with moderate levels of parent conflict.

MALTREATING AND NEGLECTING FAMILIES AND INFANTILE OUTCOMES

Studies of parent–child interactions among maltreating families have revealed maladaptive behaviors, compared to nonmaltreating families. Maltreating parents manifest less satisfaction with their children as they perceive infant rearing as more conflictual and less gratifying and use more controlling educational methods. Abusive parents do not support and sometimes interfere in the development of their children's autonomy, obliging them to live in an isolated family context (Azar, 2002; Rogosch, Cicchetti, Shields, & Toth, 1995; Trickett, Aber, Carlson, & Cicchetti, 1991; Trickett & Sussman,1988). Observing behaviors of abusive parents, they show fewer physical and verbal behaviors to attract and direct their children's attention (Alessandri, 1992; Bousha & Twentyman, 1984) and show inadequate expectations toward their child (Putallaz, Costanzo, Grimes, & Sherman, 1998), as they attribute more negative intentions to their child's behavior in comparison to nonmaltreating parents (Dixon, Hamilton-Giachritsis, & Browne, 2005; Zeanah & Zeanah, 1989).

The parent–infant interaction influences the building of attachment among maltreated infants, as has been demonstrated by the Strange Situation paradigm (Ainsworth & Wittig, 1969), with more consistent insecure attachments to caregivers in maltreated infants than in nonmaltreated infants (Cicchetti & Barnett, 1991; Crittenden, 1985; Egeland & Sroufe, 1981; Lamb, Gaensbauer, Malkin, & Schultz, 1985; Schneider-Rosen, Braunwald, Carlson, & Cicchetti, 1985). Utilizing the traditional classification for attachment relationships—in which children may be classified as Type A, anxious avoidant; Type B, securely attached; or Type C, anxious resistant (Ainsworth et al., 1978)—these early studies have found that two-thirds of maltreated infants have displayed insecure attachment (Types A or C), compared with the distribution in nonmaltreated infants (Schneider-Rosen et al., 1985; Youngblade & Belsky, 1989).

As we have already discussed, the attachment behaviors of maltreated children have been frequently described as difficult to fit within this original attachment classification schema (Egeland & Sroufe, 1981) because maltreated children have shown inconsistent, contradictory, or disorganized strategies in facing separations and reunions with their caregivers. Consequently, the observation of the attachment behaviors of maltreated children has led to the identification of an additional pattern of attachment, defined disorganized attachment, or Type D, by Main and Solomon (1990). As inconsistent care is characteristic of maltreating families, parenting can be insensitively overstimulating and insensitively understimulating, pervading parents–infant interactions (Belsky, Rovine, & Taylor, 1984; Crittenden,1985; Lyons-Ruth, Connell, Zoll, & Stahl, 1987).

The combination of these two contradictory caregiving styles could lead to the inconsistent strategy of attachment typical of Type D attachment (Cicchetti & Lynch, 1995). Beyond disorganization, infants with Type D attachment often display bizarre behaviors in the presence of their caregiver, such as interrupted movements and expressions, apprehension, dazing, freezing, and stilling behaviors (Fraiberg, 1982).

Several investigations have examined the overall affective climate of maltreating homes and have found evidence of parents expressing fewer positive and more negative emotions (Herrenkohl, Herrenkohl, Egolf, & Wu, 1991; Kavanaugh, Youngblade, Reid, & Fagot, 1988; Lyons-Ruth et al., 1987), with high rates of verbally and physically aggressive interactions between family members (Bousha & Twentyman,1984; Crittenden, 1981). Abusive mothers have been described as more controlling, interfering, and hostile with their infants (Cerezo, 1997; Crittenden, 1981, 1985), compared to nonabusive mothers. These behaviors are frequently reciprocated by infants, provoking more negative and rageful lasting exchanges than in nonabusive families (Loeber, Felton, & Reid, 1984). Serious distorted dynamics in the parent–child relationship have often been observed in maltreating families and frequently children have to face the parent's misrepresentations that the child could behave as a caretaker for him or her (Howes & Cicchetti, 1993).

Interesting research evidence has shown that maltreated children manifest less accurate recognition of emotions than nonmaltreated children, independently of their cognitive capacity (Camras et al., 1988; Camras, Grow, & Ribordy, 1983). Further investigation has revealed that, despite overall deficits in emotion recognition, maltreated children have a hypersensitivity toward the detection of anger (Camras et al., 1990). Several studies over the past decade by Pollak, Cicchetti, Hornung, and Reed (2000) have examined the emotion recognition capacities of maltreated school-aged children. These investigators have hypothesized that physically abused children manifest an increased sensitivity to anger-related cues, probably associated with decreased attention and recognition of other emotional cues. For physically abused children, displays of anger are often experienced as the most salient feature of their environment, as it is the greatest predictor of intervening threat and danger.

Research has not only explored alterations in facial affect processing in maltreated children but also the effects of maltreatment on neurobiological processes connected with facial emotion recognition using event-related potentials (ERPs) (Curtis & Cicchetti, 2011). ERPs provide a direct index of neural functioning connected with a facial stimulus. Research has demonstrated the effects of maltreatment on neural indices of emotional processing not only early in development, at 30 months of age (Cicchetti & Curtis, 2005), but also later, at 42 months of age (Curtis & Cicchetti, 2011). ERP waveforms appear in a higher degree over occipital areas that are considered face sensitive. P1 component evidenced in ERP, which is elicited by angry faces, differentiates maltreated and nonmaltreated children with a greater amplitude in maltreated children. The results of the study are consistent with the hypothesis that maltreated children are more sensitized to angry faces (Curtis & Cicchetti, 2011), not only because they are more familiar with this kind of emotion but also because angry faces have a particular importance in these children's everyday lives. Of course, these data have implications for intervention programs in abused children who need a protective support but also an emotional learning and training, in order to stimulate the recognition of emotions that they are not familiar with.

Traumatic events, like maltreatment, abuse, family conflict, and violence, provoke a failure to integrate these experiences into the organization of the self with a severe distortion in self-representation and agency (Ogawa, Sroufe, Weinfield, Carlson, & Egeland, 1997). The consequences of dissociation, denial, and repression are characterized by a lack of integration of the self, which is disrupted in its emotional and cognitive functioning. Of course, the period of life in which the trauma has been recognized is a critical aspect, as demonstrated by Ogawa and colleagues, according to whom "those participants (in the research) who first experienced trauma in infancy had higher dissociation scores at all time periods" (1997, p. 872). In this context, experiencing maltreatment or sexual abuse during infancy is a strong predictor of dissociation that shall appear later in adolescence, while parental unavailability during infancy causes dissociative phenomena to manifest during adulthood. From a psychological and psychopathological point of view, dissociation is a typical reaction during infancy to different adversities, as young children use fantastic mental functioning or play during conflict. Later in life, fantasy can assume a psychopathological meaning also because it can become a routine response, a psychic retreat (Steiner, 1993), whenever there is a difficulty, thus weakening the organization of the self and creating multiple models of the self, as has been described by Bowlby (1969, 1982).

In this regard, Schore commented: "In states of pathological dissociation the right brain's 'red phone line' is dead. The right brain is fundamentally involved in an avoidant defensive mechanism for coping with emotional stress, including the passive survival strategy of dissociation" (2010, p. 36). In particular, infant abuse interferes with the limbic system maturation in the right brain, generating dissociation (Symonds, Gordon, Bixby, & Mande, 2006).

Regarding psychological dynamics in neglecting families, careless mothers tend to express few expectations for their child, may be inconsistent in their response to him or her, and are not able to set appropriate limits when the infant is upset (Crittenden, 1988). Neglecting attitude in families, characterized by the lack of many forms of basic care and increased family stressors (Connell-Carrick & Scannapieco, 2006; Crittenden, 1981), is frequently associated with high levels of family conflict, negative affect, and domestic violence compared with non-neglectful families (Connell-Carrick & Scannapieco, 2006; Gaudin, Polansky, Kilpatrick, & Shilton, 1996).

An interesting observation has been made by Shi, Bureau, Easterbrooks, Zhao, and Lyons-Ruth (2012) about the influence of maternal withdrawal on the infantile development and its outcome 20 years later. Maternal withdrawal is characterized by silent interacting behaviors, failing to greet the infant, and using toys instead of the self to soothe the infant, producing "an affectively dead, emotionally distanced feel to the interaction and would seem to communicate to the infant the parent's reluctance to participate in a physical close and emotionally engaged relationship" (Shi et al., 2012, p. 64). Such a distant and unavailable mother reminds us of the psychoanalytic concept of the dead mother described by André Green (1983/1986): The mother does not invest emotionally and libidinally in her child, who, in turn, does not understand her coldness and distancing, and mirrors his or her maternal object, identifying with the dead mother.

Such experience is predictive of future antisocial personality disorder features, independently of childhood abuse (Shi et al., 2012). It would be interesting to explore the biological consequences of maternal withdrawal for the regulation of a child's stressful arousal. Research with animals has evidenced that less attentive early care produces an increase of stress responses in the HPA (Barr et al., 2004; Francis et al., 1999) and affects the metabolism of noradrenalin, dopamine, and serotonin negatively.

RISK, VULNERABILITY, AND RESILIENCE

The predominant focus of the research is on the negative psychological consequences of children from high-conflict families, while children who develop normally without particular vulnerabilities in the face of interparental adversity have not been adequately studied (Cummings & Davies, 1994). Thus, it would be useful to build a model of risk and vulnerability by studying protection and resilience and identifying incidences of resilience and the underlying factors and processes that intervene in child adaptation in high-conflict families. In identifying resilient children, assessments should be sensitive enough to capture the dynamic nature of resilience, with particular recognition that some resilient children may experience considerable problems over time (Luthar & Cicchetti, 2000).

Abuse and maltreatment represent the most negative and stressful experiences for children, and most of them are negatively affected by them (Cicchetti & Lynch, 1995), but not all children who are victims of maltreatment manifest a severe outcome (Cicchetti & Rogosch, 2012). To explain the resilience factors of children who do not manifest negative consequences, psychosocial factors have been studied; these include personality characteristics, secure attachment relationships, self-regulation, parental support, and positive social context (Haskett, Sabourin Ward, Nears, & McPherson, 2006). A study by Cicchetti and Rogosch

(1997) has shown that the most sensitive predictors of resilience are the personal characteristics of ego overcontrol (the capacity to monitor and control impulses and regulate affects) and ego resilience (personal flexibility in affects and behavior). Other levels of analysis have also been performed: the investigation of electroencephalographic (EEG) asymmetry, for example. Curtis and Cicchetti (2007) evidenced that resilience in maltreated children is associated with EEG asymmetry with left hemispheric hyperactivation. In another study (Cicchetti & Rogosch, 2007), adrenal steroid hormones metabolism was explored. Physically abused children with high morning cortisol manifest higher resilient functioning than physically abused children with lower levels of morning cortisol. Other biological systems are negatively involved by abuse and maltreatment, among these brain structure and functioning (De Bellis, 2001, 2005) and stress neurobiology (Cicchetti, Rogosch, Gunnar, & Toth, 2010).

The described stressful experiences represent risk factors for infantile development and predict a higher rate of negative consequences. While initially the focus of research has been directed to the consequences of a single risk factor, later it has become evident that risk factors co-occur with others risk factors configuring a cumulative risk. At the same time, research has evidenced that among children at risk, some have a better adjustment. This has stimulated the research of the factors associated with more positive outcomes and of the underlying processes implicated (Masten & Powell, 2003). These attributes have been defined as protective factors, which can be identified on the basis of their specificity, "correlates of better competence under adverse conditions" (Masten & Powell, 2003, p. 13) and regard personal competences, capacity of relationship, context, and community resources. But frequently the concept of protective factors has been used to describe effects involving interactions. According to Rutter, "resilience can be defined as a reduced vulnerability to environmental risk experiences, the overcoming of a stress or adversity, or a relatively good outcome despite risk experiences. . . . Thus, it is an *interactive* concept in which the presence of resilience has to be *inferred* from individual variations in outcome among individuals who have experienced significant major stress or adversity" (2012, p. 336, italics in original).

In defining the conceptual framework about risk, protective factors, and resilience, it should be underlined that these concepts are sometimes unclear and confusing. A distinction should be made between the term *resilience*, which should be used when we refer to the process of competence despite adversity, while *resiliency* should be used when we refer to a specific personality trait.

A good illustration of resilience is the gene–environment (G × E) interaction. Through molecular genetic methods, individual susceptibility genes which interact with environmentally mediated risks for psychopathology have been identified (Moffitt, Caspi, & Rutter, 2005). The studies of Caspi and colleagues (2002, 2003, 2005) have evidenced that there is no significant main effect of genes, a marginally significant main effect of environment, but a relevant significant effect of the G × E interaction. A convincing confirmation of the G × E interaction comes from the research by Caspi and colleagues (2002), who studied a large sample of male children from birth to adulthood in order to understand why most victims of maltreatment develop antisocial behaviors while others do not. In the study, the genetic susceptibility to maltreatment has been explored by testing individual differences at functional polymorphism in the promoter of the monoamine oxidase A (MAOA). The MAOA gene encodes the MAOA enzyme, which intervenes in the metabolism by inactivating neurotransmitters such as norepinephrine, serotonin, and dopamine. It has been suggested that childhood maltreatment could predispose children to adult antisocial behavior if their level of MAOA is insufficient to limit the influence of maltreatment in the neurotransmitter system. The research has shown that the effect of childhood maltreatment on antisocial behavior is significantly reduced among males with high MAOA activity than among males with low MAOA activity.

A further confirmation of the G × E interaction derives from another longitudinal study by Caspi and colleagues (2003), which explored why stressful experiences lead to depression in some people but not in others. This research has found a polymorphism in the promoter region of the serotonin transporter (5-HTT) gene, whose short allele (single or double) does not protect toward depressive symptoms in relation to stressful life events confronted with double long allele of 5-HTT.

In further studies about different types of stressors, it has been evidenced that in the case of serotonin transporter promoter gene there is a marginally significant G × E with life events, while there is a highly significant G × E with maltreatment (Karg, Burmeister, Shedden, & Sen, 2011). The conclusion of this study has highlighted the importance of serious environmental risk factors that could intervene in the first years of life. Another conclusion of all replicated studies is that no main genetic effect has been found and the genetic effect is not a predisposition for a particular mental disorder but a susceptibility to environmental influences. Regarding environmental influences, the findings have confirmed that the main risk effects depend on serious and chronic adversity such as maltreatment rather than from acute stresses (Rutter, 2012). Of course, this G × E interaction operates long before the onset of the disorder predisposing to a psychopathological liability.

The G × E interaction is closely connected with differential susceptibility to the environment and rearing experiences (Ellis & Boyce, 2011). Boyce and Ellis (2005) have advanced the theory of biological sensitivity to context, originated from observations of differences in children's autonomic and adrenocortical reactivity, which has some overlap with the differential susceptibility theory proposed by Belsky (2005). This differential susceptibility is rooted in differences in the personal functioning of neurobiological circuitry. In this regard, Whittle and colleagues (2011) demonstrated that differences in the structure of the hippocampus may be related to vulnerability in adverse contexts and the volume of the hippocampus may predict positive outcomes when there is a favorable environment. According to Whittle and colleagues (2011) the hippocampus could play a central role for sensitivity to context also for its connection with learning and memory. Another system involved in contextual susceptibility is represented by the neuroendocrine stress response system.

Until now, the dominant paradigm in this field has been the diathesis-stress model (Sameroff, 1983), which suggests that some individuals, because of a specific vulnerability, are particularly negatively affected by environmental stressors. So the diathesis represents a risk for the future development if it interacts with environmental risk with a synergistic effect.

With a different perspective, the biological sensitivity to context theory (Ellis & Boyce, 2011) and the differential susceptibility theory (Belsky, Bakermans-Kranenburg, & van IJzendoorn, 2007) focus on person–environment interaction, stressing the value of organismic characteristics in moderating the effects of both stressful and supportive environmental conditions. Ellis and Boyce (2011) identified a physiological mechanism of susceptibility based on autonomic, adrenocortical, and immune reactivity. An interesting distinction has been suggested between more susceptible children, also called "orchid children" (Ellis & Boyce, 2011, p. 11), with heightened sensitivity to positive and negative environmental influences and children with low reactivity, called "dandelion children" (Ellis & Boyce, 2011, p. 11), the latter adequately functioning in a wide range of situations, including adverse ones.

However, maltreated infants usually grow up in a multiproblem context, characterized by poverty, parental violence, parental psychopathology, criminality, drug and alcohol abuse, and dangerous neighborhood conditions (Appel & Holden, 1998; Jaffee, 2005; Lynch & Cicchetti, 1998; Sedlak & Broadhurst, 1996). Under these conditions of severe stress adequate functioning of children may not be possible, even possessing individual strengths, as has been proposed by the cumulative stressors model (Repetti, Taylor, & Seeman, 2002; Rutter, 1979; Seifer, Sameroff, Baldwin, & Baldwin, 1992). For example, Sameroff, Bartko, Baldwin, Baldwin, and Seifer (1998) have shown that personal protective factors have no effect on children's functioning, when children are exposed to a high numbers of environmental risk factors.

A recent confirmation of the cumulative risk model has been performed by Jaffee, Caspi, Moffitt, Polo-Tomás, and Taylor (2007), who suggest, on the basis of their research, that children from multiproblem families may not have enough personal resources to achieve a positive adjustment.

The literature about multiple risk factors does not answer the question about whether a threshold model or a linear model describes in a more relevant way the impact of cumulative risk on behavior outcomes. The cumulative risk models affirm that the accumulation of risk factors, without considering the presence or absence of specific risk factors, provokes clinical outcomes, as has been evidenced in the classic study of Rutter (1979) in the Isle of Wight or in the Rochester Longitudinal Study (Sameroff, 2000). To explain the maladaptive outcome, two models have been suggested. The first one affirms that there is a threshold effect, so after a certain number of risk factors a dramatic increase of behavioral problems occurs (Rutter, 1979). The second model affirms an additive or linear perspective, so the negative effect increases more and more.

In recent research by Appleyard, Egeland, van Dulmen, and Sroufe (2005), based on a longitudinal study, the findings support the cumulative risk model according to which the number of risks in early childhood predicts behavioral problems in adolescence. The conclusion is that the more risk present, the worse the child's outcome.

CHAPTER 8

Conclusion

We have highlighted the value of intersubjectivity in human relations and have specifically explored the rise and development of intersubjectivity in the relationship between parents and child during pregnancy, after birth, and during the child's first years. Our reference framework comprises the contributions of relational psychology, of cognitivism, of infant research, and of neurobiology. These different fields have all confronted the rise and development of intersubjectivity, which is characterized, according to the "transactional model" perspective (Sameroff & Chandler, 1975), by multiple interacting systems that are expressed by the dynamic interactions between the child, the family, and the social context.

"Understanding how infants and their parents influence each other over time," as Sameroff wrote, "is a necessary prologue to the understanding of developmental problems and recommendations for appropriate treatment" (2004, p. 11). Since multiple systems interact, we may identify different ports of entry in the context of parents–infant interactions, which receive special attention from preventing and supporting interventions (Stern, 1995) but inevitably influence the whole system.

As we have seen, the first port of entry is the parents' psychic world, the mother's especially, where representations of self as mother and of future child develop. These are both strongly rooted in the mother's experience and physical dimension, where the first exchanges between mother and child occur.

Mothers often start thinking for two as early as pregnancy; they dialogue with the child within them, attribute to the child a face, an identity, desires, and intentions, making the child their secret companion during those long days of waiting. But fathers create a representation of their child as well, and, as seen earlier, need to be confirmed in their paternal identity since the child exists in their mind but not in their body. During this waiting period, a thinking for three develops, as demonstrated with the reported interview, in which both parents dialogue with the child and support each other in the affiliation process. We have also discussed how parents interact with their future child in front of the ultrasound image, which intersects with the mental image of the child established in them by an affiliation process and testified by the parents' imitative behaviors, as they reenact their children's gestures. One of the fathers in our study, during the interaction with the child visualized through the ultrasound, spoke these words to him: "You're in there now, nice and cozy, but we hope you'll come out soon and meet us. We've prepared a room, with your bed and all your toys."

The waiting period represents a privileged port of entry because both parents are strongly motivated to direct their focus to the child, to talk about the child, and to imagine and bring the child to life in their dreams. States of anxiety, depression, or obsessive-compulsive states are already recognizable in this phase and may interfere with the waiting for the child (Ammaniti et al., 2006).

Parents may be supported both through counseling and through the parents' exploration with a doll, as in the Prenatal Lausanne Trilogue Play (Carneiro et al., 2006); or with the ultrasound image of the baby, as we did in our own research (Ammaniti et al., 2010).

For all parents, the pregnancy period is characterized by the rise of new "mental constellations" (Stern, 1995) that reorganize maternal and paternal psychic worlds, reactivating the matrixes of their childhood experiences with their own parents. This makes pregnancy a sensitive period in which interventions may be very effective.

As neurobiology research has shown, certain areas of the mother's brain circuit are activated, such as the hippocampus, the limbic system, and the orbitofrontal cortex, which intervene in the reactivation of past memories and incite a strong emotional involvement. This notion can be used in supporting interventions for the parents. And in this phase, because of the parents' positive attitude, a relationship of trust that favors supporting action can be established and then maintained after the child's birth.

After the child's birth, there are other ports of entry to the parents–child system and among these the attachment area is a very significant one. Supporting interventions in the relationship between parents and child aim at favoring the attachment ties, as has been carried out in many programs.

These interventions tend to stimulate parents' sensitivity to those behaviors of the child that are relevant for attachment, such as eye-to-eye contact, crying, and physical contact, especially in difficult moments for the child, when the parent seems to be leaving or leaves or when the child is living a moment of fatigue or distress. While parents with secure attachment are capable of reading their child's requests of protection and reassurance, the situation is different for parents who have a dismissing, enmeshed, or unresolved attachment. For a series of reasons, these parents are not capable of reading and adequately responding to their child's attachment requests (Lyons-Ruth & Easterbrooks, 2006; Olds, 2006).

Considering the framework of attachment, the home visitor intervenes in the natural context of the family, providing the parents with a secure base (Bowlby, 1988), which allows them to read and interpret the signals and behaviors of the child. The intervention strategy aims at promoting parents–infant interaction by facilitating parents' personal and couple potentialities and intuitive behaviors, while avoiding any direct advice. Parents are encouraged to improve their competence and sensitivity toward the child, to observe their interactions with the child, and to realize the importance of their influence on the child's development. An example of an attachment-based intervention is the Circle of Security Project, performed by Marvin, Cooper, Hoffman, and Powell (2002). The Project is based on concepts and ideas derived from developmental theories, attachment, and early parents–child interaction. A particular emphasis is given to emotion regulation, interactive synchrony, states of mind regarding attachment, and reflective functioning. In this context the central core of the intervention is the concept of a Secure Base and a Haven of Safety (Ainsworth et al., 1978).

The framework of attachment is particularly relevant during critical and stressing situations, when the infant is distressed, hungry, or tired. In these moments, the child expresses his or her bids for attachment and the protection and caring of parents is decisive.

Different early-intervention programs have confirmed that infancy represents a critical period that is particularly sensitive and rewarding to supporting interventions, which may have far-reaching behavioral outcomes (Swain, Thomas, Leckman, & Mayes, 2008). These early interventions have been proven to reduce maladaptive behaviors and to improve attachment behaviors and emotional regulation.

A third port of entry is connected with the area of intersubjectivity and mentalization, which could represent either a more general motivational system underlying other motivational systems or a developing specific competence stimulated by attachment security (Fonagy, 1998). If the caregiver is supported in observing the continuous changes in the infant's mental state, the child shall develop mentalizing capacity. As Fonagy (1998) wrote, "the caregiver's perception of the child as an intentional being lies at the root of sensitive caregiving" (p. 140).

The mentalizing approach, as in the "Minding the Baby" Program described by Slade (2006), has the aim of supporting parents in keeping their child in mind and in learning to think about the child in terms of his or her internal experience rather than of his or her behavior. Frequently, parents belonging to risk populations manifest the tendency to perceive and respond to the child's behavioral characteristics rather than to the child's mental experiences. In these situations, the home visitor's approach will be to give voice to the child's internal experience, so the parents can be stimulated to reframe their representation and perception of the baby. At the same time, parental curiosity about the child's experience is facilitated, helping parents to recognize that the infant's experience is separate from their own.

Other ports of entry to the parents–child system can be identified by observing the data that emerge from neurobiological research. This is the field of translational research, which includes two areas of translation. One is the process of applying discoveries generated by laboratory research and preclinical studies to the development of trials and studies in humans. The second area of translation concerns research aimed at enhancing the adoption of best practices in the community, such as interventions in the parents–child interaction system. As Curtis and Cicchetti (2011) documented, maltreatment during infancy has an impact on neurofunctional processes underlying the identification of anger, as these children have more experience of anger in their families. As Curtis and Cicchetti (2011) pointed out, these neurobiological data in maltreated children should inform prevention and intervention programs. A preventive intervention might support the learning of facial affect recognition in maltreated children, so that the salience of anger can be reduced and the negative cascade of effects on brain development avoided.

Another possible translation of neurobiological research, especially connected with the discovery of the mirror neurons system, is exemplified by the work of Beebe (2004) as is documented in the article "Faces in Relation: A Case Study." The central focus of the intervention is the matching concept as conceptualized by Stern and Trevarthen. According to them, this concept is based on the capacity of each partner to be aware of the other's feelings, expressing a matching without words that emphasizes time, form, and intensity.

Before bringing the book to a close, we would like to stress the importance of preventive and supportive interventions in the relationship between parents and children carried out during the first phase of infancy. This phase is an extremely sensitive and receptive one and may bear very significant results in later development phases as well. As demonstrated by James Heckman, the Nobel Prize–winning professor of economics at the University of Chicago, the economic return of these interventions must be kept in mind as well.

Early interventions during infancy, as Heckman (2000) highlighted, have a consistent effectiveness in disadvantaged families. They promote schooling, reduce crime, foster workplace productivity, and reduce teenage pregnancy. These interventions are estimated to have a high benefit-to-cost ratio and rates of return. As we know, the life cycle is dynamic: Cognitive abilities influence socioeconomic success, as well as socioemotional competence, attention, motivation, and self-confidence. The longer society waits to support and help infants and parents in disadvantaged families, the higher the costs will be when trying to later remedy children's and adolescents' disadvantage.

The best conclusion for our book is what John Bowlby wrote in 1951 in *Maternal Care and Mental Health*, published by the World Health Organization, which still remains valid: "Just as children are absolutely dependent on their parents for sustenance, so in all but the most primitive communities, are parents, especially their mothers, dependent on a greater society for economic provision. If a community values its children it must cherish their parents" (p. 84).

References

Abelin-Sas, G. (1992). To mother or not to mother: Abortion and its challenges. *Journal of Clinical Psychoanalysis, 1,* 607–622.

Aber, J. L., Belsky, J., Slade, A., & Crnic, K. (1999). Stability and change in mothers' representations of their relationship with their toddlers. *Developmental Psychology, 35,* 1038–1047.

Aber, L., Slade, A., Berger, B., Bresgi, I., & Kaplan, M. (1985). *The Parent Development Interview.* Unpublished manuscript, Barnard College, New York, NY.

Adams, R. E., Bromet, E. J., Panina, N., Golovakha, E., Goldgaber, D., & Gluzman, S. (2002). Stress and well-being in mothers of young children 11 years after the Chernobyl nuclear power plant accident. *Psychological Medicine, 32,* 143–156.

Adolphs, R., Damasio, H., Tranel, D., Cooper, G., & Damasio, A. R. (2000). A role for somatosensory cortices in the visual recognition of emotion as revealed by three-dimensional lesion mapping. *Journal of Neuroscience, 20,* 2683–2690.

Adolphs, R., Tranel, D., & Damasio, A. R. (2003). Dissociable neural systems for recognizing emotions. *Brain and Cognition, 52,* 61–69.

Afonso, V. M., Sison, M., Lovic, V., & Fleming, A. S. (2007). Medial prefrontal cortex lesions in the female rat affect sexual and maternal behavior and their sequential organization. *Behavioral Neuroscience, 121,* 515–526.

Aglioti, S. M., Cesari, P., Romani, M., & Urgesi, C. (2008). Action anticipation and motor resonance in elite basketball players. *Nature Neuroscience, 11,* 1109–1116.

Ahern, T. H., & Young, L. J., (2009). The impact of early life family structure on adult social attachment, alloparental behavior, and the neuropeptide systems regulating affiliative behaviors in the monogamous prairie vole (Microtus ochrogaster). *Frontiers in Behavioral Neuroscience, 3,* 17.

Ainsworth, M. D. S. (1967). *Infancy in Uganda: Infant care and the growth of love.* Baltimore, MD: Johns Hopkins University Press.

Ainsworth, M. D. S., & Bell, S. M. (1974). Mother-infant interaction and the development of competence. In K. Connolly & J. Bruner (Eds.), *The growth of competence* (pp. 97–118). New York, NY: Academic Press.

Ainsworth, M. D. S., Blehar, M., Waters, E., & Wall, S. (1978). *Patterns of attachment: A psychological study of the strange situation.* Hillsdale, NJ: Erlbaum.

Ainsworth, M. D. S., & Wittig, B. A. (1969). Attachment and exploratory behavior of one-year-olds in a strange situation. In B. M. Foss (Ed.), *Determinants of infant behavior* (Vol. 4, pp. 113–136). London, UK: Methuen.

Alessandri, S. M. (1992). Mother-child interactions correlates of maltreated and nonmaltreated children's play behavior. *Development and Psychopathology, 4*, 257–270.

Alexander, G. E., & Crutcher, M. D. (1990). Neural representations of the target (goal) of visually guided arm movements in three motor areas of the monkey. *Journal of Neurophysiology, 64*, 164–178.

Alhusen, J. (2008). A literature update on maternal-fetal attachment. *Journal of Obstetric, Gynaecologic and Nursing, 37*, 315–328.

Ammaniti, M., & Tambelli, R. (2010). Prenatal self-report questionnaires, scales and interviews. In S. Tyano, M. Keren, H. Herrman, & J. Cox (Eds.), *Parenthood and mental health: A bridge between, infant and adult psychiatry* (pp. 109–120). Oxford, UK: Wiley-Blackwell.

Ammaniti, M., Candelori, C., Pola, M., & Tambelli, R. (1999). *Maternité et grossesse*. Paris, France: Presses Universitaires de France.

Ammaniti, M., Mazzoni, S., & Menozzi, F. (2010). Ecografia in gravidanza: Studio della co-genitorialità. *Infanzia e Adolescenza, 9*, 151–157.

Ammaniti, M., Speranza, A. M., Tambelli, R., Muscetta, S., Lucarelli, L., Vismara, L., . . . Cimino, S. (2006). A prevention and promotion intervention program in the field of mother-infant relationship. *Infant Mental Health Journal, 27*, 70–90.

Ammaniti, M., Tambelli, R., & Odorisio, F. (2013). Exploring maternal representations during pregnancy in normal and at-risk samples: The use of the Interview for Maternal Representations during pregnancy. *Infant Mental Health Journal, 34*, 1–10.

Ammaniti. M., & Trentini, C. (2009). How new knowledge about parenting reveals the neurobiological implications of intersubjectivity: A conceptual synthesis of recent research. *Psychoanalytic Dialogues, 19*, 537–555.

Appel, A. E., & Holden, G. W. (1998). The co-occurrence of spouse and physical child abuse: A review and appraisal. *Journal of Family Psychology, 12*, 578–599.

Appleyard, K., Egeland, B., van Dulmen, M. H. M., & Sroufe, L. A. (2005). When more is not better: The role of cumulative risk in child behavior outcomes. *Journal of Child Psychology and Psychiatry, 46*, 235–245.

Armenian, H. K., Morikawa, M., Melkonian, A. K., Hovanesian, A., Akiskal, K., & Akiskal, H. S. (2002). Risk factors for depression in the survivors of the 1988 earthquake in Armenia. *Journal of Urban Health, 79*, 373–382.

Arnott, B., & Meins, E. (2008). Continuity in mind-mindedness from pregnancy to the first year of life. *Infant Behavior and Development, 31*, 647–654.

Azar, S. T. (2002). *Parenting and child maltreatment*. Mahwah, NJ: Erlbaum.

Baird, J. A., & Baldwin, D. A. (2001). Making sense of human behavior: Action parsing and intentional inferences. In B. F. Malle, L. J. Moses, & D. A. Baldwin (Eds.), *Intentions and intentionality* (pp. 193–206). Cambridge, MA: MIT Press.

Bakeman, R., & Adamson, L. B. (1984). Coordinating attention to people and objects in mother-infant and peer-infant interaction. *Child Development, 55*, 1278–1289.

Bakermans-Kranenburg, M. J., & van Ijzendoorn, M. H. (2007). Genetic vulnerability or differential susceptibility in child development: The case of attachment. *Journal of Child Psychology and Psychiatry, 48*, 1160–1173.

Bakermans-Kranenburg, M. J., van Ijzendoorn, M. H., & Juffer, F. (2003). Less in more:

Meta-analysis of sensitivity and attachment interventions in early childhood. *Psychological Bulletin, 129,* 195–215.

Baldwin, D. A., Baird, J. A., Saylor, M. M., & Clark, M. A. (2001). Infants parse dynamic action. *Child Development, 72,* 708–717.

Bales, K. L., Kim, A. J., Lewis-Reese, A. D., & Sue Carter, C. (2004). Both oxytocin and vasopressin may influence alloparental behavior in male prairie voles. *Hormones and Behavior, 45,* 354–361.

Baron-Cohen, S., Leslie, A. M., & Frith, U. (1985). Does the autistic child have a "theory of mind"? *Cognition, 21,* 37–46.

Baron-Cohen, S., Wheelwright, S., Hill, J., Raste, Y., & Plumb, I. (2001). The "Reading the Mind in the Eyes" Test revised version: A study with normal adults, and adults with Asperger syndrome or high-functioning autism. *Journal of Child Psychology and Psychiatry, 42,* 241–251.

Barr, C. S., Newman, T. K., Shannon, C., Parker, C., Dvoskin, R. L., Becker, M. L., . . . Higley, J. D. (2004). Rearing condition and rh5-HTTLPR interact to influence limbic-hypothalamic-pituitary-adrenal axis response to stress in infant macaques. *Biological Psychiatry, 55,* 733–738.

Bartels, A., & Zeki, S. (2000). The neural basis of romantic love. *Neuroreport, 11,* 3829–3834.

Bartels, A., & Zeki, S. (2004). The neural correlates of maternal and romantic love. *Neuroimage, 21,* 1155–1166.

Bateson, M. C. (1971). The interpersonal context of infant vocalization. *Quarterly Progress Report of the Research Laboratory of Electronics, 100,* 170–176.

Bateson, M. C. (1979). The epigenesis of conversational interaction: A personal account of research development. In M. Bullowa (Ed.), *Before speech: The beginning of human communication* (pp. 63–77). Cambridge, UK: Cambridge University Press.

Bateson, P., Barker, D., Clutton-Brock, T., Deb, D., D'Udine, B., Foley, R. A., . . . Sultan, S. E. (2004). Developmental plasticity and human health. *Nature, 430,* 419–421.

Beck Black, R. (1992). Seeing the baby: The impact of ultrasound technology. *Journal of Genetic Counseling, 1,* 45–54.

Beebe, B. (1982). Micro-timing in mother-infant communication. In M. Key (Ed.), *Nonverbal communication today: Current research* (pp. 169–195). New York, NY: Mouton.

Beebe, B. (1998). A procedural theory of therapeutic action: Commentary of the symposium "Interventions that affect change in psychotherapy." *Infant Mental Health Journal, 19,* 333–340.

Beebe, B. (2004). Faces in relation: A case study. *Psychoanalytic Dialogues, 14,* 1–51.

Beebe, B., Jaffe, J., Markese, S., Buck, K., Chen, H., Cohen, P., . . . Feldstein, S. (2010). The origins of 12-month attachment: A microanalysis of 4-month mother-infant interaction. *Attachment and Human Development, 12,* 3–141.

Beebe, B., & Lachmann, F. (1988). The contribution of mother-infant mutual influence to the origins of self and object representations. *Psychoanalytic Psychology, 5,* 305–337.

Beebe, B., & Lachmann, F. (1994). Representation and internalization in infancy: Three principles of salience. *Psychoanalytic Psychology, 11,* 127–165.

Bekkering, H., Wohlschläger, A., & Gattis, M. (2000). Imitation of gestures in children is goal-directed. *Quarterly Journal of Experimental Psychology, 53A,* 153–164.

Bell, D. C., & Richard, A. J. (2000). Caregiving: The forgotten element in attachment. *Psychological Inquiry, 11,* 69–83.

Belsky, J. (1984). The determinants of parenting: A process model. *Child Development*, 55, 83–96.

Belsky, J. (2005). Differential susceptibility to rearing influences: An evolutionary hypothesis and some evidence. In B. Ellis & D. Bjorklund (Eds.), *Origins of the social mind: Evolutionary psychology and child development* (pp. 139–163). New York, NY: Guilford Press.

Belsky, J., Bakermans-Kranenburg, M. J., & van IJzendoorn, M. H. (2007). For better and for worse: Differential susceptibility to environmental influences. *Current Directions in Psychological Science*, 16, 300–304.

Belsky, J., Crnic, K., & Gable, S. (1995). The determinants of coparenting. *Child Development*, 66, 629–642.

Belsky, J., & Fearon, R. M. P. (2004). Exploring marriage-parenting typologies and their contextual antecedents and developmental sequalae. *Development and Psychopathology*, 16, 501–523.

Belsky, J., & Rovine, M. (1987). Temperament and attachment security in the strange situation: An empirical rapprochement. *Child Development*, 58, 787–795.

Belsky, J., Rovine, M., & Taylor, D. G. (1984). The Pennsylvania Infant and Family Development Project, III: The origins of individual differences in infant-mother attachment: Maternal and infant contribution. *Child Development*, 55, 718–728.

Benjamin, J. (1998). *The shadow of the other: Intersubjectivity and gender in psychoanalysis*. New York, NY: Routledge.

Benoit, D., Parker, K., & Zeanah, C. H. (1997). Mothers' representations of their infants assessed prenatally: Stability and association with infants' attachment classifications. *Journal of Child Psychology, Psychiatry and Allied Disciplines*, 38, 307–313.

Bergman, K., Sarkar, P., Glover, V., & O'Connor, T. G. (2008). Quality of child-parent attachment moderates the impact of antenatal stress on child fearfulness. *Journal of Child Psychology and Psychiatry*, 49, 1089–1098.

Bergman, K., Sarkar, P., O'Connor, T. G., Modi, N., & Glover, V. (2007). Maternal stress during pregnancy predicts cognitive ability and fearfulness in infancy. *Journal of American Academy of Child and Adolescent Psychiatry*, 46, 1454–1463.

Berlucchi, G., & Aglioti, S. (1997). The body in the brain: Neural bases of corporeal awareness. *Trends in Neurosciences*, 20, 560–564.

Bibring, G. L. (1961). A study of the psychological processes in pregnancy and of the earliest mother-child relationship. *The Psychoanalytic Study of the Child*, 16, 9–72.

Bird, C. M., Castelli, F., Malik, O., Frith, U., & Husain, M. (2004). The impact of extensive medial frontal lobe damage on "theory of mind" and cognition. *Brain*, 127, 914–928.

Blakemore, S.-J., Bristow, D., Bird, G., Frith, C., & Ward, J. (2005). Somatosensory activations during the observation of touch and a case of vision-touch synaesthesia. *Brain*, 128, 1571–1583.

Blakemore, S.-J., & Choudhury, S. (2006). Development of the adolescent brain: Implications for executive function and social cognition. *Journal of Child Psychiatry and Psychology*, 47, 296–312.

Blanke, O., Mohr, C., Michel, C. M., Pascual-Leone, A., Brugger, P., Seeck, M., . . . Thut, G. (2005). Linking out-of-body experience and self processing to mental own-body imagery at the temporoparietal junction. *Journal of Neuroscience*, 25, 550–557.

Blasco, M. A. (2005). Telomeres and human disease: Ageing, cancer and beyond. *Nature Reviews Genetics*, 6, 611–622.

Bonini, L., Rozzi, S., Serventi, F. U., Simone, L., Ferrari, P. F., & Fogassi, L. (2010). Ventral premotor and inferior parietal cortices make distinct contribution to action organization and intention understanding. *Cerebral Cortex, 20*, 1372–1385.

Börjesson, K., Ruppert, S., Wager, J., & Bågedahl-Strindlund, M. (2007). Personality disorder, psychiatric symptoms and experience of childbirth among childbearing women in Sweden. *Midwifery, 23*, 260–268.

Bornstein, M. (2002). *Handbook of parenting biology and ecology (Vol. 2).* Mahwah, NJ: Erlbaum.

Bornstein, M. (2004). Child and family research in cross-cultural perspective. *International Society for the Study of Behavioural Development Newsletter, 3*, 17–20.

Botvinick, M., & Cohen, J. (1998). Rubber hands "feel" touch that eyes see. *Nature, 391*, 756.

Botvinick, M., Jha, A. P., Bylsma, L. M., Fabian, S. A., Solomon, P. E., & Prkachin, K. M. (2005). Viewing facial expressions of pain engages cortical areas involved in the direct experience of pain. *Neuroimage, 25*, 312–319.

Bousha, D. M., & Twentyman, C. T. (1984). Mother-child interactional style in abuse, neglect, and control groups: Naturalistic observations in the home. *Journal of Abnormal Psychology, 93*, 106–114.

Bowlby, J. (1951). *Maternal care and mental health.* [WHO Monograph Series, No. 2]. Geneva, Switzerland: World Health Organization.

Bowlby, J. (1956). The growth of independence in the young child. *Royal Society of Health Journal, 76*, 587–591.

Bowlby, J. (1958). The nature of a child's tie to his mother. *International Journal of Psychoanalysis, 39*, 350–373.

Bowlby, J. (1969). *Attachment and loss, Vol. 1. Attachment.* London, UK: Hogarth Press.

Bowlby, J. (1973). *Attachment and loss, Vol. 2. Separation, anxiety and anger.* New York, NY: Basic Books.

Bowlby, J. (1979). *The making and breaking of affectional bonds.* London, UK: Tavistock.

Bowlby, J. (1980). *Attachment and loss, Vol. 3. Loss, sadness and depression.* London, UK: Hogarth Press.

Bowlby, J. (1982). *Attachment and loss, Vol. 1. Attachment* (2nd ed.). New York, NY: Basic Books.

Bowlby, J. (1988). *A secure base: Parent-child attachment and healthy human development.* New York, NY: Basic Books.

Bowman, R. E., MacLusky, N. J., Sarmiento, Y., Frankfurt, M., Gordon, M., & Luine, V. N. (2004). Sexually dimorphic effects of prenatal stress on cognition, hormonal responses, and central neurotransmitters. *Endocrinology, 145*, 3778–3787.

Boyce, W. T., & Ellis, B. J. (2005). Biological sensitivity to context: I. An evolutionary-developmental theory of the origins and functions of stress reactivity. *Development and Psychopathology, 17*, 271–301.

Bradley, M., Cuthberth, B. N., & Lang, P. J. (1996). Lateralized startle probes in the study of emotion. *Psychophysiology, 33*, 156–161.

Brandon, A. R., Pitts, S., Denton, W. H., Stringer, C. A., & Evans, H. M. (2009). A history of the theory of prenatal attachment. *Journal of Prenatal and Perinatal Psychology and Health, 23*, 201–222.

Brass, M., Schmitt, R. M., Spengler, S., & Gergely, G. (2007). Investigating action understanding: Inferential processes versus action simulation. *Current Biology, 17*, 2117–2121.

Bråten, S. (1988). Dialogic mind: The infant and the adult in protoconversation. In M. Carvallo (Ed.), *Nature, cognition and system* (Vol. 1, pp. 187–205). Dordrecht, The Netherlands: Kluwer Academic.

Bråten, S. (1992). The virtual other in infants' minds and social feelings. In H. Wold (Ed.), *The dialogical alternative* (pp. 77–97). Oslo, Norway: Scandinavian University Press.

Bråten, S. (2007). *On being moved: From mirror neurons to empathy.* Amsterdam, The Netherlands and Philadelphia, PA: John Benjamins.

Bredy, T. W., Lee, A. W., Meaney, M. J., & Brown, R. E. (2004). Effect of neonatal handling and paternal care on offspring cognitive development in the monogamous California mouse (Peromyscus californicus). *Hormones and Behavior, 46,* 30–38.

Bressi, C., Taylor, G., Parker, J., Bressi, S., Brambilla, V., Aguglia, E., . . . Invernizzi, G. (1996). Cross validation of the factor structure of the 20-item Toronto Alexithymia scale: An Italian multicenter study. *Journal of Psychosomatic Research, 41,* 551–559.

Bretherton, I. (1991). The roots and growing points of attachment theory. In C. M. Parkes, J. Stevenso-Hinde, & P. Harris (Eds.), *Attachment across the life cycle* (pp. 9–32). London, UK: Routledge.

Bretherton, I., & Waters, E. (1985). Growing points of attachment theory and research. *Monographs of the Society for Research in Child Development, 50*(1–2, Serial No. 209).

Briere, J, & Elliott, D. (2000). Prevalence, characteristics, and long-term sequelae of natural disaster exposure in the general population. *Journal of Traumatic Stress, 13,* 661–679.

Broad, K. D., Curley, J. P., & Keverne, E. B. (2006). Mother-infant bonding and the evolution of mammalian social relationships. *Philosophical Transactions of the Royal Society of London Series B, Biological Sciences, 361,* 2199–2214.

Brockway, R. (2003). Evolving to be mentalists: The "mind-reading myms" hypothesis. In K. Sterelny & J. Fitness (Eds.), *From mating to mentality: Evaluating evolutionary psychology* (pp. 95–123). New York, NY: Psychology Press.

Bruner, J. (1986). *Actual minds, possible words.* Cambridge, MA: Harvard University Press.

Bruner, J. (1996). *The culture of education.* Cambridge, MA: Harvard University Press.

Buber, M. (1923/1970). *I and thou.* (W. Kaufman, Trans.). New York, NY: Touchstone.

Buccino, G., Binkofski, F., Fink, G. R., Fadiga, L., Fogassi, L., Gallese, V., . . . Freund, H. J. (2001). Action observation activates premotor and parietal areas in a somatotopic manner: An fMRI study. *European Journal of Neuroscience, 13,* 400–404.

Buccino, G., Lui, F., Canessa, N., Patteri, I., Lagravinese, G., Benuzzi, F., . . . Rizzolatti, G. (2004). Neural circuits involved in the recognition of actions performed by nonconspecifics: An fMRI study. *Journal of Cognitive Neuroscience, 16,* 114–126.

Bürgin, D., & Von Klitzing, K. (1995). Prenatal representation and postnatal interactions of a threesome (mother, father and baby). In J. Blitzer & M. Stauber (Eds.), *Psychosomatic obstetrics and gynaecology* (pp.185–191). Bologna, Italy: Monduzzi.

Buss, C., Davis, E. P., Muftuler, L. T., Head, K., & Sandman, C. A. (2010). High pregnancy anxiety during midgestation is associated with decreased gray matter density in 6–9-year-old children. *Psychoneuroendocrinology, 35,* 141–153.

Caggiano, V., Fogassi, L., Rizzolatti, G., Thier, P., & Casile, A. (2009). Mirror neurons differentially encode the peripersonal and extrapersonal space of monkeys. *Science, 324,* 403–406.

Calder, A. J., Keane, J., Manes, F., Antoun, N., & Young, A. W. (2000). Impaired recognition and experience of disgust following brain injury. *Nature Neuroscience, 3,* 1077–1078.

Caldji, C., Diorio, J., & Meaney, M. J. (2000). Variations in maternal care in infancy regulate the development of stress reactivity. *Biological Psychiatry, 48,* 1164–1174.

Calvo-Merino, B., Glaser, D. E, Grèzes, J., Passingham, R. E., & Haggard, P. (2005). Action observation and acquired motor skills: An fMRI study with expert dancers. *Cerebral Cortex, 15,* 1243–1249.

Calvo-Merino, B., Grèzes, J., Glaser, D. E., Passingham, R. E., & Haggard, P. (2006). Seeing or doing? Influence of visual and motor familiarity in action observation. *Current Biology, 16,* 1905–1910.

Cameron, N. M., Champagne, F. A., Parent C., Fish, E. W., Ozaki-Kuroda, K., & Meaney, M. J. (2005). The programming of individual differences in defensive responses and reproductive strategies in the rat through variations in maternal care. *Neuroscience and Biobehavioral Reviews, 29,* 843–865.

Campbell, S. (2006). 4D and prenatal bonding: Still more questions than answers. *Ultrasound Obstetrics and Gynecology, 27,* 243–244.

Camras, L., Grow, G., & Ribordy, S. (1983). Recognition of emotion expressions by abused children. *Journal of Clinical and Child Psychology, 12,* 325–328.

Camras, L., Ribordy, S., Hill, J., Martino, S., Sachs, V., Spaccarelli, S., & Stefani, R. (1990). Maternal facial behavior and the recognition and production of emotional expression by maltreated and nonmaltreated children. *Developmental Psychology, 26,* 304–312.

Camras, L., Ribordy, S., Hill, J., Martino, S., Spaccarelli, S., & Stefani, R. (1988). Recognition and posing of emotional expressions by abused children and their mothers. *Developmental Psychology, 24,* 776–781.

Cancedda, L., Putignano, E., Sale, A., Viegi, A., Berardi, N., & Maffei, L. (2004). Acceleration of visual system development by environmental enrichment. *Journal of Neuroscience, 24,* 4840–4848.

Cannella, B. L. (2005). Maternal-fetal attachment: An integrative review. *Journal of Advanced Nursing, 50,* 60–68.

Carandini, M. (2012). From circuits to behavior: A bridge too far? *Nature Neurocience, 15,* 507–509.

Carlson, V., Cicchetti, D., Barnett, D., & Braunwald, K. (1989). Disorganized-disoriented attachment relationships in maltreated infants. *Developmental Psychology, 25,* 525–531.

Carneiro, C., Corboz-Warnery, A., & Fivaz-Depeursinge, E. (2006). The Prenatal Lausanne Trilogue Play: A new observational assessment tool of the prenatal co-parenting alliance. *Infant Mental Health Journal, 27,* 207–228.

Carpenter, M., Call, J., & Tomasello, M. (2005). Twelve- and 18-month-olds copy actions in terms of goals. *Developmental Science, 8,* F13–F20.

Carr, L., Iacoboni, M., Dubeau, M.-C., Mazziotta, J. C., & Lenzi, G. L. (2003). Neural mechanisms of empathy in humans: A relay from neural systems for imitation to limbic areas. *Proceedings of the National Academy of Sciences USA, 100,* 5497–5502.

Carter, C. S., & Keverne, E. B. (2002). The neurobiology of social affiliation and pair bonding. *Hormones, Brain and Behavior, 1,* 299–337.

Casile, A., & Giese, M. A. (2006). Nonvisual motor training influences biological motion perception. *Current Biology, 16,* 69–74.

Caspi, A., McClay, J., Moffitt, T. E., Mill, J., Martin, J., Craig, I. W., . . . Poulton, R. (2002). Role of genotype in the cycle of violence in maltreated children. *Science, 297,* 851–854.

Caspi, A., Moffitt, T. E., Cannon, M., McClay, J., Murray, R., Harrington, H., . . . Craig, I. W. (2005). Moderation of the effect of adolescent-onset cannabis use on adult psychosis by a functional polymorphism in the catechol-o-methyltransferase gene: Longitudinal evidence of a gene environment interaction. *Biological Psychiatry, 57,* 1117–1127.

Caspi, A., Sugden, K., Moffitt, T. E., Taylor, A., Craig, I. W., Harrington, H., . . . Poulton, R. (2003). Influence of life stress on depression: Moderation by a polymorphism in the 5-HTT gene. *Science, 301,* 386–389.

Cassidy, J. (2008). The nature of the child's ties. In J. Cassidy & P. R. Shaver (Eds.), *Handbook of attachment: Theory, research, and clinical applications* (2nd ed., pp. 3–22). New York, NY: Guilford Press.

Castiello, U., Becchio, C., Zoia, S., Nelini, C., Sartori, L., Blason, L., . . . Gallese, V. (2010). Wired to be social: The ontogeny of human interaction. *PLoS ONE, 5,* e13199.

Cattaneo, L., Caruana, F., Jezzini, A., & Rizzolatti, G. (2009). Representation of goal and movements without overt motor behavior in the human motor cortex: A transcranial magnetic stimulation study. *Journal of Neuroscience, 29,* 11134–11138.

Cattaneo, L., & Rizzolatti, G. (2009). The mirror neuron system. *Archives of Neurology, 5,* 557–560.

Cattaneo, L., Sandrini, M., & Schwarzbach, J. (2010). State-dependent TMS reveals a hierarchical representation of observed acts in the temporal, parietal, and premotor cortices. *Cerebral Cortex, 20,* 2252–2258.

Cerezo, M. A. (1997). Abusive family interactions: A review. *Aggression and Violent Behavior, 2,* 215–240.

Champagne, D. L., Bagot, R. C., van Hasselt, F., Ramakers, G., Meaney, M. J., de Kloet, E. R., . . . Krugers, H. (2008). Maternal care and hippocampal plasticity: Evidence for experience-dependent structural plasticity, altered synaptic functioning, and differential responsiveness to glucocorticoids and stress. *Journal of Neuroscience, 28,* 6037–6045.

Champagne, F. A., Chretien, P., Stevenson, C. W., Yuan Zhang, T., Gratton, A., & Meaney, M. J. (2004). Variations in nucleus accumbens dopamine associated with individual differences in maternal behavior in the rat. *Journal of Neuroscience, 24,* 4113–4123.

Chang, H. L., Chang, T. C., Lin, T. Y., & Kuo, S. S. (2002). Psychiatric morbidity and pregnancy outcome in a disaster area of Taiwan 921 earthquake. *Psychiatry and Clinical Neurosciences, 56,* 139–144.

Charman, T., Swettenham, J., Baron-Cohen, S., Cox, A., Baird, G., & Drew, A. (1997). Infants with autism: An investigation of empathy, pretend play, joint attention, and imitation. *Developmental Psychology, 33,* 781–789.

Chartrand, T. L., & Bargh J. A. (1999). The chameleon effect: The perception-behavior link and social interaction. *Journal of Personality and Social Psychology, 76,* 893–910.

Chiba, T., Kayahara, T., & Nakano, K. (2001). Efferent projections of infralimbic and prelimbic areas of the medial prefrontal cortex in the Japanese monkey, Macaca fuscata. *Brain Research, 888,* 83–101.

Chiron, C., Jambaque, I., Nabbout, R., Lounes, R., Syrota, A., & Dulac, O. (1997). The right brain hemisphere is dominant in human infants. *Brain, 120,* 1057–1065.

Chiron, C., Raynaud, C., Mazière, B., Zilbovicius, M., Laflamme, L., Masure, M. C., . . . Syrota, A. (1992). Changes in regional cerebral blood flow during brain maturation in children and adolescents. *Journal of Nuclear Medicine, 33,* 696–703.

Cho, M. M., DeVries, A. C., Williams, J. R., & Carter, C. S. (1999). The effects of oxytocin and vasopressin on partner preferences in male and female prairie voles (Microtus ochrogaster). *Behavioral Neuroscience, 113,* 1071–1079.

Chugani, H. T. (1996). Neuroimaging of developmental nonlinearity and developmental pathologies. In R. W. Thatcher, G. Reid Lyon, J. Rumsey, & N. Krasnegor (Eds.), *Developmental neuroimaging: Mapping the development of brain and behavior* (pp. 187–195). San Diego, CA: Academic Press.

Cicchetti, D., & Barnett, D. (1991). Attachment organization in preschool-aged maltreated children. *Development and Psychopathology, 3,* 397–411.

Cicchetti, D., & Curtis, W. J. (2005). An event-related potential study of the processing of affective facial expressions in young children who experienced maltreatment during the first year of life. *Development and Psychopathology, 17,* 641–677.

Cicchetti, D., & Lynch, M. (1995). Failures in the expectable environment and their impact on individual development: The case of child maltreatment. In D. Cicchetti & D. Cohen (Eds.), *Developmental psychopathology: Risk, disorder, and adaptation* (Vol. 2, pp. 32–71). New York, NY: Wiley.

Cicchetti, D., & Rogosch, F. A. (1997). The role of self-organization in the promotion of resilience in maltreated children. *Development and Psychopathology, 9,* 797–815.

Cicchetti, D., & Rogosch, F. A. (2012). Gene by environment interaction and resilience: Effects of child maltreatment and serotonin, corticotropin releasing hormone, dopamine, and oxytocin genes. *Development and Psychopathology, 24,* 411–427.

Cicchetti, D., Rogosch, F. A., Gunnar, M. R., & Toth, S. L. (2010). The differential impacts of early abuse on internalizing problems and daytime cortisol rhythm in school-aged children. *Child Development, 81,* 252–269.

Cicchetti, D., Rogosh, F. A., & Toth, S. L. (2006). Fostering secure attachment in infants in maltreating families through preventive interventions. *Development and Psychopathology, 18,* 623–649.

Cismaresco, A. S., & Montagner, H. (1990). Mothers' discrimination of their neonates' cry in relation to cry acoustics: The first week of life. *Early Child Development and Care, 65,* 3–11.

Cohen, L. J., & Slade, A. (2000). The psychology and psychopathology of pregnancy: Reorganization and transformation. In C. H. Zeanah (Ed.), *Handbook of infant mental health* (2nd ed., pp. 20–36). New York, NY: Guilford Press.

Cohn, J. F., & Tronick, E. Z. (1987). Mother-infant face-to-face interaction: The sequence of dyadic states at 3, 6, and 9 months. *Developmental Psychology, 23,* 68–77.

Coiro, M. J., & Emery, R. E. (1998). Do marriage problems affect fathering more than mothering? A quantitative and qualitative review. *Clinical Child and Family Psychology Review, 1,* 23–40.

Committeri, G., Pitzalis, S., Galati, G., Patria, F., Pelle, G., Sabatini, U., . . . Pizzamiglio, L. (2007). Neural bases of personal and extrapersonal neglect in humans. *Brain, 130,* 431–441.

Condon, J. T. (1993). The assessment of antenatal emotional attachment: Development of a questionnaire instrument. *British Journal of Medical Psychology, 66,* 167–183.

Condon, J. T., & Corkindale, C. (1997). The correlates of antenatal attachment in pregnant women. *British Journal of Medical Psychology, 70,* 359–372.

Connell-Carrick, K., & Scannapieco, M. (2006). Ecological correlates of neglect in infant and toddlers. *Journal of Interpersonal Violence, 21,* 299–316.

Conrad, J. (1950). *Heart of darkness and The secret sharer.* New York, NY: Signet Classic. (Original work published 1909)

Corter, C., & Fleming, A. S. (1995). Fathers' and mothers' responsiveness to newborns: The role of attitudes, experience and infant odors. In M. Bornstein (Ed.), *Handbook of parenting, Vol. 2. Biology and ecology of parenting* (pp. 87–116). Hillsdale, NJ: Erlbaum.

Cox, D. N., Wittmann, B. K., Hess, M., Ross, A. G., Lind, J., & Lindahl, S. (1987). The psychological impact of diagnostic ultrasound. *Obstetrics and Gynecology, 70,* 673–676.

Cox, M. J., Paley, B., & Harter, K. (2001). Interparental conflict and parent-child relationships. In J. H. Grych & F. D. Fincham (Eds.), *Interparental conflict and child development: Theory, research, and application* (pp. 249–272). New York, NY: Cambridge University Press.

Cranley, M. S. (1981). Development of a tool for the measurement of maternal attachment during pregnancy. *Nursing Research, 30,* 281–284.

Crittenden, P. M. (1981). Abusing, neglecting problematic and adequate dyads: Differentiating by patterns of interaction. *Merrill-Palmer Quarterly, 27,* 201–208.

Crittenden, P. M. (1985). Maltreated infants: Vulnerability and resilience. *Journal of Child Psychology and Psychiatry, 26,* 85–96.

Crittenden, P. M. (1988). Relationships at risk. In J. Belsky & T. Nezworksi (Eds.), *Clinical implications of attachment* (pp. 136–174). Hillsdale, NJ: Erlbaum.

Cross, E. S., Hamilton, A. F., & Grafton, S. T. (2006). Building a motor simulation de novo: Observation of dance by dancers. *Neuroimage, 31,* 1257–1267.

Crutcher, M. D., & Alexander, G. E. (1990). Movement-related neuronal activity selectively coding either direction or muscle pattern in three motor areas of the monkey. *Journal of Neurophysiology, 64,* 151–163.

Csibra, G., Birò, S., Koòs, O., & Gergely, G. (2003). One-year-old infants use teleological representations of actions productively. *Cognitive Science, 27,* 111–133.

Csibra, G., Gergely, G., Birò, S., Koòs, O., & Brockbank, M. (1999). Goal attribution without agency cues: The perception of "pure reason" in infancy. *Cognition, 72,* 237–267.

Cummings, E. M., & Davies, P. (1994). Maternal depression and child development. *Journal of Child Psychology and Psychiatry, 35,* 73–112.

Curtis, W. J., & Cicchetti, D. (2007). Emotion and resilience: A multilevel investigation of hemispheric electroencephalogram asymmetry and emotion regulation in maltreated and nonmaltreated children. *Development and Psychopathology, 19,* 811–840.

Curtis, W. J., & Cicchetti, D. (2011). Affective facial expression processing in young children who have experienced maltreatment during the first year of life: An event-related potential study. *Development and Psychopathology, 23,* 373–395.

Dalgleish, T. (2004). The emotional brain. *Nature Reviews Neuroscience, 5,* 583–589.

Damasio, A. R. (1994). *Descartes' error: Emotion, reason, and the human brain.* New York, NY: Putnam.

Damasio, A. R. (1999). *The feeling of what happens: Body and emotion in the making of consciousness.* New York, NY: Harcourt Brace.

Damasio, A. R. (2003). *Looking for Spinoza: Joy, sorrow and the feeling brain*. New York, NY: Harcourt.

Darnaudéry, M., & Maccari, S. (2008). Epigenetic programming of the stress response in male and female rats by prenatal restraint stress. *Brain Research Reviews, 57*, 571–585.

Darwin, C. (1872). *The expression of the emotions in man and animals*. Chicago, IL: University of Chicago Press.

David, D. H., & Lyons-Ruth, K. (2005). Differential attachment responses of male and female infants to frightening maternal behavior: Tend or befriend versus fight or flight. *Infant Mental Health Journal, 21*, 1–18.

Davidson, R. J. (1998). Affective style and affective disorders: Perspectives from affective neuroscience. *Cognition Emotion, 12*, 307–330.

Davidson, R. J., & Irwin, W. (1999). The functional neuroanatomy of emotion and affective style. *Trends in Cognitive Science, 3*, 11–21.

Davis, E. P., Glynn, L. M., Schetter, C., Hobel, C., Chicz-DeMet, A., & Sandman, C. A. (2007). Prenatal exposure to maternal cortisol influences infant temperament. *Journal of American Academy of Child and Adolescent Psychiatry, 46*, 737–746.

Dayton, C. J., Levendosky, A. A., Davidson, W. S., & Bogat, G. A. (2010). The child as held in the mind of the mother: The influence of prenatal maternal representations on parenting behaviors. *Infant Mental Health Journal, 31*, 220–241.

De Bellis, M. D. (2001). Developmental traumatology: The psychobiological development of maltreated children and its implications for research, treatment, and policy. *Development and Psychopathology, 13*, 539–564.

De Bellis, M. D. (2005). The psychobiology of neglect. *Child Maltreatment, 10*, 150–172.

De Preester, H. (2008). From ego to alter ego: Husserl, Merlau-Ponty, and a layered approach to intersubjectivity. *Phenomenology and the Cognitive Sciences, 7*, 133–142.

de Vignemont, F., & Singer, T. (2006). The emphatic brain: How, when, and why? *Trends in Cognitive Sciences, 10*, 435–441.

de Waal, F. B. M. (1998). No imitation without identification. *Behavioral and Brain Sciences, 21*, 689.

de Waal, F. B. M. (2012). A bottom-up view of empathy. In F. B. M. de Waal & P. F. Ferrari (Eds.), *The primate mind* (pp. 121–138). Cambridge, MA: Harvard University Press.

de Weerth, C., van Hees, Y., & Buitelaar, J. (2003). Prenatal maternal cortisol levels and infant behavior during the first 5 months. *Early Human Development, 74*, 139–151.

de Wolff, M. S., & van Ijzendoorn, M. H. (1997). Sensitivity and attachment: A meta-analysis on parental antecedents of infant attachment. *Child Development, 68*, 571–591.

Decety, J., & Jackson, P. L. (2004). The functional architecture of human empathy. *Behavioral and Cognitive Neuroscience Reviews, 3*, 71–100.

Decety, J., & Meyer, M. (2008). From emotion resonance to empathic understanding: A social developmental neuroscience account. *Development and Psychopathology, 20*, 1053–1080.

Decety, J., & Sommerville, J. A. (2003). Shared representations between self and other: A social cognitive neuroscience view. *Trends in Cognitive Science, 7*, 527–533.

Dehaene, S., Kerszberg, M., & Changeux, J. P. (1998). A neuronal model of a global workspace in effortful cognitive tasks. *Proceedings of the National Academy of Sciences USA, 95*, 14529–14534.

Dehaene-Lambertz, G., Dehaene, S., & Hertz-Pannier, L. (2002). Functional neuroimaging of speech perception in infants. *Science, 298,* 2013–2015.

Derogatis, L. R. (1977). *SCL-90-R: Administration, scoring and procedures manual.* Baltimore, MD: Clinical Psychometrics Research.

Desai, M., Gayle, D., Babu, J., & Ross, M. G. (2005). Progammed obesity in intrauterine growth-restricted newborns: Modulation by newborn nutrition. *American Journal of Physiology: Regulatory, Integrative and Comparative Physiology, 288,* R91–R96.

Diamond, D., Blatt, S. J., Stayner, D., & Kaslow, N. (1991). *Self-other differentiation of object representations.* Unpublished research manual, Yale University, New Haven, CT.

Diatkine, G. (2000). Book reviews. Le Séminaire. Livre V. Les formations de l'inconscient [The Seminar. Book V. The formations of the unconscious] (1957–1958): Jacques Lacan. Paris, France: Seuil, 1998, pp. 518. *International Journal of Psychoanalysis, 81,* 1025–1032.

Dimberg, U. (1982). Facial reactions to facial expressions. *Psychophysiology, 19,* 643–647.

Dimberg, U., & Thunberg, M. (1998). Rapid facial reactions to emotion facial expressions. *Scandinavian Journal of Psychology, 39,* 39–46.

Dimberg, U., Thunberg, M., & Elmehed, K. (2000). Unconscious facial reactions to emotional facial expressions. *Psychological Science, 11,* 86–89.

DiPietro, J. A., Novak, M. F., Costigan, K. A., Atella, L. D., & Reusing, S. P. (2006). Maternal psychological distress during pregnancy in relation to child development at age two. *Child Development, 77,* 573–587.

Dixon, L., Hamilton-Giachritsis, C. E., & Browne, K. D. (2005). Behavioural measures of parents abused as children: A mediational analysis of the intergenerational continuity of child maltreatment (Part II). *Journal of Child and Psychiatry, 46,* 58–68.

Doan, H. M., & Zimmerman, A. (2003). Conceptualizing prenatal attachment: Toward a multidimensional view. *Journal of Prenatal and Perinatal Psychology and Health, 18,* 109–129.

Domes, G., Heinrichs, M., Michel, A., Berger, C., & Herpertz, S. C. (2007). Oxytocin improves "mind-reading" in humans. *Biological Psychiatry, 61,* 731–733.

Douglas, A. J., & Meddle, S. L. (2008). Fast delivery: A central role for oxytocin. In R. S. Bridges (Ed.), *Neurobiology of the parental brain* (pp. 225–234). New York, NY: Academic Press, Elsevier.

Draper, J. (2002). It's the first scientific evidence: Men's experience of pregnancy confirmation. *Journal of Advanced Nursing, 39,* 563–570.

Dumbar, R. I. M. (1992). Neocortex size as a constraint on group size in primates. *Journal of Human Evolution, 22,* 469–493.

Dushanova, J., & Donoghue, J. (2010). Neurons in primary motor cortex engaged during action observation. *European Journal of Neuroscience, 31,* 386–398.

Ebisch, S. J. H., Ferri, F., Salone, A., D'Amico, L., Perrucci, M. G., Ferro, F. M., . . . Gallese, V. (2011). Differential involvement of somatosensory and interoceptive cortices during the observation of affective touch. *Journal of Cognitive Neuroscience, 23,* 1808–1822.

Ebisch, S. J. H., Perrucci, M. G., Ferretti, A., Del Gratta, C., Romani, G. L., & Gallese, V. (2008). The sense of touch: Embodied simulation in a visuo-tactile mirroring mechanism for the sight of any touch. *Journal of Cognitive Neuroscience, 20,* 1611–1623.

Ebisch, S. J. H., Salone, A., Ferri, F., De Berardis, D., Mantini, D., Ferro, F. M., & Gallese, V. (2012). Out of touch with reality? Social perception in first episode schizophrenia. *Social Cognitive and Affective Neuroscience*, doi: 10.1093/scan/nss012.

Egeland, B., & Sroufe, L. A. (1981). Developmental sequelae of maltreatment in infancy. In R. Rizley & D. Cicchetti (Eds.), *Developmental perspectives in child maltreatment* (pp. 77–92). San Francisco, CA: Jossey Bass.

Eibl-Eibesfeldt, I. (1989). *Human ethology*. New York, NY: Aldine de Gruyter.

Ekelin, M., Crang Svalenius, E., & Dykes, A. K. (2004). A qualitative study of mothers' and fathers' experiences of routine ultrasound examination in Sweden. *Midwifery, 20*, 335–344.

Ellis, B. J., & Boyce, W. T. (2011). Differential susceptibility to the environment: Toward an understanding of sensitivity to developmental experiences and context. *Development and Psychopathology, 23*, 1–5.

Emde, R. N. (1994a). Three roads intersecting: Changing viewpoints in the psychoanalytic story of Oedipus. In M. Ammaniti & D. N. Stern (Eds.), *Psychoanalysis and development* (pp. 97–110). New York, NY: New York University Press.

Emde, R. N. (1994b). Commentary: Triadification experiences and a bold new direction for infant mental health. *Infant Mental Health Journal, 15*, 90–95.

Emde, R. N. (2007). Embodiment and our immersion with others: Commentary on Fonagy and Target. *Journal of the American Psychoanalytic Association, 55*, 485–492.

Emde, R. N. (2009). From ego to "we-go": Neurobiology and questions for psychoanalysis—commentary on papers by Trevarthen, Gallese, and Ammaniti & Trentini. *Psychoanalytic Dialogues, 19*, 556–564.

Entringer, S., Buss, C., & Wadhwa, P. D. (2010). Prenatal stress and developmental programming of human health and disease risk: Concepts and integration of empirical findings. *Current Opinion in Endocrinology, Diabetes and Obesity, 17*, 507–516.

Entringer, S., Epel, E. S., Kumsta, R., Lin, J., Hellhammer, D. H., Blackburn, E. H., . . . Wadhwa, P. D. (2011). Stress exposure in intrauterine life is associated with shorter telomere length in young adulthood. *Proceedings of the National Academy of Sciences USA, 108*, E513–E518.

Entwisle, D. R., & Doering, S. G. (1981). *The first birth, a family turning point*. Baltimore, MD: Johns Hopkins University Press.

Epel, E. S., Blackburn, E. H., Lin, J., Dhabhar, F. S., Adler, N. E., Morrow, J. D., & Cawthon, R. M. (2004). Accelerated telomere shortening in response to life stress. *Proceedings of the National Academy of Sciences USA, 101*, 17312–17315.

Epel, E., Lapidus, R., McEwen, B., & Brownell, K. (2001). Stress may add bite to appetite in women: A laboratory study of stress-induced cortisol and eating behavior. *Psychoneuroendocrinology, 26*, 37–49.

Falck-Ytter, T., Gredeback, G., & von Hofsten, C. (2006). Infant predict other people's action goals. *Nature Neuroscience, 9*, 878–879.

Fava Vizziello, G., Antonioli, M. E., Cocci, V., & Invernizzi, R. (1993). From pregnancy to motherhood: The structure of representative and narrative change. *Infant Mental Health Journal, 14*, 4–16.

Fava Vizziello, G., Righetti, P. L., & Cristiani, F. M. (2003). Prima filii imago. In P. L. Righetti (Ed.), *Elementi di psicologia prenatale* (pp. 170–181). Rome, Italy: Edizioni Magi. (Original work published 1997)

Feinberg, M. E. (2002). Coparenting and the transition to parenthood: A framework for prevention. *Clinical Child and Family Psychology Review, 5*, 173–195.

Feldman, R. (2003). Infant-mother and infant-father synchrony: The coregulation of positive arousal. *Infant Mental Health Journal, 24,* 1–23.

Feldman, R. (2006). From biological rhythms to social rhythms: Physiological precursors of mother-infant synchrony. *Developmental Psychology, 42,* 175–188.

Feldman, R. (2007). Parent-infant synchrony and the construction of shared timing: Physiological precursors, developmental outcomes, and risk conditions. *Journal of Child Psychology and Psychiatry, 48,* 329–354.

Feldman, R., Gordon, I., Schneiderman, I., Weisman, O., & Zagoory-Sharon, O. (2010). Natural variations in maternal and paternal care are associated with systematic changes in oxytocin following parent-infant contact. *Psychoneuroendocrinology, 35,* 1133–1141.

Feldman, R., Greenbaum, C. W., & Yirmiya, N. (1999). Mother-infant affect synchrony as an antecedent of the emergence of self-control. *Developmental Psychology, 35,* 223–231.

Feldman, R., Weller, A., Zagoory-Sharon, O., & Levine, A. (2007). Evidence for a neuro-endocrinological foundation of human affiliation. *Psychological Science, 18,* 965–970.

Ferenczi, S. (1926). Vermin as a symbol of pregnancy. In S. Ferenczi, J. Rickman, & J. I. Suttie (Eds.), *Further contributions to the theory and technique of psychoanalysis* (p. 361). New York, NY: Boni and Liveright. (Original work published 1914)

Ferrari, P. F., Coudé, G., Gallese, V., & Fogassi, L. (2008). Having access to others' mind through gaze: The role of ontogenetic and learning processes in gaze-following behavior of macaques. *Social Neuroscience, 3,* 239–249.

Ferrari, P. F., & Fogassi, L. (2012). The mirror neuron system in monkeys and its implications for social cognitive functions. In F. B. M. de Waal & P. F. Ferrari (Eds.), *The primate mind* (pp. 13–31). Cambridge, MA: Harvard University Press.

Ferrari, P. F., Kohler, E., Fogassi, L., & Gallese, V. (2000). The ability to follow eye gaze and its emergence during development in macaque monkeys. *Proceedings of the National Academy of Sciences USA, 97,* 13997–4002.

Ferrari, P. F., Paukner, A., Ionica, C., & Suomi, S. J. (2009). Reciprocal face-to-face communication between rhesus macaque mothers and their newborn infants. *Current Biology, 19,* 1768–1772.

Ferrari, P. F., Vanderwert, R., Herman, K., Paukner, A., Fox, N. A., & Suomi, S. J. (2008). EEG activity in response to facial gestures in 1-7 days old infant rhesus macaques. *Society for Neuroscience Meetings, 297.13.*

Ferrari, P. F., Vanderwert, R. E., Paukner, E., Bower, S., Suomi, S. J., & Fox, N. (2012). Distinct EEG amplitude suppression to facial gestures as evidence for a mirror mechanism in newborn monkeys. *Journal of Cognitive Neuroscience, 24,* 1165–1172.

Ferrari, P. F., Visalberghi, E., Paukner, A., Fogassi, L., Ruggiero, A., & Suomi, S. J. (2006). Neonatal imitation in rhesus macaques. *PLoS Biology, 4,* e302.

Ferris, C. F., Kulkarni, P., Sullivan, J. M. Jr., Harder, J. A., Messenger, T. L., & Febo, M. (2005). Pup suckling is more rewarding than cocaine: Evidence from functional magnetic resonance imaging and three-dimensional computational analysis. *Journal of Neuroscience, 25,* 149–156.

Field, T., Diego, M., Hernadez-Reif, M., Gil, K., Vera, Y., Schanberg, S., . . . Gonzalez-Garcia, A. (2004). Prenatal maternal biochemistry predicts neonatal biochemistry. *International Journal of Neuroscience, 114,* 933–945.

Field, T., Diego, M., Hernandez-Reif, M., Schanberg, S., Kuhn, C., Yando, R., & Bendell, D. (2003). Pregnancy anxiety and comorbid depression and anger: Effects on the fetus and neonate. *Depression and Anxiety, 17,* 140–151.

Field, T., Fox, N., Pickens, J., & Nawrocki, T. (1995). Relative right frontal EEG activation in 3- to 6-month-old infants of "depressed" mothers. *Developmental Psychology, 31*, 358–363.

Field, T., Pickens, J., Fox, N., Nawrocki, T., & Gonzalez, J. (1995). Vagal tone in infants of depressed mothers. *Development and Psychopathology, 7*, 227–231.

Field, T. M., Woodson, R., Greenberg, R., & Cohen, D. (1982). Discrimination and imitation of facial expression by neonates. *Science, 218*, 179–181.

Finnbogadòttir, H., Crang Svalenius, E., & Persson, E. K. (2003). Expectant first-time fathers' experiences of pregnancy. *Midwifery, 19*, 96–105.

Fivaz-Depeursinge, E. (2001). Corps et intersubjectivité [Body and intersubjectivity]. *Psichothérapies, 21*, 63–69.

Fivaz-Depeursinge, E., & Corboz-Warnery, A. (1999). *The primary triangle: A developmental systems view of mothers, fathers, and infants.* New York, NY: Basic Books.

Fivaz-Depeursinge, E., Favez, N., & Lavanchy, C. (2005). Four-month-olds make triangular bids to father and mother during trilogue play with still-face. *Social Development, 14*, 361–378.

Fivaz-Depeursinge, E., Frascarolo, F., & Corboz-Warnery, A. (2010). Observational tool: The prenatal Lausanne Trilogue Play. In S. Tyano, M. Keren, H. Herrman, & J. Cox (Eds.), *Parenthood and mental health: A bridge between infant and adult psychiatry* (pp. 121–128). Oxford, UK: Wiley-Blackwell.

Fivaz-Depeursinge, E., Lavanchy-Scaiola, C., & Favez, N. (2010). The young infant's triangular communication in the family: Access to threesome intersubjectivity? Conceptual considerations and case illustrations. *Psychoanalytic Dialogues, 20*, 125–140.

Fleming, A. S., O'Day, D. H., & Kraemer, G. W. (1999). Neurobiology of mother-infant interactions: Experience and central nervous system plasticity across development and generations. *Neuroscience and Biobehavioral Reviews, 23*, 673–685.

Fleming, A. S., Ruble, D., Krieger, H., & Wong, P. Y. (1997). Hormonal and experiential correlates of maternal responsiveness during pregnancy and the puerperium in human mothers. *Hormones and Behavior, 31*, 145–158.

Flinn, M. V., Geary, D. C., & Ward, C. V. (2005). Ecological dominance, social competition, and coalitionary arms races: Why humans evolved extraordinary intelligence. *Evolution and Human Behavior, 26*, 10–46.

Fodor, J. (1975). *The language of thought.* New York, NY: Thomas Y. Crowell.

Fodor, J. (1981). *Representations.* Cambridge, MA: MIT Press.

Fodor, J. (1983). *The modularity of mind.* Cambridge, MA: MIT Press.

Fogassi, L., Ferrari, P. F., Gesierich, B., Rozzi, S., Chersi, F., & Rizzolatti, G. (2005). Parietal lobe: From action organization to intention understanding. *Science, 308*, 662–667.

Fogel, A. (2003). Remembering infancy: Accessing our earliest experiences. In G. Bremner & A. Slater (Eds.), *Theories of infant development* (pp. 204–232). Cambridge, MA: Blackwell.

Fogel, A., & Thelen, E. (1987). Development of early expressive and communicative action: Reinterpreting the evidence from a dynamic systems perspective. *Developmental Psychology, 23*, 747–761.

Fonagy, P. (1998). Prevention, the appropriate target of infant psychotherapy. *Infant Mental Health Journal, 19*, 124–150.

Fonagy, P. (2001a). *Attachment theory and psychoanalysis.* New York, NY: Other Press.

Fonagy, P. (2001b). The human genome and the representational world: The role of early mother-infant interaction in creating an interpersonal interpretive mechanism. *Bulletin of the Menninger Clinic, 65,* 427–448.

Fonagy, P., Gergely, G., Jurist, E. L., & Target, M. (2002). *Affect regulation, mentalization and the development of the self.* New York, NY: Other Press.

Fonagy, P., Steele, H., Moran, G., Steele, M., & Higgitt, A. (1991). The capacity for understanding mental states: The reflective self in parent and child and its significance for security of attachment. *Infant Mental Health Journal, 12,* 201–218.

Fonagy, P., Steele H., & Steele, M. (1991). Maternal representations of attachment during pregnancy predict the organization of infant-mother attachment at one year of age. *Child Development, 62,* 891–905.

Fonagy, P., & Target, M. (1998). An interpersonal view of the infant. In A. Hurry (Ed.), *Psychoanalysis and Developmental Therapy* (pp. 3–31). London, UK: Karnac Books.

Fontaine, R. (1984). Imitative skills between birth and six months. *Infant Behavior and Development, 7,* 323–333.

Fox, N. A., Kimmerly, N. L., & Shafer, W. D. (1991). Attachment to mother/attachment to father: A meta-analysis. *Child Development, 52,* 210–225.

Fraiberg, S. H. (1980). *Clinical studies in infant mental health.* New York, NY: Basic Books.

Fraiberg, S. H. (1982). Pathological defenses in infancy. *Psychoanalytic Quarterly, 51,* 612–634.

Fraiberg S. H., Edelson, E., & Shapiro, V. (1975). Ghosts in the nursery: A psychoanalytic approach to the problem of impaired infant-mother relationships. *Journal of the American Academy of Child Psychiatry, 14,* 387–422.

Francis, D. D., Diorio, J., Liu, D., & Meaney, M. J. (1999). Nongenomic transmission across generations of maternal behavior and stress responses in the rat. *Science, 286,* 1155–1158.

Francis, D. D., Young, L. J., Meaney, M. J., & Insel, T. R. (2002). Naturally occurring differences in maternal care are associated with the expression of oxytocin and vasopressin (V1a) receptors: Gender differences. *Journal of Neuroendocrinology, 14,* 349–353.

Frazier, C. R., Trainor, B. C., Cravens, C. J., Whitney, T. K., & Marler, C. A., (2006). Paternal behavior influences development of aggression and vasopressin expression in male California mouse offspring. *Hormones and Behavior, 50,* 699–707.

Freeman, A. (2000). The influences of ultrasound-stimulated paternal-fetal bonding and gender identification. *Journal of Diagnostic Medical Sonography, 16,* 237–241.

Freud, S. (1955). The "uncanny." In J. Strachey (Ed., & Trans.), *The standard edition of the complete psychological works of Sigmund Freud* (Vol. 17, pp. 217–256). London, UK: Hogarth Press. (Original work published 1919)

Freud, S. (1955). Group psychology and the analysis of the ego. In J. Strachey (Ed., & Trans.), *The standard edition of the complete psychological works of Sigmund Freud* (Vol. 17, pp. 65–144). London, UK: Hogarth Press. (Original work published 1921)

Freud, S. (1957). Five lectures on psychoanalysis. In J. Strachey (Ed., & Trans.), *The standard edition of the complete psychological works of Sigmund Freud* (Vol. 11, pp 7–55). London, UK: Hogarth Press. (Original work published 1910)

Freud, S. (1957). On narcissism: An introduction. In J. Strachey (Ed., & Trans.), *Standard Edition of the complete psychological works of Sigmund Freud* (Vol. 14, pp 67–102). London, UK: Hogarth Press. (Original work published 1914)

Freud, S. (1958). Formulations on the principles of mental functioning. In J. Strachey (Ed., & Trans.), *The standard edition of the complete psychological works of Sigmund Freud* (Vol. 12, pp. 213–236). London, UK: Hogarth Press. (Original work published 1911)

Freud, S. (1959). Creative writers and day-dreaming. In J. Strachey (Ed., & Trans.), *The standard edition of the complete psychological works of Sigmund Freud* (Vol. 9, pp. 141–154). London, UK: Hogarth Press. (Original work published 1908)

Freud. S. (1959). Delusions and dreams in Jensen's Gradiva. In J. Strachey (Ed., & Trans.), *Standard edition of the complete psychological works of Sigmund Freud* (Vol. 9, pp.1–96). London, UK: Hogarth Press. (Original work published 1907)

Freud, S. (1961). The ego and the id. In J. Strachey (Ed., & Trans.), *The standard edition of the complete psychological works of Sigmund Freud* (Vol. 19, pp. 1–66). London, UK: Hogarth Press. (Original work published 1923)

Fries, A. B. W., Ziegler, T. E., Kurian, J. R., Jcoris, S., & Pollak, S. D. (2005). Early experience in humans is associated with changes in neuropeptides critical for regulating social behavior. *Proceedings of the National Academy of Sciences USA, 102,* 17237–17240.

Frith, C. D., & Frith, U. (2012). Mechanisms of social cognition. *Annual Review of Psychology, 63,* 287–313.

Frith, U., & Frith, C. D. (2003). Development and neurophysiology of mentalizing. *Philosophical Transactions of the Royal Society of London, 358,* 459–473.

Frith, U., & Happé, F. (1994). Autism: Beyond "theory of mind." *Cognition, 50,* 115–132.

Gallese, V. (2000). The inner sense of action: Agency and motor representations. *Journal of Consciousness Studies, 7,* 23–40.

Gallese, V. (2001) The "shared manifold" hypothesis: From mirror neurons to empathy. *Journal of Consciousness Studies, 8,* 33–50.

Gallese, V. (2003a). The manifold nature of interpersonal relations: The quest for a common mechanism. *Philosophical Transactions of the Royal Society of London Series B, Biological Sciences, 358,* 517–528.

Gallese, V. (2003b). The roots of empathy: The shared manifold hypothesis and the neural basis of intersubjectivity. *Psychopatology, 36,* 171–180.

Gallese, V. (2005). "Being like me": Self-other identity, mirror neurons and empathy. In S. Hurley & N. Chater (Eds.), *Perspectives on imitation: From cognitive neuroscience to social science* (Vol. 1, pp. 101–118). Cambridge, MA: MIT Press.

Gallese, V. (2006). Intentional attunement: A neurophysiological perspective on social cognition and its disruption in autism. *Brain Research, 1079,* 15–24.

Gallese, V. (2007). Before and below theory of mind: Embodied simulation and the neural correlates of social cognition. *Philosophical Transactions of the Royal Society of London Series B, Biological Science, 362,* 659–669.

Gallese, V. (2009a). Mirror neurons, embodied simulation, and the neural basis of social identification. *Psychoanalytic Dialogues, 19,* 519–536.

Gallese, V. (2009b). Motor abstraction: A neuroscientific account of how action goals and intentions are mapped and understood. *Psychological Research, 73,* 486–498.

Gallese, V. (2011). Neuroscience and phenomenology. *Phenomenology and Mind, 1,* 33–48.

Gallese, V., & Rochat, M. (2009). Motor cognition: The role of the motor system in the phylogeny and ontogeny of social cognition and its relevance for the understanding of autism. In P. D. Zelazo, M. Chandler, & E. Crone (Eds.), *Developmental social cognitive neuroscience*. New York, NY: Psychology Press.

Gallese, V., Fadiga, L., Fogassi, L., & Rizzolatti, G. (1996). Action recognition in the premotor cortex. *Brain, 119*, 593–609.

Gallese, V., Fogassi, L., Fadiga, L., & Rizzolatti, G. (2002). Action representation and the inferior parietal lobule. In W. Prinz & B. Hommel (Eds.), *Common mechanisms in perception and action: Attention and performance* (Vol. 19, pp. 334–355). Oxford, UK: Oxford University Press.

Gallese, V., Keysers, C., & Rizzolatti, G. (2004). A unifying view of the basis of social cognition. *Trends in Cognitive Science, 8*, 396–403.

Gallese, V., Rochat, M., Cossu, G., & Sinigaglia, C. (2009). Motor cognition and its role in the phylogeny and ontogeny of action understanding. *Develomental Psychology, 45*, 103–113.

Gallese, V., & Sinigaglia, C. (2011a). How the body in action shapes the self. *Journal of Consciousness Studies, 18*, 117–143.

Gallese, V., & Sinigaglia, C. (2011b). What is so special with embodied simulation. *Trends in Cognitive Sciences, 15*, 512–519.

Garcia, J., Bricker, L., Henderson, J., Martin, M. A., Mugford, M., Nielson, J., & Roberts, T. (2002). Women's view of pregnancy ultrasound: A systematic review. *Birth, 29*, 225–250.

Gaudin, J. M., Polansky, N. A., Kilpatrick, A. C., & Shilton, P. (1996). Family functioning in neglectful families. *Child Abuse and Neglect, 20*, 363–377.

Gazzola, V., Aziz-Zadeh, L., & Keysers, C. (2006). Empathy and the somatotopic auditory mirror system in humans. *Current Biology, 16*, 1824–1829.

Gazzola, V., Rizzolatti, G., Wicker, B., & Keysers C. (2007). The anthropomorphic brain: The mirror neuron system responds to human and robotic actions. *Neuroimage, 35*, 1674–1684.

Gazzola, V., van der Worp, H., Mulder, T., Wicker, B., Rizzolatti, G., & Keysers C. (2007). Aplasics born without hands mirror the goal of hand actions with their feet. *Current Biology, 17*, 1235–1240.

George, C., Kaplan, N., & Main, M. (1985). *Adult Attachment Interview protocol* (2nd ed.). Unpublished manuscript, University of California, Berkeley.

George, C., & Solomon, J. (1996). Representational models of relationships: Links between caregiving and attachment. *Infant Mental Health Journal, 17*, 198–216.

George, C., & Solomon, J. (2008). The caregiving system: A behavioral systems approach to parenting. In J. Cassidy & P. R. Shaver (Eds.), *Handbook of attachment: Theory, research, and clinical applications* (2nd ed., pp. 833–856). New York, NY: Guilford Press.

Gergely, G. (2007). The social construction of the subjective self: The role of affect-mirroring, markedness, and ostensive communication in self development. In L. Mayes, P. Fonagy, & M. Target (Eds.), *Developmental science and psychoanalysis: Integration and innovation* (pp. 45–82). London, UK: Karnac.

Gergely, G., & Watson, J. S. (1996). The social biofeedback theory of parental affect-mirroring: The development of emotional self-awareness and self-control in infancy. *The International Journal of Psychoanalysis, 77*, 1–31.

Gervai, J., Novak, A., Lakatos, K., Toth, I., Danis, I., Ronai, Z., . . . Lyons-Ruth, K. (2007). Infant genotype may moderate sensitivity to maternal affective communications: Attachment disorganization, quality of care, and the DRD4 polymorphism. *Social Neuroscience, 2,* 1–13.

Gianino, A., & Tronick, E. (1988). The mutual regulation model: The infant's self and interactive regulation coping and defense. In T. Field, P. McCabe, & N. Schneiderman (Eds.), *Stress and coping* (pp. 47–68). Hillsdale, NJ: Erlbaum.

Gintzler, A. R. (1980). Endorphin-mediates increases in pain threshold during pregnancy. *Science, 210,* 193–195.

Gitau, R., Cameron, A., Fisk, N. M., & Glover, V. (1998). Fetal exposure to maternal cortisol. *Lancet, 352,* 707–708.

Gitau, R., Fisk, N. M., & Glover, V. (2004). Human fetal and maternal corticotrophin releasing hormone responses to acute stress. *Archives of Disease in Childhood. Fetal and Neonatal Edition, 89,* F29–F32.

Gitau, R., Fisk, N. M., Teixeira, J. M., Cameron, A., & Glover, V. (2001). Fetal hypothalamic-pituitary-adrenal stress responses to invasive procedures are independent of maternal responses. *Journal of Clinical Endocrinology and Metabolism, 86,* 104–109.

Glocker, M. L., Langleben, D. D., Ruparel, K., Loughead, J. W., Gur, R. C., & Sachser, N. (2009a). Baby schema in infant faces induces cuteness perception and motivation for caretaking in adults. *Ethology, 115,* 257–263.

Glocker, M. L., Langleben, D. D., Ruparel, K., Loughead, J. W., Valdez, J. N., Griffin, M. D., . . . Gur, R. C. (2009b). Baby schema modulates the brain reward system in nulliparous women. *Proceedings of the National Academy of Sciences USA, 106,* 9115–9119.

Glosser, G., Zwil, A. S., Glosser, D. S., O'Connor, M. J., & Sperling, M. R. (2000). Psychiatric aspects of temporal lobe epilepsy before and after anterior temporal lobectomy. *Journal of Neurology, Neurosurgery and Psychiatry, 68,* 53–58.

Glynn, L., Wadhwa, P., Dunkel-Schetter, C., Chicz-Demet, A., & Sandman, C. (2001). When stress happens matters: Effects of earthquake timing on stress responsivity in pregnancy. *American Journal of Obstetrics and Gynecology, 184,* 637–642.

Goldberg, A. D., Allis, C. D., & Bernstein, E. (2007). Epigenetics: A landscape takes shape. *Cell, 128,* 635–638.

Goldberg, S., Benoit, D., Blokland, K., & Madigan, S. (2003). Atypical maternal behavior, maternal representations, and infant disorganized attachment. *Development and Psychopathology, 15,* 239–257.

Goldman, A. (2006). *Simulating minds: The philosophy, psychology and neuroscience of mindreading.* Oxford, UK: Oxford University Press.

Goldman, A., & Gallese, V. (2000). Reply to Schulkin. *Trends in Cognitive Sciences, 4,* 255–256.

Gordon, I., & Feldman R. (2008). Synchrony in the triad: A microlevel process model of coparenting and parent-child interactions. *Family Process, 47,* 465–479.

Gordon, I., Zagoor-Sharon, O., Leckman, J. F., & Feldman, R. (2010). Oxytocin and the development of parenting in humans. *Biological Psychiatry, 68,* 4, 377–82.

Green, A. (1986). The dead mother. In A. Green (Ed.), *On private madness* (pp. 222–253). London, UK: Hogarth Press and the Institute of Psychoanalysis. (Original work published 1983)

Grewen, K. M., Girdler, S. S., Amico, J., & Light, K. C. (2005). Effects of partner support on resting oxytocin, cortisol, norepinephrine, and blood pressure before and after warm partner contact. *Psychosomatic Medicine, 67,* 531–538.

Grienenberger, J. E., Kelly, K., & Slade, A. (2005). Maternal reflective functioning, mother-infant affective communication, and infant attachment: Exploring die link between mental states and observed caregiving behavior in the intergenerational transmission of attachment. *Attachment and Human Development, 7,* 299–311.

Grossmann, T., Johnson, M. H., Farroni, T., & Csibra, G. (2007). Social perception in the infant brain: Gamma oscillatory activity in response to eye gaze. *Social Cognitive and Affective Neuroscience, 2,* 284–291.

Gubernick, D. J., Winslow, J. T., Jensen, P., Jeanotte, L., & Bowen, J., (1995). Oxytocin changes in males over the reproductive cycle in the monogamous, biparental California mouse, Peromyscus californicus. *Hormones and Behavior, 29,* 59–73.

Gunnar, M. R. (2001). Effects of early deprivation: Findings from orphanage-reared infant and children. In C. A. Nelson & M. Luciana (Eds.), *Handbook of developmental cognitive neuroscience.* Cambridge, MA: MIT Press.

Gunnar, M. R. (2003). Integrating neuroscience and psychological approaches to the study of early experiences. *Annals of the New York Academy of Sciences, 1008,* 238–247.

Harris A., & Seckl, J. (2010). Glucocorticoids, prenatal stress and the programming of disease. *Hormones and Behavior, 59,* 279–89.

Harris, P. L. (1989). *Children and emotion.* Oxford, UK: Basil Blackwell.

Harville, E. W., Xiong, X., Pridjian, G., Elkind-Hirsch, K., & Buekens, P. (2011). Combined effects of Hurricane Katrina and Hurricane Gustav on the mental health of mothers of small children. *Journal of Psychiatric and Mental Health Nursing, 18,* 288–296.

Haskett, M. E., Sabourin Ward, C., Nears, K., & McPherson, A. (2006). Diversity in adjustment of maltreated children: Predictors of resilient functioning. *Clinical Psychology Review, 26,* 796–812.

Haslinger, B., Erhard, P., Altenmuller, E., Schroeder, U., Boecker, H., & Ceballos-Baumann, A. O. (2006). Transmodal sensorimotor networks during action observation in professional pianists. *Journal of Cognitive Neuroscience, 17,* 282–293.

Haxby, J. V., Hoffman, E. A., & Gobbini, M. I. (2000). The distributed human neural system for face perception. *Trends in Cognitive Sciences, 4,* 223–233.

Heckman, J. J. (2000). Plicies to foster human capital. *Research in Economics, 54,* 3–56.

Henry, J. P. (1993). Psychological and physiological responses to stress: The right hemisphere and the hypothalamo-pituitaryadrenal axis, an inquiry into problems of human bonding. *Integrative Physiological and Behavioral Science, 28,* 369–387.

Hepp-Reymond, M.-C., Hüsler, E. J., Maier, M. A., & Qi, H.-X. (1994). Force-related neuronal activity in two regions of the primate ventral premotor cortex. *Canadian Journal of Physiology and Pharmacology, 72,* 571–579.

Herrenkohl, R. C., Herrenkohl, E. C., Egolf, B. P., & Wu, P. (1991). The developmental consequences of child abuse: The Lehigh longitudinal study. In R. H. Starr & D. A. Wolfe (Eds.), *The effects of child abuse and neglect: Issues and research* (pp. 57–80). New York, NY: Guilford Press.

Hesse, E. (2008). The Adult Attachment Interview. In J. Cassidy & P. R. Shaver (Eds.), *Handbook of attachment: Theory, research, and clinical applications* (2nd ed., pp. 552–598). New York, NY: Guilford Press.

Hesse, E., & Main, M. (2006). Frightened, threatening, and dissociative parental behavior in low-risk samples: Description, discussion, and interpretations. *Development and Psychopathology, 18,* 309–343.

Heyes, C. (2010). Where do mirror neurons come from? *Neuroscience and Biobehavioral Reviews, 34,* 575–583.

Hillshouse, W., & Grammatopoulos, D. K. (2002). Role of stress peptides during human pregnancy and labour. *Reproduction, 124,* 239–323.

Hobson, P. (2002). *The cradle of thought: Exploration of the origins of thinking.* Oxford, UK: Macmillan.

Hobson, P. (2005). The interpersonal foundations of thinking. *Behavioral and Brain Sciences, 28,* 703–704.

Hofer, M. A. (1990). Early symbiotic processes: Hard evidence from a soft place. In A. Glick & S. Bone (Eds.), *Pleasure beyond the pleasure principle* (pp. 55–78). New Haven, CT: Yale University Press.

Hofer, M. A. (1994). Hidden regulators in attachment, separation, and loss. In N. A. Fox (Ed.), The development of emotion regulation: Behavioral and biological considerations. *Monographs of the Society for Research in Child Development,* 59(2–3, Serial No. 240), 192–207.

Hofer, M. A. (1995). Hidden regulators implications for a new understanding of attachment, separation, and loss. In S. Goldberg, R. Muir, & J. Kerr. (Eds.), *Attachment theory: Social, developmental and clinical perspectives* (pp. 203–230). Hillsdale, NJ: Analytic Press.

Hofer, M. A. (2006). Psychobiological roots of early attachment. *Current Direction in Psychological Science, 15,* 84–88.

Hoffman, M. (1977). Sex differences in empathy and related behaviors. *Psychological Bulletin, 84,* 712–722.

Horton, P. C. (1995). The comforting substrate and the right brain. *Bulletin of the Menninger Clinic, 59,* 480–486.

Howard, M. F., & Reggia, J. A. (2007). A theory of the visual system biology underlying development of spatial frequency lateralization. *Brain and Cognition, 64,* 111–123.

Howes, C., & Spieker, S. (2008). Attachment relationships in the context of multiple caregivers. In J. Cassidy & P. R. Shaver (Eds.), *Handbook of attachment: Theory, research, and clinical applications* (2nd ed., pp. 317–332). New York, NY: Guilford Press.

Howes, P. W., & Cicchetti, D. (1993). A family/relational perspective on maltreating families: Parallel processes across systems and social policy implications. In D. Cicchetti & S. L. Toth (Eds.), *Child abuse, child development, and social policy* (pp. 249–300). Norwood, NJ: Ablex.

Hrdy, S. B. (2009). *Mothers and others: The evolutionary origins of mutual understanding.* Cambridge, MA: Harvard University Press.

Hughes, P., Turton, P., Hopper, E., McGauley, G. A., & Fonagy, P. (2001). Disorganized attachment behavior among infants born subsequent to stillbirth. *Journal of Child Psychology and Psychiatry, 42,* 791–801.

Huizink, A. C., Mulder, E. J., & Buitelaar, J. K. (2004). Prenatal stress and risk for psychopathology: Specific effects or induction of general susceptibility? *Psychological Bulletin, 130,* 115–42.

Husserl, E. (1977). *Cartesian meditations.* Dordrecht, The Netherlands: Kluwer Academic.

Husserl, E. (1989). *Ideas pertaining to a pure phenomenology and to a phenomenological philosophy: Second Book: Studies in the phenomenology of constitution.* Dordrecht, The Netherlands: Kluwer Academic.

Hutchison, W. D., Davis, K. D., Lozano, A. M., Tasker, R. R., & Dostrovsky, J. O. (1999). Pain related neurons in the human cingulate cortex. *Nature Neuroscience, 2,* 403–405.

Huth-Bocks, A. C., Levendosky, A. A., & Bogat, G. A. (2002). The effects of domestic violence during pregnancy on maternal and infant health. *Violence and Victims, 17,* 169–185.

Huth-Bocks, A. C., Levendosky, A. A., Theran, S., & Bogat, G. A. (2004). The impact of domestic violence on mothers' prenatal representations of their infants. *Infant Mental Health Journal, 25,* 79–98.

Iacoboni, M., & Dapretto, M. (2006). The mirror neuron system and the consequences of its dysfunction. *Nature, 7,* 942–951.

Iacoboni, M., Koski, L. M., Brass, M., Bekkering, H., Woods, R. P., Dubeau, M. C., . . . Rizzolatti, G. (2001). Reafferent copies of imitated actions in the right superior temporal cortex. *Proceedings of the National Academy of Sciences USA, 98,* 13995–13999.

Iacoboni, M., Molnar-Szakacs, I., Gallese, V., Buccino, G., Mazziotta, J., & Rizzolatti, G. (2005). Grasping the intentions of others with one's own mirror neuron system. *PLoS Biology, 3,* 529–535.

Iacoboni, M., Woods, R. P., Brass, M., Bekkering, H., Mazziotta, J. C., & Rizzolatti, G. (1999). Cortical mechanisms of human imitation. *Science, 286,* 2526–2528.

Innamorati, M., Sarracino, D., & Dazzi, N. (2010). Motherhood constellation and representational change in pregnancy. *Infant Mental Health Journal, 31,* 379–396.

Insel, T. R., & Young, L. J. (2001). The neurobiology of attachment. *Nature Reviews Neuroscience, 2,* 129–136.

Isabella, R. A. (1993). Origins of attachment: Maternal interactive behavior across the first year. *Child Development, 64,* 605–621.

Isabella, R. A. (1998). Origins of attachment: The role of context, duration, frequency of observation, and infant age in measuring maternal behavior. *Journal of Social and Personal Relationships, 15,* 538–554.

Jabbi, M., Bastiaansen, J., & Keysers, C. (2008). A common anterior insula representation of disgust observation, experience and imagination shows divergent functional connectivity pathways. *PLoS ONE, 3,* e2939.

Jackson, P. L., Meltzoff, A. N., & Decety, J. (2005). How do we perceive the pain of others: A window into the neural processes involved in empathy. *Neuroimage, 24,* 771–779.

Jacob, S., Byrne, M., & Keenan, K. (2009). Neonatal physiological regulation is associated with perinatal factors: A study of neonates born to healthy African American women living in poverty. *Infant Mental Health Journal, 30,* 82–94.

Jaenisch, R., & Bird, A. (2003). Epigenetic regulation of gene expression: How the genome integrates intrinsic and environmental signals. *Nature Genetics, 33,* 245–254.

Jaffe, J., Beebe, B., Feldstein, S., Crown, C., & Jasnow, M. (2001). Rhythms of dialogue in infancy. *Monographs of the Society for Research in Child Development, 66*(2, Serial No. 264), 1–132.

Jaffee, S. R. (2005). Family violence and parent psychopathology: Implications for children's socioemotional development and resilience. In S. Goldstein & R. Brooks (Eds.), *Handbook of resilience in children* (pp. 149–163). New York, NY: Kluwer.

Jaffee, S. R., Caspi, A., Moffitt, T. E., Polo-Tomás, M., & Taylor, A. (2007). Individual, family, and neighborhood factors distinguish resilient from non-resilient maltreated children: A cumulative stressors model. *Child Abuse and Neglect, 31*, 231–253.

Ji, E. K., Pretorius, D. H., Newton, R., Uyan, K., Hull, A. D., Hollenbach, K., & Nelson, T. R. (2005). Effect of ultrasound on maternal-fetal bonding: A comparison of two- and three-dimensional imaging. *Ultrasound in Obstetrics and Gynecology, 25*, 473–477.

Johnson, M. H., Dziurawiec, S., Ellis, H., & Morton, J. (1991). Newborns' preferential tracking of face-like stimuli and its subsequent decline. *Cognition, 40*, 1–19.

Jones, E. (1951). The Madonna's conception through the ear. A contribution to the relation between aesthetics and religion. In E. Jones (Ed.), *Essays in applied psychoanalysis* (Vol. 2, pp. 266–270). London, UK: Hogarth Press. (Original work published 1914)

Jordan, J. V. (1991). Empathy and the mother-daughter relationship. In J. V. Jordan, A. G. Kaplan, J. B. Miller, I. P. Stiver, & J. L. Surrey (Eds.), *Women's growth in connection* (pp. 28–34). New York, NY: Guilford Press.

Joseph, R. (1996). *Neuropsychiatry, neuropsychology, and clinical neuroscience* (2nd ed.). Baltimore, MD: Williams & Wilkins.

Jurist, E. L. (2008). Minds and yours: New directions for mentalization theory. In E. L. Jurist, A. Slade, & S. Bergner (Eds.), *Mind to mind. Infant research, neuroscience and psychoanalysis* (pp. 88–114). New York, NY: Other Press.

Kaffman, A., & Meaney, M. J. (2007). Neurodevelopmental sequelae of postnatal care in rodents: Clinical and research implications of molecular insights. *Journal of Child Psychology and Psychiatry, 48*, 224–244.

Kaitz, M., Lapidot, P., Bronner, R., & Eidelman, A. I. (1992). Parturient women can recognize their infants by touch. *Developmental Psychology, 28*, 35–39.

Kakei, S., Hoffman, D. S., & Strick, P. L. (1999). Muscle and movement representations in the primary motor cortex. *Science, 285*, 2136–2139.

Kakei, S., Hoffman, D. S., & Strick, P. L. (2001). Direction of action is represented in the ventral premotor cortex. *Nature Neuroscience, 4*, 1020–1025.

Kammers, M. P. M., de Vignemont, F., Verhagen, L., & Dijkerman, H. C. (2009). The rubber hand illusion in action. *Neuropsychologia, 47*, 204–211.

Kanwisher, N., McDermott, J., & Chun, M. (1997). The fusiform face area: A module in human extrastriate cortex specialized for the perception of faces. *Journal of Neuroscience, 17*, 4302–4311.

Kanwisher, N., & Yovel, G. (2006). The fusiform face area: A cortical region specialized for the perception of faces. *Philosophical Transactions of the Royal Society, 361*, 2109–2128.

Karg, K., Burmeister, M., Shedden, K., & Sen, S. (2011). The serotonin transporter promoter variant (5-HTTLPR), stress, and depression meta-analysis revisited: Evidence of genetic moderation. *Archives of General Psychiatry, 68*, 444–454.

Katz, L. F., & Gottman, J. M. (1996). Spillover effects of marital conflict: In search of parenting and coparenting mechanisms. In J. P. McHale & P. A. Cowan (Eds.), *Understanding how family-level dynamics affect children's development: Studies of two parents families* (pp. 57–76). San Francisco, CA: Jossey-Bass.

Kavanaugh, K. A., Youngblade, L., Reid, J. B., & Fagot, B. I. (1988). Interactions between children and abusive versus control parents. *Journal of Clinical Child Psychology, 17*, 137–142.

Kaye, K. (1982). *The mental and social life of babies*. Chicago, IL: University of Chicago Press.

Kaye, K., & Wells, A. (1980). Mothers' jiggling and the burst-pause pattern in neonatal sucking. *Infant Behavior and Development, 3*, 29–46.

Kendrick, K. M. (2000). Oxytocin, motherhood and bonding. *Experimental Physiology, 85*(Spec No.), 111S–124S.

Kendrick, K. M., Keverne, E. B., & Baldwin, B.A. (1987). Intracerebroventricular oxytocin stimulates maternal behaviour in the sheep. *Neuroendocrinology, 46*, 56–61.

Kennell, J. H., Slyter, H., & Klaus, M. H. (1970). The mourning response of parents to the death of a newborn infant. *New England Journal of Medicine, 283*, 344–349.

Keverne, E. B. (2005). Neurobiological and molecular approaches to attachment and bonding. In C. S. Carter, L. Ahnert, K. E. Grossman, S. B. Hrdy, M. E. Lamb, S. W. Porges, & N. Sachser (Eds.), *Attachment and bonding: A new synthesis* (pp. 101–118). Cambridge, MA: MIT Press.

Keysers, C., & Perrett, D. I. (2004). Demystifying social cognition: A Hebbian perspective. *Trends in Cognitive Science, 8*, 501–507.

Keysers, C., Wicker, B., Gazzola, V., Anton, J.-L., Fogassi, L., & Gallese, V. (2004). A touching sight: SII/PV activation during the observation and experience of touch. *Neuron, 42*, 335–346.

Kim, P., Leckman, J. F., Mayes, L. C., Feldman, R., Wang, X., & Swain, J. E. (2010). The plasticity of human maternal brain: Longitudinal changes in brain anatomy during the early postpartum period. *Behavioral Neuroscience, 124*, 695–700.

King, S., & Laplante, D. P. (2005). The effects of prenatal maternal stress on children's cognitive development: Project Ice Storm. *Stress, 8*, 35–45.

Kinsley, C. H., & Amory-Meyer, E. (2011). Why the maternal brain? *Journal of Neuroendocrinology, 23*, 974–983.

Kinsley, C. H., & Lambert, K. G. (2006). The maternal brain. *Scientific American, 294*, 72–79.

Kinsley, C. H., Madonia, L., Gifford, G. W., Tureski, K., Griffin, G. R., Lowry, C., . . . Lambert, K. G. (1999). Motherhood improves learning and memory. *Nature, 402*, 137–138.

Klein, G. S. (1967). Peremptory ideation: Structure and force in motivated ideas. *Psychological Issues, 5*, 80–130.

Klein, M. (1928). Early stages of Oedipus conflict. *International Journal of Psychoanalysis, 9*, 167–180.

Klein, M. (1946). Notes on some schizoid mechanisms. *International Journal of Psychoanalysis, 27*, 99–110.

Kofman, O. (2002). The role of prenatal stress in the etiology of developmental behavioural disorders. *Neuroscience and Biobehavioral Reviews, 26*, 457–470.

Köhler, E., Keysers, C., Umiltà, M. A., Fogassi, L., Gallese, V., & Rizzolatti, G. (2002). Hearing sounds, understanding actions: Action representation in mirror neurons. *Science, 297*, 846–848.

Kohut, H. (1971). *The analysis of the self*. New York, NY: International Universities Press.

Kraskov, A., Dancause, N., Quallo, M. M., Shepherd, S., & Lemon, R. N. (2010). Corticospinal neurons in macaque ventral premotor cortex with mirror properties: A potential mechanism for action suppression? *Neuron, 64*, 922–930.

Kringelbach, M. L. (2005). The human orbitofrontal cortex: Linking reward to hedonic experience. *Neuroscience, 6*, 691–702.

Kringelbach, M. L., & Berridge, K. C. (2009). Towards a functional neuroanatomy of pleasure and happiness. *Trends in Cognitive Sciences, 13*, 479–487.

Kringelbach, M. L., Lehtonen, A., Squire, S., Harvey, A. G., Craske, M. G., Holliday, I. E., . . . Stein, A. (2008). A specific and rapid neural signature for parental instinct. *PLoS ONE, 3*, e1664.

Kugiumutzakis, G. (1999). Genesis and development of early human mimesis to facial and vocal models. In J. Nadel & G. Butterworth (Eds.), *Imitation in infancy* (pp. 36–59). Cambridge, UK: Cambridge University Press.

Kugiumutzakis, G., Kokkanaki, T., Markodimitraki, M., & Vitalaki, E. (2005). Emotions in early mimesis. In J. Nadel & D. Muir (Eds.), *Emotional development* (pp. 161–182). Oxford, UK: Oxford University Press.

Kuhl, P.K. (2004). Early language acquisition: Cracking the speech code. *Nature Reviews Neuroscience, 5*, 831–843.

Kurata, K., & Tanji, J. (1986). Premotor cortex neurons in macaques: Activity before distal and proximal forelimb movements. *Journal of Neuroscience, 6*, 403–411.

Kurjak, A., Miskovic, B., Andonotopo, W., Stanojevic, M., Azumendi, G., & Vrcic, H. (2007). How useful is 3D and 4D ultrasound in perinatal medicine? *Journal of Perinatal Medicine, 35*, 10–27.

Lacan, J. (1953). Fonction et champ de la parole et du langage en psychanalyse. In *Écrits* (pp. 237–322). Paris, France: Éditions du Seuil.

Lacan, J. (1998). *Le Séminaire. Le Livre V. Les formations de l'inconscient* [The Seminar. Book 5. The formation of the unconscious]. Paris, France: Seuil. (Original work published 1957–1958)

Lakatos, K., Toth, I., Nemoda, Z., Ney, K., Sasvari-Szekely, M., & Gervai, J. (2000). Dopamine D4 receptor (DRD4) gene polymorphism is associated with attachment disorganization in infants. *Molecular Psychiatry, 5*, 633–637.

Lamb, M. E., Gaensbauer, T. J., Malkin, C. M., & Schultz, L. (1985). The effects of abuse and neglect on security of infant-adult attachment. *Infant Behavior and Development, 8*, 35–45.

Landry, S. H. (1995). The development of joint attention in premature low birth weight infants: Effects of early medical complications and maternal attention-directing behaviors. In C. Moore & P. J. Dunham (Eds.), *Joint attention: Its origins and role in development* (pp. 223–250). Hillsdale, NJ: Erlbaum.

Langley-Evans, S. C., & McMullen, S. (2010). Developmental origins of adult disease. *Medical Principles and Practice, 19*, 87–98.

Larsen, T., Nguyen, T. H., Munk, M., Svendsen, L., & Teisner, L. (2000). Ultrasound screening in the 2nd trimester: The pregnant woman's background knowledge, expectations, experiences and acceptances. *Ultrasound in Obstetrics and Gynecology, 15*, 383–386.

Lebovici, S. (1983). *Le Nourrisson, la mere et le psychanalyste. Les interactions précoces.* Paris, France: Le Centurion.

Leckman, J. F., Feldman, R., Swain, J. E., Eicher, V., Thompson, N., & Mayes, L. C. (2004). Primary parental preoccupation: Circuits, genes, and the crucial role of the environment. *Journal of Neural Transmission, 111*, 753–771.

Leckman J. F., Goodman, W. K., North, W. G., Chappell, P. B., Price, L. H., Pauls, D. L., . . . McDougle, C. J. (1994). Elevated levels of cerebrospinal oxytocin in obsessive-compulsive disorder: Comparison with Tourette's syndrome and healthy controls. *Archives of General Psychiatry, 51*, 782–792.

Leckman, J. F., & Herman, A. E. (2002). Maternal behavior and developmental psychopathology. *Biological Psychiatry, 51*, 27–43.

Leckman, J. F., & Mayes, L. C. (1999). Preoccupations and behaviors associated with romantic and parental love: Perspectives on the origin of obsessive-compulsive disorder. *Child and Adolescent Psychiatry Clinics of North America, 8*, 635–665.

Leckman, J. F., Mayes, L. C., Feldman, R., Evans, D. W., King, R. A., & Cohen, D. J. (1999). Early parental preoccupations and behaviours and their possible relationship to the symptoms of obsessive-compulsive disorder. *Acta Psychiatrica Scandinavica, S396*, 1–26.

Legerstee, M. (1991). The role of person and object in eliciting early imitation. *Journal of Experimental Child Psychology, 51*, 423–433.

Legerstee, M. (2005). *Infants' sense of people: Precursors to a theory of mind.* Cambridge, UK: Cambridge University Press.

Legerstee, M. (2009). The role of dyadic communication in social cognitive development. *Advances in Child Development and Behavior, 37*, 1–53.

Leibenluft, E., Gobbini, M. I., Harrison, T., & Haxby, J. V. (2004). Mothers' neural activation in response to pictures of their children and other children. *Biological Psychiatry, 56*, 225–232.

Leifer, M. (1977). Psychological changes accompanying pregnancy and motherhood. *Genetics Psychology and Monographs, 95*, 55–96.

Lenzi, D., Trentini, C., Pantano, P., Macaluso, E., Iacoboni, M., Lenzi, G. L., & Ammaniti, M. (2009). Neural basis of maternal communication and emotional expression processing during infant preverbal stage. *Cerebral Cortex, 19*, 1124–1133.

Lenzi, D., Trentini, C., Pantano, P., Macaluso, E., Lenzi, G. L., & Ammaniti, M. (2012). Attachment models affect brain responses in areas related to emotions and empathy in nulliparous women. *Human Brain Mapping*, doi: 10.1002/hbm.21520

Lepage, J. F., & Théoret, H. (2007). The mirror neuron system: Grasping other's actions from birth? *Developmental Science, 10*, 513–529.

Levine, A., Zagoory-Sharon, O., Feldman, R., & Weller, A. (2007). Oxytocin during pregnancy and early postpartum: Individual patterns and maternal-fetal attachment. *Peptides, 28*, 1162–1169.

Levine, S. (2005). Developmental determinants of sensitivity and resistance to stress. *Psychoneuroendocrinology, 30*, 939–946.

Lichtenberg, J. D. (1989). *Psychoanalysis and motivation.* Hillsdale, NJ: Analytic Press.

Lis, A., Zennaro, A., Mazzeschi, C., & Pinto, M. (2004). Parent styles in prospective fathers: A research carried out using a semistructured interview during pregnancy. *Infant Mental Health Journal, 25*, 149–162.

Loeber, R., Felton, D. K., & Reid, J. B. (1984). A social learning approach to the reduction of coercive processes in child abusive families: A molecular analysis. *Advances in Behaviour Research and Therapy, 6*, 29–45.

Loewald, H. (1960). On the therapeutic action of psychoanalysis. In H. Loewald (Ed.), *Papers on psychoanalysis* (pp. 221–256). New Haven, CT: Yale University Press.

Lonstein, J. S., & De Vries, G. J., (1999). Comparison of the parental behavior of pair-bonded female and male prairie voles (Microtus ochrogaster). *Physiology and Behavior, 66*, 33–40.

Lorberbaum, J. P., Newman, J. D., Dubno, J. R., Horwitz, A. R., Nahas, Z., Teneback, C. C., . . . George, M. S. (1999). Feasibility of using fMRI to study mothers responding to infant cries. *Depression and Anxiety, 10*, 99–104.

Lorenz, K. (1943). Die angeborenen Formen Möglicher Erfahrung [Innate forms of potential experience]. *Zeitschrift fur Tierpsychologie, 5*, 235–519.

Love, G., Torrey, N., McNamara, I., Morgan, M., Banks, M., Hester, N. W., . . . Lambert, K. G. (2005). Maternal experience produces long-lasting behavioral modifications in the rat. *Behavioral Neuroscience, 119,* 1084–1096.

Lovejoy, C. O. (1981). The origin of man. *Science, 211,* 341–350.

Lumley, J. (1972). *The development of maternal-fetal bonding in the first pregnancy.* International Congress, Psychosomatic Medicine in Obstetrics and Gynaecology. Basel, Switzerland: Karger.

Lumley, J. M. (1982). Attitudes to the fetus among primigravidae. *Australian Pediatric Journal, 18,* 106–109.

Lumley, J. M. (1990). Through a glass darkly: Ultrasound and prenatal bonding. *Birth, 17,* 214–217.

Lundqvist, L., & Dimberg U. (1995). Facial expressions are contagious. *Journal of Psychophysiology, 9,* 203–211.

Luppino, G., & Rizzolatti, G. (2000). The organization of the frontal motor cortex. *News in Physiological Sciences, 15,* 219–224.

Luthar, S. S., & Cicchetti, D. (2000). The construct of resilience: Implications for interventions and social policies. *Development and Psychopathology, 12,* 857–885.

Lynch, M., & Cicchetti, D. (1998). An ecological-transactional analysis of children and contexts: The longitudinal interplay among child maltreatment, community violence, and children's symptomatology. *Development and Psychopathology, 10,* 235–257.

Lyons-Ruth, K. (1998). Implicit relational knowing: Its role in development and psychoanalytic treatment. *Infant Mental Health Journal, 19,* 282–289.

Lyons-Ruth, K. (2006). The interface between attachment and intersubjectivity: Perspective from the longitudinal study of disorganized attachment. *Psychoanalytic Inquiry, 26,* 595–616.

Lyons-Ruth, K., Bronfman, E., & Atwood, G. (1999). A relational-diathesis model of hostile-helpless states of mind: Expressions in mother-infant interaction. In J. Solomon & C. George (Eds.), *Attachment disorganization* (pp. 33–70). New York, NY: Guilford Press.

Lyons-Ruth, K., Connell, D., Zoll, D., & Stahl, J. (1987). Infants at social risk: Relations among infant maltreatment, maternal behavior, and infant attachment behavior. *Developmental Psychology, 23,* 223–232.

Lyons-Ruth, K., & Easterbrooks, M. A. (2006). Assessing mediated models of family change in response to infant home visiting: A two-phase longitudinal analysis. *Infant Mental Health Journal, 27,* 55–69.

Lyons-Ruth, K., & Jacobvitz, D. (2008). Attachment disorganization: Genetic factors, parenting contexts, and developmental transformation from infancy to adulthood. In J. Cassidy & P. R. Shaver (Eds.), *Handbook of attachment: Theory, research, and clinical applications* (2nd ed., pp. 666–697). New York, NY: Guilford Press.

Lyons-Ruth, K., Yellin, C., Melnick, S., & Atwood, G. (2005). Expanding the concept of unresolved mental states: Hostile-helpless states of mind on the Adult Attachment Interview are associated with disrupted mother-infant communication and infant disorganization. *Development and Psychopathology, 17,* 1–23.

MacDonald, K. (1992). Warmth as a developmental construct: An evolutionary analysis. *Child Development, 63,* 753–773.

Macfie, J., Houts, R. M., Pressel, A. S., & Cox, M. J. (2008). Pathways from infant exposure to marital conflict to parent-toddler role reversal. *Infant Mental Health Journal, 29,* 297–319.

Madigan, S., Moran, G., & Pederson, D. R. (2006). Unresolved states of mind, disorganized attachment relatioships, and disrupted interactions of adolescent mothers and their infants. *Developmental Psychology, 42*, 293–304.

Maestripieri, D., Hoffman, C. L., Anderson, G. M., Carter, C. S., & Higley, J. D. (2009). Mother-infant interactions in free-ranging rhesus macaques: Relationships between physiological and behavioral variables. *Physiology and Behavior, 96*, 613–619.

Mahler, M. S., Pine, F., & Bergman, A. (1975). *The psychological birth of the human infant.* New York, NY: Basic Books.

Main, M. (1991). Metacognitive knowledge, metacognive monitoring, and singular (coherent) vs. multiple (incoherent) models of attachment: Findings and directions for future research. In P. Harris, J. Stevenson-Hinde, & C. Parkes (Eds.), *Attachment across the life cycle* (pp. 127–159). New York, NY: Routledge.

Main, M., & Goldwyn, R. (1997). *Adult Attachment Interview: Scoring and classification systems.* Unpublished manuscript, University of California, Berkeley.

Main, M., & Hesse, E., (1990). Parents' unresolved traumatic experiences are related to infant disorganized attachment status: Is frightened and/or frightening parental behavior the linking mechanism? In M. Greeberg, D. Cicchetti, & E. M. Cumming (Eds.), *Attachment in the preschool years: Theory, research and intervention* (pp.161–184). Chicago, IL: University of Chicago Press.

Main, M., & Solomon, J. (1990). Procedures for identifying infants as disorganized/disoriented during the Ainsworth strange situation. In M. Greeberg, D. Cicchetti, & E. M. Cumming (Eds.), *Attachment in the preschool years: Theory, research and intervention* (pp. 121–160). Chicago, IL: University of Chicago Press.

Maina, G., Albert, U., Bogetto, F., Vaschetto, P., & Ravizza, L. (1999). Recent life events and obsessive-compulsive disorder (OCD): The role of pregnancy/delivery. *Psychiatry Research, 89*, 49–58.

Mancia, M. (2004). *Feeling the words. Resonant archives of the implicit memory and musicality of the transference.* Hove, UK: Routledge.

Mancia, M. (2006). Implicit memory and early unrepressed unconscious: Their role in the therapeutic process (how the neurosciences can contribute to psychoanalysis). *International Journal of Psychoanalysis, 87*, 83–103.

Manning, J. T., Trivers, R. L., Thornhill, R., Singh, D., Denman, J., Eklo, M. H., & Anderton, R. H. (1997). Ear asymmetry and left-side cradling. *Evolution and Human Behavior, 18*, 327–340.

Marvin, R. S., & Britner, P. A. (2008). Normative development: The ontogeny of attachment. In J. Cassidy & P. R. Shaver (Eds.), *Handbook of attachment: Theory, research, and clinical applications* (2nd ed., pp. 269–294). New York, NY: Guilford Press.

Marvin, R. S., Cooper, G., Hoffman, K., & Powell, B. (2002). The Circle of Security project: Attachment-based intervention with caregiver-preschool child dyads. *Attachment and Human Development, 4*, 107–124.

Masi, F. D. (2004). The psychodynamic of panick attacks: A useful integration of psychoanalysis and neuroscience. *International Journal of Psycho-Analysis, 85*, 311–336.

Masten, A. S., & Powell, J. L. (2003). A resilience frame work for research, policy and practice. In S. S. Luthar (Ed.), *Resilience and vulnerability: Adaptation in the context of childhood adversities* (pp. 1–28). New York, NY: Cambridge University Press.

Matelli, M., Luppino, G., & Rizzolatti, G. (1985). Patterns of cytochrome oxidase activity in the frontal agranular cortex of the macaque monkey. *Behavioral Brain Research, 18*, 125–137.

Matthiesen, A. S., Ransjo-Arvidson, A. B., Nissen, E., & Uvnas-Moberg, K. (2001). Post-partum maternal oxytocin release by newborns: Effects of infant hand massage and sucking. *Birth, 28,* 13–19.

Mattson, B. J., Williams, S. E., Rosenblatt, J. S., & Morrell, J. L. (2001). Comparison of two positive reinforcing stimuli: Pups and cocaine throughout the postpartum period. *Behavior and Neuroscience, 115,* 683–694.

Mayes, L. C., Swain, J. E., & Leckman, J. F. (2005). Parental attachment systems: Neural circuits, genes, and experiential contributions to parental engagement. *Clinical Neuroscience Research, 4,* 301–313.

Mayseless, O. (2006). Studying parenting representations as a window to parents' internal working model of caregiving. In O. Mayseles (Ed.), *Parenting representations* (pp. 3–40). New York, NY: Cambridge University Press.

McDougle, C. J., Barr, L. C., Goodman, W. K., & Price, L. H. (1999). Possible role of neuropeptides in obsessive compulsive disorder. *Psychoneuroendocrinology, 24,* 1–24.

McHale, J. P. (2007). When infants grow up in multiperson relationship systems. *Infant Mental Health Journal, 28,* 370–392.

McHale, J. P., Kuersten-Hogan, R., & Rao, N. (2004). Growing points for coparenting theory and research. *Journal of Adult Development, 11,* 221–234.

McHale, J. P., & Rasmussen, J. L. (1998). Coparental and family group-level dynamics during infancy: Early family precursor of child and family functioning during pre-school. *Development and Psychopathology, 10,* 39–59.

McHale, J. P., & Rotman, T. (2007). Is seeing believing? Expectant parents' outlooks on coparenting and later coparenting solidarity. *Infant Behavior and Development, 30,* 62–81.

Meaney, M. J., (2001). Maternal care, gene expression, and the transmission of individual differences in stress reactivity across generations. *Annual Review of Neuroscience, 24,* 1161–1192.

Mednick, S. A., Machon, R. A., Huttunen, M. O., & Bonett, D. (1988). Adult schizophrenia following prenatal exposure to an influenza epidemic. *Archives of General Psychiatry, 45,* 189–192.

Meins, E. (1997). Security of attachment and maternal tutoring strategies: Interaction within the zone of proximal development. *British Journal of Developmental Psychology, 15,* 129–144.

Melnick, S., Finger, B., Hans, S., Pathrick, M., & Lyons-Ruth, K. (2008). Hostile-helpless states of mind in the Adult Attachment Interview (AAI): A proposed additional AAI category with implications for identifying disorganized infant attachment in high-risk samples. In H. Steele & M. Steele (Eds.), *Clinical applications of the Adult Attachment Interview* (pp. 399–423). New York, NY: Guilford Press.

Meltzoff, A. N. (1985). Immediate and deferred imitation in fourteen-and-twenty-four-month-old infants. *Child Development, 56,* 62–72.

Meltzoff, A. N. (1990). Foundations for developing a concept of self: The role of imitation in relating self to other and the value of social mirroring, social modeling, and self practice in infancy. In D. Cicchetti & M. Beeghly (Eds.), *The self in transition: Infancy to childhood* (pp. 139–164). Chicago, IL: University of Chicago Press.

Meltzoff, A. N. (1995). Understanding the intentions of others: Re-enactment of intended acts by 18-months-old children. *Developmental Psychology, 31,* 838–850.

Meltzoff, A. N. (2002). Imitation as a mechanism of social cognition: Origins of empathy, theory of mind, and the representation of action. In U. Goshwami (Ed.), *Blackwell handbook of childhood cognitive development* (pp. 6–25). Oxford, UK: Blackwell.

Meltzoff, A. N., & Brooks, R. (2001). "Like me" as a building block for understanding other minds: Bodily acts, attention, and intention. In B. F. Malle, L. J. Moses, & D. A. Baldwin (Eds.), *Intentions and intentionality: Foundations of social cognition* (pp. 171–191). Cambridge, MA: MIT Press.

Meltzoff, A. N., & Moore, M. K. (1977). Imitation of facial and manual gestures by human neonates. *Science, 198,* 75–78.

Meltzoff, A. N., & Moore, M. K. (1992). Early infant imitation within a functional framework: The importance of person identity, movement, and development. *Infant Behavior and Development, 15,* 479–505.

Meltzoff, A. N., & Moore, M. K. (1998). Infant inter-subjectivity: Broadening the dialogue to include imitation, identity and intention. In S. Bråten (Ed.), *Intersubjective communication and emotion in early ontogeny* (pp. 47–62). Paris, France: Cambridge University Press.

Meltzoff, A. N., & Prinz, W. (2002). *The imitative mind: Development, evolution, and brain bases.* Cambridge, UK: Cambridge University Press.

Merleau-Ponty, M. (1962). *Phenomenology of perception.* (C. Smith, Trans.). London, UK: Routledge.

Minagawa-Kawai, Y., Matsuoka, S., Dan, I., Naoi, N., Nakamura, K., & Kojima, S. (2009). Prefrontal activation associated with social attachment: Facial-emotion recognition in mothers and infants. *Cerebral Cortex, 19,* 284–292.

Minuchin, P. (1985). Families and individual development: Provocations from the field of family therapy. *Child Development, 56,* 289–302.

Missonnier, S. (1999). L'échographie obstétricale: Un rituel séculier d'initiation à la parentalité? In M. Soulé, L. Gourand, S. Missonnier, & M. J. Soubieux (Eds.), *Ecoute voir . . . L'échographie de la grossesse: les enjeux de la relation* (pp. 133–161). Ramonville Saint-Agne, France: Érès.

Mitchell, J. P. (2008). Activity in right temporo-parietal junction is not selective for theory of mind. *Cerebral Cortex, 18,* 262–271.

Mitchell, S. A. (1988). *Relational concepts in psychoanalysis: An integration.* Cambridge, MA: Harvard University Press.

Mitchell, S. A. (2000). *Relationality: From attachment to intersubjectivity.* Hillsdale, NJ: Analytic Press.

Moffitt, T. E., Caspi, A., & Rutter, M. (2005). Strategy for investigating interactions between measured genes and measured environments. *Archives of General Psychiatry, 62,* 473–481.

Moore, G. A. (2010). Parent conflict predicts infants' vagal regulation in social interaction. *Developmental Psychopathology, 22,* 23–33.

Morton, J., & Johnson, M. H. (1991). CONSPEC and CONLERN: A two-process theory of infant face recognition. *Psychological Review, 98,* 164–181.

Moshe, M., & Feldman, R. (2006, July). *Maternal and infant heart rhythms and mother-infant synchrony.* Paper presented at the Biennial Conference of the 10th World Association for Infant Mental Health, Paris, France.

Mukamel, R., Ekstrom, A. D., Kaplan, J., Iacoboni, M., & Fried, I. (2010). Single-neuron responses in humans during execution and observation of actions. *Current Biology, 20,* 750–756.

Müller, M. E. (1990). *The development and testing of the Müller Prenatal Attachment Inventory.* Unpublished Ph.D. Dissertation, University of California, San Francisco.

Müller, M. E. (1993). Development of the prenatal attachment inventory. *Western Journal of Nursing Research, 15,* 199–215.

Myowa-Yamakoshi, M., & Takeshita, H. (2006). Do human fetuses anticipate self-directed actions? A study by four-dimensional (4D) ultrasonography. *Infancy, 10,* 289–301.

Myowa-Yamakoshi, M., Tomonaga, M., Tanaka, M., & Matsuzawa, T. (2004). Imitation in neonatal chimpanzees (Pan troglodytes). *Developmental Science, 7,* 437–442.

Nadel, J., & Tremblay-Leveau, H. (1999). Early perception of social contingencies and interpersonal intentionality: Dyadic and triadic paradigms. In P. Rochat (Ed.), *Early social cognition: Understanding others in the first months of life* (pp. 189–212). Mahwah, NJ: Erlbaum.

Nagy, E., Compagne, H., Orvos, H., Pal, A., Molnar, P., Janszky, I., . . . Bardos, G. (2005). Index finger movement imitation by human neonates: Motivation, learning, and left-hand preference. *Pediatric Research, 58,* 749–753.

Nakata, H., Sakamoto, K., Ferretti, A., Perrucci, G. M., Del Gratt, C., Kakigi, R., & Luca Romani, G. (2008). Somato-motor inhibitory processing in humans: An event-related functional MRI study. *Neuroimage, 39,* 1858–1866.

Neisser, U. (1988). Five kinds of self-knowledge. *Philosophical Psychology, 1,* 35–59.

Neumann, I. D. (2008). Brain oxytocin: A key regulator of emotional and social behaviours in both females and males. *Journal of Neuroendocrinology, 20,* 858–865.

Niedenthal, P. M. (2007). Embodying emotion. *Science, 316,* 1002–1005.

Nitschke, J. B., Nelson, E. E., Rusch, B. D., Fox, A. S., Oakes, T. R., & Davidson, R. J. (2004). Orbitofrontal cortex tracks positive mood in mothers viewing pictures of their newborn infants. *Neuroimage, 21,* 583–592.

Noriuchi, M., Kikuchi, Y., & Senoo, A. (2008). The functional neuroanatomy of maternal love: Mother's response to infant's attachment behaviors. *Biological Psychiatry, 63,* 415–423.

Norris, F. H., Friedman, M. J., Watson, P. J., Byrne, C. M., Diaz, E., & Kaniasty K. (2002). 60,000 disaster victims speak: Part I. An empirical review of the empirical literature, 1981–2001. *Psychiatry, 65,* 207–239.

North, C. S., Kawasaki, A., Spitznagel, E. I., & Hong, B. A. (2004). The course of PTSD, major depression, substance abuse, and somatization after a natural disaster. *Journal of Nervous and Mental Disease, 192,* 823–829.

Numan, M., & Insel, T. R. (2003). *The neurobiology of parental behavior.* New York, NY: Springer-Verlag.

Ogawa, J. R., Sroufe, L. A., Weinfeld, N. S., Carlson, E. A., & Egeland, B. (1997). Development and the fragmented self: Longitudinal study of dissociative symptomatology in a nonclinical sample. *Development and Psychopathology, 9,* 855–879.

Olds, D. L. (2006). The nurse-family partnership: An evidence-based preventive intervention. *Infant Mental Health Journal, 27,* 5–25.

Olson, I. R., Plotzker, A., & Ezzyat, Y. (2007). The enigmatic temporal pole: A review of findings on social and emotional processing. *Brain, 130,* 1718–1731.

Ongur, D., Ferry, A. T., & Price, J. L. (2003). Architectonic subdivision of the human orbital and medial prefrontal cortex. *Journal of Comparative Neurology, 460,* 425–449.

Ongur, D., & Price, J. L. (2000). The organization of networks within the orbital and medial prefrontal cortex of rats, monkeys and humans. *Cerebral Cortex, 10,* 206–219.

Panksepp, J. (1998). *Affective neuroscience: The foundation of human and animal emotions*. New York, NY: Oxford University Press.

Panksepp, J. (2001). The long-term psychobiological consequences of infant emotions: Prescriptions for the twenty-first century. *Infant Mental Health Journal, 22*, 132–173.

Papousek, H., & Papousek, M. (1975). Cognitive aspects of preverbal social interaction between human infants and adults. *Ciba Foundation Symposium, 33*, 241–269.

Papousek, H., & Papousek, M. (1987). Intuitive parenting: A dialectic counterpart to the infant's integrative competence. In J. D. Osofsky (Ed.), *Handbook of infant development* (pp. 669–720). New York, NY: Wiley.

Papousek, M. (2007). Communication in early infancy: An arena of intersubjective learning. *Infant Behavior and Development, 30*, 258–266.

Parsons, C. E., Young, K. S., Murray, L., Stein, A., & Kringelbach, M. L. (2010). The functional neuroanatomy of the evolving parent infant relationship. *Progress Neurobiology, 91*, 220–241.

Patočka, J. (1998). *Body, community, language, world*. Chicago and La Salle, IL: Carus.

Patterson, C.J. (1992). Children of lesbian and gay parents. *Child Development, 63*, 1025–1042.

Pauen, M. (2012). The second-person perspective. *Inquiry, 55*, 33–49.

Perner, J., Ruffman, T., & Leekam, S. (1994). Theory of mind is contagious: You catch it from your sibs. *Child Development, 65*, 1228–1238.

Person, E. S. (1995). *By force of fantasy*. New York, NY: Penguin Books.

Pfeifer, M., Fisk, N., Teixeira, J., Cameron, A., & Glover, M. (2002). Continuity and change in inhibited and unhibited children. *Child Development, 73*, 1474–1485.

Phillips, M. L., Drevets, W. C., Rauch, S. L., & Lane, R. (2003). Neurobiology of emotion perception I: The neural basis of normal emotion perception. *Biological Psychiatry, 54*, 504–514.

Picard, N., & Strick, P. L. (1996). Motor areas of the medial wall: A review of their location and functional activation. *Cerebral Cortex, 6*, 342–353.

Pines, D. (1972). Pregnancy and motherhood: Interaction between fantasy and reality. *British Journal of Medical Psychology, 45*, 333–343.

Pines, D. (1982). The relevance of early psychic development to pregnancy and abortion. *International Journal of Psychoanalysis, 63*, 311–319.

Piontelli, A. (2010). *Development of normal fetal movements*. Milan, Italy: Springer-Verlag.

Pollak, S. D., Cicchetti, D., Hornung, K., & Reed, A. (2000). Recognizing emotion in faces: Developmental effects of child abuse and neglect. *Developmental Psychology, 36*, 679–688.

Porges, S. W. (2007). The polyvagal perspective. *Biological Psychology, 74*, 116–143.

Premack, D., & Woodruff, G. (1978). Does the chimpanzee have a theory of mind? *Behavioral and Brain Sciences, 1*, 515–526.

Preston, S. D., & de Waal, F. B. M. (2002). Empathy: Its ultimate and proximate bases. *Brain and Behavioral Sciences, 25*, 1–72.

Propper, C. B., & Moore, G. A. (2006). The influence of parenting on infant emotionality: A multi-level psychobiological perspective. *Developmental Review, 26*, 427–460.

Propper, C. B., Moore, G. A., Mills-Koonce, W. R., Halpern, C., Hill, A., Calkins, S. D., . . . Cox, M. (2008). Gene-environment contributions to the development of vagal functioning: An examination of DRD2 and maternal sensitivity. *Child Development*, 78, 1378–1395.

Proverbio, A. M., Zani, A., & Adorni, R. (2008). Neural markers of a greater female responsiveness to social stimuli. *BMC Neuroscience*, 9, 56.

Purhonen, M., Kilpelainen-Lees, R., Paakkonen, A., Ypparila, H., Lehtonen, J., & Karhu, J. (2001). Effects of maternity on auditory event-related potentials to human sound. *Neuroreport*, 12, 2975–2979.

Purhonen, M., Paakkonen, A., Ypparila, H., Lehtonen, J., & Karhu, J. (2001). Dynamic behavior of the auditory N100 elicited by a baby's cry. *International Journal of Psychophysiology*, 41, 271–278.

Putallaz, M., Costanzo, P. R., Grimes, C. L., & Sherman, D. M. (1998). Intergenerational continuities and their influences on children's social development. *Social Development*, 7, 389–427.

Pylyshyn, Z. W. (1984). *Computation and cognition: Toward a foundation for cognitive science*. Cambridge, MA: MIT Press.

Quirk, G. J., & Beer, J. S. (2006). Prefrontal involvement in the regulation of emotion: Convergence of rat and human studies. *Current Opinion in Neurobiology*, 16, 723–727.

Quirk, G. J., Likhtik, E., Pelletier, J. G., & Pare, D. (2003). Stimulation of medial prefrontal cortex decreases the responsiveness of central amygdala output neurons. *Journal of Neuroscience*, 23, 8800–8807.

Rachman, S., & de Silva, P. (1978). Abnormal and normal obsessions. *Behavior Research and Therapy*, 16, 233–248.

Radloff, L. S. (1977). The CES-D Scale. *Applied Psychological Measurements*, 1, 385.

Rakic, P. (1995). Corticogenesis in human and nonhuman primates. In M. S. Gazzaniga (Ed.), *The cognitive neurosciences* (pp. 127–145). Cambridge, MA: MIT Press.

Ramchandani, P. G., Richter, L. M., Norris, S. A., & Stein A. (2010). Maternal prenatal stress and later child behavioral problems in an urban South African setting. *Journal of America Academy of Child and Adolescent Psychiatry*, 49, 239–247.

Ranote, S., Elliott, R., Abel, K. M., Mitchell, R., Deakin, J. F., & Appleby, L. (2004). The neural basis of maternal responsiveness to infants: An fMRI study. *Neuroreport*, 15, 1825–1829.

Raos, V., Evangeliou, M. N., & Savaki, H. E. (2007). Mental simulation of action in the service of action perception. *Journal of Neuroscience*, 27, 12675–12683.

Raphael-Leff, J. (1993). *Pregnancy. The inside story*. London, UK: Sheldon Press.

Raphael-Leff, J. (2010). Mothers' and fathers' orientations: Patterns of pregnancy, parenting and the bonding process. In S. Tyano, M. Keren, H. Herrman, & J. Cox (Eds.), *Parenthood and mental health: A bridge between infant and adult psychiatry* (pp. 9–30). Oxford, UK: Wiley-Blackwell.

Reddy, V. (2008). *How infants know minds*. Cambridge, MA: Harvard University Press.

Repetti, R. L., Taylor, S. E., & Seeman, T. E. (2002). Risky families: Family social environments and the mental and physical health of offspring. *Psychological Bulletin*, 128, 330–366.

Ricciardi, E., Bonino, D., Sani, L., Vecchi, T., Guazzelli, M., Haxby, J. V., . . . Pietrini, P. (2009). Do we really need vision? How blind people "see" the actions of others. *Journal of Neuroscience*, 29, 9719–9724.

Rizzolatti, G., Camarda, R., Fogassi, L., Gentilucci, M., Luppino, G., & Matelli, M.

(1988). Functional organization of inferior area 6 in the macaque monkey. II. Area F5 and the control of distal movements. *Experimental Brain Research, 71*, 491–507.

Rizzolatti, G., Fadiga, L., Gallese, V., & Fogassi, L. (1996). Premotor cortex and the recognition of motor actions. *Cognitive Brain Research, 3*,131–41.

Rizzolatti, G., Fogassi, L., & Gallese, V. (2000). Cortical mechanisms subserving object grasping and action recognition: A new view on the cortical motor functions. In M. S. Gazzaniga (Ed.), *The cognitive neurosciences* (2nd ed., pp. 539–552). Cambridge, MA: MIT Press.

Rizzolatti, G., Fogassi, L., & Gallese, V. (2001). Neurophysiological mechanisms underlying the understanding and imitation of action. *Nature Reviews Neuroscience, 2*, 661–670.

Rizzolatti, G., & Gallese, V. (1997). From action to meaning. In J.-L. Petit (Ed.), *Les Neurosciences et la Philosophie de l'Action* [Neuroscience and the philosophy of action] (pp. 217–229). Paris, France: Librairie Philosophique.

Rizzolatti, G., Gentilucci, M., Camarda, R. M., Gallese, V., Luppino, G., Matelli, M., & Fogassi, L. (1990). Neurons related to reaching-grasping arm movements in the rostral part of area 6 (area 6a beta). *Experimental Brain Research, 82*, 337–350.

Rizzolatti, G., Luppino, G., & Matelli, M. (1996). The classic supplementary motor area is formed by two independent areas. *Advances in Neurology, 70*, 45–56.

Rizzolatti, G., Scandolara, C., Matelli, M., & Gentilucci, M. (1981). Afferent properties of periarcuate neurons in macaque monkeys. II. Visual responses. *Behavioral Brain Research, 2*, 147–163

Rizzolatti, G., & Sinigaglia, C. (2007). *Mirrors in the brain. How our minds share actions, emotions, and experience.* Oxford, UK: Oxford University Press.

Rizzolatti, G., & Sinigaglia, C. (2008). *Mirrors in the brain. How our minds share actions and emotions.* Oxford, UK: Oxford University Press.

Rizzolatti, G., & Sinigaglia, C. (2010). The functional role of the parieto-frontal mirror circuit: Interpretations and misinterpretations. *Nature Review Neuroscience, 11*, 264–274.

Rochat, M. J., Caruana, F., Jezzini, A., Escola, L., Intskirveli, I., Grammont, F., . . . Umiltà, M. A. (2010). Responses of mirror neurons in area F5 to hand and tool grasping observation. *Experimental Brain Research, 204*, 605–616.

Rogosch, F. A., Cicchetti, D., Shields, A., & Toth, S. L. (1995). Parenting dysfunction in child maltreatment. In M. H. Bornstein (Ed.), *Handbook of parenting* (pp. 127–159). Hillsdale, NJ: Erlbaum.

Rolls, E. T., & Grabenhorst, F. (2008). The orbitofrontal cortex and beyond: From affect to decision-making. *Progress in Neurobiology, 86*, 216–244.

Ross, L. E., & McLean, L. M. (2006). Anxiety disorders during pregnancy and the postpartum period: A systematic review. *Journal of Clinical Psychiatry, 67*, 1285–1298.

Rubin, R. (1967a). Attainment of the maternal role: Part I. Processes. *Nursing Research, 16*, 237–245.

Rubin, R. (1967b). Attainment of the maternal role: Part II. Models and referents. *Nursing Research, 16*, 342–346.

Rubin, R. (1975). Maternal tasks in pregnancy. *Maternal Child Nursing Journal, 4*, 143–153.

Rubonis, A. V., & Bickman, L. (1991). Psychological impairment in the wake of disaster: The disaster-psychopathology relationship. *Psychological Bulletin, 109*, 384–399.

Ruby, P., & Decety, J. (2003). What you believe versus what you think they believe: A neuroimaging study of conceptual perspective-taking. *European Journal of Neuroscience, 17*, 2475–2480.

Ruby, P., & Decety, J. (2004). How would you feel versus how do you think she would feel? A neuroimaging study of perspective-taking with social emotions. *Journal of Cognitive Neuroscience, 16*, 988–999.

Rueckert, L., & Naybar, N. (2008). Gender differences in empathy: The role of the right hemisphere. *Brain and Cognition, 67*, 162–167.

Rustin, M. (1997). Rigidity and stability in a psychotic patient: Some thoughts about obstacles to facing reality in psychotherapy. In M. Rustin, M. Rhode, A. Dubinsky, & H. Dubinsky (Eds.), *Psychotic states in children* (pp. 245–266). London, UK: Duckworth, Tavistock Clinic Series.

Rutter, M. (1979). Protective factors in children's responses to stress and disadvantage. In M. W. Kent & J. E. Rolf (Eds.), *Primary prevention of psychopathology: Social competence in children* (pp. 49–74). Hanover, NH: University Press of New England.

Rutter, M. (2006). Implications of resilience concepts for scientific understanding. *Annals of the New York Academy of Sciences, 1094*, 1–12.

Rutter, M. (2012). Resilience as a dynamic concept. *Development and Psychopathology, 254*, 335–344.

Sameroff, A. J. (1983). Developmental systems: Contexts and evolution. In P. Müssen (Ed.), *Handbook of child psychology* (Vol. 1, pp. 237–294). New York, NY: Wiley.

Sameroff, A. J. (2000). Dialectical processes in developmental psychopathology. In A. Sameroff, M. Lewis, & S. Miller (Eds.), *Handbook of developmental psychopathology* (2nd ed., pp. 23–40). New York, NY: Kluwer Academic/Plenum.

Sameroff, A. J. (2004). Ports of entry and the dynamics of mother-infant interventions. In A. J. Sameroff, S. C. McDonough, & K. L. Rosenblum (Eds.), *Treating parent-infant relationship problem* (pp. 3–28). New York, NY: Guilford Press.

Sameroff, A. J., Bartko, W. T., Baldwin, A., Baldwin, C., & Seifer, R. (1998). Family and social influence on the development of child competence. In M. Lewis & C. Feiring (Eds.), *Families, risk, and competence* (pp. 161–185). Mahwah, NJ: Erlbaum.

Sameroff, A. J., & Chandler, M. J. (1975). Reproductive risk and the continuum of caretaking casualty. In F. D. Horowitz, M. Hetherington, S. Scarr-Salapatek, & G. Siegel (Eds.), *Review of child development research* (pp. 187–244). Chicago, IL: University of Chicago Press.

Sander, K., Frome, Y., & Scheich, H. (2007). fMRI activations of amygdala, cingulate cortex, and auditory cortex by infant laughing and crying. *Human Brain Mapping, 28*, 1007–1022.

Sander, L. (1962). Issues in early mother-child interaction. *Journal of the American Academy of Child Psychiatry, 3*, 231–264.

Sander, L. (1977). The regulation of exchange in the infant-caretaker system and some aspects of the context-content relationship. In M. Lewis & L. Rosenblum (Eds.), *Interaction, conversation, and the development of language* (pp. 133–156). New York, NY: Wiley.

Sander, L. (1985). Toward a logic of organization in psycho-biological development. In H. Klar & L. Siever (Eds.), *Biologic response styles: Clinical implications* (pp. 20–36). Washington, DC: American Psychiatric Press.

Sandler, J. (1976). Actualization and object relationships. *Journal of Philadelphia Association of Psychoanalysis, 3*, 59–70.

Sandler, J., & Rosenblatt, B. (1962). The concept of the representational world. In J.

Sandler (Ed.), *From safety to superego: Selected papers of Joseph Sandler*. London, UK: Karnac Books.

Sandler, J., & Sandler, A. (1998). *Internal objects revisited*. Madison, CT: International University Press.

Saxe, R., & Kanwisher, N. (2003). People thinking about thinking people: fMRI investigations of theory of mind. *Neuroimage, 19*, 1835–1842.

Saxe, R., & Powell, L. J. (2006). It's the thought that counts: Specific brain regions for one component of theory of mind. *Psychological Science, 17*, 692–699.

Saxe, R., & Wexler, A. (2005). Making sense of another mind: The role of the right temporo-parietal junction. *Neuropsychologia, 43*, 1391–1399.

Saxena, S., & Rauch, S. L. (2000). Functional neuroimaging and the neuroanatomy of obsessive-compulsive disorder. *Psychiatric Clinics of North America, 23*, 563–586.

Schafer, R. (1959). Generative empathy in the treatment situation. *Psychoanalytic Quarterly, 28*, 342–373.

Schneider-Rosen, K., Braunwald, K., Carlson, V., & Cicchetti, D. (1985). Current perspectives in attachment theory: Illustrations from the study of maltreated infants. In I. Bretherton & E. Waters (Eds.), Growing points in attachment theory. *Monographs of the Society for Research in Child Development, 50*(1-2, Serial No. 209), 194–210.

Schoppe-Sullivan, S. J., Mangelsdorf, S. C., Brown, G. L., & Sokolowski, M. S. (2007). Goodness-of-fit in family context: Infant temperament, marital quality, and early coparenting behavior. *Infant Behavior and Development, 30*, 82–96.

Schore, A. N. (1996). The experience-dependent maturation of a regulatory system in the orbital prefrontal cortex and the origin of developmental psychopathology. *Development and Psychopathology, 8*, 59–87.

Schore, A. N. (2000). Attachment and the regulation of the right brain. *Attachment and Human Development, 2*, 23–47.

Schore, A. N. (2001). Effects of a secure attachment relationship on right brain development affect regualtion, and infant mental health. *Infant Mental Health Journal, 22*, 7–66.

Schore, A. N. (2002). The right brain as the neurobiological substratum of Freud's dynamic unconscious. In D. Scharff (Ed.), *Freud at the millennium: The evolution and application of psychoanalysis* (pp. 61–88). New York, NY: Other Press.

Schore, A. N. (2003). *Affect regulation and the repair of the self*. New York, NY: Norton.

Schore, A. N. (2010). Relational trauma and the developing right brain: The neurobiology of broken attachment bonds. In T. Baradon (Ed.), *Relational trauma in infancy* (pp. 19–47). London, UK: Routledge.

Schore, A. N. (2011). The right brain implicit self lies at the core of psychoanalysis. *Psychoanalytic Dialogues, 21*, 75–100.

Sears, R. R., Maccoby, E. E., & Levin, H. (1957). *Patterns of child rearing*. Evanston, IL: Row, Peterson.

Sedlak, A. J., & Broadhurst, D. D. (1996). *Executive summary of the third national incidence study of child abuse and neglect*. Washington, DC: U. S. Department of Health and Human Services.

Seifer, R., Sameroff, A. J., Baldwin, C. P., & Baldwin, A. (1992). Child and family factors that ameliorate risk between 4 and 13 years of age. *Journal of the American Academy of Child and Adolescent Psychiatry, 31*, 893–903.

Seifritz, E., Esposito, F., Neuhoff, J. G., Luthi, A., Mustovic, H., Dammann, G., . . . Di

Salle, F. (2003). Differential sex-independent amygdala response to infant crying and laughing in parents versus nonparents. *Biological Psychiatry, 54,* 1367–1375.

Seip, K. M., & Morrell, J. I. (2007). Increasing the incentive salience of cocaine challenges preference for pup-over cocaine-associated stimuli during early postpartum: Place preference and locomotor analyses in the lactating female rat. *Psychopharmacology, 194,* 309–319.

Seligman, S. (1991, April). *What is structured in psychic structure? Affect, internal representations and the relational self.* Paper presented at the Spring Meeting of the Division of Psychoanalysis (39), American Psychological Association, Chicago, IL.

Seligman, S. (1999). Integrating kleinian theory and intersubjective infant research: Observing projective identification. *Psychoanalytic Dialogues, 9,* 129–159.

Settis, S. (1990). *Giorgione's tempest.* Chicago, IL: University of Chicago Press.

Shamay-Tsoory, S. G., Tomer, R., & Aharon-Peretz, J. (2005). The neuroanatomical basis of understanding sarcasm and its relationship to social cognition. *Neuropsychology, 19,* 288–300.

Shen, L., & Alexander, G. E. (1997). Preferential representation of instructed target location versus limb trajectory in dorsal premotor area. *Journal of Neurophysiology, 77,* 1195–1212.

Shepherd, S. V., Klein, J. T., Deaner, R. O., & Platt, M. L. (2009). Mirroring of attention by neurons in macaque parietal cortex. *Proceedings of the National Academy of Sciences USA, 106,* 9489–9494.

Shi, Z., Bureau, J. F., Easterbrooks, M. A., Zhao, X., & Lyons-Ruth, K. (2012). Childhood maltreatment and prospectively observed quality of early care as predictors of antisocial personality disorder features. *Infant Mental Health Journal, 33,* 55–69.

Shieh, C., Kravitz, M., & Wang, H. H. (2001). What do we know about maternal-fetal attachment? *Kaohsiung Journal of Medical Science, 17,* 448–454.

Shimada, S., & Hiraki, K. (2006). Infant's brain responses to live and televised action. *Neuroimage, 32,* 930–939.

Sieratzki, J. S., & Woll, B. (1996). Why do mothers cradle babies on their left? *Lancet, 347,* 1746–1748.

Singer, J. L. (1966). *Daydreaming: An introduction to the experimental study of inner experience.* New York, NY: Random House.

Singer, T., & Hein, G. (2012). Human empathy through the lens of psychology and social neuroscience. In F. B. M. de Waal & P. F. Ferrari (Eds.), *The primate mind* (pp. 158–174). Cambridge, MA: Harvard University Press.

Singer, T., Seymour, B., O'Doherty, J., Kaube, H., Dolan, R. J., & Frith, C. D. (2004). Empathy for pain involves the affective but not sensory components of pain. *Science, 303,* 1157–1162.

Singer, T., Seymour, B., O'Doherty, J. P., Stephan, K. E., Dolan, R. J., & Frith, C. D. (2006). Empathic neural responses are modulated by the perceived fairness of others. *Nature, 439,* 466–469.

Slade, A. (2004). The move from categories to process: Attachment phenomena and clinical evaluation. *Infant Mental Journal, 25,* 269–283.

Slade, A. (2005). Parental reflective functioning: An introduction. *Attachment and Human Development, 7,* 269–281.

Slade, A. (2006). Reflective parenting programs: Theory and development. *Psychoanalytic Inquiry, 26,* 640–657.

Slade, A. (2008). Mentalization as a frame for working with parents in child psychotherapy. In E. L. Jurist, A. Slade, & S. Bergner (Eds.), *Mind to mind. Infant research, neuroscience and psychoanalysis* (pp. 307–334). New York, NY: Other Press.

Slade, A., Belsky, J., Aber, J., & Phelps, J. L. (1999). Mothers' representation of their relationships with their toddlers: Links to adults' attachment and observed mothering. *Developmental Psychology, 35,* 611–619.

Slade, A., Cohen, L. J., Sadler, L. S., & Miller, M. (2009). The psychology and psychopathology of pregnancy: Reorganization and transformation. In C. H. Zeanah (Ed.), *Handbook of infant mental health* (3rd ed., pp. 22–39). New York, NY: Guilford Press.

Solms, M., & Panksepp J. (2012). The id knows more than the ego admits: Neuropsychoanalytic and primal consciousness perspectives on the interface between affective and cognitive neuroscience. *Brain Sciences, 2,* 147–175.

Sommerville, J. A., & Woodward A. (2005). Pulling out the intentional structure of action: The relation between action processing and action production in infancy. *Cognition, 95,* 1–30.

Sommerville, J. A., Woodward, A., & Needham, A. (2005). Action experience alters 3-month-old perception of other's actions. *Cognition, 96,* 1–11.

Sonnby-Borgstrom, M. (2002). Automatic mimicry reactions as related to differences in emotional empathy. *Scandinavian Journal of Psychology, 43,* 433–443.

Soulé, M. (1991). La mère qui tricote suffisamment. *Revue Médecine et Enfance, 11,* 190–196.

Southgate, V., Johnson, M. H., & Csibra, G. (2008). Infants attribute goals even to biomechanically impossible actions. *Cognition, 107,* 1059–1069

Southgate, V., Johnson, M. H., El Karoui, I., & Csibra, G. (2010). Motor system activation reveals infants' on-line prediction of others' goals. *Psychological Science, 21,* 355–359.

Sowell, E. R., Thompson, P. M., Tessner, K. D., & Toga, A. W. (2001). Mapping continued brain growth and gray matter density reduction in dorsal frontal cortex: Inverse relationships during postadolescent brain maturation. *Journal of Neuroscience, 2,* 8819–8829.

Spinoza, B. (1955). *Ethics, part 2. Of the nature and origin of the mind. Proposition 13* (R. H. M. Elwes, Trans.). New York, NY: Dover Press. (Original work published 1677)

Sprengelmeyer, R., Perrett, D. I., Fagan, E. C., Cornwell, R. E., Lobmaier, J. S., Sprengelmeyer, A., . . . Young, A. W. (2009). The cutest little baby face: A hormonal link to sensitivity to cuteness in infant faces. *Psychological Science, 20,* 149–154.

Sroufe, L. A. (1990). An organizational perspective on the self. In D. Cicchetti & M. Beeghly (Eds.), *The self in transition: Infancy to childhood* (pp. 281–307). Chicago, IL: University of Chicago Press.

Sroufe, L. A., Egeland, B., Carlson, E., & Collins, W. (2005). *The development of the person: The Minnesota study of risk and adaptation from birth to adulthood.* New York, NY: Guilford Press.

Sroufe, L. A., Fox, N., & Pancake, V. (1983). Attachment and dependency in developmental perspective. *Child Development, 54,* 1615–1627.

Sroufe, L. A., & Waters, E. (1977). Attachment as an organizational construct. *Child Development, 48,* 1184–1199.

Stadimayr, W., Boukydis, C. F., Bishsel, S., Kappeler, S., Gurber, S., Surbek, D., & Tutschek, B. (2009). A micro-analytic evaluation of parents watching a non-diagnostic ultrasound-based video of their fetus at mid-gestation. *Ultrasound in Obstetrics and Gynecology, 34,* S148.

Steiner, J. (1993). *Psychic retreats: Pathological organizations of the personality in psychotic, neurotic, and borderline patients.* London, UK: Routledge.

Stern, D. N. (1971). A microanalysis of the mother-infant interaction. *Journal of the American Academy of Child Pscychiatry, 10,* 501–507.

Stern, D. N. (1974). Mother and infant at play: The dyadic interaction involving facial, vocal and gaze behaviors. In M. Lewis & L. Rosenblum (Eds.), *The effect of the infant on its caregiver* (pp. 187–213). New York, NY: Wiley.

Stern, D. N. (1977). *The first relationship: Mother and infant.* Cambridge, MA: Harvard University Press.

Stern, D. N. (1985). *The interpersonal world of the infant.* New York, NY: Basic Books.

Stern, D. N. (1988). Affect in the context of the infant's lived experience: Some considerations. *International Journal of Psychoanalysis, 69,* 233–238.

Stern, D. N. (1993). L'amore infantile e l'amore di transfert: relazione e implicazioni. In D. N. Stern & M. Ammaniti (Eds.), *Psicoanalisi dell'amore* (pp. 100–114). Rome-Bari, Italy: Laterza.

Stern, D. N. (1995). *The motherhood constellation: A unified view of parent-infant psychopathology.* New York, NY: Basic Books.

Stern, D. N. (2004). *The present moment in psychotherapy and everyday life.* New York, NY: Norton.

Stern, D. N. (2010). *Forms of vitality: Exploring dynamic experience in psychology, the arts, psychotherapy, and development.* New York, NY: Oxford University Press.

Stifter, C. A., & Corey, J. M. (2001). Vagal regulation and observed social behavior in infancy. *Social Development, 10,* 189–201.

Stolorow, R., Brandchaft, B., & Atwood, G. (1987). *Psychoanalytic treatment: An intersubjective approach.* Hillsdale, NJ: Analytic Press.

Strathearn, L., Li, J., & Montague, P. R. (2005). An fMRI study of maternal mentalization: Having the baby's mind in mind. *Neuroimage, 26,* S25.

Suess, P. E., Porges, S. W., & Plude, D. J. (1994). Cardiac vagal tone and sustained attention in school-age children. *Psychophysiology, 31,* 17–22.

Swain, J. E., Leckman, J. F., Mayes, L. C., Feldman, R., Constable, R. T., & Schultz, R. T. (2003, December). *The neural circuitry of parent–infant attachment in the early postpartum.* Paper presented at the 42nd American College of Neuropsychopharmacology Annual Meeting, San Juan, Puerto Rico.

Swain, J. E., Leckman, J. F., Mayes, L. C., Feldman, R., Constable, R. T., & Schultz, R. T. (2004). Neural substrates and psychology of human parent-infant attachment in the postpartum. *Biological Psychiatry, 55,* S153.

Swain, J. E., Leckman, J., Mayes, L. C., Feldman, R., & Schultz, R. (2006). Functional neuroimaging and psychology of parent-infant attachment in the early postpartum. *Annals of General Psychiatry, 5,* S85.

Swain, J. E., & Lorberbaum, J. P. (2008). Imaging the human parental brain. In R. S. Bridges (Ed.), *Neurobiology of the parental mind* (pp. 83–100). London, UK: Academic Press.

Swain, J. E., Lorberbaum, J. P., Kose, S., & Strathearn, L. (2007). Brain basis of early parent-infant interactions: Psychology, physiology, and *in vivo* functional neuroimaging studies. *Journal of Child Psychology and Psychiatry, 48,* 262–287.

Swain, J. E., Thomas, P., Leckman, J. F., & Mayes, L. C. (2008). Parent-infant attachment systems. Neural circuits and early life programming. In E. Jurist, A. Slade, & S. Bergner (Eds.), *Mind to mind: Infant research, neuroscience and psychoanalysis* (pp. 264–306). New York, NY: Other Press.

Symonds, L. L., Gordon, N. S., Bixby, J. C., & Mande, M. M. (2006). Right-lateralized pain processing in the human cortex: An fMRI study. *Journal of Neurophysiology, 95,* 3823–3830.

Talbot, J. A., Baker, J. K., & McHale, J. P. (2009). Sharing the love: Prebirth adult attachment status and coparenting adjustment during early infancy. Parenting. *Science and Practice, 9,* 56–77.

Talge, N. M., Neal, C., & Glover, V. (2007). Antenatal maternal stress and long-term effects on child neurodevelopment: How and why? *Journal of Child Psychology and Psychiatry, 48,* 245–261.

Taylor, G. J., Bagby, R. M., & Parker, J. D. (1992). The Revised Toronto Alexithymia Scale: Some reliability, validity, and normative data. *Psychotherapy and Psychosomatics, 57,* 34–41.

Taylor, S. E., Klein, L. C., Lewis, B. P., Gruenewald, T. L., Gurung, R. A., & Updegraff, J. A. (2000). Biobehavioral responses to stress in females: Tend-and-befriend, not fight-or-flight. *Psychological Review, 107,* 411–429.

Theodosis, D. T., Shachner, M., & Neumann, I. D. (2004). Oxytocin neuron activation in NCAM-deficient mice: Anatomical and functional consequences. *European Journal of Neuroscience, 20,* 3270–3280.

Theran, S. A., Levendosky, A. A., Bogat, G. A., & Huth-Bocks, A. C. (2005). Stability and change in mothers' internal representations of their infants over time. *Attachment and Human Development, 7,* 1–16.

Thompson, R. A. (2008). Early attachment and later development familiar questions, new answers. In J. Cassidy & P. R. Shaver (Eds.), *Handbook of attachment: Theory, research, and clinical applications* (2nd ed., pp. 348–365). New York, NY: Guilford Press.

Tkach, D., Reimer, J., & Hatsopoulos, N. G. (2007). Congruent activity during action and action observation in motor cortex. *Journal of Neuroscience, 27,* 13241–13250.

Tomasello, M. (1999). *The cultural oringins of human cognition.* Cambridge, MA: Harvard University Press.

Tomasello, M., Carpenter M., Call J., Behne T., & Moll H. (2005). Understanding and sharing intentions: The origins of cultural cognition. *Behavioral and Brain Sciences, 28,* 675-735.

Tomasello, M., Hare, B., Lehamann, H., & Call, J. (2006). Reliance on head versus eyes in the gaze following of great apes and human infants: The cooperative eye hypothesis. *Journal of Human Evolution, 3,* 314–320.

Tremblay, H., & Rovira, K. (2007). Joint visual attention and social triangular engangement at 3 and 6 months. *Infant Behavior and Development, 30,* 366–379.

Trentini, C. (2008). *Rispecchiamenti. L'amore materno e le basi neurobiologiche dell'empatia.* Roma, Italy: Il Pensiero Scientifico Editore.

Trevarthen, C. (1974). The psychology of speech development. *Neurosciences Research Program Bulletin, 12,* 570–585.

Trevarthen, C. (1977). Descriptive analyses of infant communicative behavior. In H. R. Schaffer (Ed.), *Studies in mother-infant interaction* (pp. 227–270). London, UK: Academic Press.

Trevarthen, C. (1979). Communication and cooperation in early infancy: A description of primary intersubjectivity. In M. Bullowa (Ed.), *Before speech: The beginning of interpersonal communication* (pp. 321–347). Cambridge, UK: Cambridge University Press.

Trevarthen, C. (1982). The primary motives for cooperative understanding. In G. Butterworth & P. Light (Eds.), *Social cognition: Studies of the development of understanding* (pp. 77–109). Brighton, UK: Harvester Press.

Trevarthen, C. (1987). Sharing makes sense: Intersubjectivity and the making of an infant's meaning. In R. Steele & T. Threadgold (Eds.), *Language topics: Essays in honour of Michael Halliday* (pp. 177–199). Amsterdam, The Netherlands and Philadelphia, PA: John Benjamins.

Trevarthen, C. (1988). Universal cooperative motives: How infants begin to know language and skills and culture. In G. Jahoda & I. M. Lewis (Eds.), *Acquiring culture: Cross-cultural studies in child development* (pp. 37–90). London, UK: Croom Helm.

Trevarthen, C. (1989). Development of early social interactions and the effective regulation of brain growth. In C. Von Euler, H. Forssberg, & H. Langercrantz (Eds.), *Neurobiology of early infant behavior* (pp. 191–216). New York, NY: Stockton Press.

Trevarthen, C. (1993). The self born in intersubjectivity: An infant communicating. In U. Neisser (Ed.), *The perceived self* (pp. 121–173). New York, NY: Cambridge University Press.

Trevarthen, C. (1998). The concept and foundations of infant intersubjectivity. In S. Bråten (Ed.), *Intersubjective communication and emotion in early ontogeny* (pp. 15–46). Cambridge, UK: Cambridge University Press.

Trevarthen, C. (2003). Infant psychology is an evolving culture. *Human Development, 46,* 233–246.

Trevarthen, C. (2009). The intersubjective psychobiology of human meaning: Learning of culture depends on interest for co-operative practical work-and affection for the joyful art of good company. *Psychoanalytic Dialogues, 19,* 507–518.

Trevarthen, C., & Aitken, K. J. (2001). Infant intersubjectivity: Research, theory, and clinical applications. *Journal of Child Psychology and Psychiatry, 42,* 3–48.

Trevarthen, C., & Hubley, P. (1978). Secondary intersubjectivity: Confidence, confiding and acts of meaning in the first year. In A. Lock (Ed.), *Action, gesture and symbol: The emergence of language* (pp. 183–229). London, UK: Academic Press.

Trickett, P. K., Aber, J. L., Carlson, V., & Cicchetti, D. (1991). The relationship of socioeconomic status to the etiology and developmental sequelae of physical child abuse. *Developmental Psychology, 27,* 148–158.

Trickett, P. K., & Sussman, E. J. (1988). Parental perceptions of child-rearing practices in physically abusive and non abusive families. *Developmental Psychology, 24,* 270–276.

Tronick, E. Z. (1989). Emotions and emotional communication in infants. *American Psychologist, 44,* 112–119.

Tronick, E. Z. (1998). Dyadically expanded states of consciousness and the process of therapeutic change. *Infant Mental Health Journal, 19,* 290–299.

Tronick, E. Z., Als, H., & Adamson, L. (1979). The communicative structure of face-to-face interaction. In M. Bullowa (Ed.), *Before speech: The beginnings of human communication* (pp. 349–372). Cambridge, UK: Cambridge University Press.

Tronick, E. Z., Als, H., Adamson, L., Wise, S., & Brazelton, T. (1978). The infant's response to entrapment between contradictory messages in face-to-face interaction. *Journal of the American Academy of Child and Adolescent Psychiatry, 17,* 1–13.

Tronick, E. Z., & Cohn, J. F. (1989). Infant-mother face-to-face interaction: Age and gender differences in coordination and the occurrence of miscoordination. *Child Development, 60,* 85–92.

Tronick, E. Z., & Gianino, A. F. (1986a). Interactive mismatch and repair: Challenges to the coping infant. *Zero to Three, 6,* 1–6.

Tronick, E. Z., & Gianino, A. F. (1986b). The transmission of maternal disturbance to the infant. *New Directions for Child Development, 34,* 5–11.

Tsakiris, M., Costantini, M., & Haggard, P. (2008). The role of the right temporo-parietal junction in maintaining a coherent sense of one's body. *Neuropsychologia, 46,* 3014–3018.

Tsao, D. Y., Freiwald, W. A., Tootell, R. B., & Livingstone, M. S. (2006). A cortical region consisting entirely of face-selective cells. *Science, 311,* 670–674.

Tyano, S., Keren, M., Herrman, H., & Cox, J. (2010) *Parenthood and mental health: A bridge between infant and adult psychiatry.* Oxford, UK: Wiley-Blackwell.

Tzourio-Mazoyer, N., De Schonen, S., Crivello, F., Reutter, B., Avjard, Y., & Mazoyer, B. (2002). Neural correlates of woman face processing by 2-month-old infants. *Neuroimage, 15,* 454–461.

Umiltà, M. A., Kohler, E., Gallese, V., Fogassi, L., Fadiga, L., Keysers, C., & Rizzolatti, G. (2001). I know what you are doing: A neurophysiological study. *Neuron, 31,* 155–165.

Uvnas-Moberg, K. (1998). Oxytocin may mediate the benefits of positive social interaction and emotions. *Psychoneuroendocrinology, 23,* 819–835.

van Bussel, J. C. H., Spitz, B., & Demyttenaere, K. (2009). Depressive symptomatology in pregnant and postpartum women: An exploratory study of the role of maternal antenatal orientations. *Archives of Women's Mental Health, 12,* 155–166.

van der Meer, A. L. H. (1997). Keeping the arm in the limelight: Advanced visual control of arm movements in neonates. *European Journal of Paediatric Neurology, 4,* 103–108.

van Egeren, L. A. (2003). Prebirth predictors of coparenting experiences in early infancy. *Infant Mental Health Journal, 24,* 278–295.

van Egeren, L. A. (2004). The development of the coparenting relationship over the transition to parenthood. *Infant Mental Health Journal, 25,* 453–477.

van Egeren, L. A., & Hawkins, D. P. (2004). Coming to terms with coparenting: Implications of definition and measurement. *Journal of Adult Development, 11,* 165–178.

van Elk, M., van Schieb, H. T., Hunnius, S., Vesperc, C., & Bekkering, H. (2008). You'll never crawl alone: Neurophysiological evidence for experience-dependent motor resonance in infancy. *Neuroimage, 43,* 808–814.

van IJzendoorn, M. H. (1995). Adult attachment representations, parental responsiveness, and infant attachment: A meta-analysis on the predictive validity of the Adult Attachment Interview. *Psychological Bulletin, 117,* 387–403.

van Ijzendoorn, M. H., & De Wolff, M. S. (1997). In search of the absent father: Meta-analysis of infant-father attachment. A rejoinder to our discussants. *Child Development, 60,* 71–91.

van Ijzendoorn, M. H., Sagi, A., & Lambermon, M. W. (1992). The multiple caregiver paradox: Data from Holland and Israel. *New Directions for Child Development, 57,* 5–27.

van Ijzendoorn, M. H., Schuengel, C., & Bakermans-Kranenburg, M. J. (1999). Disorganized attachment in early childhood: Meta-analysis of precursors, concomitants, and sequelae. *Development and Psychopathology, 11,* 225–249.

Van Overwalle, F. (2009). Social cognition and the brain: A meta-analysis. *Human Brain Mapping, 30,* 829–858.

Vaughn, B. E., Bost, K. K., & van Ijzendoorn, M. H. (2008). Attachment and temperament: Additive and interactive influences on behavior, affect, and cognition during infancy and childhood. In J. Cassidy & P. R. Shaver (Eds.), *Handbook of attachment: Theory, research, and clinical applications* (2nd ed., pp. 192–216). New York, NY: Guilford Press.

Vogt, S., Buccino, G., Wohlschläger, A. M., Canessa, N., Shah, N. J., Zilles, K., . . . Fink, G. R. (2007). Prefrontal involvement in imitation learning of hand actions: Effects of practice and expertise. *Neuroimage, 37,* 1371–1383.

von Hofsten, C. (1982). Eye-hand coordination in newborns. *Developmental Psychology, 18,* 450–461.

von Hofsten, C. (2007). Action in development. *Developmental Science, 10,* 54–60.

von Klitzing, K., & Burgin, D. (2005). Parental capacities for triadic relationship during pregnancy: Early predictors of children's behavioral and representational functioning at preschool age. *Infant Mental Health, 26,* 19–39.

von Klitzing, K., Simoni, H., & Burgin, D. (1999). Child development and early triadic relationships. *International Journal of Psychoanalysis, 80,* 71–89.

Wadhwa, P. D. (2005). Psychoneuroendocrine processes in human pregnancy influence fetal development and health. *Psychoneuroendocrinology, 30,* 724–743.

Wadhwa, P. D., Sandman, C. A., & Garite, T. J. (2001). The neurobiology of stress in human pregnancy: Implications for prematurity and development of the fetal central nervous system. *Progress in Brain Research, 133,* 131–142.

Wang, Z. W., Liu, Y., Young, L. J., & Insel, T. R. (2000). Hypothalamic vasopressin gene expression increases in both males and females postpartum in a biparental rodent. *Journal of Neuroendocrinology, 12,* 111–120.

Waterland, R. A., & Jirtle, R. L. (2003). Transposable elements: Targets for early nutritional effects on epigenetic gene regulation. *Molecular and Cellular Biology, 23,* 5393–5300.

Watson, J. B., Mednick, S. A., Huttunen, M., & Wang, X. (1999). Prenatal teratogens and the development of adult mental illness. *Development and Psychopathology, 11,* 457–466.

Weaver, I. C. G., Cervoni, N., Champagne, F. A., D'Alessio, A. C., Sharma S., Secki, J. R., . . . Meaney, M. J. (2004). Epigenetic programming by maternal behavior. *Nature Neuroscience, 7,* 847–854.

Weinberg, M. K. (1992). *Sex differences in 6-month-old infants' affect and behavior: Impact on maternal caregiving.* Unpublished Ph.D. dissertation, University of Massachusetts, Boston.

Weinfield, N. S., Sroufe, L. A., Egeland, B., & Carlson, E. (2008). Individual difference in infant-caregiver attachment: Conceptual and empirical aspects of security. In J. Cassidy & P. R. Shaver (Eds.), *Handbook of attachment: Theory, research, and clinical applications* (2nd ed., pp. 78–101). New York, NY: Guilford Press.

Weinstock, M. (2007). Gender differences in the effects of prenatal stress on brain development and behaviour. *Neurochemical Research, 32,* 1730–1740.

Weinstock, M. (2008). The long-term behavioural consequence of prenatal stress. *Neuroscience and Biobehavioral Reviews, 59*(4), 1073–1086.

Whittle, S., Yap, M. B. H., Sheeber, L., Dudgeon, P., Yücel, M., Pantelis, C., . . . Allen, N. B. (2011). Hippocampal volume and sensitivity to maternal aggressive behavior: A prospective study of adolescent depressive symptoms. *Development and Psychopathology*, *23*, 115–129.

Wicker, B., Keysers, C., Plailly, J., Royet, J.-P., Gallese, V., & Rizzolatti, G. (2003). Both of us disgusted in my insula: The common neural basis of seeing and feeling disgust. *Neuron*, *40*, 655–664.

Williams, K. E., & Koran, L. M. (1997). Obsessive-compulsive disorder in pregnancy, the puerperium, and the premenstruum. *Journal of Clinical Psychiatry*, *58*, 330–334.

Wimmer, H., & Perner, J. (1983). Beliefs about beliefs: Representation and constraining function of wrong beliefs in young children's understanding of deception. *Cognition*, *13*, 103–128.

Winnicott, D. W. (1953). Transitional objects and transitional phenomena: A study of the first not-me possession. *International Journal of Psychoanalysis*, *34*, 89–97.

Winnicott, D. W. (1958). Hate in the countertransference. In D. W. Winnicott (Ed.), *Collected papers* (pp. 194–203). London, UK: Tavistock. (Original work published 1947)

Winnicott, D. W. (1958). Primary maternal preoccupation. In D. W. Winnicott (Ed.), *Collected papers* (pp. 300–305). London, UK: Tavistock. (Original work published 1956)

Winnicott, D. W. (1960). The theory of the parent-infant relationship. *International Journal of Psychoanalysis*, *41*, 585–595.

Winnicott, D. W. (1965a). The development of the capacity for concern. In D. W. Winnicott (Ed.), *The maturational processes and the facilitating environment* (pp. 73–82). London, UK: Hogarth Press. (Original work published 1963)

Winnicott, D. W. (1965b). The maturational processes and the facilitating environment: Studies in the theory of emotional development. In M. Masud Khan (Ed.), *The international psychoanalytic library* (Vol. 64, pp. 1–276). London, UK: Hogarth Press and the Institute of Psychoanalysis.

Winnicott, D. W. (1969). Mother's madness appearing in clinical material as an ego-alien factor. In C. Winnicott, R. Shepherd, & M. Davis (Eds.), *Psychoanalytic explorations* (pp. 375–382). London, UK: Karnac.

Winnicott, D. W. (1971a). Mirror-role of mother and family in child development. In D. W. Winnicott (Ed.), *Playing and reality* (pp. 111–118). London, UK: Tavistock. (Original work published 1967)

Winnicott, D. W. (1971b). *Playing and reality*. London, UK: Tavistock.

Winnicott, D. W. (1975). *Through pediatrics to psychoanalysis*. New York, NY: Basic Books.

Winter, S. K. (1970). Fantasies at breast feeding time. *Psychology Today*, *3*, 31–32.

Wittling, W. (1997). The right hemisphere and the human stress response. *Acta Physiologica Scandinavica*, *640*, 55–59.

Woodward, A. L. (1998). Infants selectively encode the goal object of an actor's reach. *Cognition*, *69*, 1–34.

Wynne-Edwards, K. E. (2001). Hormonal changes in mammalian fathers. *Hormones and Behavior*, *40*, 139–145.

Wynne-Edwards, K. E., & Timonin, M. E. (2007). Paternal care in rodents: Weakening support for hormonal regulation of the transition to behavioral fatherhood in rodent animal models of biparental care. *Hormones and Behavior*, *52*, 114–121.

Xerri, C., Stern, J. M., & Merzenich, M. M. (1994). Alterations of the cortical representation of the rat ventrum by nursing behavior. *Journal of Neuroscience*, *14*, 1710–1721.

Yehuda, R., Engel, S. M., Brand, S. R., Seckl, J., Marcus, S. M., & Berkowitz, G. S. (2005). Transgenerational effects of posttraumatic stress disorder in babies of mothers exposed to the World Trade Center attacks during pregnancy. *Journal of Clinical Endocrinology and Metabolism*, 90, 4115–4118.

Young, L. J., Lim, M. M., Gingrich, B., & Insel, T. R. (2001). Cellular mechanisms of social attachment. *Hormones and Behavior*, 40, 133–138.

Youngblade, L. M., & Belsky, J. (1989). Child maltreatment, infant-parent attachment security, and dysfunctional peer relationships in toddlerhood. *Topics in Early Childhood Special Education*, 9, 1–15.

Yu, I. T., Lee, S. H., Lee, Y. S., & Son, H. (2004). Differential effects of corticosterone and dexamethasone on hippocampal neurogenesis in vitro. *Biochemical and Biophysical Research Communications*, 317, 484–490.

Zahavi, D. (2001). Beyond empathy: Phenomenological approaches to intersubjectivity. *Journal of Consciousness Studies*, 8, 151–167.

Zaki, J., & Ochsner, K. N. (2012). The neuroscience of empathy: Progress, pitfalls and promise. *Nature Neuroscience*, 15, 675–680.

Zald, D. H. (2003). The human amygdala and the emotional evaluation of sensory stimuli. *Brain Research Reviews*, 41, 88–123.

Zeanah, C. H., & Benoit, D. (1995). Clinical applications of a parent perception interview. *Infant Mental Health Child and Adolescent Psychiatric Clinics of North America*, 4, 539–554.

Zeanah, C. H., Benoit, D., Hirshberg, L., Barton, M. L., & Regan, C. (1994). Mothers' representations of their infants are concordant with infant attachment classifications. *Developmental Issues in Psychiatry and Psychology*, 1, 9–18.

Zeanah, C. H., & Zeanah, P. D. (1989). Intergenerational transmission of maltreatment: Insights from attachment theory and research. *Psychiatry*, 52, 177–196.

Zhang, T. Y., Parent, C., Weaver, I., & Meaney, M. J. (2004). Maternal programming of individual differences in defensive responses in the rat. *Annals of the New York Academy of Sciences*, 1032, 85–103.

Ziegler, T. E. (2000). Hormones associated with non-maternal infant care: A review of mammalian and avian studies. *Folia Primatologica*, 71, 6–21.

Zlatev, J., Persson, T., & Gärdenfors, P. (2005). Triadic bodily mimesis is the difference. *Behavioral and Brain Sciences*, 28, 720–721.

Zoia, S., Blason, L., D'Ottavio, G., Bulgheroni, M., Pezzetta, E., Scabar, A., & Castiello, U. (2007). Evidence of early development of action planning in the human foetus: A kinematic study. *Experimental Brain Research*, 176, 217–226.

Index

The letter *f* following a page number denotes a figure.

For details, a complete list of books in the Series, and to order online, please visit
www.tiny.cc/1zrsfw